Over Here

Over Here

THE FIRST WORLD WAR
AND AMERICAN SOCIETY

DAVID M. KENNEDY

OXFORD UNIVERSITY PRESS
Oxford   New York   Toronto   Melbourne

OXFORD UNIVERSITY PRESS
Oxford   London   Glasgow
New York   Toronto   Melbourne   Auckland
Delhi   Bombay   Calcutta   Madras   Karachi
Kuala Lumpur   Singapore   Hong Kong   Tokyo
Nairobi   Dar es Salaam   Cape Town

and associate companies in
Beirut   Berlin   Ibadan   Mexico City   Nicosia

Library of Congress Cataloging in Publication Data
Kennedy, David M.
Over here.
Bibliography: p.   Includes index.
1. European War, 1914–1918–United States.
2. United States–History–1913–1921.   3. United
States–Social conditions–1865–1918.   I. Title.
D570.1.K43   940.3'73   80-11753
ISBN 0-19-502729-9
ISBN 0-19-503209-8 (pbk.)

Printing (last digit):   9 8

Printed in the United States of America

For Judy

Preface

This book provides a reasonably complete account of events in the United States during the nineteen months of American belligerency in the First World War, but it also seeks to do more than that. I have used the occasion of the war as a window through which to view early twentieth-century American society. From that vantage point, I believe, some familiar historical landscape can be seen in a new light, and perhaps some new terrain identified. The book, therefore, is not a comprehensive chronicle of all that happened in wartime America, though the pages that follow contain much of that sort of detail. Neither is it, strictly speaking, a study of the impact of the war on American society, though dimensions of that impact are frequently examined. The book might best be described as a discussion of those aspects of the American experience in the First World War that I take to be crucial for an understanding of modern American history.

The paramount theme of any account of American participation in the Great War of 1914–18 must be the historic departure of the United States from isolation and all that isolation implied. That departure not only spelled the abandonment of nearly a century and a half of American diplomatic practice, a commonplace observation to which I offer neither dissent nor elaboration. It also compelled the United States, as almost never before, to measure itself against Europe, even to compete with Europe for a definition of the war's meaning and for the fruits of victory. Moreover, the war temporarily required the United States—though not as insistently as it required the Old World combatants—to discipline and mobilize its citizens in a manner from which history and geography had theretofore singularly spared them.

For the Americans, the drama of the war was enacted on a smaller stage, and in fewer acts, than for the Europeans. Yet somehow millions of persons in the strikingly voluntaristic and fragmented society that was early twentieth-century America (as described in the Prologue) had to be made to perform in concert their appointed parts. How—or indeed whether—that task was accomplished is a question that has intrigued me. The answers to it reveal much about the historical moment through which American society was then passing, about the peculiarities of American history when contrasted with the experiences of other peoples, and even, I argue, about abiding features of the American national character, especially national attitudes toward the authority of the government. These topics comprise the substance of Chapters One and Two, and part of Chapter Three.

The story both begins and ends in the Old World, where for some 50,000 young American men it ended forever. No small part of the significance of the war is to be found in the forced exposure of millions of Americans to foreign lands and modern battle. That development, as well as some of its implications for imaginative literature, is discussed in Chapters Three and Four.

Chapter Five deals chiefly with a number of social groups, including workers, women, and blacks, who entertained high expectations of the war's beneficial results. Those expectations were, in the main, far from fulfilled in the war's aftermath, as were the optimistic predictions of many reformers that the war would usher in a new era of liberalism and justice at home.

Chapter Six addresses the widespread wartime anticipation that American economic strength would both prosper Americans in postwar world markets and assist Woodrow Wilson in his effort to promote American principles at the Paris peace table. I hope that the account here will illumine what I take to be the cardinal truth of this matter: that American economic power was not used effectively during the war or the peace negotiations, nor was it used particularly profitably in the international field after the war.

The Epilogue recounts Woodrow Wilson's efforts to influence the peace talks at Paris, and his campaign on behalf of the League of Nations at home, which ended in political and personal tragedy. I have also tried in the Epilogue to evoke some of the ways in which the war was remembered in the decade following the Armistice.

What follows is in many ways a sad story, a tale of death, broken hopes, frustrated dreams, and of the curious defeat-in-victory that was Woodrow Wilson's, and the nation's, bitter lot. The history of American involvement in World War I stands also as a kind of prologue to American involvement in a still greater war a generation later. But that is another story, for telling another time.

Stanford, California   D. M. K.
May 1980

Acknowledgments

The American Council of Learned Societies on two separate occasions supported my research on this project, and I am therefore doubly grateful to the Council. I wish also to record my appreciation for a John Simon Guggenheim Memorial Foundation fellowship that allowed me to devote an uninterrupted year to writing. My thanks go as well to five bodies at Stanford University which contributed materially to my work on this book: the Hoover Institution on War, Revolution and Peace; the Center for Research in International Studies; the Graduate Division; the School of Humanities and Sciences; and the Institute of American History.

I was fortunate to have two research assistants, William T. Generous, Jr., in the initial stages of research, and Daniel B. Smith, in the final stages, whose thorough professionalism added substantially to my understanding of the war era. Several colleagues generously responded to my appeals for critical readings of various sections. John Morton Blum read an early version of almost the entire manuscript. Carl N. Degler and David B. Tyack offered valuable suggestions about Chapter Two. William M. Chace twice gave me the benefit of his customarily wise counsel on the material that comprises Chapter Four and part of Chapter One. James Hoopes rescued me, I hope, from some errors in that same material. Robert O. Keohane rescued me, I know, from even larger errors in Chapter Six. Thomas A. Bailey on numerous occasions shared with me his encyclopedic knowledge of American history, and of the World War I period in particular. Susi Lilly and Emily Hallin deciphered my drafts and rendered them legible. To all of them, my warmest thanks.

Contents

Prologue: Spring, 1917

Everywhere it was a time of waiting. Cold and despair gnawed at the peoples of the Old World, where the winter of 1916–17 clung cruelly, as apparently endless as the war that had gripped Europe since August 1914. Men had then gone eagerly to battle, expecting swift victory. But two and a half years of fighting had killed five million of them. Those still living waited wearily in the frigid early months of 1917, hoping for peace.

Since the scything sweep of the German armies through Belgium and France had been stopped at the River Marne in September 1914, the Great War in Europe had settled into a grisly stalemate. Slanting from the Channel to the Swiss frontier, an unmovable line of battle had congealed across northern France. Throughout 1915, four million men burrowed into trenchworks along that line drew rivers of one another's blood, but neither the Germans on the one side nor the French and British on the other could breach the opponent's defenses.

Seeking to resolve the deadlock in 1916, Germany had launched a plan to turn the very impenetrability of the French defenses into the instrument of French destruction. The scheme was as logical as it was horrible: attack at a point which the enemy must defend at whatever costs; besiege that point indefinitely, bleeding France dry; thus rely, ultimately, on the numerical superiority of German manpower as the guarantor of victory. So began the siege of Verdun in February 1916.

3

When it ended five months later, 350,000 Frenchmen and 330,000 Germans lay dead. France had not fallen. The front had not moved.

In the valley of the Somme River a hundred miles northwest of Verdun, the British launched their greatest assault of the war on July 1, 1916. By October it too had ground to an ineffective halt, at a price of more than one million dead on both sides. Many of them had drowned in the mud that swallowed men, machines, and horses without a trace. To the south, at the head of the Adriatic Sea, the Italians and the Austrians stood in checkmate on either side of the Isonzo River. Far to the east, in Poland and Galicia, the Central Powers had inflicted two million casualties on the Czar's armies in 1915, and there the battle lines moved more measurably across the map. But still the Russians were not driven from the field. Underequipped and often untrained, Russian troops continued to absorb punishment on a terrifying scale. From one end of the continent to the other, the military stand-off had made a charnel house of Europe.

Inside Germany, inflation laid waste the economy, as the British cinched ever tighter the noose of the blockade first thrown across the north German ports in 1914. From the Baltic to the Danube, women and children tramped through the chill streets of the villages and towns, seeking scarce food. The Germans called it the "turnip winter," in mock tribute to one of the few available sources of nutriment. Farmers had begun to slaughter milch cows for meat. A cut in the bread ration in April brought rioters into the streets of German cities, and on April 12 the Austrian foreign minister confided that his country could not fight another year. The people of Germany and Austria were slowly starving to death.

In the German Reichstag, wartime solidarity had begun to crack in 1916. The Social Democrats voted in growing numbers against war credits, and increasingly demanded social and political reforms as the price of their continued support for the war. Knowing the sorry situation of his armies and his people, Chancellor Theobald von Bethmann Hollweg had put out a cautious peace feeler in December 1916. Doubting his intentions and still hoping for military victory, Britain and France had rebuffed Bethmann Hollweg's overtures. His armies deadlocked and his diplomacy checked, the German chancellor was forced to a last desperate gamble to break the stalemate at sea.

At a meeting on January 9, 1917, at General Paul von Hindenburg's field headquarters at Pless, in Silesia, Bethmann Hollweg yielded to the demand of his military chiefs for a resumption of unrestricted submarine warfare in the Atlantic. The risks were great. More than once since 1914, submarine attacks on merchant and passenger ships had brought the United States to the brink of war with Germany, most notably in 1915 when the *Lusitania* was sunk, killing more than a hundred Americans. But Hindenburg and General Erich von Ludendorff argued that merciless U-boat warfare would bring England to her knees within six months, well before a distant and unprepared America could field an effective force in France. "If success beckons," Bethmann Hollweg conceded, "we must follow."[1] On January 31, Johann von Bernstorff, the German ambassador at Washington, informed Secretary of State Robert Lansing that commencing the next day German submarines would sink on sight and without warning all merchant ships, including neutral vessels, bound for Britain or France.

In his offices in Berlin, Bethmann Hollweg now waited impatiently as the winter grudgingly relaxed its grip and gave way to spring. He scanned his daily reports with both satisfaction and anxiety. His submarine commanders were sinking several British merchantmen daily. But they were torpedoing American vessels as well—*Housatonic* in early February, *City of Memphis, Illinois,* and *Vigilancia* in mid-March. President Woodrow Wilson had severed diplomatic relations with Germany, but still there was no American declaration of war. Would the German gamble pay off? Would Wilson hesitate long enough for the U-boats mortally to cripple Britain?

In the frost-clad fields of Champagne, veteran French troops huddled in their winter greatcoats. They waited anxiously for warmer weather to permit the opening of the spring campaign. Their commanders promised it was to be the last great drive of the war, the decisive turn of the military tide. That turn must come soon. The French people, too, though less famished than their foes, had wearied of the war. The ordeal of Verdun had excited deep civilian resentment and sapped the morale of the army. Peace advocates were growing bolder; some mingled with front-bound troops at the Gare de l'Est and Gare du Nord in Paris, distributing anti-war pamphlets and urging desertion. The government of Prime Minister Aristide Briand had barely survived

1. Quoted in Arthur S. Link, *Wilson: Campaigns for Progressivism and Peace 1916–1917* (Princeton: Princeton University Press, 1965), 245.

through 1916, and finally fell in March 1917. General Joseph Joffre, the "victor of the Marne," had relinquished supreme military command in December 1916 to Robert Nivelle, who proposed to end the tortuous war of attrition and break the deadlock in the trenches with a massive attack on the German salient north of Reims. But when General Nivelle flung his immense forces forward in mid-April, they stumbled headlong into a German trap. Ludendorff had a few weeks earlier withdrawn to a shorter, more defensible line across the chord of the salient's arc, and had systematically devastated the land as he retreated. Buildings were burned, trees toppled, wells poisoned, and booby-traps scattered through the destruction. After two weeks of futile slaughter on this hellish terrain, the French troops began to mutiny. Nivelle was dismissed. The fear-struck French high command ordered executions of mutineers, some chosen by lot, in a desperate attempt to keep the remaining troops at their posts in the trenches.[2] The abortive Nivelle offensive once again buried the dream of a military breakthrough. No number of mere men, it seemed, could overcome the advantage that the machine gun—"concentrated essence of infantry," it was called— gave to the defensive position. The French, exhausted and demoralized, could only wait for relief from another quarter.

Across the Channel in London, British Prime Minister David Lloyd George also waited. When he had heard on February 4, 1917, of Wilson's response to the unrestricted submarine warfare campaign, Lloyd George had exploded: "And so he is not going to fight after all! He is awaiting another insult before he actually draws the sword."[3] In the ensuing weeks, those insults were delivered, in the form of torpedoed American vessels. But still, as February passed into March, and March into April, only silence came from Washington. German submarines, meanwhile, were sinking over half a million tons of Allied shipping per month. Grain reserves in the United Kingdom fell to a bare six-week ration. Britain, Lloyd George knew, could not hold out much longer.

The war had already changed the face of British life. Food shortages had not reached the starvation levels of Germany, but Britons felt the

2. This episode inspired a moving novel by Humphrey Cobb, *Paths of Glory* (New York: Viking Press, 1935).
3. Quoted in Sterling J. Kernek, "Distractions of Peace During War: The Lloyd George Government's Reactions to Woodrow Wilson, December, 1916–November, 1918," *Transactions of the American Philosophical Society*, n.s. 65, part 2 (Apr. 1975), 36.

pinch of privation. Feeding precious food to pigeons was prohibited, as was the throwing of rice at weddings. Scarcities of coal, sugar, and potatoes in early 1917 brought the introduction of a social phenomenon destined to become a permanent feature of the British scene: the queue.

Less visibly, the war had begun to work transformations in the very character of British society. Britain in the Victorian and Edwardian eras was seemingly a model of harmonious social and economic progress guaranteed by the sacred principles of laissez-faire. Liberal and Conservative governments succeeded one another with decorous regularity. Leaders of both parties were drawn from the upper class, and they shared values sanctified in the rituals of aristocratic education. True, the working class had begun to stir toward the end of the nineteenth century, and by 1900 had given birth to a fledgling political organization, the Labour Party. But on the eve of the war the few Labourites in Parliament were still barely distinguishable from their Liberal brethren. In fact, the Liberal government that had come to power in 1906 had proceeded in the following ten years to pursue a reform program designed to accommodate many of Labour's aspirations: home rule for Ireland, tax equalization, and a national insurance plan for workers. Given time and peace, the Liberals might well have continued to manage the modernization of Britain at a gentlemanly, leisurely pace that would have peacefully assimilated the Labourites into the existing political system. But the war, as one historian has said, "had blown the bottom out of the hourglass."[4] Frustrated that the conflict in Europe had slowed their progress toward home rule, Irish nationalists rose in rebellion during Easter 1916. Workers chafed increasingly at Liberal rule as the government proved unable to curb inflation. Their resentment intensified in 1916 when the Asquith cabinet, however reluctantly, resorted to the unprecedented imposition of military conscription. Male workers watched sullenly as the draft calls thinned their ranks and compelled the "dilution" of the work force with women. And conscription was but the most noxious of the many departures from laissez-faire that the tightening demands of the war forced on the London government. Slowly but unremittingly, the state was closing its hand over ever larger areas of British life. By 1917 the government had decreed

4. Arthur Marwick, *The Deluge: British Society and the First World War* (New York: Norton, 1970), 186. For a comparative discussion, see John Williams, *The Home Fronts: Britain, France, and Germany, 1914–1918* (London: Constable, 1972).

food rationing, shipping controls, liquor regulation, and a host of other measures.

Among the casualties of these war-born stresses was the Liberal government of H. H. Asquith, which gave way in December 1916 to a coalition cabinet headed by David Lloyd George. Prominent among the members of the newly reorganized and centralized War Cabinet was Arthur Henderson, secretary of the Labour Party. His presence symbolized the full entry into the British political elite of a new type of man, the labor politician, representing a newly assertive laboring class. Henderson's presence in the innermost councils of state also evidenced the older elite's growing fear that it might lose the willing collaboration of labor in the war effort, and hence lose the war itself. Henderson did not allay that fear when he returned from a journey to Russia after the Revolution of March 1917 and endorsed the Russians' proposal for a conference of socialists from all the warring nations to discuss peace terms.

As the will of the British people to continue the struggle seeped inexorably away, so did their fund of fiscal resources. Once mighty international bankers, Britons by early 1917 had deeply mortgaged themselves to American creditors as they bought enormous quantities of war munitions for themselves and their allies. In the London countinghouses in the spring of 1917 men knew that the day of reckoning was near. It was only a matter of weeks until all the coffers in Britain would be empty. Spiritual and financial exhaustion, together with the murderous depredations of the submarine, might soon force Britain to accept peace on the enemy's terms.

By early 1917, in all of the belligerent countries, the war's frozen battlefronts and the seemingly endless drain of men and material into the trenches had drawn taut the lines of political tension. In Russia, those lines snapped in the last week of the fateful winter of 1916–17. War had already proved to be the mother of revolution in Russia. Defeat at the hands of the Japanese in 1905 had ignited the torch of insurrection that lighted the way for the first faltering steps toward Russian parliamentary democracy. Now the far greater disaster of the war in Europe touched off a veritable bonfire of rage. Soldiers had been slaughtered by the millions, peasants had been herded unarmed into battle, civilians had been subjected to unspeakable suffering—and yet the Czar's government remained aloof and inscrutable, unwilling or unable to give moral purpose and efficient organization to the Russian war effort. In December 1916, Rasputin, the mysterious adviser to the court, was assassinated, and the Czar began to set in motion the heavy apparatus of repression. Machine guns were issued to the police, and the Russian parliament, the Duma, was adjourned. On January 22, 1917 (the same day that Woodrow Wilson delivered his "Peace Without Victory" speech in Washington), over 100,000 strikers filled the streets of Petrograd. On March 8 food riots erupted, soon developing into a general strike that shut all the city's factories. The army refused to fire on the insurrectionaries, and when the Czar tried to return to Petrograd from the front his own troops turned back the imperial train. On March 15, he abdicated. Two days later, Russia became a republic, headed by a Provisional Government that promised to implement liberal reforms.

News of these events in Petrograd exhilarated the western allies. The overthrow of the Czar heralded the long overdue entry of his vast and backward land into the modern political world—and raised the hope that a newly invigorated Russia would now prosecute the war with more energy and effect. Here, perhaps, was the break for which western leaders had been so desperately waiting.

In Germany, Bethmann Hollweg was also assessing the implications of the Russian developments. The new government in Petrograd, he knew, was riven with factionalism, and it held in precarious equilibrium the contending revolutionary forces that pulsed in Russian society. Germany, the Chancellor concluded, ought somehow to support the most extreme elements in Russia and thus encourage the chaos that would cripple the Russian military effort. He accordingly arranged for the return to Russia of a group of radical political exiles living in Switzerland. They would travel through Germany on a "sealed" train; no one would be allowed to embark or disembark on German territory. The radical virus that was the train's cargo would be released only on arrival in Russia.

In Zurich, the leader of the little colony of Russian émigrés, V. I. Lenin, prepared excitedly as arrangements went forward for his departure. A professional revolutionary, he had awaited this opportunity all his adult life and he intended to use it well. When he stepped onto the platform at Petrograd's Finland Station in mid-April, he would damn the "bourgeois" Provisional Government and summon the workers to arms. Soon he would demand withdrawal from the war, insulating Russia from the imminent European collapse. The new Soviet state could

then serve as the fountain of socialist revolution that Lenin hoped
would flood across Europe's ruins in the wake of the war.

Even as Lenin waited tensely in his cramped lodgings in the house
of a Zurich shoemaker, Woodrow Wilson waited in the White House in
Washington. Through the month of March the insults from Germany
had at last become too many and too grievous to endure. On March 1,
the newspapers had published an intercepted telegram, sent by German
Foreign Secretary Arthur Zimmerman to his ambassador in Mexico.
The message proposed to Mexico that it join Germany in war against
the United States, with Mexico's reward to be the reconquest of "lost
territory" in New Mexico, Texas, and Arizona. The revelation further
inflamed American public opinion, already incensed by the U-boat attacks on United States ships. Meeting with his cabinet on March 20,
the President found his advisers unanimously in favor of war with Germany. The following day the President called the newly elected 65th
Congress into special session on April 2 to receive his war message.

Now the President waited through the long afternoon of April 2. He
had planned to go to the Capitol at 2:00 P.M. to deliver his war address,
but shortly after luncheon a messenger informed him that the House
was still electing its officers and was not yet prepared to hear him. The
President passed the hours chatting with his adviser, Colonel Edward
House; late in the afternoon he walked to the Navy Department and to
the office of Secretary of State Robert Lansing. Word finally arrived
that the Congress could receive him in the evening, and he prepared
to go at 8:20. After dinner, accompanied by a troop of cavalry, the
President motored swiftly through the rain up Pennsylvania Avenue.
Flag-waving crowds of people, held back by mounted police with
drawn sabers, were visible through the windows of the automobile.
Soon the President could see the Capitol itself, its white dome starkly
illuminated by searchlights against the dark gray sky. In a moment he
would be in the House chamber, asking the Congress of the United
States to declare war on Germany.

This was the fifth time since the beginning of 1917 that Wilson had
made the short trip to Capitol Hill to speak about America's relation to
the war in Europe. On January 22 he had explained to the Senate his
proposal for "peace without victory." On February 3, Wilson returned
to Congress and announced his response to the German proclamation
of submarine warfare: he would cut diplomatic ties, but there would

be no request for a declaration of war. (Wilson "is afraid," wrote Henry Cabot Lodge, "he flinches in the presence of danger, physical and moral.")[5] Then, on February 26, Wilson had gone in person to ask Congress for the authority to arm merchant ships, a request tenaciously opposed in the Senate by what Wilson called "a little group of willful men." In that charged atmosphere, on March 5, under unusually heavy guard, Wilson had made the ceremonial journey to the rostrum on the east façade of the Capitol to deliver his second inaugural address. There, referring to the conflict in Europe, he had said, "Our own fortunes as a nation are involved, whether we would have it so or not." But still the President had waited; he did not ask for a declaration of war.

Wilson had waited so long for war with reason. "It was necessary for me," he wrote a friend, "by very slow stages indeed and with the most genuine purpose to avoid war to lead the country on to a single way of thinking."[6] Since the guns had first sounded in Europe in August 1914, Americans had profoundly disagreed about the conflict and about America's relation to it. Moreover, the United States in 1917 stood at the end of two decades of extraordinarily divisive political and social upheaval. Deep social fissures had been opened by the enormous concentration of private capital and economic power in "trusts," by the efforts of progressive reformers to bring the corporations under public control, by labor disturbances, and by the arrival in America of over twelve million immigrants since the turn of the century. In the face of these already severe stresses, Wilson understandably hesitated to submit the country to the added strain of war. He well knew what the protracted conflict was doing to the political and social structures of the European belligerent countries, especially to Liberal England. "Every reform we have won," Wilson had said as early as 1914, "will be lost if we go into this war. We have been making a fight on special privilege. We have got new tariff and currency and trust legislation. We don't yet know how they will work. They are not thoroughly set."[7] As recently as March 15, just six days before Wilson summoned the special congressional session, the railroad unions had threatened to throw the nation's

5. Quoted in Link, *Campaigns for Progressivism and Peace*, 303.
6. Woodrow Wilson to Cleveland H. Dodge, Apr. 4, 1917, Woodrow Wilson Papers, Library of Congress, Washington, D.C. (hereafter WWP).
7. Quoted in Ray Stannard Baker, *Woodrow Wilson: Life and Letters*, 8 vols. (Garden City and New York: Doubleday, Page, and Doubleday, Doran, 1927–39), V, 77 (hereafter RSB).

transportation system into chaos by calling a general strike to force compliance with new federal legislation establishing the eight-hour work day. And Wilson himself, acutely sensitive to the problems that millions of foreign-born residents posed, had spoken urgently throughout his presidency about the question of loyalty. In 1916 he had tried to make "Americanism" the controlling motif of his re-election campaign.

That presidential campaign had been particularly bitter, revealing the depth of the divisions in American society. The Republican candidate, Charles Evans Hughes, strongly attacked Wilson's labor policies and charged him with softness in defending American rights in Mexico and Europe. The Democrats insinuated that Hughes was pro-German, and Wilson, shamelessly exploiting the issue of "100 percent Americanism," openly slandered as "disloyal Americans" those who accused him of pro-British sympathies. By election day, the war issue had come to dominate all else, and most observers agreed that Wilson owed his victory to the effect of the Democratic slogan, "He Kept Us Out of War." Those words would soon become like ashes in the mouth.

The electoral margin was disconcertingly narrow. A difference of fewer than 4000 votes in California would have removed Woodrow Wilson from the White House. And his party fared no better; though Democrats enjoyed a majority of nine seats in the Senate, the voters returned but 216 Democrats to the House of Representatives, along with 210 Republicans and 6 Independents.

When the new Congress met on April 2 to hear Wilson's address, therefore, it was by no means clear which party would control the organization of the House. Democrats took heart early in the morning when an independent Progressive Republican from Minnesota nominated Champ Clark of Missouri for the key position of Speaker of the House. Clark was a long-time foe of Woodrow Wilson, but nevertheless a Democrat. "Should the Republican party succeed in organizing the House, evenly divided as it is," said the Minnesotan, "with a Democratic Senate and a Democratic President, it could accrue no possible advantage. . . ."[8] But Republicans were not so easily convinced. Clark won the Speakership by a tiny margin, and the parties were so nearly balanced that the Republican minority leader, hoping to exploit temporary Democratic absences from the floor, repeatedly demanded roll-call votes for the election of all other House officers. Nothing more vividly

8. *Congressional Record*, House, 65th Congress, 1st sess., Apr. 2, 1917, 107.

exemplified the persistent vigor of contesting forces in American society than this tedious wrangling in the Capitol on the very day of President Wilson's war message.

Wilson, meanwhile, had been made to wait through the afternoon. Finally at 8:32 in the evening, after composing himself briefly in a Capitol anteroom, he strode through the swinging doors into the House chamber. Newly elected Speaker Clark announced, "The President of the United States," and the packed hall erupted in emotional applause.

But if the setting was dramatic, the President's manner was not. He knew the trial of leadership he faced, and feared the ordeal that the nation must unavoidably undergo. The day's exasperating delays had urgently reminded him of the contending factions he had somehow to harness to the war effort. Wilson, therefore, forsook his usually elaborate platform style. As he spoke, noted an observer, "There was neither rhetorical artifice nor oratorical surge of personality. His voice was not strong. His manner was solemn and burdened."[9]

"I have called the Congress into extraordinary session," the President began, "because there are serious, very serious, choices of policy to be made." He referred first, of course, to the declaration of war itself, though on this point he merely urged that Congress "formally accept the status of belligerent which has thus been thrust upon it." The difficult choices of policy, he made clear, would not simply concern the question of peace or war, but the ways in which America should wage the war.

Belligerency would require, he warned, "the organization and mobilization of all the material resources of the country." The Treasury would have to grant massive credits to the other governments at war with Germany, and Wilson at once announced his intention to raise those credits, "so far as they can equitably be sustained by the present generation, by well-conceived taxation." In other words, he intended to keep government borrowing to a minimum, while increasing taxes and very probably revising the tax structure itself. Wilson next called for gigantic additions to the armed services, and here, too, he immediately let it be known that those additions should be made "upon the principle of universal liability to service," or a manpower draft. Measures for the accomplishment of those objectives, Wilson said, were being drawn up in the Executive branch and would soon be submitted to the appropri-

9. *The Outlook* 115 (Apr. 11, 1917), 646.

ate congressional committees. There had already been battles between President and Congress on the issue of military preparedness, and Wilson now made it clear that in wartime he would insist more than ever on the preeminence of the Executive, "upon which the responsibility of conducting war and safeguarding the nation will most directly fall." Finally, Wilson touched again on the issue of loyalty. There were "millions of men and women of German birth and native sympathy who live amongst us," he said, and he knew that most were loyal to America. But, he warned, "if there should be disloyalty, it will be dealt with with a firm hand of repression." An explosion of applause greeted that remark. "It is a fearful thing," the President concluded, "to lead this great peaceful people into war, into the most terrible and disastrous of all wars, civilization itself seeming to be in the balance."[10]

It was a fearful thing indeed. Wilson had asked the Congress to commit the United States to a distant war that had already butchered men by the millions, shredded the social and economic fabric of the Old World, and shaken the very foundations of every belligerent government. The President had also called for a bold tax program, for the compulsory draft of hundreds of thousands of young men into the national service, for the enforced loyalty of all Americans in a cause to which many were indifferent or openly hostile, and, by implication, at least, for congressional acquiescence in the expansion of presidential power. The country would have to gird not only for war in Europe, but for many battles on the home front as well.

Some domestic skirmishes had already been fought. In the days immediately preceding April 2, pro-war and anti-war groups had met and marched and demonstrated and declaimed in several cities, each group aiming to persuade the government to adopt its preferred policy. The Emergency Peace Federation, a hastily assembled pacifist organization, had in early March summoned to the East from his home in California its champion platform speaker, David Starr Jordan, retired president of Stanford University. During the last ten days of March, Jordan stumped from Boston to Baltimore on behalf of peace. On Sunday, April 1, the eve of Wilson's war address, a Baltimore mob of nearly a thousand persons stormed the building in which Jordan was speaking, and started to rush the stage. The pro-peace audience sang "The Star-Spangled

10. Albert Shaw, ed., *The Messages and Papers of Woodrow Wilson,* 2 vols. (New York: Review of Reviews Corp., 1924), I, 372–83.

Banner," compelling the zealous patriots to stop and stand at attention in mid-aisle long enough for Jordan to slip away. But the mob hunted him, unsuccessfully, through the streets of Baltimore well into the night, chanting, "We'll hang Dave Jordan to a sour apple tree."[11] The following morning, twelve special Baltimore and Ohio railroad cars brought other members of the Emergency Peace Federation from New York to Washington, where they spent the day pleading with Senators and Representatives not to approve the expected request for a declaration of war. One youthful pleader for peace accosted Massachusetts Republican Senator Henry Cabot Lodge in the corridor outside his Senate office and told him: "Anyone who wants to go to war is a coward. You're a damned coward!" To which Lodge, then in his sixty-seventh year, replied: "You're a damned liar!" and underlined his statement with a swift punch to the youth's jaw. The protester, unpacifistically, returned the blow. The ensuing scuffle ended shortly when bystanders hauled the pacifist away and badly beat him.[12]

Wilson's sensitivity to such passions dictated his subdued manner on the evening of April 2. He knew that every point he made would provoke controversy—not just the matter of war itself, but his proposals for heavy taxation, for universal military training, for the repression of supposed disloyalty, and for the paramountcy of the Executive in wartime. Wilson could see for himself the evidence of tension as he spoke from the rostrum. Two powerful Senators, Mississippi's James K. Vardaman and Wisconsin's Robert M. La Follette, had chosen not to wear on their lapels the small American flag that their Senate colleagues had donned for the occasion, and the absence was conspicuous. At the conclusion of the address, as his arch-foe Henry Cabot Lodge shook his hand, Wilson could notice the slight puffiness in the Senator's face, the result of Lodge's afternoon fisticuffs. As the President proceeded from the House chamber, he could also see Senator La Follette standing motionless, quietly chewing gum, his arms folded high on his chest in a studied posture of opposition to what Wilson had said.

Financing America's military mobilization had occasioned hot argument even before April 1917. Early in the preceding year the administra-

---

11. David Starr Jordan, *The Days of a Man,* 2 vols. (Yonkers-on-Hudson, N.Y.: World Book Co., 1922), II, 727–29.
12. John A. Garraty, *Henry Cabot Lodge, a Biography* (New York: Knopf, 1965), 333–35.

tion had sought to revise the tax laws in order to provide an additional $300 million in revenues for the limited preparedness program Wilson had endorsed. Southern and Western legislators seized the opportunity to increase the income tax—a revenue-producing device made possible just three years earlier, in 1913, by the passage of the Sixteenth Amendment. Led by North Carolina Representative Claude Kitchin in the House and La Follette in the Senate, a coalition of progressives sought tax reform in the summer of 1916 with two goals in mind: blunting the force of the preparedness movement, and moving the federal tax structure to a more egalitarian basis. "I am persuaded to think," Kitchin wrote to William Jennings Bryan, "that when the New York people are thoroughly convinced that the income tax will have to pay for the increase in the army and navy, they will not be one-half so frightened over the future invasion by Germany and that preparedness will not be so popular with them as it now is."[13] The existing tax system, only mildly progressive in character, gathered more than half its receipts from persons earning less than $20,000 per year. Secretary of the Treasury William Gibbs McAdoo proposed changes aimed primarily at increasing receipts, without significant effect on the distribution of the tax burden among different economic groups. But once the issue was raised, the administration could no longer fully control it. The final legislation in 1916 shifted more than 95 percent of the federal tax obligation to those with incomes greater than $20,000. The new tax plan was a great victory for Southern and Western progressive reformers, and a great defeat for conservative forces, heavily based in the Northeast.

Thus when Wilson proposed still more drastic tax revision in his war message, he knew full well that he was reopening a sectional and class issue of the first magnitude, one which he had already shown himself incapable of managing. Professional economists lined up on opposite sides of the question: some favored maximum use of the graduated income tax; others advocated the kind of heavy borrowing to which most of the European belligerents had resorted. The socialist press called for the outright appropriation of all income in excess of $10,000. J. P. Morgan, on the other hand, advised Secretary McAdoo to seek no more than 20 percent of war revenues from taxation; the remainder should be raised by loans to which the wealthy, he assured the Secretary,

13. Quoted in Link, *Campaigns for Progressivism and Peace,* 62.

would patriotically subscribe. The *Wall Street Journal* favored lowering the amount of income exempted from taxation from $4000 to $1000, "and bring home the war to all the people." The *Journal* agreed with Morgan that bonds were the preferred instrument for financing the war: "It is not right," said an editorial, "that the present generation should bear the whole burden of a conflict fought for the freedom of our children's children." Clearly, there was no consensus in the spring of 1917 about who should provide the money for American participation in the war, or how that money might be collected. Yet Wilson appeared to be aligning himself with the progressive side in the looming fight over revenue policy.[14]

Even more pointed disagreement attended the question of recruiting and training troops. Here too, on the evening of April 2, Wilson rather surprisingly committed himself to a highly controversial position when he endorsed the idea of "universal liability to service." A year earlier the President's opposition to just that idea had cost him the resignation of his first Secretary of War, Lindley M. Garrison. The Secretary, along with many military men such as Generals Hugh Scott and Leonard Wood, as well as prominent pro-preparedness civilians like Theodore Roosevelt and Henry L. Stimson, had championed a proposal to reorganize the Army into a so-called "continental" force, superseding the obsolescent National Guard as the nation's first line of defense. The proponents of the continental force aimed first at improving military effectiveness, but the provisions for obligatory military service in Garrison's proposal revealed that its backers had broad social purposes in mind as well. Universal military training, they believed, could be an effective homogenizing agent in what they regarded as a dangerously diverse society. Shared military service, one advocate colorfully argued, was the only way to "yank the hyphen" out of Italian-Americans or Polish-Americans or other such imperfectly assimilated immigrants. "The military tent where they all sleep side by side," Theodore Roosevelt preached, "will rank next to the public school among the great agents of democratization."[15] Compulsory military training, said a Representative in 1917, "is a melting pot which will . . . break down

14. *Literary Digest* 54 (Apr. 21, 1917), 1150; see also Charles Gilbert, *American Financing of World War I* (Westport, Conn.: Greenwood, 1970), 79–89.
15. Quoted in Chase C. Mooney and Martha E. Lyman, "Some Phases of the Compulsory Military Training Movement, 1914–1920," *Mississippi Valley Historical Review* 38 (1952), 41.

distinctions of race and class and mold us into a new nation and bring forth the new Americans."[16]

Opponents of the continental force had objected to the weakening effect it would have on the National Guard, which was virtually autonomous in each of the several states and hence a favorite institution of the friends of states' rights. But those opponents had objected even more strongly to the compulsory-service features of Garrison's plan. Conscription, they argued, menaced historic American ideals of individual freedom and voluntarism. Some had still darker fears. The chairman of the House Military Affairs Committee told the President that "many Southern members fear it because they believe it will be the means of enlisting large numbers of negroes." On the question of compulsion the continental force scheme finally foundered. "I do not at all agree with you in favoring compulsory enlistment for training," the President wrote to Garrison in the letter that precipitated Garrison's resignation, "and I fear the advocacy of compulsion before the Committee of the House . . . has greatly prejudiced the House against the proposal for a continental army. . . ."[17] The President thus sided in 1916 with those Southern and Western Democrats who so fiercely resisted the idea of obligatory military service.

In his war message, Wilson now appealed to those same elements in his party when he announced his intention to finance the war effort insofar as possible through taxation. But he enraged them when he reversed his stand of the preceding year and called for conscription. In the House of Representatives his party virtually deserted him on this issue. Speaker Champ Clark railed that "in the estimation of Missourians there is precious little difference between a conscript and a convict."[18] Majority leader Claude Kitchin angrily denounced the conscription bill. The Democratic chairman of the House Military Affairs Committee refused to sponsor the bill and relegated its management to the ranking Republican member of the committee, Julius Kahn of California.

The sounds of discord within the President's own party cheered the opposition. Senator Lodge magnanimously announced on the Senate

16. *Congressional Record*, House, 65th Congress, 1st sess., Apr. 5, 1917, 319.
17. The episode is fully discussed in Arthur S. Link, *Wilson: Confusions and Crises, 1915–1916* (Princeton: Princeton University Press, 1964), chap. 2.
18. Quoted in Frederic L. Paxson, *American Democracy and the World War,* 3 vols. (Boston: Houghton Mifflin, 1936–48), II, 4.

floor on April 4 that "when the country is at war, party lines will disappear. . . . Both Democrats and Republicans must forget party in the presence of the common danger."[19] But in reality neither party, and especially not the Republicans, had any such intention. Beneath the veneer of apparent cooperation, Lodge had devised an artfully simple strategy for gaining maximum partisan advantage from the war crisis: he would keep up a drumfire of criticism against the Democrats for their insufficient vigor in the prosecution of the war, and against Wilson for his inability to bring his own party into line. For Lodge, in fact, the war afforded a compound political opportunity. Not only did it provide the occasion for a running attack on the opposition party on patriotic grounds, but it could also be used to flay the pacifistic Republican minority, bothersome progressives like La Follette and Senator George W. Norris of Nebraska.

The Republican Party had been badly divided since the schism of 1912, when Theodore Roosevelt had split the GOP by leading a newly formed Progressive Party against the Republican candidate, President William Howard Taft. By 1917 neither the conservative Eastern nor the progressive Midwestern faction was in undisputed control, though the Easterners seemed to have the upper hand. Lodge lost no chance, therefore, to use war issues both to discipline his own party and to needle the Democrats. He ostentatiously condemned La Follette and Norris for their opposition to the armed-ship bill in March 1917. In April he championed the effort of Theodore Roosevelt, then nearly sixty years of age and in failing health but as enamored as ever with the romance of war, to raise a volunteer regiment to be sent immediately to France. Roosevelt's regiment, Lodge hoped, would exemplify a Republican bellicose fervor that would contrast sharply with the spectacle of Democrats in Congress attempting to cripple draft legislation. Most ominously, Lodge blessed the introduction by his Massachusetts colleague, Senator John W. Weeks, of a resolution to create a Joint Committee on the Conduct of the War. To Wilson, the proposal raised the terrible specter of the Wade-Chandler committee in the Civil War, which had badly harassed Abraham Lincoln. So determined was Wilson to avoid Lincoln's problems with such a committee that he went in person to the Capitol on April 9 and persuaded the Rules Committee to bury the bill, at least temporarily. But it remained, writes one his-

19. All quotations from the congressional debate are from *Congressional Record*, 65th Congress, 1st sess., Apr. 3–6, 1917.

torian, "like a Damoclean sword poised over the President's head in the bitter controversy that was gathering momentum in connection with the war program."[20]

Controversy was the keynote from the moment the Congress began to discuss the war resolution. War with Germany was by then a foregone conclusion, but the certain outcome of the congressional debate diminished neither its vigor nor its significance for an understanding of the character of American society in wartime. The often heated views exchanged on the floors of the House and Senate during that first week of April 1917 foretold much about the months and years that followed. In that debate, the pro-war forces had the telling advantage of overwhelming numbers, while of their opponents it can be said that they possessed in greater abundance the virtues of consistency, clarity of purpose, and prophetic accuracy.

Many who spoke on behalf of American entry figured the war as a contest between democracy and autocracy, a profound ideological struggle in which America was at last aligning herself, selflessly and as a matter of principle, with the forces of right. Others, such as Ohio's Senator Warren G. Harding, subordinated questions of principle to hard considerations of national interest. "I want especially to say," Harding noted, "that I am not voting for war in the name of democracy. . . . It is my deliberate judgment that it is none of our business what type of government any nation on this earth may choose to have. I am voting for war tonight for the maintenance of just American rights. . . ." Not two years of increasingly precarious neutrality, nor the mounting crises of early 1917, nor even Wilson's moving address of April 2 had fully dispelled the cloud of confusion about America's interest in the Great War, even among those who unhesitatingly wanted her in it. That confusion persisted in the minds of many for the duration of the conflict, and would endure even after the guns had fallen silent.

Anti-war spokesmen saw only hypocrisy in the demand for war in the name of democracy. That cry, they noted, came from the lips of men like Senator Lodge who had been among the most tenacious opponents of progressive efforts to extend democratic ideas and institutions in America. It was no accident, said an Illinois Representative, that interventionists came predominantly from the Northeastern states where

20. Seward W. Livermore, *Politics Is Adjourned: Woodrow Wilson and the War Congress, 1916–1918* (Middletown, Conn.: Wesleyan University Press, 1966), 16.

commercial and financial ties to Great Britain were the strongest. War fever, said an Arkansas Senator, had been whipped up by "the Eastern papers yonder." Senator Norris blistered the ears of his colleagues with an impassioned declaration that

> belligerency would benefit only the class of people who will be made prosperous should we become entangled in the present war, who have already made millions of dollars, and who will make many hundreds of millions more if we get into the war. To whom does war bring prosperity . . . ? Not to the soldier . . . not to the broken hearted widow . . . not to the mother who weeps at the death of her brave boy. . . . War brings no prosperity to the great mass of common patriotic citizens. It increases the cost of living of those who toil and those who already must strain every effort to keep soul and body together.
> We are going into war upon the command of gold . . . I feel that we are about to put the dollar sign on the American flag.

Shouts of "Treason! Treason!" greeted Norris's speech, and the Senators heaped equal invective upon Robert La Follette, who on April 4 made a lengthy address accusing the administration of having forced war through a policy of imperfect neutrality that had favored Great Britain. Like Norris, he charged that the war was to be fought for the benefit of the dominant economic classes, to the certain harm of the broad mass of the American public. La Follette's speech "was absolutely worthy of Bethmann Hollweg in the Reichstag," cried Senator John Sharp Williams of Mississippi. "I heard from him a speech which was pro-German, pretty nearly pro-Goth, and pro-Vandal, which was anti-American President and anti-American Congress, and anti-American people."

Opponents of the war resolution made three kinds of arguments. The first proceeded from a careful fidelity to the principles of traditional American isolationism. Many anti-war legislators declared themselves perfectly willing to fight in defense of American rights, and they had accordingly voted for Wilson's armed-ship proposals in March. But in full-scale belligerency they saw the danger of entangling alliances with European powers in the service of aims irrelevant or even antithetical to historic American values. "For defense of American rights on land and sea, let millions be called and billions voted," said Representative Charles Sloan of Nebraska; "for an allied European war of aggression, no men, no money." A second objection to war derived from the perception that certain sections and classes had a disproportionate interest in American participation, and the fear that they would exploit the crisis to their particular advantage. Norris and La Follette dogged this question with remarkable tenacity, but they were only the most prominent spokesmen for a feeling that pervaded much of the populace and was particularly evident in many of the Western states. Charles Nagel, Secretary of Commerce in the Taft administration and a prominent Missourian, wrote to a friend in early 1917 that "some sections of the West may be open to the charge that they desire peace at any price. It is at least as true that large sections of the East are open to the charge that they demand war at any price. The result is not a happy one. The chasm is widening. . . ."[21] Closely coupled with this sectional animosity was an element of class antagonism with historical roots going back at least as far as the Populist upheaval of the late nineteenth century. To many in the West in 1917, American entry into the war represented what the gold standard had signified to William Jennings Bryan's supporters in the 1896 election: a conspiracy by Eastern plutocrats to fasten suffering on the common people for the benefit of big capital. Many found proof of the conspiratorial and unpopular character of American belligerency in the fact that the administration had introduced legislation, even before the declaration of war had been formally approved, providing for government censorship of the newspapers and other curtailments of the right of free speech.

Others made a similar argument about compulsory military service. "I have thought that in a Republic like ours," said one anti-war Senator, "where the public sentiment was supposed to control, a cause for war must be so plain and so just and so necessary that the people would rise as one man and volunteer their lives to support the cause. Do you find any such proposition suggested in the United States Senate or in this Congress today? No! We must, in order to raise and arm troops, adopt this same militarism that we have denounced and decried. In order to raise an army we must make compulsory universal military service." Representative Ernest Lundeen of Minnesota predicted that "This may prove to be the most unpopular war in our history. Conscription, always distasteful to a free people, may soon stalk through the land, hand in hand with his brothers, war and death. If you conscript men for war, conscript wealth for war." A. J. Gronna of North Dakota seconded that proposal when he read to the Senate a telegram he had

21. Charles Nagel to Edward A. Rumely, Feb. 24, 1917, Nagel Papers, Sterling Library, Yale University, New Haven, Conn.

received from the Non-Partisan League, a militant farmers' organization in the upper Midwest, urging that Congress "compel those having property useful to the Government for the carrying on of war to surrender the same to the Government . . . , such property to include factories, shipyards, munitions plants, armor-plate mills, flour mills, arms factories, packing plants, supplies and equipment, cloth factories, steel mills, and iron mills. . . ." The list, listeners might have noted, was virtually a complete roster of the Populists' ancient adversaries.

A third source of anti-war sentiment was to be found in the simple conviction that no cause could sanctify the wanton bloodletting of modern warfare. There were those in the Congress in 1917 who knew that carnage at first hand. "My experience in the Civil War has saddened all my life," said the venerable Isaac Sherwood. "I had my soul rent with indescribable agony, as I stood in the presence of comrades who were maimed, mangled, and dying on 42 battlefields of this Republic. As I love my country, I feel it is my sacred duty to keep the stalwart young men of today out of a barbarous war 3,500 miles away, in which we have no vital interest." On the House floor on April 6, Jeannette Rankin, the first woman ever to sit in the United States Congress, made her maiden speech with tears in her eyes as she answered the roll for the vote on the war resolution: "I want to stand by my country, but I cannot vote for war," she said. "I vote no."

Six Senators and fifty Representatives finally voted against war. Some observers felt that those figures understated the true extent of congressional opposition to the war. Representative Frederick Britten of Illinois thought that there was "something in the air, gentlemen, destiny, or some superhuman movement, something stronger than you and I can realize or resist . . . forcing us to vote for this declaration of war when away down deep in our hearts we are just as opposed to it as are our people back home." Several legislators said they would vote against war if they thought it would do any good, but had concluded that opposition was futile. By the same token, nearly all the ballots against the resolution were accompanied by statements that opposition would cease once war was officially declared.

There seemed indeed to be something inexorable in the air, some sucking wind from across the Atlantic, drawing the United States into the vortex of the gruesome conflict. Some who had tried to stand against that gale scented the noxious odors of repression and hysteria that it was already spreading across the land. "For my vote I shall be not only criticized," said Claude Kitchin, "but denounced from one end of the country to the other. The whole yelping pack of defamers and revilers in the nation will at once be set upon my heels."

Woodrow Wilson himself had helped to spread the bacillus of fear. To be sure, he and the nation were not without provocation. During the period of American neutrality, German agents had committed acts of sabotage and tried to foment labor troubles in East Coast ports and factories, in order to disrupt the delivery of war material to the Allies. In 1915 Wilson had expelled the German military and naval attachés from the country for their connection with those intrigues. But the President had not stopped with reprisals against representatives of the German government. He had gone on in late 1915 and 1916 to launch a broad attack against so-called hyphenated Americans. "There are citizens of the United States, I blush to admit," Wilson told the Congress in his third annual message, "born under other flags but welcomed under our generous naturalization laws to the full freedom and opportunity of America, who have poured the poison of disloyalty into the very arteries of our national life. . . . Such creatures of passion, disloyalty, and anarchy must be crushed out. . . . [T]he hand of our power should close over them at once."[22] In an otherwise dull address, one observer remarked, "The most enthusiastic applause was at the beginning of his attack on hyphenated Americans."[23]

Wilson pandered in that speech to fears about the foreign-born that plagued his generation of old-stock Americans, and did so much to stain their page in history. The problem they faced was real enough. According to the census of 1910, one of every three Americans in that year had either been born abroad or had at least one parent born abroad. Of those 32 million persons from families with close foreign ties, more than ten million derived from the Central Powers. Those were far from negligible magnitudes, and no reasonable critic can fault the men and women of Wilson's day for their legitimate concern about the effect of that immigrant flood on the flow of the nation's life. But what must forcibly strike even sympathetic observers is the reflex response of repression that Wilson and so many others displayed, especially after American entry into the war.

Xenophobia was not new in America in 1917, but the war opened a wider field for its excesses. As early as June 1916, and again in the

22. Shaw, ed., *Messages and Papers of Woodrow Wilson*, I, 151.
23. Quoted in Link, *Confusion and Crises*, 37.

lame-duck 64th Congress in February 1917, Attorney General Thomas Gregory had proposed legislation to punish espionage and to curtail freedom of speech and the press. On both occasions Congress refused to pass the bills. Then, on the evening of April 2, even as the applause for Wilsons' speech faded from the corridors of the Capitol, Representative Edwin Webb of North Carolina and Senator Charles Culberson of Texas moved quickly to arm the President with the tools of "stern repression" for which he had called in his war address. The bills they introduced that momentous evening differed little from the proposals that had failed twice in the preceding year. But the war crisis quickly spurred Congress into action. Ostensibly aimed at checking espionage and treason, the Webb-Culberson legislation sought to vest the government with power to accomplish three objectives: censorship of the press; punishment of any interference with the activities of the armed services, including recruitment; and control of the mails to prevent their use for the dissemination of allegedly treasonable material.

The press censorship provision proved the most controversial. The American Newspaper Publishers petitioned Congress to delete that section from the bill. Senator Hiram Johnson of California voiced the fears of many when he said that censorship such as the bill envisaged would "render impossible legitimate criticism . . . of those who may lead during this war, and lead in incompetence and inefficiency." It was "outrageous, shameful and tyrannical," Johnson wrote to a friend. "I am burning with indignation concerning it."[24] President Wilson burned equally with fervor to possess censorship powers. "I want to say again," the President wrote to Representative Webb, "that it seems to me imperative that powers of this sort should be granted." At the same time he assured noted journalist Arthur Brisbane: "I shall not expect or permit any part of this law to apply to me or any of my official acts, or in any way to be used as a shield against criticism."[25]

Significantly, much of the support for censorship came from the ethnic and foreign-language press, most of whose publishers, conscious of their vulnerability, were anxious to do anything, including submission

24. Quoted in H. C. Peterson and Gilbert Fite, *Opponents of War, 1917–1918* (Seattle: University of Washington Press, 1968), 16; and Hiram Johnson to C. K. McClatchey, Apr. 21, 1917, Johnson Papers, Bancroft Library, University of California, Berkeley.
25. Wilson to Edwin Webb, May 22, 1917, and Wilson to Arthur Brisbane, Apr. 25, 1917, WWP.

to censorship, that might protect them from charges of disloyalty.[26]
Thus when Congress, over Wilson's objections, eventually removed the
censorship provisions from the final version of the bill, it did not act
from friendship for the foreign element or from principled devotion to
the ideal of a free press. Congress was moved more by considerations
of political interest—by the wish to keep the press available as a forum
for partisan criticism of the Wilson administration's conduct of the war.
Calculations such as those united in opposition to censorship such
otherwise dissimilar figures as the progressive Hiram Johnson and the
conservative Henry Cabot Lodge.

The Espionage Act, as it was known when finally enacted into law
on June 5, 1917, furnished the government with ample instrumentalities
for the suppression of those who opposed the war. It provided for
$10,000 fines and imprisonment up to twenty years for persons obstruct-
ing military operations in wartime, and $5,000 fines and up to five years'
imprisonment for use of the mails in violation of the statute. Postmaster
General Albert Burleson was to use his power under the Act to break
the backs of groups dependent on the mails to circulate news among
their members, including ethnic communities, radical labor organizations, and minority political parties.

The Socialist Party was among the first groups to feel the whip of
official wrath. The party in 1917 claimed an active membership of
nearly 70,000 persons; it had polled almost 600,000 votes for its presidential candidate the preceding year, and had elected a sizable number
of mayors and other municipal officials in a variety of cities in the years
immediately before the war. Thrown into momentary ideological confusion by the outbreak of war in 1914 (and by the unseemly haste with
which most European socialists had abandoned the principles of international working-class solidarity and embraced nationalist war programs), the American Socialist Party had by 1916 unequivocally committed itself to an anti-war position. Meeting in emergency convention
in St. Louis on April 7, 1917, party delegates passed a resolution brand-
ing the previous day's declaration of war "a crime against the people
of the United States," and urging "vigorous resistance" to conscription,
censorship, and curtailment of labor's right to strike. The membership
soon voted overwhelmingly to ratify the convention's action.

The party therefore stood, in the spring of 1917, as the largest center

26. See, for example, Gustave Kosik, publisher of the *Slovak Catholic Sokol*, to
Wilson, May 25, 1917, WWP.

of organized opposition to American participation in the war. Socialists thus called down upon themselves the heavy fist of governmental repression, gloved, after June 1917, in the legal authority of the Espionage Act. Burleson began to ban socialist publications from the mails even before the Act had passed, and at an accelerating pace thereafter.[27] During the summer months of 1917, the Post Office Department withdrew the mailing privileges of more than a dozen socialist publications, including major organs like *Appeal to Reason*, which had a prewar weekly circulation of more than half a million. Assaults on the socialist press and socialist leadership multiplied in number and severity as the war progressed, blows from which the American socialist movement never fully recovered.

Many socialist intellectuals anticipated those blows at the outset of American belligerency, and sought refuge in the Wilson administration's welcoming embrace. Following the example of their brethren in the right wing of the Second International in Europe, they hoped by collaboration both to avoid the extremes of repression and to use the war emergency to further the socialist cause. Though pro-war socialists were a small minority within the party, their ranks included nearly all the more prominent radical theorists and publicists. In the days after the St. Louis convention, nationally known figures on the left like Charles Edward Russell, Upton Sinclair, A. M. Simons, Allen Benson, William English Walling, Rose Pastor Stokes, W. J. Ghent, Robert Hunter, and John Spargo all dissociated themselves from the manifesto issued by the convention, and declared their support of the war effort.

This split in socialist ranks over American involvement in the war raised immediate problems for the American Federation of Labor and its shrewd, calculating president, Samuel Gompers. A pacifist himself in his younger days, Gompers had painlessly shed the principles of his youth as he began to see after 1914 the advantages to be gained from his support for the war. Encouraged by emissaries from pro-war British unions, by representatives of the House of Morgan and the House of Rothschild, by Herbert Hoover, and by Woodrow Wilson himself, Gompers came out four-square for preparedness in 1916. Wilson rewarded Gompers's efforts to prepare the American working class for possible participation in war by naming him in October 1916 to the

27. James Weinstein, *The Decline of Socialism in America, 1912–25* (New York: Vintage, 1969), chap. 3; see also Peterson and Fite, *Opponents,* chap. 5.

Advisory Commission of the Council of National Defense, the body formed in August of that year to mount a mobilization program.

Support for the war, Gompers believed, provided the opportunity to gain for labor a voice in the making of defense policy, a modicum of assurance that, as he told the A.F. of L. executive committee, war measures would not be exclusively drawn up by people "out of sympathy with the needs and ideals of the workers."[28] In return for its cooperation, Gompers reasoned, the trade-union movement could ask for stronger government guarantees of the right to organize and bargain collectively, and for the preservation of union standards of pay and working conditions. Gompers called a special conference of A.F. of L. leaders in Washington on March 12, 1917, to issue a proclamation pledging labor's support for the government in wartime on condition that those guarantees be provided. The conference unanimously endorsed the statement, but with considerable reluctance. Andrew Furuseth of the Seamen's Union told Gompers that the resolution "sounds the death-knell of the American Federation of Labor, and your forty years of work for labor you have destroyed today." The heads of several major unions, including the United Mine Workers, had refused even to attend the conference, believing that the proper course for labor was to prevent American belligerency, not underwrite it. "In my broad travels," the president of the Mine Workers wrote to Gompers, "I find little sentiment among the working people in favor of this terrible war."[29]

Gompers knew that to realize the opportunities the war afforded, he needed a united labor movement behind him. The hesitation and the absences at the Washington meeting in March dangerously weakened the wall of working-class unity that Gompers hoped to construct. But the vigorous anti-war manifesto of the socialists at St. Louis threatened even greater trouble. Long Gompers's mortal enemies in the contest for control of the labor movement, the socialists seemed poised in April 1917 to take full advantage of anti-war sentiment among workers and wrest leadership of the labor movement from Gompers's conservative hands. He grew still more alarmed in May when the anti-war socialists joined forces with the Emergency Peace Federation to create the People's Council of America for Democracy and Peace. The Council

28. Quoted in Marc Kerson, *American Labor Unions and Politics, 1900–1918* (Carbondale: Southern Illinois University Press, 1958), 94.
29. Quoted in Bernard Mandel, *Samuel Gompers* (Yellow Springs, O.: Antioch Press, 1963), 362.

hoped to commit American workers to the recently announced peace program of the Russian Bolsheviks, which called for an immediate negotiated settlement without annexation, indemnities, or vindictive features of any kind. Gompers denounced the Council's founders as "conscious or unconscious agents of the Kaiser," and so commenced against the Council a campaign of defamation based on the charge of disloyalty that grew more bitter as the war progressed. Fearing particularly the Council's potential appeal among German-American, Irish-American, and Russian-American workers, Gompers established in August a counter-organization, the American Alliance for Labor and Democracy, dedicated to increasing working-class enthusiasm for the war.[30]

By the summer of 1917 Gompers was engaged in his own two-front battle. On the one side he sought through cooperation with the government's mobilization program to force concessions from capital for labor's benefit. But to accomplish that objective he must first surely weld to the war effort and the Wilson administration the loyalties of a broad spectrum of the working class. That loyalty could by no means be taken for granted in 1917. So Gompers, and his allies in government, fought too on the left, with the pacifists and socialists within the labor movement, who saw in the war possibilities far more terrifying than those that Gompers so hopefully contemplated.

Fissure lines like those that the war widened in the ranks of socialism and labor soon appeared throughout American society, separating the pacifistic from the bellicose, creating in some cases unbridgeable chasms between those who feared and those who welcomed the consequences of American belligerency. Many blacks, for example, contemplated with horror the prospect of a war-fueled wave of lynching and terrorism, as rumors swept the South in the spring of 1917 of a German plot to set the country ablaze with a black insurrection. But other blacks saw in the war a great opportunity, "a God-sent blessing," as one Negro newspaper put it, to earn white regard and advance the standing of the race by valiant wartime service. The Central Committee of Negro College Men petitioned Woodrow Wilson and the War Department "to establish a special officers' training camp for the training of Colored officers for the Colored regiments in the New Federal Army." Though their ultimate goal was the eradication of Jim Crow, said the committee, "our

30. See Frank L. Grubbs, Jr., *The Struggle for Labor Loyalty: Gompers, the A.F. of L., and the Pacifists, 1917–1920* (Durham, N.C.: Duke University Press, 1968.)

young men are so anxious to serve their country in this crisis that they are willing to accept a separate camp."[31]

Analogous divisions of opinion about the anticipated effects of war appeared everywhere in the spring of 1917. All knew that the conflict would define an extraordinary moment in the nation's life, but none could as yet see clearly who would be the beneficiaries and who the victims. Thrust toward a future whose only certainty was tumult, countless groups in the first weeks of war found themselves in a scrambling struggle for position.

Some had begun their maneuvering well before the spring of 1917. In the so-called "preparedness" controversy of the neutral years may be seen the outline of the confrontations whose marks would be stamped boldly on the history of 1917–18. From the outset, the questions at issue in those confrontations reached far beyond the immediate problems of war, as those problems became intertwined with all manner of aspirations and anxieties for the future of American society.

Feminists had been among the first to take the field. Even while the guns of the war's opening battles in Belgium and East Prussia still boomed, on August 29, 1914, some 1500 black-clad women marched in dirge time down New York's Fifth Avenue. Stepping to the beat of muffled drums, they carried a large white flag depicting a dove holding an olive branch, the simple emblem of their pacifist principles. But the organizers of the demonstration, including Fanny Garrison Villard, daughter of abolitionist William Lloyd Garrison, were moved by more than broad humanitarian opposition to war. They felt that war, which would glorify the martial and virile virtues, posed a particular threat to the feminist movement, struggling as it was to minimize sexual differences and to discredit the spurious claim that male primacy in the sexual order derived from the primeval prowess of men as warriors. Within a few months, Villard and some of the country's leading feminists, including suffragist Carrie Chapman Catt and social worker Jane Addams, formed the Woman's Peace Party. It sought both to blunt the drive for American military build-up and to strengthen the cause of American feminism. It was soon joined by a host of newly formed peace societies, including the League To Enforce Peace and the American League To Limit Armaments. In varying degrees those societies, like the Woman's Peace Party, fused the anti-preparedness goals that were their ostensi-

31. Committee of 100 Colored Citizens on the War to Wilson, May 11, 1917, WWP.

ble reasons for being with one or another program for social reform. Thus the first impact of war on the progressive left had been to give its myriad elements new organizational energy and spine.

Contesting with those new organizations for preeminence in the public mind, and for influence at the seats of power, was a sizable array of preparedness lobbies. They were summoned into being, like their pacifist adversaries, by the war drums that began to sound in Europe in 1914. The best-heeled and most formidable of the preparedness groups was the National Security League (NSL), brainchild of New York corporation lawyer S. Stanwood Menken and a number of prominent associates, including preacher-publicist Lyman Abbott, former Secretary of War Henry L. Stimson, and onetime ambassador to Great Britain Joseph H. Choate. Based principally in the cities of the Eastern seaboard, comprised largely of men associated with the nation's leading banking and commercial houses, bankrolled by big capitalists like Cornelius Vanderbilt, Henry C. Frick, and Simon Guggenheim, the NSL was as intimately tied to conservative interests as the peace groups were to progressive elements.

Though its members might admit in private that they were "earnestly sympathetic with the purposes of the Allies," the NSL did not at first openly agitate for American intervention.[32] It did push for measures to militarize American society: a bigger army, an expanded navy, and, above all, a system of universal military training. But, at least in the beginning, the NSL regarded the war less as an immediate problem and more as an occasion to advance long-standing social goals. The NSL's bylaws described its objectives not in material but in spiritual terms: "to promote patriotic education and national sentiment and service among the people of the United States."[33] In practice, those lofty sentiments translated into well-heeled campaigns opposing the election of various Congressmen suspected of criticizing J. P. Morgan or of favoring labor unions or government ownership of the railroads. Taken in sum, one student of the NSL concludes, its policies constituted "a counterattack, in the name of conservative business interests, against political and economic liberalism. . . ."[34]

Progressive pacifists sensed acutely this polarization of domestic po-

32. George Haven Putnam to Theodore Stanton, Feb. 23, 1915, Putnam Papers, Butler Library, Columbia University, N.Y.
33. "National Security League," *Hearings* before a Special Committee of the House of Representatives, 65th Congress, 3rd sess. (1919), 4–5.
34. Robert D. Ward, "The Origin and Activities of the National Security League, 1914–1919," *Mississippi Valley Historical Review* 47 (1960), 60–61.

litical forces around the charged issue of war. The American plutocracy, warned reformer Amos Pinchot, was "using the preparedness campaign as an excuse for preaching the sanctity of American industrial absolutism."[35] Men of Pinchot's persuasion, already attracted by the domestic reform achievements of Woodrow Wilson since 1912, were drawn still more closely to him by the President's steady resistance to the preparedness agitation in 1914 and early 1915. Reformers reassured themselves that they had a like-minded man in the White House, one who took frequent counsel with the representatives of liberal causes, who appreciated the irrelevance of the European war to American affairs, and who was sensitive to the threat that militarism posed to progressive strivings. Oswald Garrison Villard, pacifist son of Fanny Villard and progressive publisher of the New York *Evening Post,* gushed at the time of the *Lusitania* crisis in the spring of 1915 that "every American should give thanks with a full heart that Woodrow Wilson is in the White House at this time."[36]

But Wilson was to prove an inconstant friend of the liberal antipreparedness forces. By the late summer of 1915, moving to protect his vulnerable right political flank, he had begun to indicate his support for what he called "reasonable preparedness." Only four months after Villard had waxed rapturous at the idea of Wilson's occupancy of the White House, the publisher informed the President of "my most profound regret that you have decided to go on the side of the large armament people. . . . The new departure seems to me . . . anti-moral,

35. C. Roland Marchand, *The American Peace Movement and Social Reform, 1898–1918* (Princeton: Princeton University Press, 1973), 245. Though there was much weight to Pinchot's charge, at least some preparedness advocates believed so genuinely in their cause that they were willing to compromise their positions in the social order, if need be, in order to secure a strong military establishment. The attitude of some conservative preparedness enthusiasts toward Theodore Roosevelt made that clear. A champion of reform at the head of the Progressive Party ticket in 1912, and hence a threat to many conservative interests, Roosevelt had emerged after 1914 as an even more aggressive champion of military build-up and, eventually, American intervention. This development threw many preparedness advocates into a quandary, but in some cases it revealed where their real priorities lay. "A new outbreak of Rooseveltism would be a serious thing for us," wrote one pro-preparedness Wall Streeter, "but, in the way the issue is being shaped up now, I am not at all sure that I would not vote for him." Lucius H. Beers to George Haven Putnam, Nov. 20, 1915, Putnam Papers.

36. Osward Garrison Villard to Woodrow Wilson, June 7, 1915, Villard Papers, Houghton Library, Harvard University, Cambridge, Mass.

anti-social and anti-democratic, and the burdens rest primarily on the already overtaxed and overgoverned masses. . . . You are sowing the seeds of militarism, raising up a military and naval caste, and the future alone can tell what the further growth will be and what the eventual blossoms."[37] On November 4, 1915, Wilson publicly announced his intention to submit to Congress proposals for military and naval expansion; he made those proposals the centerpiece of his third annual message on December 7, and the following month he set out on a "swing around the circle," characteristically taking the case for his preparedness program directly to the people. No doubt anticipating the likely sources of greatest resistance to that program, he concentrated his speech-making fire in the Midwest. Everywhere Wilson hammered at the same theme: there was no imminent threat to American security —but the country must ready itself to survive in a world being transformed on the battlefields of Europe. Significantly, the President at this stage did not cry emergency and demand a reflex response. Instead, like the citizen pacifist and preparedness advocates, he set his proposals in a broad historical context, encouraging his listeners to take the long view, to reflect on the complex implications of the war for American society and the postwar world. In St. Louis he even invited his opponents to hire their own meeting halls in which to air their views.[38]

Wilson's deliberate detachment as he took up the preparedness issue was among the many luxuries afforded by America's safe distance from the shooting in Europe. But the President's cool manner was small comfort to his progressive followers, stunned by his abrupt abandonment of his anti-preparedness position.

In all the gathering places and forums of the liberal reformers, men and women agonized over their champion's sudden apostasy. "To break with this man who has been the embodiment of so much hope is hard," said a reform journal, "yet to follow him in the new course he has laid may be harder."[39] Many, at first, chose opposition. Less than two weeks after Wilson's November 4 pro-preparedness announcement, a group of reformers associated with Lillian Wald's Henry Street Settlement in New York came together to form the "Anti-Militarism Committee," soon to be renamed the American Union Against Militarism. The roster of the AUAM's charter members comprised a virtual *Who's Who* of ad-

37. Villard to Wilson, Oct. 30, 1915, Villard Papers.
38. Lillian D. Wald, *Windows on Henry Street* (Boston: Little, Brown, 1934), 302.
39. Quoted in Link, *Confusions and Crises*, 26.

vanced progressive leadership, including Jane Addams, Edward T. De-
vine, John Haynes Holmes, Frederic C. Howe, Florence Kelley, Paul U.
Kellogg, George Kirchwey, Owen Lovejoy, and Rabbi Stephen Wise.
They shared a conviction, as Wald put it, that war was "inevitably disastrous to the humane instincts which had been asserting themselves in
the social order."[40] Howe wrote about this time that war "is usually
identified with a reaction at home. It checks social legislation. . . . The
program that has been going on during the last ten years is likely to be
checked with this new emphasis on overseas interests."[41] Moreover,
Howe and others charged, the preparedness advocates deliberately
aimed to crush the reform movement at home and extend imperial
dominion abroad. The preparedness drive, an AUAM delegation told
President Wilson in May 1916, was a "dangerous expression of class and
national aggression." Thus the AUAM declared its intention to "throw
. . . a monkey wrench into the machinery of preparedness."[42]

The analysis seemed sound enough, and the AUAM's consequent position in 1915 and 1916 appeared appropriately uncompromising. But
doctrinaire resistance did not sit well with such irrepressibly hopeful
souls, eager always to find means for positive accomplishment. The
AUAM could not long maintain a united phalanx of unyielding opposition to the war. Paul Kellogg exemplified the endemic progressive disposition to view events positively when he wrote to Lillian Wald in
early 1916 that "the time is ripe . . . to take both the war scare and
the lesson which the military leaders of Europe are giving us in developing human and natural resources, as two motive factors in pushing
through a program for human conservation and national growth that
might otherwise take years to develop." He outlined to Wald a sweeping reform program that the war might make possible, including a
civilian conservation brigade to undertake land reclamation, a revitalized army to serve as a vast vocational school for the nation's youth, the
curtailment of child labor, and an improved income-tax system.[43]

By early 1917 the AUAM's anti-war lines were wavering badly in the
face of the beckoning call to arms for an idealistic crusade. Some members, such as Jane Addams and Max Eastman, stayed true to their paci-

40. Marchand, *The American Peace Movement,* 223.
41. Frederic C. Howe, "Democracy or Imperialism—the Alternative That Confronts Us," *Annals of the American Academy of Political and Social Science* 66 (1916), 252 (hereafter *Annals*).
42. Marchand, *The American Peace Movement,* 241.
43. Paul U. Kellogg to Lillian D. Wald, Feb. 17, 1916, Wald Papers, Butler Library, Columbia University, N.Y.

fist principles. But the conviction grew in the minds of many others that the war was in fact an opportunity to pursue reform policies—at home and abroad—by other means. It was a trying time—a time, Kellogg noted, "when men's nerves were on edge and so many fellowships snapped under the strain."[44] Rabbi Wise was among the first openly to break ranks. At a dramatic meeting that Kellogg described as "the most gripping experience I have ever been through," Wise, his perspiring face registering the strain of the decision, announced to the other members of the Henry Street group that he had determined to declare his support for the war. Kellogg himself soon followed suit, convinced at last that Wilson had "lifted the plane of our entrance into the war from that of neutral rights to an all-impressing fight for democracy."[45] "I do want to have a hand in fighting it," he wrote to Lillian Wald, "along civil lines, by a drive for a liberal statement of peace terms and a negotiated, liberal peace."[46]

Here was the classic liberal dilemma: whether to oppose a distasteful policy on principle and work against it whatever the pain, or to swallow the bitter pill, seek somehow to make it palatable, retain one's "effectiveness," and push for good policies to temper or counter-balance the bad. The preparedness debate that erupted in late 1915 impaled the progressive left on the horns of that dilemma, where it writhed for more than a year. The declaration of war in April 1917 intensified the agony, and, as Kellogg noted, in the ensuing months the prolonged suffering took a terrible toll in friendships as well as in the spirit and the institutional solidarity of the reform forces.

The AUAM, from its inception a cockpit of controversy over these issues, became during the war a bloody arena for battles among pro-war moderates and anti-war radicals. In the end, few survived intact. The AUAM, in fact, may be taken as a case study of the fragmenting impact of the crisis on the broad pre-1917 base of liberal reform. As the war progressed, many of its members drifted into the People's Council of America for Democracy and Peace, a group so apparently radical that the AUAM's leadership, seeking safety in a volatile time, tried to put distance between themselves and the Council by protesting that "we are not a party of opposition . . . we are not, by habit or tempera-

44. Clarke A. Chambers, *Paul U. Kellogg and the "Survey": Voices for Social Reform and Social Justice* (Minneapolis: University of Minnesota Press, 1971), 61.
45. *Ibid.*, 56–61; see also Marchand, *The American Peace Movement*, 252.
46. Kellogg to Wald, June 6, 1917, Wald Papers.

ment, troublemakers."[47] This was a far cry from the determination to put a monkey wrench in the preparedness machinery, so boldly announced in 1915. Lillian Wald, freshly prudent, put down the radical pacifists as "free lances," without "weighty responsibilities" such as she carried at Henry Street and Kellogg carried as editor of *Survey*.[48] In June 1917, Kellogg, also feeling the weight of responsibility, protested the militancy of the AUAM's Civil Liberties Bureau, headed by Roger Baldwin, which he worried would "so throw the organization out of balance, both in our own absorption in it and in the public estimation as to put us in a position of attempting to paralyze the government and incapacitate us for constructive action."[49] Soon the Bureau was severed from the AUAM, to become the American Civil Liberties Bureau (later the American Civil Liberties Union). In July 1917 Wald resigned from the AUAM, and other desertions followed. A few members persisted to form the Foreign Policy Association in 1921, but the original AUAM, like so many elements of the pre-1917 progressive coalition, pounded and riven by the effects of the war, was rapidly disintegrating into its constituent parts. Soon it was but a crumbled ruin, standing as an empty monument to a lost era of better will and stronger resolve among men and women of good hope.

The preparedness dispute foreshadowed much of the history of the reform cause during the war period. Wilson's turnabout on defense policy in the autumn of 1915, and the attendant anguish it inflicted on his progressive followers, merely hinted at the havoc the war itself would wreak upon the left. Many reformers would be destroyed. Some would be driven further left. The majority, who with fear and trembling decided to take their stand with Wilson, began almost immediately to feel the withering effect of war on the liberal spirit.

The skirmishes of the neutrality period also revealed that, just as in the wars of the French Revolution more than a century earlier, the Great War of 1914 worked to exacerbate conflicts already cleaving American society. Though they owed their formal existence to the war crisis, both the National Security League and the AUAM, for example, represented opposing interests and aspirations that considerably antedated the war. When the war clouds finally rolled across the Atlantic in 1917, those contending forces would be hurled into sometimes violent confrontation.

47. Marchand, *The American Peace Movement*, 253.
48. Wald, *Windows on Henry Street*, 307ff.
49. Kellogg to Wald, June 6, 1917, Wald Papers.

There were other parallels with the era of the wars of the French Revolution. On that distant occasion, Thomas Jefferson had in the same breath lamented the bloodshed in Europe and prayed that the combatants might eat a great deal of American foodstuffs. So too in 1914. No one rejoiced in the catastrophe breaking over the Old World, but many commercial and financial interests recognized, as the New York *Sun* put it, that "anything resembling a general European war would seem likely to guarantee that the economic future will belong to the American continents, especially to North America."[50] The European war, said another newspaper, was "a supreme opportunity for American manufacturers to gain world-wide markets."[51] "It is the opportunity of a century," proclaimed another writer, "of an opening and new century latent with undreamed possibilities for the United States."[52] Government officials shared those heady visions of American commercial advance at the expense of the European belligerents. "It would seem plain," said Secretary of Commerce William C. Redfield in 1915, "that our resources are undiminished, our capital secure, our labor safe, that we are saving when others are losing, that we are living when others are dying, that with us the path is upward and with them it is in large measure downward. It seems certain that one result is to be our own greater industrial independence."[53] Secretary of Agriculture David Houston said in 1916 that it was "unthinkable" that Europe after the war "should be in a position to compete with this country. . . . It is impossible that there should be in any of these nations a great reservoir of useful commodities which the nations themselves have not long ago consumed."[54] America, he concluded, could look forward confidently to a postwar period in which a shattered Europe would yield all its economic advantages to a vigorous, unscathed United States.

American businessmen had tried to profit from the neutrality period in four related ways. They diminished the expatriation of profits by purchasing great quantities of American stocks and bonds thrown on the exchanges by foreign belligerents desperate for cash. In turn, they

50. *Literary Digest* 49 (Aug. 8, 1914), 215.
51. *Literary Digest* 49 (Aug. 15, 1914), 256.
52. Agnes C. Laut, "Will the Shipping Bill Help or Hurt Our Commerce?" *The Outlook* 109 (Feb. 3, 1915), 292.
53. William C. Redfield, "America's International Trade as Affected by the European War," *Annals* 60 (1915), 15.
54. David Houston, "European Competition After the War," n.d., copy in Houston Papers, Houghton Library, Harvard University, Cambridge, Mass.

recaptured many of the dollars so paid out by selling war material and foodstuffs to the warring governments, principally to the Allies. When that dollar supply had been exhausted, they offered large loans to the combatants, thus reversing America's historic credit subserviency to a previously capital-rich Europe. Finally, Americans made strenuous efforts to take over the traditionally European-dominated foreign commerce that the war had disrupted, particularly with Latin America. Those policies had paid off; the economy had been lifted out of recession in 1913–14, and factories hummed at full capacity as America entered the war. Board room charts everywhere showed corporate profits soaring to unprecedented heights.

When neutrality ended in April 1917 businessmen moved to preserve and extend the enviable position they had enjoyed for more than two years. They sought first of all to ensure that mobilization would go forward with as little disturbance as possible to the lucrative arrangements that private enterprise had crafted since 1914. They were determined not to lose the competitive advantages or the high profits of the neutrality period. They resolved further to bind the government more closely to their efforts, both at home and abroad. Many entertained ambitions that could only be called imperial. "Need an American be ashamed to confess that he wishes his country to become the great empire of the 20th century . . . ," asked Henry A. Wise Wood, a prominent inventor and member of the Naval Consulting Board, "that he covets for it a power great as was that of Rome, beneficent as is that of the British Empire, youthful, creative and altruistic as is that of buoyant America . . . ? If we but grasp these, our opportunities," said Wood, "we shall be made able to satisfy at our profit the needs of all nations, and draw on ever increasing income from the industry of other peoples." For the accomplishment of that end, Wood insisted, government must cooperate with business, by helping to build a great merchant fleet, by subsidizing the training of men to manage a far-flung commercial empire, and by securing America's overseas enterprises through force of arms if necessary. "We therefore must hold superior power," Wood concluded. "The aegis of America must protect the American, as did that of Rome, the Roman. Upon no other terms can a nation win either the respect or the trade of the world."[55]

Such was the opportunity that war promised to some Americans. But

55. Henry A. Wise Wood, "Planning the Future America," *Annals* 72 (1917), 19–23.

others had quite opposite views. The then progressive journalist Walter Lippmann sounded a warning in July 1917 about "the forces of reaction" who hoped to turn the war to their advantage. "There are political and commercial groups," he said, "who see in this whole thing nothing but opportunity to secure concessions, manipulate tariffs and extend the bureaucracies. We shall know how to deal with them."

For Lippmann, as for many others, especially those men and women who found in the pages of the recently established *New Republic* the highest expression of progressive political wisdom, the war's opportunities were not to be pursued in the kingdom of commerce but in the realm of the spirit. The chastening rigors of collective martial endeavor would, they thought, forge a new American community, its social and political life lifted to a higher and nobler plane. Lippmann and his colleagues at the *New Republic* in 1917 eagerly accepted the role of prophets for that vision of a purified American democracy. "Out of this horror," said Lippmann,

> ideas have arisen to possess men's souls. There are times . . . when new sources of energy are tapped, when the impossible becomes possible, when events outrun our calculations. This may be such a time. The Alliance to which we belong has suddenly grown hot with the new democracy of Russia and the new internationalism of America. It has had an access of spiritual force which opens a new prospect in the policies of the world. We can dare to hope for things which we never dared to hope for in the past. In fact if those forces are not to grow cold and frittered they must be turned to a great end and offered a great hope. . . . That great hope is nothing less than the Federation of the World.

At home, Lippmann concluded, "we shall stand committed as never before to the realization of democracy in America. . . . We shall turn with fresh interest to our own tyrannies—to our Colorado mines, our autocratic steel industries, our sweatshops and our slums. We shall call that man un-American and no patriot who prates of liberty in Europe and resists it at home. A force is loose in America as well. Our own reactionaries will not assuage it with their Billy Sundays or control through lawyers and politicians of the Old Guard."[56]

Liberals of the *New Republic* stamp repeated those sentiments in countless forums in the early weeks of the war. The National Women's Trade Union League of America sent to President Wilson in June a

56. Walter Lippmann, "The World Conflict in Relation to American Democracy," *Annals* 72 (1917), 1–10.

copy of its war program, which called for nationalization of railroads, strengthening of labor's rights to organize and bargain collectively, and "conscription of wealth through heavy taxes on incomes, particularly those unearned, excessive business profits." The *New Republic* had since 1914 endorsed similar reforms, including extensive governmental regulation of industrial, agricultural, and financial life, as well as social welfare measures like the abolition of child labor. The magazine frankly advocated in 1917 that the war should serve "as a pretext to foist innovations upon the country."[57]

Of course, the exploitation of the opportunity for social reform necessitated support for the war. This was no time to be crying in the wilderness of futile opposition. Like the pro-war socialists and Samuel Gompers, many liberals in 1917 quickly shelved their pacifistic principles and resolved to cooperate with the government's war program in order to turn it to progressive purposes. Thus did Arthur M. Schlesinger, Sr., then a fledgling historian at Ohio State University, congratulate John Spargo for his defection from the Socialist Party. "The Socialist Party has tarred itself without justification with copperheadism," wrote Schlesinger. "The times call imperiously for the marshalling of the liberals of the country for the purpose of making the war an instrument for the promotion of social justice and public ownership. I believe that the liberal forces of the country are ripe for the formation of a party which, holding the Socialist commonwealth as its goal, would bring an enlightened and fearless opportunism to the solution of public questions and which will permit and encourage freedom of opinion and speech within its own ranks. Many of us are awaiting an opportunity to cooperate with such a movement."[58]

Practical politicians were less sanguine than the intellectuals and professors about the prospects for liberal success in wartime. Hiram Johnson, ex-governor of California and Theodore Roosevelt's running mate on the Progressive Party's national ticket in 1912, arrived in Washington as a freshman Senator on April 2, 1917, intending to "progressivize" the Republican Party. He hoped to purge its reactionary elements and commit the party to the advanced social and economic views of the Bull

57. Copy of N.W.T.U.L. Resolution in WWP; *New Republic* remark quoted in Charles Hirschfeld, "Nationalist Progressivism and World War I," *Mid-America* 45 (1963), 146.
58. A. M. Schlesinger to John Spargo, June 3, 1917, copy in A. M. Schlesinger Memoir, Columbia University Oral History Collection, Butler Library, Columbia University, N.Y.

Moose bolters of 1912. But to his dismay, Johnson soon discovered that the atmosphere in Washington smothered all efforts to rekindle the fires of reform. "Everything here is war," he wrote on April 10 to a California friend. "To suggest a social program or a domestic policy would simply afford an opportunity to those who believe in none to boll [sic] you over."[59] Johnson met with a small band of progressives, including Raymond Robins, Harold Ickes, and Donald Richberg, at the home of Gifford Pinchot on April 20. They issued a statement advocating a number of progressive policies, such as guarantees of the rights of labor, price controls, an excess-profits tax, a steeply graduated income tax, and woman suffrage. But Johnson was not hopeful. "Our group has dwindled to very, very few," Johnson wrote after the meeting. Any comprehensive progressive program, he concluded, "will die of inanition. There are not enough of our people left to carry out such a plan."[60]

Whether the war would confirm Lippmann's hopes or Johnson's fears was a question over whose outcome people would fight fiercely in the months ahead. Americans went to war in 1917 not only against Germans in the fields of France but against each other at home. They entered on a deadly serious contest to determine the consequences of the crisis for the character of American economic, social, and political life.

They struggled also to grasp the symbolic meaning of the war, to cast the conflict in terms that would command loyalty or, in the case of the dissenters, compel opposition. George Creel's Committee on Public Information would be the most visible and official organ in the contest to mantle the war with a transcendent ideological significance; scores of other contenders also took to the field in early 1917. Some, such as the pro-preparedness National Security League, had been active for years. Others sprang suddenly into existence with the declaration of war, like "The Vigilantes," a group of authors and artists, including Mark Sullivan and James Montgomery Flagg, who purposed "to drive the peace-at-any-price men to cover, to arouse the youth of the nation to their duties in peace and war, and to carry on a propaganda that will thrill the country."[61]

Despite the historic appeal and plausibility of the anti-war arguments, those notions proved weak weapons indeed when confronted by the arsenal of principles invoked to legitimate American participation in

59. Hiram Johnson to Charles H. Rowell, Apr. 10, 1917, Johnson Papers.
60. Hiram Johnson to Meyer Lissner, Apr. 23, 1917, Johnson Papers.
61. *Literary Digest* 54 (Apr. 14, 1917), 1061.

the war. Woodrow Wilson had brandished the most potent of those principles when he intoned on April 2 that "the world must be made safe for democracy." Interventionists had attempted since 1914 to justify American entry on the grounds that the European war was a fight to the death between the forces of popular government and arbitrary government. Such spokesmen had been embarrassed, until March 1917, by the presence of Czarist Russia in the Allied camp. But the March revolution swept away that troublesome monarchical encumbrance. Wilson in his war address spoke of "the wonderful and heartening things that have been happening . . . in Russia," and the *Literary Digest* proclaimed that "a thrilling change has come over the moral aspect of the war with the Russian revolution."[62] A second revolution in November 1917 would confound those calculations, but for a season the events in Petrograd confirmed in the minds of many a picture of the war as an epic contest between democracy and autocracy, an image that fitted well with the American sense of history.

Pro-war propagandists invoked other dearly held American myths. Most significantly, they nullified the isolationist claim that American entry violated the ancient rule of no entanglement in European affairs by suggesting that the United States was going to war not simply against Germany but against Europe itself, against the very *idea* of Europe and all that Europe historically represented in the American mind: coercive government, irrationality, barbarism, feudalism. "We are resisting an effort to thrust mankind back," said Henry Cabot Lodge, "to forms of government, to political creeds and methods of conquest which we had hoped had disappeared forever from the world."[63] America, in other words, was going to war against the past.

A hundred years earlier, speaking of the Monroe Doctrine, the British statesman George Canning had boasted: "I called the New World into existence to redress the balance of the Old." Americans had always resented the spirit of that remark, but in 1917 they were acutely conscious of themselves as a new, youthful force in the planet's affairs, girding not merely to redress the balance of the Old World but to redeem it. Thus would Wilson refuse to make the United States a formal ally of France and Britain. America would fight, rather, as an "Associated Power," preserving at least in part her unique mission as savior to a decrepit old order. Thus did *The Outlook* distinguish America from her co-belligerents in characteristic terms; there was no crowd in the

62. *Literary Digest* 54 (Apr. 21, 1917), 1156.
63. *Congressional Record*, Senate, 65th Congress, 1st sess., Apr. 4, 1917, 208.

world like an American one, said the magazine. A French crowd might have "fervor," and a British gathering "dignity and pride," but an American crowd was remarkable for its "brightness, its zest—a quality that Americans themselves call 'pep.'"[64] Thus did journalist Frederick Lewis Allen, in a notable intellectual stock-taking in the face of war, affirm that "the spirit of America has remained the spirit of youth," and it stood in hopeful contrast to the senile obsolesence of Europe. There was much confidence to be found in the image of a young United States rescuing decadent Europe from the burden of her feudal past, and many Americans cheerfully accepted that view of the war, with its implications of a new world order in which their country could at last take its rightfully premier place.

But others had their doubts. Frederick Lewis Allen, despite his sanguineness, found much to worry him in the prospect of American belligerency. The image of youth connoted immaturity as well as exuberance. "We must admit that we are undisciplined, careless of law, too ready to disrespect authority and upset orders," warned Allen. "In great measure our democracy has been ineffectual, and our blind optimism has allowed us to surrender too easily to the irresponsible commercialism which has grown up around it."

> The question [Allen continued] is whether we can remain true to the American tradition in time of war. War necessitates organization, system, routine, and discipline. The choice is between efficiency and defeat. . . . The executive side of the Administration will have to be strengthened by the appointment of trained specialists. Socialism will take tremendous strides forward. A new sense of the obligations of citizenship will transform the spirit of the nation. But it is also inevitable that the drill sergeant will receive authority. We shall have to give up much of our economic freedom. We shall be delivered into the hands of officers and executives who put victory first and justice second. We shall have to lay by our good-natured individualism and march in step at their command. The only way to fight Prussianism is with Prussian tools. The danger is lest we forget the lesson of Prussia: that the bad brother of discipline is tyranny. . . . It would be an evil day for America if we threw overboard liberty to make room for efficiency.[65]

Allen touched on a problem that had preoccupied thoughtful Americans for at least a generation before the war began: the proper relation

64. *The Outlook* 115 (Apr. 4, 1917), 604.
65. F. L. Allen, "The American Tradition and the War," *Nation* 104 (Apr. 26, 1917), 484–85.

of the rights of individual freedom and the claims of national need. Progressive intellectuals, such as Herbert Croly, author of *The Promise of American Life* and a founder of the *New Republic,* had long lamented the excessive individualism and consequent chaotic drift of American life. Many progressives yearned for some experience that would heighten social consciousness and tighten social bonds. Woodrow Wilson's successor as president of Princeton, John Grier Hibben, had worried as early as 1914 that Europe might emerge from the war "chastened and purified," while Americans, "far removed from these grim and desperate scenes, should remain insensible to our great opportunities and responsibilities, and continue in our habits of self-seeking and self-indulgence and self-concern."[66] Many intellectuals, in short, welcomed war as the forge in whose fires they might shape a new ethos of social duty and civic responsibility.

There was a dilemma here. Europe had always represented to Americans a version of that very ethos—a perverted version, to be sure, one that exemplified the perils of regimentation, the miseries of individual unfreedom from which millions had fled westerly across the Atlantic, but a model nonetheless of the social philosophy that many people found so harmfully absent in the United States. Could Americans now recross the ocean on a mission that was at once to redeem the old continent and make America more like her? Did not the achievement of American maturity imply loss of innocence and even assimilation to Europe? Those questions, turning always on the relation of the Old World to the New, evoked no certain answers in the spring of 1917.

66. *Literary Digest* 49 (Oct. 17, 1914), 741.

1

The War for the American Mind

"If the war didn't happen to kill you," one of George Orwell's characters observed, "it was bound to start you thinking."[1] The remark might have been applied with special accuracy to Americans. Safely distant from the war zone, they had unique opportunities for reflection. In Europe the swift crisis of 1914 had swept both governments and peoples over the brink with scant time for thought about the war's meaning. In the months that followed, the proximity of the fighting had helped to keep men's minds fastened closely on the war's immediate tasks, rather than its ultimate significance. But during more than two and a half years of neutrality, Americans felt no such restraints on their thinking, and they elaborated vigorous and quite various ideas about the war and its meaning for America. Even the submarine attacks that finally provoked the United States to belligerency had a certain remoteness, and did not instantly clear the national mind about America's relation to the European conflict. President Wilson himself had responded deliberately, even haltingly, to the U-boat assaults, first severing diplomatic relations and then arming American merchant ships before at last asking for a declaration of war. The congressional debate on the war resolution had further reflected the persistent confusion

---

1. George Orwell, *Coming Up for Air* (New York: Harcourt Brace, 1950), 144.

about America's stake in the fighting, and about the precise causes and purposes of American entry.

More than the other belligerent governments, the Wilson administration was compelled to cultivate—even to manufacture—public opinion favorable to the war effort. Lacking the disciplinary force of quick-coming crisis or imminent peril of physical harm, Wilson had to look to other means to rally his people: to the deliberate mobilization of emotions and ideas. Here, the Great War was peculiarly an affair of the mind.

Wilson seemed to sense that fact as early as 1914, when he had called not merely for legal neutrality but for neutral "thought" and "sentiments" as well. The plea had been in vain, for Americans began to divide about the war and its implications for their country as soon as they received the first news of the European armies clashing in Belgium and East Prussia in the summer of 1914. But if Wilson found those divisions of opinion unfortunate in peacetime, he regarded them as intolerable after April 1917. "Woe be to the man or group of men that seeks to stand in our way," he warned peace advocates in June 1917. They had small idea, as yet, just how much woe was to befall them.

Many factors contributed to the intense concern to create a "correct" public opinion in 1917–18. Foremost, of course, was the simple fact that no such opinion could be easily taken for granted, given the conflicting loyalties of America's diverse accumulation of ethnic groups, and given the wrenching departure from usual American diplomacy that entrance into a European war constituted. Other factors, too, had roots deep in the nation's past. America had from the first been a society extraordinarily preoccupied with the problem of like-mindedness. William Bradford had worried at Plymouth Plantation in the early seventeenth century that the independent settlers "on their particular" might corrupt the godly community he was struggling to build in the wilderness. The witch hunts at Salem later in that century further testified to an aggressive concern for uniformity of spirit. In the nineteenth century, some radical abolitionists, like William Lloyd Garrison, had deemed differences of opinion over slavery sufficient reason to dissolve the social contract itself. Garrison on that ground had damned the Constitution as a "covenant with death and an agreement with hell." As Alexis de Tocqueville had observed in the 1830s, few countries displayed less genuine independence of mind and real freedom of discussion than America. Those deep-running historical currents, darkly moving always beneath the surface of a society more created than given, more bonded by principles than by traditions, boiled once more to the surface of American life in the crisis of 1917–18.

Concern for sameness of opinion, for commonality of mind as the indispensable prerequisite for a stable community, carried with it a corollary, especially evident in the reform agitation of the prewar years: that social change should come about primarily through education and the appeal to people's enlightened, better selves. For progressive reformers particularly, faith in publicity as the chief instrument of reform was axiomatic. Underlying that faith was the hopeful premise that men and women in the mass were rational beings, uniformly responsive to reasoned argument and incapable of serious disagreement in the face of scientifically demonstrated facts. Its crowning appeal was the assurance that informed public opinion could substitute for radical institutional reordering or for the naked brandishing of state power as a solution to the problems of the day. Education could cancel out class antagonisms, improve the efficiency of workers, and assimilate immigrants. Publicity could tame the trusts and extinguish corruption; it could settle strikes and pass legislation; it could clean up the slums and end "white slavery." These were comforting beliefs in a society wracked by new social ills but reluctant to repudiate the laissez-faire, anti-statist heritage that Americans prized.

Even Herbert Croly's influential progressive tract of 1909, *The Promise of American Life*, had in its closing pages abruptly attenuated its argument for enlarging the power of government, and had instead called for an educational campaign to "nationalize" the consciousness of the American people. The faith in education, preached most prominently by philosopher John Dewey, was revolutionizing the nation's schools in the prewar era. The faith in publicity animated the countless exposés of the muckrakers as well as the crusades of Theodore Roosevelt against the "malefactors of great wealth." Thomas W. Gregory, Woodrow Wilson's Attorney General, declared flatly that America was a "country governed by public opinion," small exaggeration in an era when the formal instrumentalities of government were so feeble." In the progressive era, under the press of necessity and in the absence of more formal alternatives, the manipulation of mass opinion for political purposes was becoming a highly refined art—and Woodrow Wilson

2. *Annual Report of the Attorney General of the United States for the Year 1918* (Washington, D.C.: Government Printing Office, 1918), 21.

was its consummate practitioner. He had used publicity adroitly to discipline the Congress in the struggle for his "New Freedom" legislation in 1913 and 1914. Now he would use it to discipline the country in the struggle to win the war.

Wilson brought to this effort great gifts—and liabilities. He had all his life been a moralizing evangelist who longed with a religious fervor to sway the public mind with the power of his person and his rhetoric. The war furnished him with a wider stage for the ultimate performance of the act he had long been perfecting. Moreover, Wilson was in many ways an outsider in American politics, an educator who had taken no significant part in public life until his campaign for the New Jersey governorship in 1910. His late start in a political career, and his rocket-like rise to the presidency only two years later, made him an unfamiliar figure in the national corridors of power, and reinforced his already considerable obsession with popular opinion. By temperament he was a traditionalist and by training a conservative historian with a refined appreciation of the value of inherited institutions. But Wilson was a political newcomer who knew not how to manipulate the traditional levers of influence, nor how to move comfortably within existing structures of power. So handicapped, without well-established bases in either party or in Congress, he still had one constituency to which to turn: the public at large, whose collective opinion he repeatedly sought to shape and direct to his political ends. From the beginning of his political career to the end, from his attack on lobbyists in the tariff fight of 1913 and his swing around the circle for preparedness in 1916, to his futile appeal to the Italian people during the Paris peace negotiations about Fiume, down to his self-destructive speaking tour on behalf of the League of Nations in 1919, Wilson had a single master strategy: appeal directly to the people, unify their convictions, awaken their emotional energy, and turn this great massed force on his recalcitrant foes.[3] So Wilson, for all his reverence toward order and formality, was frequently forced by his own peculiar political circumstance to circumvent established forms. He subverted the more or less orderly processes of politics by stirring and heating the volatile cauldron of public opinion.

3. "The real people I was speaking to," Wilson typically said after his "peace without victory" address to the Senate in January 1917, "was neither the Senate nor foreign governments, as you will realize, but the *people* of the countries now at war." Wilson to J. P. Gavit, Jan. 29, 1917, quoted in Arthur S. Link, *Wilson: Campaigns for Progressivism and Peace, 1916–1917* (Princeton: Princeton University Press, 1965), 271.

Therein lay both his greatest political genius and a major source of his eventual downfall.

When Wilson summoned the American people to arms in April 1917, he strained even his large talents for swaying men's minds. Only months earlier he had won re-election to the presidency as the man who "kept us out of war." Now, just as he had reversed himself on the preparedness question in 1915, he reversed his stand on the ultimate question of war itself. And just as that earlier shift had visited special cruelties on Wilson's progressive supporters, so did he now inflict on those same persons what John Dewey called "the immense moral wrench involved in our passage from friendly neutrality to participation in war."[4] For the progressive men and women who had devoted themselves to the settlement house movement, to the campaigns against civic corruption and corporate power, to the struggles for political reform and economic justice, for workers' rights and immigrant education, to all the schemes to civilize the cities and to tame capitalism—for those people in particular the war had seemed distant, repugnant, malicious. They saw it as a regression to medieval violence, a kind of lunatic vestige from the feudal past that had incredibly intruded its way into the modern world, a vile eruption from the pit of corruption that was Europe. As citizens of the New World, believers in the future, in progress and intelligence, they wanted no part of such madness. The immense popularity of Norman Angell's 1910 book, *The Great Illusion*, which argued that a modern war would be monumentally insane and therefore impossible, attested to the faith of the progressive generation that the world must improve by conforming to the precepts of reason and moderation. The reformers thus found abundant moral grounds on which to condemn the war; on practical grounds, too, they naturally worried that American intervention might choke off the movement for domestic reform to which many of them had committed much of their adult lives.

Some of those persons of sensitive conscience would indeed find the passage from neutrality to war impossible to negotiate. The steadfast pacifists—like those who held to the original anti-war principles of the American Union Against Militarism—increasingly found themselves isolated in a wilderness of opposition from which nearly all their country-

4. John Dewey, "Conscience and Compulsion," in Joseph Ratner, ed., *Characters and Events: Popular Essays in Social and Political Philosophy by John Dewey*, 2 vols. (New York: Henry Holt, 1929), II, 577.

men had fled by the end of 1917. But most of the progressives, like most
other Americans, did ultimately make that passage, though the reformers only tempered, rather than abandoned, their earlier misgivings
about American belligerency.

The philosopher and educator John Dewey best articulated the ra-
tionale that helped to guide the pacifistically inclined progressives into
the ranks of enthusiasts for war. He argued that the war constituted a
"plastic juncture" in history, a time when the world was made momentarily more malleable to the guiding influence of reason. The war presented an opportunity pregnant with "social possibilities," which were
not the direct objects of the martial enterprise, but which it might be
made to yield. Dewey therefore looked hopefully to the crisis to bring
about "the more conscious and extensive use of science for communal
purposes," to throw "into relief the public aspect of every social enterprise," to create "instrumentalities for enforcing the public interest in all
the agencies of production and exchange," to temper "the individualistic tradition" and drive home the lesson of "the supremacy of public
need over private possessions."[5] So Dewey argued repeatedly throughout 1916 and 1917 in the pages of the influential *New Republic*, the
flagship of the pro-war progressives and a journal so closely aligned
with Wilson's policies that its editors—Herbert Croly, Walter Lippmann, and Walter Weyl—were sometimes suspected of being his min-
ions. That suspicion was surely exaggerated, but it is nevertheless important to note the extent to which progressive thinkers identified with
Wilson and placed their faith in his person and in his carefully stated
reasons for American belligerency. "I hardly believe the turnover could
have been accomplished under a leadership less skillful than that of
President Wilson," wrote Dewey, "so far as he succeeded in creating
the belief that just because the pacific moral impulse retained all its
validity Germany must be defeated in order that it find full fruition.
That," he concluded, "was a bridge on which many a conscience
crossed. . . ."[6]

5. John Dewey, "The Social Possibilities of War," *ibid.*, II, 551–60; see also Sidney
   Kaplan, "Social Engineers as Saviors: Effects of World War I on Some American Liberals," *Journal of the History of Ideas* 17 (1956), 347–69.
6. John Dewey, "Conscience and Compulsion," in Ratner, ed., *Characters and
   Events,* II, 577. Even pacifistic Jane Addams acknowledged that "certainly
   we were all eager to accept whatever progressive social changes came from the
   quick reorganization demanded by the war." Quoted in Stuart I. Rochester,
   American Liberal Disillusionment in the Wake of World War I (University Park:
   Pennsylvania State University Press, 1977), 41.

That so many thoughtful men and women passed so swiftly from favoring peace to embracing war testified less to the weakness of their convictions than to the deep-running consistency of the progressive mentality, able to find grounds for hopeful affirmation even in the face of unprecedented calamity. It testified equally strongly to Wilson's remarkable adroitness at figuring the war in terms congenial to the American mind, and particularly appealing to the progressives: a war for democracy, a war to end war, a war to protect liberalism, a war against militarism, a war to redeem barbarous Europe, a crusade.

Flying those seductive colors, the *New Republic* steamed into battle in 1917, its helm guided always by the lodestar of Wilson's idealism. In its wake followed legions of faithful progressives, their ears filled with Dewey's siren song. But in the summer and fall of that year, an embittered young intellectual named Randolph Bourne launched from the pages of the short-lived radical periodical *Seven Arts* a series of highly explosive salvos against Dewey's effort to pilot the progressives over the shoals of indecision and into the swelling current of support for the war. Bourne had once been Dewey's enthusiastic pupil, an active exponent of his mentor's philosophic and educational theories. If Dewey's pronouncements on the war crackled with the hot and cranky zeal of the recent convert, Bourne burned with the resentment of betrayal. He aimed his fire almost entirely to the left, at his erstwhile comrades in the progressive reform camp; he had little to say against the forces of reaction on the right, whose support for the war Bourne found altogether predictable. He proclaimed wounded indignation at "the relative ease with which the pragmatist intellectuals, with Professor Dewey at their head, have moved out their philosophy, bag and baggage, from education to war."[7] The pro-war spokesmen, Bourne charged, were sacrificing principle to expediency, values to technique, abandoning reason and endorsing violence as the instrument of social change. Most tellingly, they had in the process identified themselves "with the least democratic forces in American life."

Bourne did not merely disagree with Dewey about the war. His argument, abbreviated though it was by the closing of *Seven Arts* in late 1917, and by his own death a year later, called into question the entire intellectual system that had permitted the philosopher and his followers

---

7. This and the following quotations from Bourne are taken from Carl Resek, ed., *War and the Intellectuals: Essays by Randolph S. Bourne, 1915–1919* (New York: Harper and Row, 1964).

to endorse American belligerency. Dewey's position, said Bourne, revealed nothing less than "the inadequacy of his pragmatism as a philosophy of life in this emergency." This was truly radical criticism, taking the progressives' support for the war as but the outward sign of the
corruption at the core of their thought. Bourne's shafts at the pro-war
reformers dripped with scorn. There was, he said, "a peculiar congeni-
ality between the war and these men. It is as if the war and they had
been waiting for each other." Committed above all to staying close to
the action, they had been easily and contemptibly swung loose from
their philosophic moorings by the tide of war. Dewey, in good pragmatic fashion, had claimed that the war was a fact to be dealt with, an
ugly fact that might, however, be turned to good ends. Bourne countered with a famous question: "If the war is too strong for you to prevent, how is it going to be weak enough for you to control and mould
to your liberal purposes?" The question strongly compelled its own
answer, and its sharp point pierced close to the heart of the difficulties
in the pro-war position. History was largely to confirm the prophetic
implications of Bourne's query, and later generations have canonized
Bourne and anathematized his discredited progressive adversaries. So
thorough has been Bourne's vindication in the history books that it
takes a certain effort to recall that he did not have a monopoly on intelligence and courage in 1917.

The remarkable thing about the support that Dewey and most other
progressive thinkers gave to the war was its carefully qualified and
highly contingent character. Their conversion from peace to war signified neither stupid self-delusion nor weak-kneed whoring after "influence," as Bourne notoriously argued. They were not oblivious to the
dangers that lay athwart their path. Rather, they crossed the "bridge of
conscience" with cautious and measured step, their eyes fixed on quite
specific goals, faith in which alone secured their allegiance to the cause.
No one knew better than Woodrow Wilson how provisional was the
support of the progressives for the war. They were a significant part of
the constituency that had narrowly re-elected him in 1916, and he was
not deaf to their insistent calls for reform and a liberal peace.

Dewey wrote in August 1917 that he harbored a "vague but genuine
vision of a world somehow made permanently different by our participation in a task which taken by itself is intensely disliked. . . . But it
is ridiculous," he stressed, "to say that [progressive goals] are mere
idealistic glosses, sugar-coatings of the bitter pill of war. They present

genuine possibilities, objects of a fair adventure."[8] That language—
"possibilities," "fair adventure"—accurately caught the progressive
mood. The words suggested neither tender-minded naïveté nor swoon-
ing surrender to sonorous idealistic slogans. They suggested, rather, an
attitude of calculated risk. The progressives gambled on Wilson because they felt the stakes were high; but neither did they forget that
the odds were long. In 1917, it was not wholly unreasonable to believe
that the "fair adventure" might, just possibly, be crowned with success;
but the progressives were not so foolish as to presume that success
would be easy, an affair of pious wishes and moral incantations. They
had few illusions of that sort, though they did have abundant—if cautious—hope. Their story, therefore, is not simply a tale of innocence
rudely violated; it is a far more complex matter than that. Locked in
deadly embrace with their palladin, Woodrow Wilson, the pro-war progressives began in the spring of 1917 to trace with him an ironic circle
of history whose outcome would be the stuff of genuine tragedy.

Progressives and their pacifist former comrades, whose numbers and
will were in any case severely diminished by the declaration of war,
were not alone on the field of ideological battle in the America of 1917.
Conservative organizations, like the National Security League, and
special-interest groups of all kinds now sought to invest America's role
in the war with their preferred meaning, and to turn the crisis to their
particular advantage. All, of course, mantled their activities in the rai-
ment of patriotism. But that loose garment could be stretched to many
sizes and shapes, and the struggle to define the war's meaning often
cloaked purposes far removed from Wilson's summons to a crusade for
a liberal peace and democracy.

The nation's schools swiftly became skirmishing sites for those competing groups. Holding more than 22,000,000 impressionable young
minds, they were natural objects of attention. Dispersed through more
than 100,000 school districts, they lent themselves to a kind of ideological guerrilla warfare. The decentralized character of American education meant that the struggle to control teaching about the war had to
be waged in countless local actions, in communities scattered across the
country. Most of the groups that contended to bring their version of the
war into the classroom were themselves local in origin, like the Cham-

8. John Dewey, "What America Will Fight For," in Ratner, ed., *Characters and
Events*, II, 561–65.

bers of Commerce and Rotary Clubs. But soon national organizations were making their presence felt, among them the National Education Association, the Committee on Patriotism through Education of the National Security League, the National Industrial Conference Board, a manufacturers' association publicity arm, and the National Board for Historical Service, a group of historians devoted to the "progressive" or "New History" belief that study of the past should promote present-day social reform.

The initial victories in those skirmishes confirmed the long-voiced criticism that crabbed provincialism was the unfortunate concomitant of local control in American education. District after district did its patriotic bit for the war effort by banning the teaching of the German language. Many states did likewise; the California State Board of Education condemned German as "a language that disseminates the ideals of autocracy, brutality and hatred."[9] The anti-German animus soon extended to teachers. An Iowa politician charged that "ninety percent of all the men and women who teach the German language are traitors."[10] Loyalty oaths were increasingly demanded of school personnel. All texts that failed to condemn the Germans or that made too much of past Anglo-American friction were suspect. The New York legislature created a commission to receive complaints about "seditious" schoolbooks in "civics, economics, English, history, language and literature." Montana barred a modern history textbook for its "pro-German" views, presumably because it asserted in one passage that "Christianity advanced from the Rhine to the Elbe."[11] The perpetrators of these measures cared little for President Wilson's nice distinctions between the German government, with which the United States was at war, and the German people, toward whom Wilson wished to extend the hand of respect and conciliation. Nor did the National Industrial Conference Board appear to agree with Wilson's concept of democracy when it objected to a wartime course of study as too favorable to "the eight-hour day, old age pensions, social insurance, trade unionism, the minimum wage, and similar issues."[12]

It is against this backdrop of local excess and special-interest perver-

9. Lewis Paul Todd, *Wartime Relations of the Federal Government and the Public Schools 1917–1918* (New York: Teachers College, Columbia University, 1945), 73.
10. *Idem.*
11. *Ibid.,* 74–75.
12. Quoted in *ibid.,* 68.

sion of Wilson's war themes that the federal government's efforts to influence wartime education must be understood. Commissioner of Education P. P. Claxton at first resisted all attempts to propagandize in
the schools, and he encouraged the nation's teachers to maintain their
normal educational program. He denounced the expulsion of German
from the curriculum, and against the "hate-the-Hun" zealots he pointedly argued that "the fewer hatreds and antagonisms that get themselves embodied in institutions and policies the better it will be for us
when the days of peace return."[13] But Claxton could not long ignore
the pressures of the various "patriotic" societies. Reluctantly, he allowed
the Bureau of Education to cooperate with the National Board for Historical Service and with the official government propaganda agency, the
Committee on Public Information, in the distribution of various "war
study courses" to the nation's schools.

Those courses sought both to counter the malicious influence of the
"patriotic" groups and to present a considered version, suitable for
school-age children, of the government's view of the war. Drafted by
professional educators, many of them recruited from university history
faculties, the study plans for the courses represented unusually clear
distillations of the way the Wilson administration wished the public to
understand the conflict.

"Patriotism, heroism, and sacrifice" were made the themes of the suggested study plan for elementary school children. Americans fought,
teachers were urged to explain, to protect the victimized peoples of
France and Belgium, burned and murdered in their homes, and "to
keep the German soldiers from coming to our country and treating us
the same way." While warning against emphasis on "the terrible and
the repulsive," the government pamphlet nevertheless encouraged instructors to appeal "primarily to the imagination and to the emotions"
of their young pupils. Students in more advanced elementary grades
were to be instructed in the differences between the autocratic German
form of government and the democratic American way. Those students
were to be further edified by the study of "war biographies" of heroic
figures from the Allied countries. Prominent among the biographical
subjects was Joan of Arc, portrayed as the redemptress of a "France
overrun with enemies." Nowhere, however, was it mentioned that the
enemies then were English—an awkward instance of the untidiness of

13. *Ibid.*, 77–79.

history, knowledge of which might have sullied the bright cause of Allied unity.[14]

That omission typified the standards of scholarship that guided the government's educational work. The authors of the officially sponsored study plans spurned the right-wing hyperboles of the "patriotic" pressure groups, but they retailed simplifications of their own that were equally distorting. The approved elementary school course of study, noted one observer, presented war "as a glamorous adventure filled with deeds of 'patriotism, heroism, and sacrifice.'"[15] Neither negative notes nor ambiguities were permissible. Significantly, the National Board for Historical Service rejected one commissioned syllabus because it raised doubts about "the positive values of nationalism" and the "liberalism of Western Europe." Worse, it did not sufficiently distinguish between "predatory" imperialism and "that exemplified in the present relation of the self-governing colonies to the British Empire."[16] Nothing could be allowed to obscure the theme of autocracy *versus* democracy, principles embodied, respectively, in Imperial Germany and in the Western powers, especially, of course, in the United States. Discussion of "universal" factors like nationalism and imperialism that tended to spread responsibility for the war was not to be allowed.

This black-and-white approach also informed the government's favored war study plan for high school students. Prepared originally by Indiana University history professor Samuel B. Harding for the enlightenment of troops in the training camps, the plan was eventually distributed to nearly 800,000 secondary school teachers and students. Harding's work had the semblance of a scholarly presentation, replete with hundreds of footnotes. But most of his references cited either other publications of the Committee on Public Information, or the official propaganda statements of the Allied countries. On such evidence, Harding neatly demonstrated that Germany alone had caused the war, that German soldiers fought cruelly without regard to the laws of God or man, that Germany was a pervasively militarized society, and that the Allies sincerely wished peace, which the Germans callously scorned. Differences over war aims and peace terms among the Allies and the United States—an embarrassing subject, more difficult to simplify than the image of the bestial Hun—Harding deliberately ignored.[17]

14. "Outline of Emergency Course of Instruction on the War," reprinted in *ibid.*, 58–63.
15. *Ibid.*, 61.
16. *Ibid.*, 57.
17. *Ibid.*, 48–54.

Educators in the colleges and universities responded less swiftly and with more subtlety to the demand for instruction relevant to the war. But by the summer of 1918 mobilization had unmistakably reached the nation's campuses, with the announcement that beginning in the autumn academic term virtually all able-bodied male students in post-secondary educational institutions would be enlisted as privates in the army. As members of the Students' Army Training Corps, they would wear uniforms and live under military discipline. In addition to their regular studies, they would take several hours a week of military instruction. The colleges, in short, were to become a vast network of pre-induction centers where young men could be temporarily held prior to call-up for active military duty.

Integral to this scheme was a special "War Issues Course" which every participating institution was obliged to offer. No standard content was prescribed, though the National Board for Historical Service distributed a list of one hundred questions to be addressed, with accompanying bibliography to guide instructors in arriving at the correct answers. The course varied considerably from one institution to another, but it essentially consisted of a survey of nineteenth- and twentieth-century European history designed to expose the war's origins and fix the blame for its outbreak squarely on Germany. Everywhere the effort was made to include faculty members from a broad spectrum of disciplines, including history, philosophy, economics, political science, and literature. This cross-disciplinary collaboration, however, apparently failed to sustain the various scholars' sense of objectivity. All too frequently, the War Issues Course merchandised to captive college audiences crude historical simplifications, cultural stereotypes, hate propaganda, and reactionary political views. The fundamental purpose of the course, writes one commentator, was "to present the war as a life-and-death struggle between democracy and autocracy, upon whose outcome the future of civilization depended. This purpose was logical for a course designed to enhance the morale of students being trained for combat."[18]

18. This theme of indoctrination was also evident, in muted form, in one of the principal progeny of the War Issues Course. Educators at Columbia College welcomed the War Issues Course as an opportunity to "give to the generations to come a common background of ideas and commonly understood standards of judgment." They sought to continue that function with the creation of a required course in Contemporary Civilization, developed at Columbia in 1917 and widely imitated by American institutions of higher education in the next two generations. At least one of the founders of the Columbia course offered a

Like their colleagues at the elementary and secondary level, War Issues Course instructors had small patience with doubt-breeding complexities. At the University of Chicago, noted historian Andrew C. McLaughlin counseled his teaching staff that the students' work should be kept "below the ordinary college level." Lectures, he advised, "must be very simple, given very slowly, and thoroughly outlined . . . [because] a lot of these fellows do not know Peter the Great from Temerlane [sic] the Great, or Odessa from Petrograd."[19] Also like their fellow educators in the grade schools and high schools, the college-level teachers glided agilely around potentially embarrassing historical problems. One University of Michigan historian blamed the excesses of the French Revolution on "that same military autocracy, Prussia, which . . . goaded the French people into fury by senseless interference." The same professor blandly announced that the "subject people of France love their masters," as evidenced by the presence of so many French colonial troops at the European front.[20] For minds trained to scholarly skepticism, the War Issues Course seemed suddenly to have induced a comforting measure of unblinking certainty. Peacetime history teaching might be a matter of nuance and tempered judgment and vast impersonal forces; but the subject matter of the War Issues Course presented itself as a clear-cut contest between the forces of light and the forces of darkness. That certainty also carried over into issues only tangentially related to modern European history. Stanford's prestigious diplomatic historian Ephraim D. Adams, for example, concocted in 1918 a novel theory of "indirect treason." The perpetrators of that new crime were all those agitators—"Socialists, the Land Tax reformers, the Pacifists"— who refused to recognize "that special programs must, for the moment, be subordinated to the one great object of *winning the war*. . . . These people are traitors to our democracy."[21] As Carol S. Gruber accurately

---

frankly political justification for it. The course, as he saw it, would prepare students to "meet the arguments of the opponents of decency and sound government," thus equipping the college-educated citizen to combat effectively the "destructive element in our society." See Carol S. Gruber, *Mars and Minerva: World War I and the Uses of the Higher Learning in America* (Baton Rouge: Louisiana State University Press, 1975), 240–44.

19. *Ibid.*, 239–40.
20. *Ibid.*, 241.
21. Ephraim Douglass Adams, *Why We Are at War with Germany* (San Francisco: Liberty Loan General Executive Board, n.d.), 20.

concludes, "the course placed educators in the position of war propagandists."[22] It was not their finest hour.

Concreteness, the appearance of "research," simplification, omission for the sake of simplicity and drama, and the appeal to the emotions stood out as the chief techniques of wartime propaganda in the nation's halls of learning. But those traits, exaggerated in war propaganda, also characterized the peacetime mass-circulation publications. Such tactics had been especially evident in the "advocacy journalism" of the prewar muckrakers. Muckraking journalists had made a deep impress on American culture in the first decade and a half of the twentieth century. Their appearance had coincided with the rise of aggressively marketed popular magazines like *Collier's* and *McClure's*, and with the spread of the progressive reforming spirit. Indeed, the muckrakers helped to further both those developments. Seeking to boost circulation, magazine editors had eagerly published the muckrakers' sensational exposés of corruption in high places, such as David G. Phillips's startling attack in 1906, "The Treason of the Senate," which charged that the majority of U.S. Senators had been bought by the big corporate interests. Progressives had applauded when muckrakers laid bare the fraudulent practices of the meat-packing or patent-medicine industries, or the unfair tactics of the Standard Oil Company, or the sordid facts about child labor, racial injustice, or the white slave trade. Yet for all the energy that went into them, and for all the outrage they provoked, the writings of the muckrakers had produced few genuine reforms. Muckraking or exposé journalism was by its very nature a crude instrument, not directed precisely at the pivots of power, but rather aimed broadside, its target being the individual consciences of millions of readers. Like all scattered fire, the blasts of the muckrakers were easily defended against. Muckraking was a quintessentially progressive endeavor. It relied on publicity rather than the direct exercise of power, and it was content with agitation rather than accomplishment.

It was significant, therefore, that Woodrow Wilson chose prominent muckraker George Creel to head the Committee on Public Information. Creel surrounded himself with people like Ida Tarbell, Ernest Poole, Will Irwin, and Ray Stannard Baker—all passionate muckrakers before

22. Gruber, *Mars and Minerva*, 238; see also George T. Blakey, *Historians on the Homefront: American Propagandists for the Great War* (Lexington: University Press of Kentucky, 1970).

the war and devotees of the progressive reforming faith.[23] Creel was arrestingly handsome, outspoken, and boundlessly vital. He was also impetuous and caustic, a man of whom it was said that an open mind formed no part of his inheritance. An ardent Wilson supporter in 1912 and 1916, he boasted impeccable credentials as a fire-breathing progressive reformer. Before the war he had harnessed his prodigious energies to reform crusades in Kansas City and Denver, and now he eagerly enlisted his facile pen and organizational talents in the greatest crusade of them all.

The Secretaries of War, Navy, and State proposed an official information agency to the President in April 1917, arguing that in wartime more than ever citizens should be "given the feeling of partnership that comes with full, frank statements concerning the conduct of the public business."[24] Not censorship but publicity, they suggested, should be the keynote of the government's policy toward news and opinion. Newton D. Baker later declared that the official philosophy of the Committee on Public Information (CPI) was "faith in democracy . . . faith in the fact."[25] That formula succinctly summarized the muckrakers' creed, and George Creel gave it his wholehearted assent. He took quite seriously the traditional regard of American democracy for the individual consenting will as the cornerstone of political legitimacy and social action. He made that scrupulous voluntarism the informing motif of the CPI's activities. He shunned coercion and censorship, techniques that he scornfully dismissed as "European." In common with other wartime administrators, Creel prided himself on the formal, legal weakness of his agency. "We had no authority," he trumpeted. "Yet the American idea *worked*. And it worked better than any European *law*." Creel drew satisfaction from the contrast between a Europe stultified by statutes and a happier America where persuasion and consensus had replaced stark authority and servile submission. His opposition to censorship derived not from First Amendment principles, but from his belief "that

23. To a lesser degree, these attributes were also characteristic of the "New History" of the so-called "progressive school." See Richard Hofstader, *The Progressive Historians* (New York: Knopf, 1968), and John Higham et al., *History: The Development of Historical Studies in the United States* (Princeton: Princeton University Press, 1965), especially chap. 3.

24. Robert Lansing, Newton D. Baker, and Josephus Daniels to Woodrow Wilson, Apr. 13, 1917, WWP.

25. George Creel, *How We Advertised America* (New York: Harper and Brothers, 1920), xiv.

the desired results could be obtained without paying the price that a formal law would have demanded. . . . Better far to have the desired compulsions proceed from within than to apply them from without."[26]

Probably the most eloquent testimony to the sincerity of Creel's sentiments was the CPI's publication of the *Official Bulletin*, the first comprehensive, day-by-day guide to the proceedings of every government department and agency.[27] It was usually a dull document, perhaps, but it showed Creel's commitment to information and disclosure, pure and simple, as the preferred means to win what he unashamedly called "the fight for the *minds* of men, for the 'conquest of their convictions.' "[28] A similar attitude governed the work of the "Four-Minute Men," at least in the early months of the war. A small, fast-talking army of patriotic speechifiers, the 75,000 Four-Minute Men were selected in local communities from among applicants endorsed by at least "three prominent citizens—bankers, professional or business men."[29] Thus certified as to speaking prowess and safe political views, the men were turned loose for four-minute stints before any available audience to whip up enthusiasm for the war. But they were carefully instructed, at first, that "a statement only of patent facts will convince those who require argument more readily than 'doubtful disputations. . . .' No hymn of hate accompanies our message."[30] Before the war was over, in addition to its activities in the schools, the CPI had distributed 75 million copies in several languages of more than thirty pamphlets explaining America's relation to the war. It had sponsored war expositions in nearly two dozen cities, attended by 10 million people. It had issued 6000 press releases to assist (and to influence) the nation's newspapers in their reporting on the war.

Creel never abandoned his faith in "the fact," but as the war went forward, the CPI strayed ever farther from its original, exclusively informational mission and increasingly took on the character of a crude propaganda mill. The Committee began to place illustrated advertisements in mass magazines like the *Saturday Evening Post*, exhorting

26. *Ibid.*, 24, 16–17; italics in original.
27. *The Official Bulletin* was a kind of precursor of the now-familiar *Federal Register*, which began publication in the 1930s when the scope and importance of government's daily operations again expanded.
28. Creel, *How We Advertised*, 3.
29. *Ibid.*, 89.
30. James R. Mock and Cedric Larson, *Words That Won the War: The Story of the Committee on Public Information, 1917–1919* (Princeton: Princeton University Press, 1939), 122–23.

readers to report to the Justice Department "the man who spreads pessimistic stories . . . , cries for peace, or belittles our efforts to win the war."[31] By the beginning of 1918, the Four-Minute Men were specifically encouraged to use atrocity stories. The Committee, which early in the war had produced upbeat films like *Pershing's Crusaders* and *Our Colored Fighters*, turned to promoting movies like *The Prussian Cur*, and *The Kaiser, the Beast of Berlin*. And in a development chillingly evocative of the "Two Minutes Hate" exercise practiced by George Orwell's Oceanians in his novel, *1984*, the CPI urged participatory "Four-Minute Singing" to keep patriotism at "white heat."[32]

The parallels between World War I America and the setting of Orwell's famous cautionary tale are instructive. The Oceania of *1984* was distant from the actual fighting (if indeed there was any actual fighting), its citizens ignorant about their country's purposes and interests, and its masters determined to use war anxieties to discipline fractious "proles" at home. So too was World War I America almost eerily distant from the battlefields. Many American citizens felt uncertain about the causes and aims of American belligerency. And conservative elements, increasingly abetted by the Wilson administration, anxiously sought to suffocate troublesome immigrant and working-class elements in an avalanche of "patriotism."

To be sure, neither George Creel nor Woodrow Wilson should be taken as models for Big Brother, nor can the content of the CPI's propaganda be closely assimilated to the creations of Orwell's Ministry of Truth. The Four-Minute Singers, after all, sang "Pack Up Your Troubles," and "There's A Long, Long Trail," tunes scarcely comparable to the ferocious chants Winston Smith and his co-workers flung at the telescreen in *1984*. But neither should the parallels be quickly dismissed. The American experience in World War I (as, indeed, the experience of many other belligerents in that war) darkly adumbrated the themes Orwell was to put at the center of his futuristic fantasy: overbearing concern for "correct" opinion, for expression, for language itself, and the creation of an enormous propaganda apparatus to nurture the desired state of mind and excoriate all dissenters. That American propaganda frequently wore a benign face, and that its creators genuinely believed it to be in the service of an altruistic cause, should not obscure those important facts.

31. *Ibid.*, 65.
32. *Ibid.*, 124 and *passim*; Creel, *How We Advertised, passim.*

Creel confessed after the Armistice, "When I think of the many voices that were heard before the war and are still heard, interpreting America from a class or sectional or selfish standpoint, I am not sure that, if the war had to come, it did not come at the right time for the preservation and reinterpretation of American ideals."[33] Clearly, the paramount ideal in Creel's mind, as in the minds of many of his countrymen, was the ancient American longing for a unanimous spirit, for a single, consensual set of values that would guarantee the social harmony, not to mention the economic efficiency, of the nation. Active always in American culture, in war that longing grew acute. And no fact seemed more insulting to the ideal of unity in 1917 than the gaudy presence in American society of millions of unassimilated immigrants. The wartime drive for unity, spearheaded by Creel's Committee, led naturally to a campaign for accelerated "Americanization" of those newcomers. That campaign soon exceeded Creel's ability, or the ability of any of the reformers who had long lobbied on behalf of the immigrants, to control it.

Few issues festered more sorely in the American body politic in 1917 than those borne by the great waves of immigration that had washed the nation's shores in the preceding generation. Down through the nineteenth century, the country had given no sustained attention to the problem of assimilating the immigrants who streamed through the coastal ports and into the virtually empty hinterland. Confidence in the equalizing effect of abundant land, and the familiar cultural backgrounds of the immigrants themselves, combined to underwrite a national policy of laissez-faire toward immigration. The melting pot, Americans believed, would automatically fuse the various foreign elements into an acceptably homogeneous national amalgam. But around the turn of the century, many people began to doubt that item of national faith. The United States was changing, providing fewer opportunities for entrepreneurship or independent farming, and sucking more and more of Europe's "surplus" people into the mines and foundries and factories of an industrial America. Increasingly, the newcomers huddled together in the great cities, where they made up not an independent yeomanry but an industrial proletariat. They also came more frequently from the strange and suspect lands southeast of the Alps and beyond the Danube and the Vistula. Beginning in the 1880s, immigrants from the "new" regions outnumbered those from the "old" areas of northwestern Europe. By the end of the century, a movement actively

33. Creel, How We Advertised, 105.

to encourage the "Americanization" of those peoples had begun to stir.

That movement sprang from two not entirely compatible sources. One comprised the settlement house workers and social reformers, among them women activists such as Lillian Wald, Jane Addams, and Josephine Roche, and many of the people eventually associated with the American Union Against Militarism. Their first concern was for the immigrants themselves. Especially prominent in this camp was Frances Kellor, guiding spirit of the Committee for Immigrants in America, founded in 1914 to promote the education of immigrants and protect them from predatory *padrones* and exploiting employers.

Reformers of this stripe, writes historian John Higham, sought "to temper as well as improve the ordinary course of assimilation by providing a receptive environment for Old World heritages. Preaching the doctrine of immigrant gifts, Jane Addams and her fellow workers concentrated less on changing the newcomers than on offering them a home."[34] The other source of the Americanization movement was a loose coalition comprised of old-stock Americans who feared for the continued ascendancy of their cultural values and social position, and businessmen who sought to discipline a troublesomely varied labor force. This type of Americanizer, Higham observes, "preached a loyalty that consisted essentially of willing submissiveness. Above all, in the words of the D.A.R., they 'taught obedience to law, which is the groundwork of true citizenship.' The main object of such self-constituted champions of America was to combat the danger of immigrant radicalism or discontent; their chief motive, fear."[35]

The war thrust those two groups into unholy collaboration, and immediately tested which attitude toward the nation's immigrant masses would prevail. At first, war conditions seemed most to benefit the cause of the liberal Americanizers, as many old-stock Americans, awakened to the need for wartime unity, made genuine efforts to bring previously excluded aliens into the life of the community. Higham reports that in at least one New England industrial town many residents in the 1930s looked back fondly on the vital social spirit that prevailed in 1917–18, "when some of the traditional ethnic and religious barriers had broken down."[36] Similarly, the Committee for Immigrants in America found its

34. John Higham, *Strangers in the Land: Patterns of American Nativism, 1860–1925* (New York: Atheneum, 1963), 236.
35. *Ibid.*, 237.
36. *Ibid.*, 216.

programs significantly advanced by the war. The Bureau of Education, in close collaboration with the Committee (even with its financial support), inaugurated an ambitious "War Americanization Plan" that sponsored English and citizenship classes in schools, community halls, and factories. The Bureau of Naturalization reported that the number of such programs tripled in 1917, "rejuvenating, rebuilding, and placing within reach of the adult immigrant . . . those opportunities which exist on every hand but from which he is shut off by the barrier of a foreign tongue and foreign traditions."[37]

At the CPI, George Creel gave heart to the liberal Americanizers when he named one of their number, social worker Josephine Roche, to head the Division of Work with the Foreign-Born. Roche, with Creel's approval, set out to organize "Loyalty Leagues" in America's many ethnic communities. The Leagues served primarily as conduits for circulating extremely simple foreign-language pamphlets on various topics related to the war. The Division also sponsored rallies and pageants, including a much-ballyhooed "pilgrimage" to Mt. Vernon, in Virginia, on July 4, 1918. There, while Irish-born tenor John McCormack sang the "Battle Hymn of the Republic," representatives of thirty-three different ethnic groups reverently filed past Washington's burial place. In addition, drawing on reports from agents abroad, the CPI undertook to provide readers of the foreign-language press with "local, sentimental and humorous matter" culled from their old-country newspapers. As a CPI official explained, "If we . . . let them have this look-in they will feed out of our hands on all the propaganda we supply."[38] To ensure that CPI propaganda was being properly digested, the Committee established a network of bilingual watchdogs (many of them university professors), assigned to monitor the foreign-language publications in their area for "material which may fall under the Espionage Act."[39] In a remarkable twist on the "Americanization" campaign at home, which hoped to root out ethnic particularity, the CPI also mobilized American ethnic groups to carry propaganda back to their European homelands. Creel encouraged General Pershing, for example, to send wounded Italian-American troops to Italy for convalescence, where they spread the Wilsonian gospel and "turned out to be our best propagandists."[40]

37. Edward George Hartmann, *The Movement To Americanize the Immigrant* (New York: AMS Press, 1967), 181.
38. Mock and Larson, *Words That Won the War*, 228.
39. Gruber, *Mars and Minerva*, 157.
40. Creel, *How We Advertised*, 244.

The Committee paid special attention to Austria-Hungary, where the doctrine of self-determination had great appeal. Creel encouraged immigrants from that polyglot empire to foment among their old-country brethren the very notions of ethnic consciousness and separatism that were under such brutal attack in the United States itself. The CPI thus showed that it cared as much about controlling and manipulating immigrant groups as it did about educating them.

Even the prewar immigrant education movement had contained illiberal and conformist elements. At Henry Ford's factory school for immigrants, the first English sentence to be mastered was "I am a good American," and the graduating pupils were made to act out a gigantic pantomime in which old-country-clad immigrants filed into a large "melting pot," while out of it poured a stream of men, "each prosperously dressed in identical suits of clothes and each carrying a little American flag."[41] But such exercises reflected, until the advent of war, subdominant themes. For the most part the impulse to Americanize through education was animated by a sincere regard for the immigrants themselves, by the desire to treat them fairly and equip them to survive and even prosper in their new land. Creel shared those sentiments, though he made clear that his highest ambition was to end "the tendency toward segregation" of ethnic communities.[42] Not pluralism but homogeneity remained his ideal, and in that preference he closely resembled many of even the most liberal Americanizers. In the last analysis, they differed with the exponents of forced assimilation more over tactics than ultimate goals.

With the quickening tempo of war, the enlightened tactic of education for immigrants steadily gave way to the harsh technique of repression. To a significant degree, the concern for preparedness and the concern for forced assimilation flowed from the same anxiety about the flabbiness of American society in a hostile world. It was not surprising, therefore, that the two campaigns had commingled. Many of the spokesmen who cried for greater military strength frequently spoke in the next breath about the necessity to create—by coercion if necessary—a strong, unifying nationalist sentiment among the immigrant masses where no such sentiment appeared to exist. Preparedness paraders on New York's Fifth Avenue in 1916, for example, had passed beneath a

41. Higham, Strangers, 248.
42. Mock and Larson, Words That Won the War, 231.

great electric sign that flashed: "Absolute and Unqualified Loyalty to Our Country."[43] And the speech in which President Wilson first presented his preparedness proposals to Congress in 1915 had also contained a vicious attack on foreign-born "creatures of passion, disloyalty, and anarchy," who, he warned, must be "crushed out."[44] Even Frances Kellor, symbol of the humane and generous approach to Americanization, took herself before a receptive National Security League audience in 1916 to raise the specter of an America imperiled from within by alien influences.[45] Indeed, the NSL itself exemplified the confounding of militaristic and anti-alien sentiments under pressure of war. Created originally to lobby for greater attention to national defense policy, the NSL had shifted its attention by war's end to a broad range of conservative concerns, especially internal security and the dangers of "hyphenated Americanism." Its educational director declared in 1918 that "the melting pot has not melted," and that "there are vast communities in the Nation thinking today not in terms of America, but in terms of Old World prejudices, theories, and animosities. . . . In the bottom of the melting pot there lie heaps of unfused metal."[46] League President Charles B. Leydecker announced in 1918 that the organization had a new set of goals, including "protecting our national legislators from dangerous proletarians."[47] Elsewhere, Leydecker defined a "proletarian" as "that member of society who is devoid of thrift, industry, or any accumulation by reason therefore. . . . Our imported people are, unfortunately, some of them of that class."[48]

That kind of rank nativism, tinged often with anti-radicalism, seeped deeper and deeper into the American mind as the war progressed, carried by the current of a newly fashioned phrase: "100 percent Americanism." The 100 percenters aimed to stamp out all traces of Old World identity among immigrants. They visited their worst excesses on German-Americans, which at first glance was scarcely surprising. But the abuse directed at German-Americans did reveal the specific roots of the era's nativism in the war. Before 1914 the Germans had been proba-

43. Higham, *Strangers*, 200.
44. Albert Shaw, ed., *The Messages and Papers of Woodrow Wilson*, 2 vols. (New York: Review of Reviews Corp., 1924), I, 151.
45. Higham, *Strangers*, 244–45.
46. "National Security League," *Hearings* before a Special Committee of the House of Representatives, 65th Congress, 3rd sess. (1919), 2013.
47. *New York Times*, Nov. 17, 1918, sec. II, 1.
48. "National Security League," 221.

bly the most esteemed immigrant group in America, regarded as easily assimilable, upright citizens. Now they found themselves the victims of a brainless fury that knew few restraints. Familiar words like "hamburger" and "sauerkraut" were replaced by "liberty sandwich" and "liberty cabbage." In Iowa, the governor forbade the speaking of German on streetcars, over the telephone, or in any public place. On the day of Wilson's war message, a man in Wyoming who exclaimed "Hoch der Kaiser" was hanged, cut down while still alive, and made to kneel and kiss the American flag.

In one of the war's most infamous cases of vigilantism, near St. Louis in April 1918, a mob seized Robert Prager, a young man whose only discernible offense was to have been born in Germany. He had, in fact, tried to enlist in the American Navy but had been rejected for medical reasons. Stripped, bound with an American flag, dragged barefoot and stumbling through the streets, Prager was eventually lynched to the lusty cheers of five hundred patriots. A trial of the mob's leaders followed, in which the defendants wore red, white, and blue ribbons to court, and the defense counsel called their deed "patriotic murder." The jury took twenty-five minutes to return a verdict of not guilty, accompanied by one jury member's shout, "Well, I guess nobody can say we aren't loyal now." The *Washington Post* commented: "In spite of excesses such as lynching, it is a healthful and wholesome awakening in the interior of the country."[49]

Suspicion, intolerance, and vigilantism were not aimed exclusively at German-Americans. Every citizen, said the head of the Iowa Council of Defense, should join a patriotic society, denounce *all* those persons who dared even to discuss peace, and generally "find out what his neighbor thinks." In short, concludes Higham, "by threat and rhetoric 100 per cent Americanizers opened a frontal assault on foreign influence in American life. They set about to stampede immigrants into citizenship, into adoption of the English language, and into an unquestioning reverence for existing American institutions. They bade them abandon entirely their Old World loyalties, customs and memories."[50]

By the time of the Armistice, the 100 percent spirit, so distant from the original Americanizing aims of people like Jane Addams and Frances Kellor, reigned supreme. Where the liberal Americanizers had looked to the government for aid in the immigrant education program,

49. H. C. Peterson and Gilbert C. Fite, *Opponents of War, 1917–1918* (Seattle: University of Washington Press, 1968), 202–7.
50. Higham, *Strangers*, 247.

100 percenters now pressed to enlist the state's authority for purposes of repression and exclusion. Significantly, the two campaigns met with markedly different fates. Both the 65th and 66th Congresses rejected bills to appropriate funds for the Bureau of Education "with the purpose . . . of giving aliens the ground work of Americanism."[51] But in 1917, Congress for the first time sustained over the President's veto a bill mandating a literacy test for prospective immigrants. And in 1921 Congress ended a phase in American history by imposing an absolute numerical limit on immigration, accompanied by a quota system based on national origin. This measure not only effectively closed the gates, but rankly discriminated against people from southern and eastern Europe. The postwar era thus began with an official salute to the 100 percent spirit the war had made ascendant.

Just as Creel's apparently good intentions toward immigrants had succumbed to the malignities of the 100 percenters, so were his sympathies for labor largely swamped by the forces of reaction. Immigrants and laborers were to a great extent the same people, but the CPI directed special attention to them in their roles as workers crucial to war production. "In every publication of the Committee," observed the historians of the CPI, "in the appeal of its Four-Minute Men, its news stories, its posters, its movies, and its syndicate features, the effect on labor was carefully considered."[52]

The government was rightly uneasy about labor's behavior. European workers had chafed increasingly at their war-harness since 1914, and especially after the Bolshevik Revolution in late 1917 the governments of the Allies as well as the Central Powers held the loyalty of their working classes only with difficulty. Though American labor was neither so well organized nor so ideologically inclined as the European working class, it was nevertheless a restive body in the prewar years, and its fitful stirrings made it seem menacing in the minds of many businessmen. The head of General Motors, for example, had confided to presidential adviser Colonel Edward House just weeks before the American declaration of war his belief that "we are sitting on a volcano and that war might cause an eruption."[53]

51. *New York Times,* Jan. 27, 1920, 7; see also Hartmann, *Movement To Americanize,* 230–33.
52. Mock and Larson, *Words That Won the War,* 231.
53. Edward M. House Diary, entry for Feb. 24, 1917, House Papers, Sterling Library, Yale University, New Haven, Conn.

Many employers who shared that fear sought to enlist the government's aid in capping the volcano. They were resolved that the war should provide no opportunity for workers to improve their wages or working conditions or, worse still, to spread the blight of unionism.

To those predictable fears on the part of businessmen was added another anxiety, even more threatening in its implications for the government's war effort. Workers were the natural recruits for the pacifist appeals of the Socialist Party. The socialists charged that the war was a capitalists' quarrel, and that America was now fixing bayonets not to make the world safe for democracy, but to redeem the loans made to the Allies by Wall Street bankers. The popularity of those charges with workers seemed to be swelling in 1917. In November, Morris Hillquit, an openly anti-war socialist candidate for Mayor of New York (reviled as a "Hillquitter" and accused by Theodore Roosevelt of cowardly cringing before the Hun), received five times the usual socialist vote. Similar dramatic gains for socialist candidates were registered in local elections in New York, Ohio, and Pennsylvania, apparently attributable to the party's emergence as the rallying point for opposition to the war.[54] In the West and in some New England mill towns, the less numerous but more militant Industrial Workers of the World (IWWs, or "Wobblies") took a similarly strong anti-war stand, which they embellished with calls for sabotage and wrathful denunciations of an alleged union-busting conspiracy between capitalists and the government.

These developments posed an immediate threat to the mobilization of industry. They also struck at the heart of the Wilson administration's campaign to define the war as a popular democratic struggle against German autocracy. But to many businessmen, the pacifism of the Wobblies and the socialists must have seemed a rare opportunity, since it allowed them to brand *all* labor agitation as disloyal and traitorous.

George Creel knew that employers were trying to bludgeon labor with the club of "patriotism," and he repeatedly condemned those efforts. Workers, he wrote, "are bitterly resentful of this sort of thing. They feel that if they are to surrender their demands in the matter of hours and overtime, that employers . . . should make like concessions in the matter of profits." While the government discouraged strikes, he noted, "it avoids very carefully any suggestion that it denies the right of labor to protest against conditions. . . . The most important task

54. See James Weinstein, *The Decline of Socialism in America, 1912–1925* (New York: Vintage, 1969), chap. 3.

we have before us today in the fight for unity is that of convincing
the great mass of workers that our interest in democracy and justice begins at home."[55] Thus Creel scrupulously distinguished between the
issues of labor's welfare and labor's loyalty. He favored the former;
but he could not leave the latter issue unattended. He must somehow
combat the socialist appeal.

Creel had an eager ally in American Federation of Labor President
Samuel Gompers. A British-born cigar-maker who had emigrated to
the United States during the Civil War, Gompers was tough and short,
his chunky body a small furnace of energy that perpetually propelled
him in dogged, single-minded pursuit of his goals. He had early in life
rejected European socialist doctrines as inappropriate to the American
working class. He spent his career promoting "pure and simple" trade
unionism, strictly divorced from ideology. For theory and for intellectuals he had the utmost contempt. Abundant jobs, better working conditions, more pay—that was Gompers's concrete program, and he
worked tirelessly, often in close collaboration with big capital, to promote those aims and simultaneously insulate the American labor movement from the disrupting effects of doctrinaire socialism. He was animated not by dreams of broad-scale social reconstruction, nor by abstract
principle, but by the relentless quest to seek and exploit opportunities
for immediate gain. In that quest, his eternal foes were the socialists.

They now added to their villainy, in Gompers's eyes, by opposing the
war. He had pledged labor's support for the war as early as 1916, and
had rather high-handedly forced his vassals to solemnize the pledge
at the Washington meeting of labor chieftains in March 1917. President Wilson duly rewarded him with a seat on the Advisory Commission of the Council of National Defense, and from that height Gompers
could happily see a new day dawning of advantageous cooperation
among labor, capital, and government. Such was the dream Gompers
headily entertained in early 1917. But the clamorings of his ancient
socialist adversaries intruded upon that lofty vision, and threatened
to knock Gompers from his perch. If the socialists could successfully
ride the anti-war issue through labor's ranks, they would divide the
working class, stiffen the enmity of capital, and call down the wrath of
the state on the backs of labor. They would thus dissipate the hopes
that Gompers had long held and that now seemed so close to realization.

Gompers accordingly undertook a massive campaign against the ac-

55. Mock and Larson, *Words That Won the War*, 210–12.

tivities of the socialists, contending with them for the soul of the American working class. George Creel quickly rallied to his side with the formation of a Division of Industrial Relations at the CPI. Creel also encouraged the creation of a special propaganda arm of the Department of Labor, headed by Boston businessman Roger W. Babson. Together, Creel and Babson flooded the nation's factories with posters, speakers, and slogans calculated to defuse the radical charge that this was a capitalists' war in which the workingman had no stake. "This, therefore, is the message that has been carried by the Department of Labor from one end of the country to the other," said Secretary of Labor William B. Wilson. "Every mediator, every employment official, every field officer of the Department, in addition to a corps of trained speakers [the Four-Minute Men] has been carrying the message to the workers of America that this is their war."[56] The President, in an unprecedented move, carried the message in person to the annual meeting of the A.F. of L. in Buffalo in November 1917, denouncing peace talk in unmistakably threatening terms. "What I am opposed to," he said, "is not the feeling of the pacifists, but their stupidity. My heart is with them, but my mind has a contempt for them. I want peace, but I know how to get it, and they do not." As for the faithful Gompers, Wilson said: "I like to lay my mind alongside of a mind that knows how to pull in harness." Gompers, evidently, was a good dray-horse to bear the administration's goods to the working class. But, Wilson pointedly warned, "the horses that kick over the traces will have to be put in the corral."[57]

Creel also bankrolled the American Alliance for Labor and Democracy, nominally labor's spontaneous answer to the allegedly disloyal socialists, but in fact the creature of Creel's Committee, carefully placed in the hands of the compliant Gompers. "In most respects," say the official historians of the CPI, "the Alliance may be considered a field organization of the CPI charged with the special responsibility of keeping labor industrious, patriotic, and quiet."[58]

"Industrious, patriotic, and quiet"—those goals for labor differed hardly at all from the intentions of the most ruthlessly anti-union employers, and the fate of labor in the war revealed how difficult it was in practice to keep the issues of welfare and loyalty separate. Conservative

56. William B. Wilson, "The Efficiency of Labor," *Annals of the American Academy of Political and Social Science* 78 (1918), 66–74.
57. Shaw, ed., *Messages and Papers of Woodrow Wilson*, I, 439–40.
58. Mock and Larson, *Words That Won the War*, 190–91.

capitalists continued to crush legitimate labor demands with the charge of disloyalty, just as they would later cry "communism" in the face of similar demands. The government itself abetted these developments with a series of spectacular raids on IWW halls in September 1917, leading to the conviction of nearly two hundred persons in three mass trials in Illinois, California, and Oklahoma.

Such furies, once unleashed, could not be easily contained by officialdom. The issue of loyalty, bound up with festering resentments of the foreign-born, with the calculated desire of capital to stamp out unions, and with hatred for pacifists who could not make the conversion to war, fed the ugly fires of vigilantism across wartime America. German-born Robert Prager, hanged by Missouri patriots, was but one victim of that violence. In the early morning hours of August 1, 1917, several vigilantes in Butte, Montana, burst into the boarding-house room of Frank Little, an IWW official trying to organize in the Butte Copper mines. Pummelled into the street, Little was tied to the rear of an automobile and dragged through the streets until his kneecaps were scraped off, then hanged from the side of a railroad trestle. The *New York Times* was among many organs of "respectable" opinion that deplored the lynching while insisting that "the IWW agitators are in effect, and perhaps in fact, agents of Germany. The Federal authorities should make short work of these treasonable conspirators against the United States." A few weeks later a mob seized pacifist clergyman Herbert S. Bigelow as he was about to address a peace gathering near Cincinnati. Bound and gagged, Bigelow was taken to a clearing in the woods and stripped to the waist. A white-robed man with a blacksnake whip lashed Bigelow's back to ribbons "in the name of the poor women and children of Belgium."[59]

Cries for undiluted loyalty and full-blown Americanism came from many lips during the war, but they were most remarkable in the mouths of the cultivated classes, the elites supposedly inoculated by education against base emotional appeals. Their demeanor and institutions allegedly embodied the values of decorum and rationality that the progressives had hoped to quicken throughout the society. But the war revealed the brittleness of their vaunted "culture." Columbia University President Nicholas Murray Butler, for example, announced in June 1917 that though the University was the safest refuge for dissident views in time of peace, with the coming of war "conditions sharply

59. Peterson and Fite, *Opponents,* 57–60, 79.

changed. What had been tolerated became intolerable now. What had been wrongheadedness was now sedition. What had been folly was now treason." Accordingly, Butler soon dismissed Professor Henry W. L. Dana for working with various peace societies, and Professor James N. Cattell for having petitioned Congress not to send conscripts to Europe. Columbia had "done its duty," exulted the *New York Times*, "by expelling two members of the faculty who . . . fomented disloyalty."[60] Theodore Roosevelt, apoplectically angry at Robert La Follette's opposition to the armed-ship bill in early 1917, had seethed that the Wisconsin Senator "has shown himself to be an unhung traitor, and if the war should come, he ought to be hung."[61] At Brooklyn's Plymouth Congregational Church, the Reverend Newell Dwight Hillis offered Christian forgiveness to the German people "just as soon as they are all shot. If you would give me happiness," he intoned from his pulpit, "just give me the sight of the Kaiser, von Tirpitz, and von Hindenburg hanging by a rope."[62]

When the nation's centers of higher learning had grown suddenly rigid with intolerance, when even an ex-President and the clergy were so given to bloody rhetorical excess, it was small wonder that popular passions exploded so frequently into violence in the wake of American belligerency. That violence grotesquely mocked the hopeful pieties about reason and education with which once-pacifistic progressives had so hesitantly enlisted on the side of war. But perhaps, in the final analysis, it was but a short step for a people who had listened for a generation to the progressive summons to fight corruption with direct democracy, now to cross a slender line and take the law into their own hands. There were frightful ironies here that ran deep, the full implications of which might have struck terror into the progressive mind, had it summoned the courage to confront them. Creel and Wilson and countless progressives repeatedly condemned vigilantism, but none of them could admit his own contribution to the cultural atmosphere in which the flames of hysteria were kindled. Much wartime violence was struck from the flint and steel of American tradition—especially from the hal-

60. Richard Hofstadter and Walter P. Metzer, *The Development of Academic Freedom in the United States* (New York: Columbia University Press, 1955), 498ff; Peterson and Fite, *Opponents*, 103.

61. Theodore Roosevelt to Henry Cabot Lodge, Feb. 20, 1917, in Elting E. Morison, ed., *The Letters of Theodore Roosevelt*, 8 vols. (Cambridge, Mass.: Harvard University Press, 1954), VIII, 1157.

62. *New York Times*, Mar. 26, 1917, 3.

lowed principles that shared convictions were the cement of society, and that persuasion was preferable to law as an instrument of governance. Those beliefs underlay American democratic culture at all times, but they had been especially operative in the movement for progressive reform, with its reliance on publicity and the appeal to conscience as the tools of social change. Now, under the stress of war, those practices could perversely sanction the most noxious kinds of oppression, both unofficial and official, inflicted in the name of popular sovereignty and often connived at by officials sworn to uphold the law. Against that awful tide neither George Creel's ebullient goodwill nor Woodrow Wilson's stiff propriety could effectively stand. The very basis of the society in freely given individual consent, it seemed, along with the consequent abhorrence for formal authority, could consume the body politic itself in the moment of crisis.

If Creel may be taken as both the agent and the symbol of a usually benign democratic impulse somehow run amok under the strain of war, it must also be noted that the government contained other souls more forthrightly malevolent than Creel, more contemptuous of man's capacity for reason and the sanctity of consent. They were less interested in propagandizing the people, and more disposed to direct methods of extinguishing dissent, by fair means or foul.

The foremost official enemy of dissidents was without doubt Postmaster General Albert Sidney Burleson. A Texan, a follower of William Jennings Bryan, a protector of small businessmen and farmers, Burleson hated, as only a certain species of white Southern Populist could, all of his fellow citizens who did not fall into one of those categories. Narrow, intolerant, so self-consciously pompous that Wilson called him "the Cardinal," Burleson, says a biographer, "acted the part he spoke, complete with black coat, wing collar, [and] rolled umbrella."[63] Colonel Edward House remarked with some consternation in 1918 that Burleson "is in a belligerent mood against the Germans, against labor, against the pacifists, etc. He is now the most belligerent member of the cabinet."[64]

The Espionage Act of June 1917 authorized the Postmaster General to ban from the mails any material violating the Act, or advocating treason, insurrection, or forcible resistance to any law of the United

63. John Morton Blum, "Albert Sidney Burleson," in *Dictionary of American Biography, Supplement Two* (New York: Scribner's, 1958), 74–75.
64. House Dairy, entry for Feb. 11, 1918, House Papers.

States. Though the zealous Burleson had begun to withdraw mailing privileges from various journals even before the Act became law, in the summer of 1917 he revealed the full dimensions of his campaign against radicals, pacifists, and the foreign-born. With the cooperation of Attorney General Thomas W. Gregory, and over Wilson's rare and timid objections, Burleson began ruthlessly to strip second-class mailing privileges from journals that dared, as he said in October, "to impugn the motives of the government and thus encourage insubordination." More specifically, Burleson added, he would deal severely with publications claiming "that the government is controlled by Wall Street or munition manufacturers, or any other special interests," or papers criticizing "improperly our Allies."[65]

Burleson, according to socialist Norman Thomas, "didn't know socialism from rheumatism," and the Postmaster General officially declared that he would not bar socialist publications from the mails—unless they contained treasonable or seditious matter.[66] But, he added, "the trouble is that most Socialist papers do contain such matter."[67] That was but a sample of the casuistic logic Burleson turned on his enemies. On another occasion, he banned from the mails a single issue of the *Masses* (a genteel anti-establishment publication that mixed political radicalism with literary and artistic avant-gardism) because it allegedly contained offensive matter. When the publisher proposed to avoid such matter in the future, Burleson still refused to restore the magazine's second-class mailing permit, on the ground that it had skipped an issue —no matter the reason—and was thus ineligible for such privileges as a regularly issued "periodical"! That high-handed action drew outraged, and ineffectual, protests from many quarters. *New Republic* editor Herbert Croly complained directly to the President, as did prominent reformer Amos Pinchot. Muckraking novelist Upton Sinclair wrote Wilson that "your Postmaster-General reveals himself a person of such pitiful and childish ignorance concerning modern movements that it is simply a calamity that [in] this crisis he should be the person to decide what may or may not be uttered by our radical press."[68]

Burleson was not the lone villain. By the autumn of 1917 Congress

65. O. A. Hilton, "Freedom of the Press in Wartime, 1917–1919," *Southwestern Social Science Quarterly* 28 (1948), 348–49.
66. Norman Thomas Memoir, Columbia University Oral History Collection, Butler Library, Columbia University, N.Y. (hereafter CUOHC).
67. Hilton, "Freedom of the Press," 349.
68. Upton Sinclair to Wilson, Oct. 22, 1917, WWP.

knew full well the harshness with which the Postmaster General was administering the censorship laws; yet in October it considerably extended his powers in the Trading-with-the-Enemy Act. That Act required foreign-language newspapers to submit to the Post Office Department, in advance of publication, English translations of all articles or editorials referring to the government, to any of the belligerent powers, or to the conduct of the war. The procedure was costly and forced crippling delays in publication—though exemptions might be issued in cases of demonstrably "loyal" publications. Burleson wielded this new authority with the same unremitting fierceness that he had shown to the radical press, with the result that the country's many foreign-language publications either converted to an unqualified and even overblown support for the government or simply shut up shop, many never to reopen.[69]

Wilson only feebly opposed the rampages of his Postmaster General. In late 1917, the President gently suggested to Burleson that "I am sure you will agree with me that we must act with the utmost caution and liberality in all our censorship."[70] Burleson did not agree, nor was he persuaded. A week later Wilson questioned the suppression of the socialist *Milwaukee Leader*, and inquired hesitantly ("I am afraid you will be shocked . . ." he timidly addressed Burleson) if the paper might be given another chance.[71] Burleson remained unperturbed, and the President showed no inclination to force the issue. When Wilson counseled leniency in the *Masses* case, Burleson threatened to resign. At that, Wilson reportedly laughed and said, "Well, go ahead and do your duty."[72] Burleson proceeded to do his duty with a vengeance. He suppressed one journal for proposing that the war be financed by higher taxes and less borrowing. He censored others for reprinting Thomas Jefferson's opinion that Ireland should be a republic, and others still for expressing doubt that Britain would keep its promise to make Palestine an independent Jewish state. In one notorious example of bureaucratic contrariness, he banned from the mails Thorstein Veblen's *Imperial Germany and the Industrial Revolution*, which Creel's

69. See Harry N. Scheiber, *The Wilson Administration and Civil Liberties, 1917–21* (Ithaca: Cornell University Press, 1960), 20, and Carl Wittke, *German-Americans and the World War* (Columbus: Ohio State Archaeological and Historical Society, 1936), 135.
70. Wilson to Burleson, Oct. 11, 1917, RSB, VII, 301.
71. Wilson to Burleson, Oct. 18, 1917, RSB, VII, 313.
72. RSB, VII, 165n.

CPI at the same time was trying to disseminate as a telling attack on the character of German society. He suspended the mailing privileges of the liberal *Nation* in September 1918, apparently because it had criticized Samuel Gompers; in this single instance, and at this late date in the war, Wilson intervened directly to overrule his Postmaster General.

A close second behind Burleson in hostility to civil liberties was Attorney General Thomas W. Gregory. A Texan like his colleague, he had made a distinguished career as an anti-trust lawyer, but had no extensive prior experience that suited him to deal sensitively with issues like freedom of speech and conscience. "May God have mercy on them," he said of war opponents, "for they need expect none from an outraged people and an avenging government."[73] He favored broad construction and vigorous application of the Espionage Act of June 1917, on one occasion publicly chastising a federal judge for instructing a jury to acquit a man who had called the President a Wall Street tool. The judge ruled that such statements, however distasteful, did not directly obstruct the army, the navy, or the Selective Service System, and hence did not violate the Espionage Act. The ruling was arguably quite consonant with the spirit of the legislation, and the spirit of the First Amendment, but it called forth incredulous disgust from the Attorney General. Gregory also professed his admiration for the Illinois State Bar Association when they condemned as "unpatriotic" and "unprofessional" an attorney who would take a draft resister as a client. Refusing counsel, in the eyes of the nation's highest law-enforcement officer, was a praiseworthy way to ensure justice in wartime.[74]

Despite their seeming extremity, such attitudes were not unfamiliar in the legal community at the time. Herbert L. Packer once distinguished between "due process" and "crime control" approaches to criminal justice. The former attends scrupulously to questions of justice and legal correctness, while the latter subordinates those values in its relentless drive to crush out criminality. Most early twentieth-century American lawyers and jurists, including the most eminent, were inclined to take the crime-control approach.[75] They came, mostly, from an older, established elite class that felt particularly menaced by ap-

---

73. Peterson and Fite, *Opponents,* 14.
74. Thomas W. Gregory, Speech to Executive Committee of American Bar Association, Apr. 16, 1918, in *Congressional Record,* 65th Congress, 2nd sess., Vol. 56, Part 6 (May 9, 1918), 6233–35.
75. Herbert L. Packer, *The Limits of the Criminal Sanction* (Stanford: Stanford University Press, 1968).

parently increasing levels of criminal unrest and political agitation. They were thus quite prepared to sweep aside the obstacles that careful attention to due process put in the way of aggressive crime control. Efficient prosecution of criminals, said leading lawyers from countless forums, was the only way to safeguard the public order. Social peace itself was threatened by a too meticulous regard for procedural refinements that effectively favored the guilty. That sentiment, with which later generations would also be familiar, fostered in this period a sympathetic attitude toward vigilantism and even lynching. Many legal writers noted the close connection between vigilantism and the concept of self-government, seeing in lynch law simply the extension of the sovereign people's will into realms where formal writ, for whatever reason, did not run. The distinguished lawyer Charles J. Bonaparte, for example, himself to be a future United States Attorney General, had said in 1890 that "Judge Lynch may make mistakes . . . but if the number of failures of justice in his court could be compared with those in our more regular tribunals, I am not sure that he need fear the result. I believe that very few innocent men are lynched, and, of those who have not committed the past offense for which they suffer, a still smaller proportion are decent members of society. It is, of course, an evil that the law should be occasionally enforced by lawless means, but it is, in my opinion, a greater evil that it should be habitually duped and evaded by means formally lawful." The underlying purpose of vigilantism, said Bonaparte, "is not to violate, but to vindicate, the law."[76] Mob violence, in this view, was strangely transformed into the visible sign of a healthy society, vigorously rooting out criminal—or at least less than "decent"—elements from its midst.

Attorney General Gregory revealed his sympathy with such sentiments in his attitude toward the wartime censorship laws. The courts construed the law broadly, convicting persons, for example, for even discussing the constitutionality of conscription, or, as happened in New Hampshire, for claiming "this was a Morgan war and not a war of the people" (a remark that earned its author a three-year prison sentence). But the administration remained uneasy about the legal basis for such sweeping application of the espionage statute.[77] Consequently, Gregory

---

76. See Richard Maxwell Brown, *Strain of Violence: Historical Studies of American Violence and Vigilantism* (New York: Oxford University Press, 1975), 144–79.

77. Zechariah Chafee, Jr., *Free Speech in the United States* (Cambridge, Mass.: Harvard University Press, 1941), 74–75.

sought an amendment that would allow him to prosecute "disloyal utterances." Legislation to that end was introduced in Congress in March
1918, in the form of amendments to the Espionage Act, proposing to
prohibit, among other new offenses, "any disloyal, profane, scurrilous, or
abusive language about the form of government of the United States,
or the Constitution of the United States, or the flag of the United States,
or the uniform of the Army or Navy," or any language that might bring
those institutions "into contempt, scorn, contumely, or disrepute." Commonly known as the Sedition Act, this legislation became the law of
the land on May 16.

Hiram Johnson was not alone in regarding the new law "a villainous
measure," and commentators ever since have rightly viewed it as a
landmark of repression in American history.[78] But the Sedition Act
warrants scrutiny as well as condemnation, for it reveals a great deal
about the popular temper at the midpoint of American belligerency,
and about the Wilson administration's relation to civil liberties issues.

Despite its harshness, Wilson and Gregory regarded the Sedition bill
as something of a compromise. They depended on it to head off congressional passage of a constitutionally dubious "court-martial bill" that
would have transferred counter-espionage responsibility from the Justice Department to the War Department, and greatly extended the
authority of courts-martial in questions of "disloyalty." The press pic-
tured the bill as part of a mounting attack on the government's alleged
inability to cope with "spies" and "traitors," and anticipated that Con-
g̱.ess would use the hearings on the bill to cause political embarrassment to the President. Like the Overman executive reorganization bill
making its way through Congress at about the same time, the Sedition
bill represented Wilson's counter-stroke against congressional critics of
his mobilization policies. In both cases, but especially in the latter, he
ceded considerable ground to his conservative foes.

Gregory, as the President's chief spear-carrier in this affair, was
obliged simultaneously to defend his Department against charges of
weakness in the pursuit of disloyalty and to justify his request for additional legislation to strengthen the Department's hand. To resolve those
apparently conflicting requirements, Gregory offered ingenious arguments, typical to his time and caste. On the one hand, he asserted, "I
do not believe there is today any country which is being more capably

78. Hiram Johnson to C. K. McClatchey, Apr. 11, 1918, Johnson Papers, Bancroft
    Library, University of California, Berkeley.

policed than is the United States."[79] "Scores of thousands of men are under constant observation throughout the country," Gregory assured a friend.[80] But on the other hand, he explained, the Espionage Act as it stood "did not reach the individual casual or impulsive disloyal utterances. These individual disloyal utterances, however, occurring with considerable frequency throughout the country, naturally irritated and angered the communities in which they occurred." Gregory made much of the recent and heavily publicized lynching of Robert Prager near St. Louis as a prime example of the harmful lengths to which popular excitement over disloyalty could run. "Consequently," he said, "there was a popular demand for such an amendment as would cover these cases."[81]

Gregory in effect argued that the government had the real problems of enemy espionage under control—but that it needed new statutory instruments to deal with the quick-tempered vigilantism of the loyal citizenry, to stay their hands from tar-bucket, torch, and rope as expressions of their patriotic impatience with the disloyal. In a remarkable revelation of the crime-control mentality, with its favorable regard for night-riders and lynch law, Gregory proposed not to prosecute the mobs but to pre-empt them, to replace crude vigilantes with trained government agents armed with the new sedition statute! Here was an inventiveness in the art of subverting free speech that rivaled the considerable accomplishments of Burleson.

The Attorney General himself was already intimately acquainted with the excesses of a quasi-vigilante organization called the American Protective League (APL), a band of amateur sleuths and loyalty enforcers which had managed to enter into an official relationship with Gregory's Department. It had begun in the spring of 1917, when Albert M. Briggs, a Chicago advertising executive, had proposed to the Justice Department's Bureau of Investigation (later the FBI) that he be allowed to form a citizens' auxiliary to the Bureau, to aid in monitoring the activities of enemy aliens. Bureau Chief A. Bruce Bielaski, short of funds and manpower but long on anxiety about national security in time of war, accepted the offer. Gregory requested that Wilson make a supplemental budget allotment of $275,000 from the President's $100 million war

79. Gregory, Speech to Executive Committee of American Bar Association, 6234.
80. Thomas W. Gregory to T. U. Taylor, Apr. 10, 1918, Gregory Papers, Library of Congress, Washington, D.C.
81. *Annual Report of the Attorney General of the United States for the Year 1918* (Washington, D.C.: Government Printing Office, 1918), 18.

emergency fund, apparently to finance the citizens' auxiliary. "I . . . request that . . . it be made in such form as will permit me wide latitude in its use," Gregory secretively suggested; "that is to say, that the approval of the Attorney General on a voucher for payment out of this fund be final and conclusive. The necessity for this I will explain to you in person."[82]

Soon Gregory was boasting that "I have today several hundred thousand private citizens—some as individuals, most of them as members of patriotic bodies, engaged in . . . assisting the heavily overworked Federal authorities in keeping an eye on disloyal individuals and making reports of disloyal utterances."[83] Thus there came into existence a nationwide network of "agents," their authority proclaimed by official-looking badges that read "American Protective League—Secret Service." By war's end they numbered 250,000. They spied on neighbors, fellow workers, office-mates, and suspicious characters of any type.

Though Gregory admiringly called the APL a "powerful patriotic organization," and claimed that it was "well-managed," the League in fact constituted a rambunctious, unruly *posse comitatus* on an unprecedented national scale. Its "agents" bugged, burglarized, slandered, and illegally arrested other Americans. They opened mail, intercepted telegrams, served as *agents provocateurs*, and were the chief commandos in a series of extralegal and often violent "slacker raids" against supposed draft evaders in 1918. They always operated behind a cloak of stealth and deception, frequently promoting reactionary social and economic views under the guise of patriotism. The League sometimes counseled its members to commit outright physical assault on dissenters. It was, in one authority's summary view, "a force for outrageous vigilantism blessed with the seal and sanction of the federal government."[84]

That an organization such as the APL was allowed to exist at all testifies to the unusual state of American society in World War I, when fear corrupted usually sober minds, and residual suspicions of strong government disposed public officials to a dangerous reliance on private means. Through the APL volunteers, the government sought to effect drastic measures without itself assuming the full formal authority to do so—a fatal reluctance in the face of supposed necessity, leading directly

82. Gregory to Woodrow Wilson, Apr. 23, 1917, Gregory Papers.
83. Gregory to Francis H. Weston, Aug. 10, 1917, *ibid*.
84. The authority is Harold Hyman, quoted in Joan M. Jensen, *The Price of Vigilance* (Chicago: Rand McNally, 1968), 309.

to a kind of officially blessed vigilantism. Wilson recognized the perils that lurked in this policy. On hearing of the American Protective League, he wrote to Gregory "that it would be very dangerous to have such an organization operating in the United States, and I wonder if there is any way in which we could stop it?"[85] But Wilson had acquiesced in Burleson's brazen disregard of presidental cautions; so now did he fail to push Gregory about the APL. Beyond that initial inquiry, the record shows few instances of Wilson's attempts to curb the citizen-watchdogs of the League. They went their meddlesome and noxious way, unmolested and even supported by the administration.

At lower administrative and judicial levels, many United States Attorneys and Federal District Judges seemed bent on outdoing both Burleson and Gregory in their aggressive enforcement of the Espionage Act. As one Justice Department official commented, "It has been quite unnecessary to urge upon the United States Attorneys the importance of prosecuting vigorously, and there has been little difficulty in securing convictions from juries."[86] Especially after the sedition amendments of May 1918, local federal attorneys had wide discretionary authority about whom they might prosecute. One observer noted that now every U.S. Attorney became "an angel of life and death clothed with the power to walk up and down in his district, saying, 'This one will I spare, and that one will I smite.' "[87] Not until the last weeks of the war were Federal District Judges instructed to refrain from prosecuting alleged Espionage Act offenders without the explicit approval of the Attorney General. This decentralization encouraged a wildly arbitrary application of justice. Anti-war speakers were indicted in one jurisdiction for repeating remarks made without objection in another. Socialist Kate Richards O'Hare, for example, was sentenced to five years' imprisonment for a speech in North Dakota that she had many times given elsewhere with impunity. At war's end, the lopsided record revealed that nearly half the prosecutions under the Espionage and Sedition acts had taken place in thirteen of the eighty-seven federal districts. Not surprisingly, those thirteen districts were to be found primarily in the Western states, especially where the IWW was most active.[88]

85. Wilson to Gregory, June 4, 1917, quoted in Peterson and Fite, *Opponents*, 19.
86. John Lord O'Brian, assistant to the Attorney General, quoted in Chafee, *Free Speech*, 67.
87. *Ibid.*, 69.
88. Scheiber, *Wilson Administration and Civil Liberties*, 46–49.

The Supreme Court did not review any Espionage Act cases until after the Armistice. By then, of course, the damage was done. Given Gregory's swift movement and the war's sudden end, the nine Justices, observed one commentator, could "only lock the doors after the Liberty Bell [was] stolen."[89] Even then, the high bench showed little inclination to undo the harm the war had inflicted on the tradition of free speech. In fairness, it must be noted that the Court in 1919 was abruptly confronted with one of the touchiest and most complex of constitutional issues. There had been virtually no judicial interpretation in this area for over one hundred years. In the brief and extraordinary period of a few months in 1919, a period still echoing with the cries of battle, the Supreme Court was forced to erect the very foundations of American case law concerning freedom of speech.

One promising precedent had been offered by Federal District Judge Learned Hand in 1917, barely six weeks after the passage of the Espionage Act. In *Masses Publishing Co. v. Patten,* Hand had issued a temporary restraining order to prevent Postmaster General Burleson from banning the radical publication, *Masses,* from the mails. Hand noted the magazine's "political agitation" against the war, but insisted that agitation could not be equated with "direct incitement to violent resistance." Only the most straightforward language urging violation of the law, Hand argued, fell outside the constitutional protections of free speech. The government, he declared, must "point with exactness to just that conduct which violates the law. It is difficult and often impossible to meet the charge that one's general ethos is treasonable."[90] Hand's ruling was quickly reversed by the Circuit Court of Appeals and, unfortunately for the cause of free speech, his formulation of First Amendment doctrine also failed to persuade the Justices of the United States Supreme Court.

In March 1919 three Espionage Act cases came before the Court.[91] In each of them, the conviction reached by the lower tribunals was unanimously upheld. In the first of those cases, *Schenck v. United States,* Justice Oliver Wendell Holmes, Jr., articulated the theory that "when a nation is at war many things that might be said in time of peace are such a hindrance to its effort that their utterance will not be endured."

89. Chafee, *Free Speech,* 80.
90. *Masses Publishing Co. v. Patten,* 244 Fed. 535 (So. Dist., N.Y., 1917).
91. The three cases were *Schenck v. United States,* 249 U.S. 47 (1919); *Frohwerk v. United States,* 249 U.S. 204 (1919); and *Debs v. United States,* 249 U.S. 211 (1919).

Accordingly, he affirmed Schenck's guilt for having mailed pamphlets urging potential army inductees to resist conscription. "The question," Holmes declared, "is whether the words used are used in such circumstances and are of such a nature as to create a clear and present danger that they will bring about the substantive evils that Congress has a right to prevent."[92]

Schenck had clearly counseled illegal action, and thus would have been convicted even under Judge Hand's definition of illicit utterances. But Holmes's famous "clear and present danger" test, despite his effort, like that of Hand, to distinguish legitimate agitation from illegitimate incitement, significantly reduced the range of protected speech that Hand had tried to encompass. To Hand's simple test of the explicitness of the language itself, Holmes added the criterion of *circumstances*, thus leaving wide latitude for judicial guesswork about the mood of an audience, the intention of the speaker, and the *probable* consequences of specific utterances.[93]

Worse still, Holmes's colleagues on the Court—and Holmes himself in some instances—violated even the "clear and present danger" standard in their subsequent decisions about free speech. In *Frohwerk v. United States*, decided shortly after *Schenck*, Holmes upheld the guilt of a Missouri German-American who had published articles questioning the constitutionality of the draft and the purposes of the war. Though the clarity and the proximity of the danger to military operations were difficult to discern in this case, Holmes nevertheless conjectured that "it is impossible to say that it might not have been found that the circulation of the paper was in quarters where a little breath would be enough to kindle a flame and that the fact was known and relied on by those who sent that paper out."[94] In the third case, *Debs v. United States*, Holmes upheld the conviction of socialist leader Eugene Victor Debs for an anti-war speech given before a convention of socialists in Canton, Ohio. Most of the speech had rehearsed standard socialist views on the evils of capitalism and the economic causes of the war. Debs had neither spoken exclusively to potential draftees, nor had he explicitly urged violation of the draft laws. Yet Holmes ruled that though most of the speech fell within the bounds of First Amendment

92. *Schenck v. United States*, 249 U.S. 47 (1919).
93. See Gerald Gunther, "Learned Hand and the Origins of the Modern First Amendment Doctrine: Some Fragments of History," *Stanford Law Review* 27 (1975), 719–73; see also Chafee, *Free Speech*, chap. 2.
94. *Frohwerk v. United States*, 249 U.S. 204 (1919).

protections, "if a part of the manifest intent of the more general utterances was to encourage those present to obstruct the recruiting service . . . the immunity of the general theme may not be enough to protect the speech."[95] Debs was packed off to the federal penitentiary in Atlanta, a martyred hero to the opponents of war, who helped give him nearly one million votes for President in the election of 1920, even while he languished in his cell.

Only in *Abrams v. United States*, later in 1919, did Holmes himself use the "clear and present danger" test to condemn a wartime conviction under the Sedition Act. Russian immigrant Jacob Abrams and four associates had printed pamphlets denouncing the American military intervention in Russia. Holmes, with his colleague Louis Brandeis, found that this action did not sufficiently threaten the American war against Germany. Whatever imaginable menace that Abrams's "poor and puny anonymities" might have posed, said Holmes in his dissenting opinion, lacked the requisite proximity and immediacy to be constitutionally punishable. Unfortunately, the majority of the Court held that the tests of proximity and immediacy were beside the point. It was enough, the Court declared, if Abrams's publications merely *tended* to encourage disruption of the American military effort.[96]

The decisions of March 1919, wrote noted First Amendment scholar Zechariah Chafee, Jr., "came as a great shock to forward-looking men and women, who had consoled themselves through the wartime trials with the hope that the Espionage Act would be invalidated when it reached the Supreme Court. They were especially grieved that the opinions which dashed this hope were written by the Justice [Holmes] who for their eyes had long taken on heroic dimensions."[97] Holmes's opinion in the *Abrams* case may have helped to redeem his reputation, but the fact remained that the nation's highest tribunal had overwhelmingly endorsed the most aggressive wartime assaults on dissenting opinion. Moreover, the effect of these decisions was to weave into the legal fabric of the nation restrictions on freedom of speech that had been unknown before 1917.

The stamp of Supreme Court approval on both the Espionage and the Sedition acts in 1919 surely seemed to have taken the attack against

95. *Debs v. United States*, 249 U.S. 211 (1919).
96. *Abrams v. United States*, 250 U.S. 616 (1919).
97. Chafee, *Free Speech*, 86.

dissent far enough to satisfy even the most fierce advocates of repression. But Woodrow Wilson, for one, was not content. In his campaign to secure American approval of the Versailles Treaty and the League of Nations, he repeatedly churned the cauldron of anti-radical and anti-alien sentiment that the war had heated. America, he declared, was not immune from the revolutionary upheavals of Europe, as "the poison of disorder, the poison of revolt, the poison of chaos," had entered "into the veins of this free people." Without a stable Europe, he warned, America might succumb to those toxins. As for the opponents of the League, he equated them with "the same sources . . . which threatened this country . . . with disloyalty. . . . Any man who carries a hyphen about with him carries a dagger that he is ready to plunge into the vitals of this Republic."[98] In December 1919 Wilson called for a peacetime sedition act to replace the wartime amendment, scheduled to expire in 1921.[99]

These postwar spasms of Wilson's hostility to dissent were consonant with his general regard for civil liberties during the war. True, he had publicly denounced lynching, and had opposed the court-martial bill.[100] And, in his annual message to Congress in 1917, he struck a Jeffersonian stance toward the "voices of dissent," proposing that "they may be safely left to strut their uneasy hour and be forgotten," noisy testimonials to the futility of opposing "the calm, indomitable power of the nation."[101]

But in practice Wilson was usually neither calm nor indifferent. He had hesitated to restrain Burleson and protested only weakly against the semi-vigilantism of the American Protective League. A friend of free speech in theory, he was its foe in fact. He surely preferred that Burleson and Gregory should go too far, rather than not far enough, in

98. Quoted in Scheiber, *Wilson Administration and Civil Liberties,* 55–56.
99. Congress refused the request, and the legislation died quietly in 1921. The Alien Registration Act of 1940 was the first modern American peacetime anti-sedition statute.
100. The bill was in any case clearly unconstitutional, according to the doctrine set down in *ex parte Milligan* (4 Wallace 2, 1866), which said that neither Congress nor the President had the authority to declare the civil courts incompetent. Wilson was familiar with the precedent, and alluded to it in discouraging the bill's supporters. See, for example, Wilson to Sen. Robert L. Owen, Feb. 1, 1918, RSB, VII, 517.
101. Shaw, ed., *Messages and Papers of Woodrow Wilson,* I, 444. Jefferson had said in his first inaugural address: "If there be any among us who would wish to dissolve this Union or to change its republican form, let them stand undisturbed as monuments to the safety with which error of opinion may be tolerated where reason is left free to combat it."

the war against dissent. He persistently ignored pleas to speak out against attacks on German-Americans.[102] He personally approved the high-handed scheme to raid IWW halls in September 1917, breaking the back of the nation's largest industrial union by mass trials and imprisonment of its leadership.[103] Like Gregory, he chafed at the imperfections in the Espionage Act before the amendments of May 1918, lamenting that the Act did not strictly permit prosecuting opponents of the conscription law unless they "stand in the way of the administration of it by any overt acts or improper influences."[104] On one occasion, he told his cabinet that a man who had been overheard wishing for Secretary of War Newton D. Baker's premature demise "ought to be punished if seditious and otherwise should be brought here by the Attorney General and given the 33rd degree and then the story of his comment given to the public so he would be forever damned by the people."[105]

Even before the Armistice, many progressives were showing signs of disenchantment with Wilson and with the war, and the administration's shabby record in the area of civil liberties was among the most powerful factors that began the process of their disillusionment. The government's policy of repressing dissent, the *New Republic*'s Herbert Croly wrote to Wilson in late 1917, was "dividing the body of public opinion into two irreconcilable classes" of war opponents and war enthusiasts. That development, Croly explained, "makes the situation of papers which occupy an intermediate position, such as the *New Republic* does, extremely difficult. We are constantly being crowded between two extremes."[106]

"An intermediate position"—there was the heart of the matter. The progressives had rallied to Wilson on the promise that he would make the center hold, that his mobilization policies would preserve reform gains at home and that his diplomacy would introduce liberal American moderation into the settlement of the conflict in Europe. Now all those aspirations were overshadowed by Wilson's determination to extinguish dissent. To speak up for immigrants or to defend the rights of

---

102. See, for example, Wilson to L. C. Dyer, Aug. 1, 1917, RSB, VII, 201.
103. See William D. Stephens to Wilson, July 9, 1917, and Gregory to Wilson, Aug. 21, 1917, WWP.
104. Wilson to Joseph Tumulty, July 26, 1917, RSB, VII, 196–97.
105. E. David Cronon, ed., *The Cabinet Diaries of Josephus Daniels, 1913–1921* (Lincoln: University of Nebraska Press, 1963), 299; entry for Apr. 15, 1918.
106. Herbert Croly to Wilson, Oct. 19, 1917, WWP.

labor was to risk being persecuted for disloyalty. And to criticize the course of the war, or to question American or Allied peace aims, was to risk outright prosecution for treason. In this atmosphere, the hopes of the progressives in 1917 that they might temper and guide Wilson's war policies were revealed as extravagant fantasies. "Wilson does not energetically enough strive to maintain liberalism," *New Republic* editor Walter Weyl confided to his diary in July 1918. "He allows liberalism to go by default . . . [while] the liberals . . . do nothing to embarrass him." By the time of the Armistice, Weyl despaired: "Liberalism is crumbling about our ears, and we are doing little or nothing."[107]

By that time, there was little or nothing that people of Weyl's persuasion could do. Wilson, Amos Pinchot wryly noted, had put "his enemies in office and his friends in jail." George Creel advised the President in late 1918, explaining the Democratic Party's congressional losses in the November elections: "All the radical or liberal friends of your anti-imperialist war policy were either silenced or intimidated. The Department of Justice and the Post-Office [Department] were allowed to silence or intimidate them. There was no voice left to argue for your sort of peace. When we came to this election the reactionary Republicans had a clean record of anti-Hun imperialistic patriotism. Their opponents, your friends, were often either besmirched or obscured."[108]

Thus the progressives and Wilson, thrust into cautious embrace in 1917, went down in defeat together at war's end. As the Paris peace negotiations loomed, the dimensions of their shared tragedy grew more apparent. "The more is the pity," reflected Wilson's erstwhile supporter, Oswald Garrison Villard, "that Wilson has made the great blunder of allowing his dull and narrow Postmaster General, his narrow Attorney General, all the other agencies under his control to suppress adequate discussion of the peace aims. . . . At the very moment of his extremest trial our liberal forces are by his own act scattered, silenced, disorganized, some in prison. If he loses his great fight for humanity, it will be because he was deliberately silent when freedom of speech and the right of conscience were struck down in America."[109]

That prospect galled the progressives who had with such trepidation

107. Quoted in Charles Forcey, *The Crossroads of Liberalism: Croly, Weyl, Lippmann and the Progressive Era, 1900–1925* (New York: Oxford University Press, 1961), 284, 288.
108. Quoted in Scheiber, *Wilson Administration and Civil Liberties,* 40.
109. Quoted in Michael Wreszin, *Oswald Garrison Villard: Pacifist at War* (Bloomington: Indiana University Press, 1965), 101.

fallen in line behind Wilson in 1917. Their gamble on Wilson's leadership had failed. They were forced to recognize the hollowness of their hopes in that first spring of war. Now, in the final days, John Dewey acknowledged that the war had encouraged a "cult of irrationality" fed by "an insidious and skilled effort . . . to detach the volume of passionate energy from its original end"—that end being the progressive dream that Dewey had helped to conjure in 1917. Instead, popular passions had been grotesquely attached to reactionary purposes, fulfilling Randolph Bourne's direst predictions. For Dewey, the conscientious warrior who had so expansively endorsed the war only nineteen months earlier, the sting of disappointment was sharp. "These reactionaries, these constitutional disbelievers in the people," he raged, had in fact gained the upper hand, blasting his liberal ideals to mist. They were now "egging on the intolerance of the people," putting "a stigma upon all whose liberalizing influence in domestic policies they dread."[110]

Disillusion with Wilson and disappointment at their own failure to protect the reform cause were not the only wounds the war inflicted on progressives. The cruelest damage was visited on their very social philosophy, their most cherished assumptions about the reasonableness of mankind, the malleability of society, and the value of education and publicity as the tools of progress. The events of the war years had mauled John Dewey's central premise that the world, even a world at war, was a plastic place that an enlightened public might shape to progressive ends. Both on the domestic and international fronts, the conflict had revealed forces loose in the world that terribly twisted the fragile hopes of men of goodwill.

Even less tenable in the aftermath of wartime hysteria was the presumption that the public at large was rational and decent. Increasingly, that benign appraisal of human nature succumbed to a more cynical assessment, and the idea of "the people," good and educable, gave way to a concept of "the masses," brutish and volatile. Publicity, in which the prewar progressives had placed so much political hope, became in the postwar decade little more than an adjunct to the new economy of consumerism, as the fledgling industry of advertising adopted the propagandists' techniques of mass communication and persuasion. George Creel, with unwitting irony, titled his postwar memoir of the CPI's activities *How We Advertised America,* and bragged that the war "gave

110. John Dewey, "The Cult of Irrationality," in Ratner, ed., *Characters and Events,* II, 587–91.

me the opportunity . . . for recognition of advertising as a real profession."[111] When John Dos Passos wrote *USA*, his bitterly disillusioned account of American life in the World War I era, he made "public relations" expert J. Ward Morehouse among the most contemptible of characters, a man who blithely urged the marketing of a worthless "health food" cereal under the banner of "selfservice, independence, individualism. . . . This is going to be more than a publicity campaign," Morehouse is made to say in grotesque mockery of the rhetorical crimes of the war, "it's going to be a campaign for Americanism."[112]

Walter Lippmann perhaps best expressed the dimensions of the disenchantment the progressives felt as they contemplated the fruits of the war for the American mind in 1917–18. Lippmann had been among the initial architects of the Committee on Public Information. In July 1918 he accepted a commission as captain in the army, joining a unit that sent a barrage of propaganda about Wilson's peace terms into the German trenches. He studied propaganda techniques both in the United States and in the Allied countries, and in 1922 published his conclusions in a trenchant essay, *Public Opinion*. He wrote, he later recalled, "as the result of my experience in psychological warfare and in seeing the war."[113] The book constituted a learned polemic against the idea that the public might ever know or act rationally in the modern world. Contemporary society had grown "too big, too complex, and too fleeting" for mankind's puny powers of comprehension, Lippmann wrote.[114] The citizens of mass societies never saw reality, only "stereotypes," or "pictures in their heads," pictures that were invariably too simple and thus distorting. The crude passions cultivated by skilled propagandists during the war had dramatically demonstrated this sobering truth. Politics, especially, was "out of reach, out of sight, out of mind," for most citizens, many of whom "are mentally children or barbarians, people whose lives are a morass of entanglements, people whose vitality is exhausted, shut-in people, and people whose experience has comprehended no factor in the problem under discussion. The stream of public opinion is stopped by them in little eddies of misunderstanding, where it is discolored with prejudices and far-fetched analogy."[115] Democratic

111. Creel, *How We Advertised*, 157.
112. John Dos Passos, *USA: The Big Money* (New York: New American Library, 1969), 494–95.
113. Walter Lippmann Memoir, CUOHC, 88.
114. Walter Lippmann, *Public Opinion* (New York: Free Press, 1965), 11.
115. *Ibid.*, 48.

theory, premised on the enlightenment and civic interest of the citizen, Lippmann declared to be built on a foundation of sand. There could be no common will, no spontaneous consensus, no such thing as an intelligently made mass decision. The solution, concluded Lippmann, was to create an "intelligence bureau," to pursue "the common interests [that] very largely elude public opinion . . . managed only by a specialized class whose personal interests reach beyond the locality."[116]

In the prewar years progressives had held in productive equilibrium the ancient tension between the political ideals of self-government on the one hand and efficient government on the other. Faith in man's reason, and reliance on the techniques of education and publicity, had sustained that equilibrium. But the war had cast dark clouds of doubt over that faith, and had shown the perverse effects that could result from abuse of those techniques. Lippmann now announced that "self-determination is only one of the many interests of a human personality," and he openly urged that democratic self-rule be subordinated to "order," "rights," and "prosperity."[117]

From reflections like this may be dated the rise of a substantial nagging fear of the people among modern liberals, a fear sharply at odds with traditional liberal purposes and one that threatened mortally to divide the liberal spirit against itself. One of the casualties of the war for the American mind thus seemed to have been the progressive soul, and the spiritual bloodletting very nearly drained the last reserves of utopianism from American social thought. The next reforming generation, after a decade of desuetude, would hearken not to the buoyant optimism of John Dewey but to the sober voice of Reinhold Niebuhr, preaching in Augustinian accents the doctrine of human imperfection and the necessity of diminished hopes. The war had killed something precious and perhaps irretrievable in the hearts of thinking men and women.

116. *Ibid.*, 195.
117. *Ibid.*, 195–96.

2

The Political Economy of War:
The Home Front

When America at last entered the stalemated war, the beleaguered Allies quickly dispatched missions of supplication across the Atlantic. Before the end of April 1917, high-level French and British delegations had arrived in Washington, seeking manpower, matériel, and, above all, money. The money was at first easily forthcoming, as Congress opened wide the doors to the United States Treasury. And the booming American economy was already supplying much of the Allied demand for munitions and foodstuffs. But manpower was another matter. Washington instantly recoiled from the request of the Europeans that American soldiers be amalgamated into the Allied armies. Instead, the War Department mounted preparations to field a force of one million Americans in France by the spring of 1918. They would not be commingled with foreign units, but would fight as an independent army. That army, officially called the American Expeditionary Force (AEF), was to be assigned its own sector of the front and supported by a distinctly American supply operation.

This plan stunned many Americans. When a prominent Senator declared in mid-April that "Congress will not permit American soldiers to be sent to Europe," no member of the administration troubled to refute him.[1] At the War Department, no plans existed for training a

1. Edward M. Coffman, *The War To End All Wars: The American Military Experience in World War I* (New York: Oxford University Press, 1968), 8.

93

large army and transporting it across the Atlantic. As the commander of the AEF later put it, when the General Staff went to look in the files for the plans for a large-scale European military operation, "the pigeon-hole was empty."[2]

The American proposal for an independent force also disconcerted the Europeans. Assembling such a force would necessarily delay the arrival of sizable contingents of fresh American troops in the trenches. And, if effectively used, a separate American military force would significantly strengthen Wilson's ability to play an independent political role. Most immediately, the decision to create the AEF meant that the United States would not function merely as a great reservoir of resources from which the Allies alone might draw. To the already considerable task of furnishing the Europeans with food and war matériel, America now added the obligation to sustain a major military effort of its own. Supplies that might otherwise have been channeled directly and quickly to the British or French were instead to be sluiced in part to American enterprises.

Thus, outfitting the AEF and meeting the Allies' continuing need for foodstuffs and munitions, as well as their increasingly desperate requests for money, made up the urgent demands on the American economy. The history of American mobilization is largely a record of successful response to those demands but it is a more interesting and significant story than that. As the first major American military endeavor since the nation had entered the industrial epoch, the First World War amplified dramatically the distinguishing features and problems of that epoch. The war forced both government and business to think and act on an unprecedentedly large and integrated scale, and the process was uniquely revealing of the character of the American economy and polity in the early twentieth century. As Robert D. Cuff has suggested, the study of wartime mobilization can disclose much about a nation's life style.[3] It can also disclose a great deal about a moment in history, and the war experience may be made to yield fresh answers to old questions about the progressive era. The war etched the lineaments of the ordinary more visibly into the historical record. It threw into high relief problems that had been imperfectly perceived or only partially resolved in the preceding two decades.

2. John J. Pershing, *My Experiences in the World War*, 2 vols. (New York: Frederick A. Stokes, 1931), I, 78.
3. Robert D. Cuff, "Organizing for War; Canada and the United States During World War I," Canadian Historical Association, *Historical Papers 1969*, 143.

Foremost among such problems was the relation of the government to the economy. The Populist and progressive movements, challenging in their various ways the laissez-faire theories and practices of the nineteenth century, had kept that issue at the head of the nation's political agenda for nearly thirty years before 1917. Yet for all the attention it had commanded, the matter was still in hot dispute as the country began to gird for war. Inevitably, the federal government would assume increased economic authority; public power would touch private enterprise in myriad new ways. Beyond that, little was certain. How would war revenues be raised? Would taxes bear more heavily on individuals or corporations? How would food production be increased? Would the government make its own munitions or draw on private sources of supply? On what legal structure would the government rely to legitimate and enforce its edicts? Would the emergency demonstrate that there was indeed a public interest in private enterprise, or would it prove, as Walter Lippmann and others feared, an opportunity seized by the "forces of reaction" to make the state the servant of corporate interests?

It does not necessarily impugn the patriotism of businessmen to acknowledge that in war as in peace they pressed their opportunities. During the neutrality period, in fact, the government had proved remarkably willing to aid in the pursuit of profits, and to come to the support of business generally. The Wilson administration had modernized the nation's banking structure when in 1914 it brought the Federal Reserve System into being; it had successfully sought legislation to create a federally owned and operated merchant marine; and in 1916 Wilson had backed the Webb-Pomerene bill, which sought to relax the anti-trust laws for businesses engaged in the export trade.[4]

This pro-business program did not go unopposed, and much of the hostility to it emanated from the President's own party, especially its huge Southern wing. "The South is clearly in the saddle, both in Congress and in the Administration," noted Presidential aide Colonel Edward House in mid-1916.[5] That Democratic stronghold was the traditional bastion of states' rights principles. Its representatives in Congress harbored deep enmity toward aggrandized federal power. The recent Populist ferment in the South only nurtured the traditional suspicion of

4. See Chapter 6 for further discussion of these developments.
5. Edward M. House Diary, entry for June 17, 1916, House Papers, Sterling Library, Yale University, New Haven, Conn.

all schemes that brought the government into closer cooperation with corporate enterprise. Recalcitrant Southern Senators had blocked passage of Wilson's shipping program for nearly two years, and in 1917 were still stalling the Webb-Pomerene legislation.

To Republicans like Henry Cabot Lodge, the regional character of the Democratic Party, with its attendant ideological implications, manifestly unfitted the Democrats for leadership in wartime, when federal power must necessarily be expanded, and government and industry made to work in harness. Lodge and other critics attempted to make Secretary of War Newton D. Baker and Secretary of the Navy Josephus Daniels the symbols of Democratic incapacity. Baker, of Southern birth and family background, had made his career in Cleveland, where he achieved a notable record as a reform mayor from 1911 to 1915. Baker's reform reputation and especially his well-known anti-militaristic views encouraged Wilson to appoint him Secretary of War in early 1916, when the President was seeking a way to bank the fires of preparedness agitation fueled by the outgoing Secretary, Lindley Garrison. But those very progressive and pacifist credentials made Baker a magnet for criticism in wartime. Localism and voluntarism, says a biographer, "were the cornerstones of his creed. . . . During the war he was seldom among those who saw the conflict as an opportunity to increase the control of the federal government over the life of the nation, and he opposed the creation of new agencies that might place more power permanently in federal hands."[6] Small of stature, gentle in speech and manner, remembered by his cabinet colleague Treasury Secretary William McAdoo as a man who "looked boyish in the company of the tall and bulky generals who were usually around him," Baker's very person could incite Republicans to paroxysms of rage. "He never talks of fighting," fumed Lodge, "but tells the country how nice everything is and garnishes it with the jargon of the Socialist and the uplifter and the platitudes of the pacifist."[7]

Josephus Daniels was, if anything, a still more controversial figure. A North Carolina newspaper man, Daniels was mercilessly lashed by his critics for his alleged ignorance about naval affairs. And as an old Bryanite schooled in Populist principles, he invited the strongest attacks for his anti-business policies, including his repeated claims that

6. Daniel R. Beaver, *Newton D. Baker and the American War Effort, 1917–1919* (Lincoln: University of Nebraska Press, 1966), 6.
7. William Gibbs McAdoo, *Crowded Years* (Boston: Houghton Mifflin, 1931), 342; Henry Cabot Lodge to John T. Morse, May 16, 1918, Lodge Papers, Massachusetts Historical Society, Boston.

private industry overcharged the Navy and his campaign for a government steel plant to make armor plate. Unlike Baker, whose performance as Secretary of War was eventually to win him grudging respect from the business community, Daniels was incessantly vilified from that quarter. He was, sneered one of Lodge's confidants, "a maggot in a putrid sore of the social organism."[8] As the gathering crisis increasingly forced business and government to work in span, Republicans intensified their charges that Wilson's Democratic Party, represented at the highest levels of leadership by men like Baker and Daniels, suffused with antiquated Jeffersonian values, and politically rooted in agrarian, Populist regions, was a terribly inadequate war horse in an industrial era.[9]

Much of the political wrangling that surrounded mobilization owed simply to the usual rivalries among parties and factions, and their disposition to exploit any advantage in the pursuit of power. That source of conflict was as timeless as politics itself. Much, too, derived from the history of the recent past, from disagreement over how best to preserve the growth in foreign commerce that neutrality had nurtured. And much of it could be ascribed to the wrestling among different regions and economic interests for shares of the crisis fattened military budget. This was but one of the many ways in which the war experience provided a glimpse of the future.

But to a significant degree the politics of mobilization also reflected enduring differences in principle about the character of American life —especially about the proper role of the state in an industrial democracy. Those differences, though a constant element in American history, were particularly sharp in the second decade of the twentieth century, when the quick coming of economic giantism was everywhere forcing intellectual and institutional adjustments. Progressive reformers had sought since the turn of the century to combat the immense new concentrations of private economic power by expanding public power. If any single premise underlay the myriad manifestations of progressive agitation, it was the conviction that government should actively pursue the public interest in a society whose private sector seemed increasingly indifferent or hostile to that interest. Beyond that general purpose, however, progressives agreed on little. Some, like Josephus Daniels, clung to Jeffersonian precepts and hoped to restore a lost world of numerous small competitors through vigorous enforcement of the anti-trust laws.

8. W. S. Bigelow to Henry Cabot Lodge, June 7, 1918, Lodge Papers.
9. See, for example, J. W. Beller to Joseph Tumulty, June 15, 1917, WWP; and Wilson to William C. Adamson, July 16, 1917, RSB, VII, 167.

Others, like Theodore Roosevelt, welcomed the efficiency of the large corporations and proposed to leave them intact while empowering federal regulatory commissions to monitor their activities. Woodrow Wilson, elected twice to the presidency on progressive platforms, appeared undecided between those contrasting progressive policies. He had helped to secure passage of the Clayton Act in 1914, strengthening the anti-trust laws. But he had also crafted a Federal Reserve Board to oversee the country's banking activities, and had aided in the birth of the Federal Trade Commission, a decidedly Rooseveltian regulatory body. Anti-progressives, such as Senator Lodge, opposed any infringement whatsoever on the prerogatives of business. If government were to enter the marketplace at all, in their view, it should come as the junior partner of private enterprise, protecting always the paramount interests of capital.

American society has not to this day resolved the competition among those principles. But in 1917, after a generation of progressive agitation, that competition was unusually acute, and mobilization would repeatedly manifest the irresolution of American political ideas. Contemporaries of all persuasions regarded mobilization as a testing ground for the principle of government involvement in the economic life of the nation. Over all the history of that effort hung unanswered questions about the proper relation of public to private power in American society. Uncertainty about those questions daily colored men's judgments about the legitimacy, legality, and permanency of wartime measures.

Uncertainty was further compounded by sheer ignorance. No one knew at the time of American entry what the precise—or even approximate—scale of the demands on the American economy would be, nor how much time was available to meet them. Moreover, reliable information on the nation's net financial reserves, aggregate industrial output, or even its transportation capacity simply did not exist. The men who must marshal the country's money and matériel and manpower went to work without benefit of comprehensive collections of data, without guiding precedents from the past, even without assurance that the other belligerents' experiences could serve as models for American mobilization.

All those elements—national self-interest, partisanship both petty and principled, as well as ignorance—came into play when the government tried to devise a war finance policy. The principal architect of that effort was Secretary of the Treasury William Gibbs McAdoo. Tall, thin-lipped, long-nosed, with high prominent cheekbones and deep-set, intense eyes that gave him a hawk-like appearance, McAdoo was a phenomenally forceful and ambitious man, who made a strong impress on the record of the Wilson administrations. He had been a prime mover in the drive to set up a government shipping line, partly because he suspected that private capital was too cautious to continue commercial operations on the submarine-threatened Atlantic. He had also urged a greater public element in the composition of the Board of Governors of the Federal Reserve System, hoping to establish a central bank that would operate out of the Treasury Department. The Federal Reserve legislation that initially passed fell short of that mark, but the war provided McAdoo with an opportunity to bend the System into closer alignment with his original intentions. "The Who, preeminently Who,/" wrote a wartime wag, "Is William Gibbs, the McAdoo. . . ./ He's always up and McAdooing./ From Sun to Star and Star to Sun,/ His Work is never McAdone . . ./ I don't believe he ever hid/ A single thing he McAdid."[10] After 1914 McAdoo was also Woodrow Wilson's son-in-law, referred to as the "Crown Prince." By virtue of both ability and family tie he enjoyed the special confidence of the President. Like his father-in-law, the Secretary was a Southerner who had made his mark in the North, as the promoter of the Hudson River tunnels linking New Jersey to New York. Raised in Georgia and Tennessee, he never lost his suspicion of the urban North, despite his successful career there. New York, he would later say, was an "imperial" city, "the citadel of privilege . . . reactionary, sinister, unscrupulous, mercenary, and sordid." That animus endeared him to the old Bryanites in his party, though McAdoo in practice, notes a biographer, "was a man of mildly progressive sentiments who easily overrode them in favor of solving the problem at hand by finding a middle way."[11]

The Secretary approached the problem of war finance in that mildly progressive but easily compromising spirit. In the spring of 1917, he later recalled, he "endeavored to form some reasonable estimate of the amount of money that would be required. With each fresh calculation

10. Mark Sullivan, *Our Times: The United States, 1900–1925*, 6 vols. (New York: Scribner's, 1933), V, 462, 464. The poet was Arthur Guiterman.
11. Otis L. Graham, Jr., "William Gibbs McAdoo," in *Dictionary of American Biography, Supplement Three* (New York: Scribner's, 1973), 479–82.

the sum had grown larger, and the figures were appalling. There were so many uncertain factors in the problem that a definite conclusion was not possible."[12] In his search for guides to policy McAdoo did not, as one might have expected, look first for enlightenment to the fiscal histories of the powers at war since 1914. To be sure, the financial representatives of the Allied governments, appearing as humble mendicants at the Secretary's desk in the Treasury Building, scarcely suggested examples to be emulated. But there was perhaps a deeper reason McAdoo's mind turned initially for inspiration to the history of the American Civil War. He seemed to act, as did so many of his colleagues, from an almost instinctual sense of the uniqueness of American society, a uniqueness so deep and durable as to render the distant American past more pertinent to the American present than the experiences of foreign peoples, no matter how modern. McAdoo further expressed this sense of a special American relation to what was popularly called the "European War" when he later explained that the United States had made massive loans to the Allies, so that they might "gain victories before American troops could be trained and put into action. The dollars that we sent through these loans to Europe were, in effect, substitutes for American soldiers, and the extent to which we were able to save the lives of the young men of America would be measured by the extent to which we could make operative, quickly and effectively, the credits the Allies needed to purchase supplies in American markets."[13] Thus the government moved promptly and generously to meet the Allies' financial needs. The British, for example, immediately received $200 million at 3 percent interest, nearly two points below what they were then accustomed to paying, and many more millions of dollars at preferred rates were to follow. But this American munificence must be understood in the context of considered calculations of American self-interest.

McAdoo, of course, was required to make other calculations as well. After hurried consultation with financial advisers, he largely rejected their counsel and in April 1917 requested a bond issue in the amount of $2 billion, with a thirty-year maturity and bearing interest at 3½ percent. Most private bankers had advised that the capital markets would be wrenched out of shape by any effort to absorb a loan of more than one billion dollars. Conventional wisdom also affirmed that issues with

12. McAdoo, *Crowded Years*, 372.
13. *Ibid.*, 376–77.

shorter maturities were more likely to sell and remain at par (face value). In the event, the first "Liberty Loan," as McAdoo artfully dubbed it, was considerably oversubscribed, as were all four subsequent loans in varying degrees. Government bonds did not, however, stay at par. By 1920 the war issues were selling in the 80s, or on an interest basis of about 6 percent.

Much of the explanation for that price erosion could be attributed to the relatively low interest rate at which the Treasury marketed its bonds, a much-criticized decision with complex consequences. "I do not like to complain of the Government," wrote prominent Boston investment banker Henry Lee Higginson in May 1917, "but that loan should have been put out at four per cent. . . . No person and no government can go into the market and borrow under the regular rates ruling."[14] Several factors shaped McAdoo's decision to make the first offering at 3½ percent. Not knowing the magnitude of the demands the financial system might be facing, he wanted to preserve his ability to make future issues, presumably to be offered in harder times, more attractive without pushing interest rates too high. This he could do only by starting out with a modest coupon rate on the first loan. The Secretary also shared with many of his contemporaries a fear of large government debt. Keeping the interest rate low would make it easier for future generations to service the indebtedness the war would inevitably create. It would also tend to minimize the future transfer of wealth from taxpayers to bondholders that was an equally unavoidable implication of large-scale debt financing. No less important was a factor that appears time and again in all aspects of the mobilization effort: McAdoo, like so many other policy-makers in government and chieftains of capital, sought emergency measures that would do the least possible violence to the monetary and business arrangements that had proved so profitable in the neutrality period. He chose the 3½ percent interest rate for the first loan, he explained, "because, for one thing, this rate was a little *lower* than the rates usually paid by savings banks. They were afraid that large withdrawals of these deposits would be made if the rate was higher."[15] He hoped, in other words, to attract lenders who would not siphon funds from other investments but would instead decrease their current consumption to buy war bonds. The twin intentions of this scheme—to preserve the structure of private capital, and to restrain

14. Henry Lee Higginson to Henry Cabot Lodge, May 9, 1917, Lodge Papers.
15. McAdoo, *Crowded Years*, 382 (italics added).

inflation by diverting moneys from current consumption—were admirable; unhappily, it proved impossible to realize them both.

From the outset, McAdoo frustrated the achievement of his own objectives because he feared that the low interest rate, however desirable its effects should they be accomplished, might itself prove the fatal impediment to the successful sale of the Liberty Loan. To offset that possibility, he attached several compensating features to the bonds: they could be paid for in installments, interest on them would be exempt from all federal income taxes, and they were to be convertible into any future issue that might bear a higher coupon rate. But the contradictory character of those provisions previewed the paradoxical course that McAdoo's policies were to take. The purpose of the first provision was to facilitate purchase by the widest possible public. But the tax-exemption feature discriminated in favor of the wealthy. McAdoo estimated in September 1917 that under the tax legislation then pending the 3½ percent tax-free return was the equivalent of a taxable return of 9½ percent for those in the highest brackets.[16] Eliminating the exemption and relying simply on a higher interest rate to make the bonds attractive was the obvious remedy for that inequity; but those steps McAdoo strongly resisted. Each of the subsequent four issues did in fact bring a rise in the interest rate, though never to a level that put the bonds on a straightforward competitive basis with the prevailing market. McAdoo thus was allowed to persist in the policy of financing the war on the cheap.

Or so it might appear. In fact, in their effort to ensure the smooth and painless progress of financial mobilization, McAdoo and Wilson followed policies that indirectly but surely inflated the cost of the war. The background to those somewhat intricate developments was provided by the inauguration of the Federal Reserve System in November 1914. The virtual simultaneity of the System's origin and the outbreak of the World War was to be a fact of the first importance. Wilson, it will be recalled, had appreciated some of the implications of that coincidence when he remarked in 1914 that the new currency legislation (the Federal Reserve Act) was "not thoroughly set," and that its workings would be strongly influenced by America's relation to the war.[17] The Act's chief function, in the words of its title, was "to furnish an

16. Charles Gilbert, *American Financing of World War I* (Westport, Conn.: Greenwood, 1970), 126.
17. See Prologue, p. 11.

elastic currency," one capable of quickly expanding or contracting in accord with commercial need. When America entered the war there swiftly came substantial transformations in the System's charter. Congress in early 1917 mandated several steps that vastly increased the liquidity of the Federal Reserve System. Required reserve levels of member banks were reduced, and all reserves were directed to be redeposited in Federal Reserve district banks, thus increasing the free reserves of both. The collateral required for securing Federal Reserve notes was diminished, enabling the System to issue them in greater numbers. Reserve requirements against government deposits were dropped altogether, and the number of banks eligible to be federal depositories was greatly expanded.[18] Thus the banking system was better equipped than ever, as America entered the war, to furnish tremendous elasticity in the supply of money. That function it performed perhaps too well.

McAdoo's stated purpose was to sell bonds to the non-banking public, to final investors who would divert their resources from other uses and put them in the service of the war effort. But his policies in practice prompted massive bank borrowing. And because debt obligations in the hands of banks provide a basis for the creation of credit—for the creation, quite simply, of new money—McAdoo's tactics produced powerfully inflationary results. The changes effected in the Federal Reserve System's regulations and procedures in the spring of 1917 provided a reservoir of financial resources ready to be tapped; the stream of government debt obligations that began to appear in April drained that pool into all the channels of commerce, straining the carrying capacity of all, bloating some nearly to the bursting point. Between 1916 and 1920, the total money supply increased about 75 percent, and the consumer price index nearly doubled.[19]

The Treasury encouraged those developments in several ways. Directly contradicting the policy of diverting rather than creating funds, McAdoo urged the public to "borrow and buy," to obtain bank loans with which to purchase bonds, using the bonds themselves as collateral. The banks, in turn, could then rediscount the same bonds at the Fed-

18. See Gilbert, *American Financing*, 177–99; and Milton Friedman and Anna Jacobson Schwartz, *A Monetary History of the United States, 1867–1960* (Princeton: Princeton University Press, 1963), 189–239.
19. Gilbert, *American Financing*, 197; *Historical Statistics of the United States* (Washington, D.C.: Government Printing Office, 1975), 164.

eral Reserve district bank; in fact, the Federal Reserve System, aiming to stimulate member bank holdings of government bonds, either on their own or their customers' accounts, offered a preferential discount rate on notes secured by government obligations rather than by commercial paper. Nor was this all; the Treasury also issued 48 series of short-term certificates of indebtedness during the war period. The scale of those operations was so large that 79.4 percent of proceeds from the five major war loans went to refund the certificates.[20] Because the interest rate on the certificates was markedly below that on comparable short-term commercial paper, they were taken almost entirely by the banks, and then only because of the preferential treatment given by the Federal Reserve to government issues. In short, as two students of the period have put it, "The Federal Reserve became to all intents and purposes the bond-selling window of the Treasury, using its monetary powers almost exclusively to that end."[21]

That close relationship between the Treasury and the central banking system, fostered generally by the war conditions into which the system was born, and crystallizing especially around the effort to float war loans at the lowest direct cost to the government, had several consequences. One was to force the Federal Reserve System rather permanently into the position of supporting the Treasury's funding operations. That subordinate role for the System largely fulfilled McAdoo's original intention to bring central banking functions under close public control. Ironically, the experience of war suggested that the System's political accessibility, an arrangement prompted by the concern of men like McAdoo for the public interest, paved the way to inflationary policies which, in the end, threatened that interest.[22]

The System's actions during and just after the war made possible the financing of a significant portion of America's war contribution by the creation of new money. In the absence of a comparable increase in the net output of consumable goods and services, the only possible result was inflation. McAdoo's borrowing practices, with the credit expansion they engendered, led as surely to that result as had the printing of greenbacks by his Civil War predecessor, Salmon P. Chase.

For the Wilson administration, financing the war through money-creation had certain advantages. However onerous its consequences, that method proved more politically palatable than drastically increas-

20. Gilbert, *American Financing*, 158.
21. Friedman and Schwartz, *A Monetary History*, 216.
22. *Ibid.*, 623ff.

ing direct taxation. It also meant that the carefully constructed edifice of private investment from which the United States hoped to command great postwar trade advantages could remain largely undisturbed. It meant, too, that the painful dislocations necessitated by shifting finite resources from peaceful to martial purposes could be partly avoided, or at least temporarily concealed. In all of those ways World War I suggested a model for later administrations in waging unpopular wars: McAdoo demonstrated that the true incidence of war costs could be hidden, at least in the short run, by inflation.

In so demonstrating, McAdoo could be said merely to have rediscovered the long-known political utility of easy money. But there was another aspect to his policies that must be acknowledged as innovative. As McAdoo studied the financial history of the Civil War, he concluded that Lincoln's Secretary of the Treasury had made a "fundamental error." Secretary Chase, McAdoo explained, had failed to recognize that "any great war must necessarily be a popular movement. It is a kind of crusade; and, like all crusades, it sweeps along on a powerful stream of romanticism. Chase did not attempt to capitalize the emotion of the people." That error McAdoo determined to avoid. "We went direct to the people," he later wrote, "and that means to everybody—to business men, workmen, farmers, bankers, millionaires, school-teachers, laborers. We capitalized the profound impulse called patriotism. It is the quality of coherence that holds a nation together; it is one of the deepest and most powerful of human motives."[23] To energize that impulse and direct it toward the purchase of Liberty bonds, McAdoo launched himself on an exhausting round of speaking tours. He caused the country to be papered with posters by noted artists like Howard Chandler Christy, Charles Dana Gibson, and James Montgomery Flagg. He induced celebrities like Douglas Fairbanks and Mary Pickford and Arthur Guy Empey to exhort monster rallies to buy bonds. He prompted "Four-Minute Men" to appear in front of movie screens, or on stages at schools, lodges, or union halls, briefly but fervently urging their auditors to support the Liberty Loans. McAdoo even accepted the bond-selling services of the nation's Boy Scouts, giving "every Scout a wonderful opportunity to do his share for his country under the slogan 'Every Scout To Save a Soldier.' "[24]

23. McAdoo, *Crowded Years*, 374–79.
24. Woodrow Wilson to Colin H. Livingstone, President of Boy Scouts of America, May 19, 1917, WWP.

All that patriotic effusion was no doubt honestly motivated and was manifestly successful in its purposes—all the bond issues, after all, were oversubscribed. But one might well ask why it was necessary. Some people at the time attempted to ask that question, but their queries were quickly drowned out by the very patriotic gales against which they tried to lift their voices. McAdoo, for example, told a crowd in California during the second loan campaign: "Every person who refuses to subscribe or who takes the attitude of let the other fellow do it, is a friend of Germany and I would like nothing better than to tell it to him to his face. A man who can't lend his government $1.25 per week at the rate of 4% interest is not entitled to be an American citizen."[25] In such an atmosphere, it was small wonder that when Senator Warren G. Harding called the loan drive "hysterical and un-seemly," he was blasted by gusts of derision and sarcasm on the Senate floor.[26]

Harding may not have spoken from the purest of motives, but the issue he tried to raise was certainly real, and profoundly troubling. The administration commenced American participation in the war with a campaign to agitate the deepest levels of the popular psyche, employ-ing all the techniques of persuasion and manipulation that the infant industries of advertising and mass entertainment could provide. The super-heated patriotism Harding remarked in the Liberty Loan cam-paigns was deliberately cultivated by the Wilson administration. It was a calculated consequence of the administration's reluctance to make the true material costs of the war visible and to lay them explicitly on the people. McAdoo's unwillingness to rely either on heavy taxation or on market-rate borrowing led directly to the effort to mobilize emo-tions instead, to substitute aroused patriotic fervor for the real economic price he would not ask the country to pay.

Many progressives, notably Robert La Follette, hoped to avoid both the inflation and the forced emotionalism that McAdoo's loan policies ultimately entailed. Paying for at least half of war costs by current taxation, they believed, would be more efficient, more rational, and above all more equitable than large-scale borrowing. The war was for

25. Quoted in a letter from Hiram Johnson to Charles K. McClatchey, Nov. 21, 1917, Johnson Papers, Bancroft Library, University of California, Berkeley.
26. *Congressional Record,* Senate, 65th Congress, 1st sess., Vol. 55, Part 4, June 8, 1917, 3325.

them an occasion to strike for a permanent tax system on progressive principles, and they had taken heart from Wilson's endorsement of those principles in his war message of April 2, 1917. McAdoo further lifted their spirits a few days later when he informed members of Congress that of his estimated $3.5 billion in increased revenue needs for the following year, he hoped new taxation would provide $1.8 billion. "As to taxation," McAdoo wrote on April 14, "my feeling has been that fifty per cent of the cost of the War should be financed by it."[27] But progressive hopes were shortly dashed; McAdoo's fidelity to his own formula proved fragile indeed, and the President, despite his rather bold profession of progressive intentions on the evening of April 2, took remarkably little interest in finance policy for a long time thereafter.

The progressive program was no secret. Based on the principle of taxation according to ability to pay, and relying heavily on graduated income and corporate taxes, it had been dramatically advanced in the years before the war—first with the passage of the Sixteenth Amendment in 1913, then with the highly progressive Revenue Act of 1916, and most recently with the introduction of an excess-profits tax in the emergency legislation of March 1917. In the key chair of the House Committee on Ways and Means sat Claude Kitchin, doubly influential as House majority leader. Son of a North Carolina Populist, reared to be suspicious of the "New South" doctrine of cooperation with the industrial Northeast, a commanding physical figure and eloquent orator, Kitchin had long been a formidable advocate of laying higher levies on the wealthy. In the Senate Committee on Finance, La Follette energetically represented the progressive cause. But the opponents of that cause, alarmed that the strategically positioned reformers might use the war crisis to inflict permanent damage on their interests, rallied in force to block the progressive tax program.

The Liberty Loan bill and the War Revenue bill were introduced in Congress at virtually the same moment. But while the first, which posed no significant threat to vested interests, passed after perfunctory discussion in less than three weeks, the tax bill took six months to reach the President's desk. The House Committee on Ways and Means reported out a bill in early May that sought to raise $1.8 billion in incremental revenues chiefly by increasing income taxes, lowering exemp-

27. McAdoo to Cleveland Dodge, Apr. 14, 1917, quoted in Gilbert, *American Financing*, 84.

tions, doubling the excess-profits levy, and imposing new excise taxes on items deemed to be luxuries, including automobiles. All of those proposals provoked painful outcries from the interests affected. A procession of special pleaders filed through the hearing room of the Senate Committee on Finance throughout the month of May. All professed patriotism and willingness to bear their fair share of the war's burdens, and all in the end begged that their share be shifted to someone else. "Our endeavors to impose heavy war profit taxes," noted Hiram Johnson, "have brought into sharp relief the skin-deep dollar patriotism of some of those who have been loudest in declamations on war and in their demands for blood."[28] Most of the conservative attack concentrated on the excess-profits provisions of the bill. Kitchin proposed simply to tax on a graduated scale all corporate profits in excess of an 8 percent return on invested capital. Such a device posed thorny administrative problems in determining what the base of invested capital actually was. But the measure appealed to progressives because it defined a potentially permanent formula for taxing corporate wealth. Business interests, however, wished to substitute a *war*-profits tax, with the base determined by the difference between earnings during wartime and average earnings in the years immediately preceding 1914. On the face of it, this was a reasonable proposal. Yet in effect it not only stressed the temporary character of the business tax, but also tended to discriminate against those sectors that had been least profitable before the war, especially agriculture and Southern textiles. Conversely, the proposal favored those firms, predominantly located in the North, whose profits had been relatively solid before the war and hence showed smaller percentage increases.

Kitchin's hard fight for his version of the excess-profits tax intensified the enmity he had already earned by his refusal to vote for the war resolution. He soon rivaled Daniels in the Republican press as the chief symbol of Southern Democratic provincialism. He had, after all, boasted to William Jennings Bryan that progressive tax legislation in 1916 was blunting the preparedness drive.[29] Now a host of critics assailed his War Revenue bill as a vindictive attempt "to pay for the war out of taxes raised north of the Mason and Dixon Line." Kitchin, said the New York *Sun*, "seems to have proceeded upon the assumption that

28. Johnson to Theodore Roosevelt, Sept. 8, 1917, Johnson Papers.
29. See Prologue, p. 16.

the war would prove unpopular, and, rather frankly, he has endeavored to make it so."[30]

Kitchin's measure nevertheless passed the House on May 23, substantially in its original form. Conservative Senators, especially Lodge and his Massachusetts colleague John W. Weeks, moving against the background of the press tattoo against the Kitchin bill, proceeded during June and early July to wheel their forces into position for the fight that loomed on the Senate floor. McAdoo, said Lodge, had put forward a "plan of perfectly exorbitant taxation" which must be somehow averted.[31] With the congressional battle lines thus shaping up, McAdoo exploded a bombshell at the end of July. Extraordinary expenditures for the new fiscal year, which the Secretary had estimated in April at $3.5 billion, plus $3 billion for loans to the allies,[32] he now projected to be $15 billion. Conspicuously absent from the Secretary's announcement was any request for a revision of the pending tax legislation, designed as it stood to provide a bit less than $2 billion. Thus McAdoo's earlier commitment to finance half the war through current taxation had collapsed by midsummer. He was now willing to settle for a much higher ratio of loans to taxes—about five to one. When the Senate opened debate on the bill on August 10, La Follette quickly condemned it as woefully inadequate to the Treasury's revised estimates of its needs, and introduced amendments aimed at restoring the original 50-50 tax-loan proportion. His efforts were of little avail. La Follette was saddled, as was Kitchin in the House, with the burden of having voted against the war itself. Like Kitchin, he laid himself open to the charge that he sought to use tax legislation to torpedo the war effort, embarrass the administration, and so vindicate his own original opposition to American entry. Other potential comrades were so sensitive to La Follette's vulnerability on this count that they hesitated to join him, though they agreed in principle with his fiscal goals. Hiram Johnson, for example, though he shared La Follette's antagonism toward the Republican Old Guard led by Lodge and Weeks, nevertheless thought that "La Follette is simply impossible. . . . His attitude upon the war and every question in connection with it has tainted him so that his

30. Quoted in Alex Mathews Arnett, *Claude Kitchin and the Wilson War Policies* (Boston: Little, Brown, 1937), 274–75.
31. Lodge to Arthur D. Hill, June 8, 1917, Lodge Papers.
32. American policy-makers at this time assumed that the loans to the Allies would be fully repaid; hence the loans were funded largely by domestic borrowing and carried as assets on the government's books.

leadership even in a just cause, or even his advocacy, will militate against that cause. I determined I would not get in his category, nor be a part of any movement which he led."[33] Their forces divided, progressives could not breach the lines of the powerful interests already arrayed against higher taxes. The final version of the legislation, enacted into law in October after four weeks of heated and often venomous Senate debate, did increase the excess-profits tax rates, but the net effect was to raise anticipated revenues only $600 million over the original House bill.

In the battle to apportion war costs between taxes and loans, the progressives clearly lost a major round in 1917, but they had an opportunity to recoup part of the loss the following year. Expenditures so outran all prior calculations that even McAdoo's revised estimates of July proved too low. In December he announced that yet another $3 billion would be needed, and Kitchin again seized the occasion to call for new tax legislation, with schedules revised sharply upward. McAdoo at first resisted the Congressman's attempt to renew the revenue fight, fearing that new tax legislation would hurt the sale of Liberty bonds. Yet by May 1918 Treasury deficits were approaching the staggering sum of a billion dollars per month—an amount greater than the annual federal budget before the war. Disbursements for fiscal 1919 were now projected at $24 billion. Overwhelmed by those magnitudes, McAdoo now convinced himself that higher tax rates, besides providing additional revenue, would in fact stimulate the sale of Liberty bonds, by enhancing the appeal of their tax-exempt feature. He accordingly appealed to Congress for legislation sufficient to provide the Treasury with eight billion tax dollars in the upcoming fiscal year.

That appeal set in motion a fateful and ironic episode. When Congress received McAdoo's message in May 1918, it stood on the verge of adjournment. Politicians were preparing for a round of spring and summer primary elections, and the November election already preoccupied political minds. Incumbents balked at the prospect of returning to their constituents fresh from a tax-raising session. Some of the stiffest resistance to the administration's request came from Democrats, especially those like Kitchin, who felt betrayed by McAdoo's inconstancy and Wilson's aloofness in the struggle over the last Revenue Act. Faced with that intransigence, McAdoo was moved to feats of persuasion. "The records in the Treasury showing up the war profiteering of the past year," he assured a Congressman, "will be a tremendous argument

33. Johnson to Charles K. McClatchey, Sept. 17, 1917, Johnson Papers.

in support of the bill and will justify any Democrat for staying in Washington to get new legislation."[34] The financial crisis, it seemed, had rekindled McAdoo's interest in taxation as a source of war revenue; it had even awakened an affinity for the progressive argument that taxes should fall most heavily on corporate profits.

McAdoo also convinced the President once again to display publicly an interest in revenue policy, and on May 27 Wilson made a dramatic appearance before a joint session of Congress and called it "a most unsound policy to raise too large a proportion" of revenues by loans. "Only fair, equitably distributed taxation . . . can prevent inflation and keep our industrial system free of speculation and waste," Wilson argued. "We shall naturally turn, therefore, I suppose, to war profits and incomes and luxuries for the additional taxes." Then, urging the assembled legislators to put fiscal duty before their hopes for an early end to the congressional session, Wilson declared that "politics is adjourned. The elections will go to those who think least of it."[35]

That phrase was to become famous, even infamous, in the months ahead. War mobilization was already an intensely partisan affair, and Wilson now grandly counseled the adjournment of partisanship even while urging action on tax policy, a notoriously divisive topic. Moreover, in order to whip their recalcitrant party into line, he and McAdoo endorsed the particular tax policies of the party's Southern, populistic wing—policies that had already called down upon the heads of Kitchin and men like him charges of fomenting sectionalism and class war. Ironically, within a few months the demons unleashed by the renewed attention to revenue policy that Wilson's address compelled would drive the President himself to the grossest violation of his own advice, in his ill-starred appeal for the election of a Democratic Congress in November.[36]

Robert La Follette hailed Wilson's May 27 speech as a "trenchant address" that "heartened and encouraged every student of War Finance."[37] La Follette and his colleagues, braced by administration backing, proceeded in the summer of 1918 toward the drafting of still

34. McAdoo to John Nance Garner, June 3, 1918, quoted in Seward W. Livermore, *Politics Is Adjourned: Woodrow Wilson and the War Congress, 1916–1918* (Middletown, Conn.: Wesleyan University Press, 1966), 134.

35. Albert Shaw, ed., *Messages and Papers of Woodrow Wilson*, 2 vols. (New York: Review of Reviews Corp., 1924), I, 493–95.

36. See Chapter 5, p. 240.

37. Belle Case La Follette and Fola La Follette, *Robert M. La Follette*, 2 vols. (New York: Macmillan, 1953), II, 747.

more progressive tax legislation. But irony intruded here, too. Despite the most intense administration exertions to achieve speedy completion of the bill, it remained in committee when the war ended on November 11. McAdoo immediately scaled down his estimated revenue needs, and Congress, facing now a peacetime tax proposal, dropped or diluted many of the progressive features of the War Revenue Act of 1918.[38] When the Republicans came to power in 1921, Secretary of the Treasury Andrew Mellon was to make the dismantling of the war-built tax structure one of his principal objectives. The excess-profits tax was repealed in 1921; income tax rates were lowered in that year and cut still further in 1924 and again in 1926. But they would never again approach the exceedingly low levels of the pre-World War I era.

Despite the attenuated character of the 1918 legislation, and Mellon's assault on the entire wartime financial legacy, World War I occasioned a fiscal revolution in the United States. Some of that revolution was ideological. The principle of progression—of laying taxes on those most able to absorb them—was permanently woven into the nation's tax system. Before the war nearly 75 percent of federal revenues came from customs and excise taxes, levies on consumption that bore most heavily on the least affluent groups. After the war the same percentage of revenues would come from taxes on incomes, profits, and estates, a decided shift in the incidence of the tax burden. Without the crisis and the huge financial demands it put upon the government, that shift in incidence and the accepted legitimacy of such a degree of progression in the tax system might have come about much more slowly, if at all. Reformers could take some comfort from that reflection. But the relative indifference of the Wilson administration, the liabilities incurred by the "pacifism" of their own leadership, the opposition of capital, and the chance of events had in the end confined their victories chiefly to the realm of principle.

Even more than the efforts of the reformers, the sheer scale of war-related revenue needs shaped the permanent fiscal legacy of the war. Federal tax receipts, for example, would never again be less than a sum five times greater than prewar levels.[39] Payments to veterans and to

38. One progressive feature that remained in the bill was a prohibitive tax on the products of child labor in interstate commerce; but the Supreme Court invalidated the tax in *Bailey v. Drexel Furniture Company*, 259 U.S. 20 (1922).
39. The Civil War had permanently multiplied annual federal tax collections to a level more than four times greater than the early nineteenth-century average. World War II had an even more dramatic effect on tax collections, lifting re-

holders of government bonds—both items derived directly from the war—comprised the bulk of the expenditures to which those receipts were applied. The federal debt increased from about a billion dollars in 1915 to over $20 billion by 1920. That growth not only put a permanent floor beneath tax rates—to Mellon's consequent chagrin—but also placed new obligations on the Federal Reserve System, whose Open-market Committee now had to deal in a government securities market whose size and centrality to the nation's financial life had been unimagined at the System's inception. The creation of a federal Bureau of the Budget in 1921 further testified to the vastly increased complexity and importance the war had imparted to the government's financial operations. The Bureau also signified a new impulse, observable in government as well as in the private economic sector, to put their commonly enlarged enterprises on a new footing of knowledge and centralized administrative control.

The absence of the knowledge essential to a well-coordinated war effort had been painfully obvious from the outset of mobilization, and the drive to overcome ignorance about large-scale aggregative phenomena in American life was one of the principal creations of the war era. Significantly, the main sources of that drive were traceable neither to government nor to the largest corporations, despite their later reputations as the chief agents of informed and amplified administrative control. Rather, the sources of this systemizing impulse were to be found in the activities of a small group of engineers. Most prominent was Howard E. Coffin, president of the Society of Automobile Engineers and vice-president of the Hudson Motor Car Company. Coffin had achieved a modicum of fame in the years after 1910 by spearheading a drive for the standardization of parts in the automobile industry. That apparently prosaic campaign in fact provided a model for much that was to happen during the war. It relied on systematic gathering of data, centralized administration, vigorous publicity, and voluntary cooperation of the interested parties—all devices that were to characterize American mobilization.

"If I heard Coffin talking in his sleep," noted an associate, "I wouldn't take the trouble to go over and listen because I would know exactly

---

ceipts to a level never less than seven times the prewar annual average. The figures clearly show the powerful—and enduring—effects of war on government finances.

what he would be saying. 'Standardize! Standardize! Standardize!' That's his motto, his slogan, his creed."[40] Appointed to the Naval Consulting Board in 1915, Coffin immediately perceived that before standardization or any appreciable degree of industrial coordination could be effected there must first be a fund of information on which to base intelligent action. That fund simply did not exist. There were, for example, 450 automobile manufacturers in the United States in 1915, and no data had been compiled on their aggregate output, their relative efficiency in employing resources, or their ability to integrate production facilities in an emergency. The same was true of virtually every industry. Consequently, Coffin inaugurated a national industrial inventory, undertaken with the cooperation of the five largest engineering societies, and blessed by President Wilson. Coffin soon acquired the services of Walter S. Gifford, a statistician at the American Telephone and Telegraph Company. The efforts of Coffin and Gifford complemented those of another engineer, Hollis Godfrey, president of the Drexel Institute in Philadelphia, who was proceeding in 1916 with his own survey of possible war needs. All of these men, in the judgment of Robert D. Cuff, "stood apart from the dominant centers of power in American social and economic life."[41] They were neither "captains of industry" nor prominent public officials. They were, rather, acolytes of the gospel of efficiency of which Thorstein Veblen was the chief exegete and Frederick Winslow Taylor the principal apostle. They were, in short, technocrats who abhorred disorder and loved efficiency with a passion that perhaps exceeded their regard for profits. The prospect of war focused the energies of these men on the imminent realization of their goals, even if their efforts carried them into dangerous proximity to some of the allegedly characteristic features of the enemy's culture. "The vision of a rationalized German society," Cuff notes, "was never far from the minds of American preparedness groups."[42]

The work of Coffin and Gifford and Godfrey, joined with the public cry for preparedness, resulted in August 1916 in the creation of the Council of National Defense and its Civilian Advisory Commission. The Council itself comprised the secretaries of war, navy, agriculture,

40. Robert D. Cuff, *The War Industries Board: Business-Government Relations During World War I* (Baltimore: Johns Hopkins University Press, 1973), 27. I am especially indebted to Cuff's thorough and penetrating analysis of the WIB.

41. Cuff, *War Industries Board*, 42.

42. *Ibid.*, 20.

commerce, labor, and interior. The Advisory Commission was designed to represent transportation, labor, general industry, finance, mining, merchandise, and medicine. Its original appointees included, in addition to Coffin and Godfrey, Daniel Willard, president of the Baltimore and Ohio Railroad; Samuel Gompers, president of the American Federation of Labor; Bernard Baruch, an independent Wall Street operator who was pursuing a second career as a statesman after accumulating a vast fortune as a stock speculator; Julius Rosenwald, president of Sears, Roebuck; and Franklin Martin, secretary general of the American College of Surgeons. Gifford was appointed director of the Commission. The composition of the Council and the Advisory Commission provided an important clue to their mandate. Military and State Department representatives had been deliberately excluded because the new body was charged not with conducting war or diplomacy but with harmonizing the American economy, especially relations between business and government. Secretaries Daniels and Baker, in fact, favored the title "Council of Executive Information," so as to forestall confusion about its intended purpose. Wilson underscored that purpose when he declared that the Advisory Commission "opens up a new and direct channel of communication and cooperation between business and scientific men and all departments of the Government. . . . The personnel of the Council's advisory members, appointed without regard to party, marks the entrance of the non-partisan engineer and professional man into American governmental affairs on a wider scale than ever before. It is responsive to the increased demand for and need of business organization in public matters and for the presence there of the best specialists in their respective fields . . . efficiency being their sole object and Americanism their only motive."[43]

The commissioners commenced their work enthusiastically but hesitantly. Their charge was at once sweeping and vague; their power potentially large but formally nil. As an advisory body, they depended for the realization of their aims on the cooperation of other government agencies, especially the military bureaus, as well as on the goodwill of industry. In the first months of the Council's existence neither the bureaus nor industry were particularly disposed to follow the Council's lead. The apparent success of Wilson's diplomacy in securing American neutrality in late 1916, and the already comfortable profits many key

43. Grosvenor B. Clarkson, *Industrial America in the World War: The Strategy Behind the Line, 1917–1918* (Boston: Houghton Mifflin, 1923), 21.

industries were reaping from war trade with the Allies, obviated any sense of urgency about getting on with the task of economic coordination. Hollis Godfrey, in fact, submitted a mobilization plan in late 1916 that would have taken five years to implement fully. With little else immediately to do, the Council directed its first efforts to organizing itself. It encouraged the formation of defense councils in every state, which in turn were to foster county councils, which again in turn would bring about "the creation of community councils of defense in the school district or a similar local unit of such small size that all the citizens in that locality can be reached through personal contact."[44]

That schema, so reminiscent of Thomas Jefferson's system of wards, was based on the premise that mobilization would require the synchronization of myriad local enterprises, all physically separate but consisting essentially of similar if not identical functions that required merely to be orchestrated. It rested, in other words, on the same premise underlying political representation: that the society consisted of so many equivalent parts, distinguished for administrative purposes simply by geography. Though sound as a principle of political equity, and appropriate to an economically homogeneous society, that organizational formula proved spectacularly irrelevant to the economic character of an industrial nation such as America was in 1917. Effective administrative networks needed now to run not along geographic lines but along lines of function. Those lines traced the connections among what might be called the new communities of production, distribution, and consumption—communities vertically organized and far-flung—that the industrial economy had brought into being. When mobilization got under way in earnest after April 1917, the obsolescence, for purposes of economic coordination, of the federal-state-county-school district organizational pyramid was quickly demonstrated. There emerged instead a host of new agencies whose titles designated their concern for specific economic sectors, such as the Food Administration, Fuel Administration, Railroad Administration, and the War Industries Board. Nothing better revealed the complex, variegated character of the American economy in the early twentieth century than its calling forth of this highly specified administrative apparatus in wartime. The Council of National Defense itself, apparently failing to catch the significance of that revelation, occasionally bemoaned the irrelevance of the neat organizational struc-

44. J. P. Lichtenberger, "The War Relief Work of the Council on National Defense," *Annals of the American Academy of Political and Social Science* 79 (1918), 230 (hereafter *Annals*).

ture it had originally erected. Secretary of War Baker complained to the President in November 1917 that the Food Administrator, the Fuel Administrator, and others had largely ignored the state organizations. "The State Councils of Defense have felt that they were not being used," said Baker, and Wilson accordingly suggested to the agencies that they work through the state councils to the maximum extent possible.[45] But that suggestion, which ignored the economic realities of modern America, had no visible effect. Mobilization continued to go forward under the aegis of the special agencies, with the several state councils largely reduced to propaganda organs, occasionally given to fostering vigilantism against local dissenters and "slackers."

The first of the agencies to take shape was the Food Administration. Like all wars that concentrate masses of men into armies, World War I greatly increased the demand for food. The Allies largely depended on the fertility of the American plains and the productivity of Midwestern farmers for their sustenance. To that already huge demand was now added the war-whetted appetite of a mobilized America gearing to place more than a million troops in the field. Poor American grain crops in 1916 and 1917 further complicated matters, as farmers anticipating a short-crop financial windfall planned to hold precious harvests on the farm in the spring of 1917 while they watched futures prices rise steeply on the exchanges. To dispel that gathering chaos Wilson named Herbert Clark Hoover Food Administrator on May 19.

In the person of Hoover, Wilson introduced onto the Washington scene a figure whose reputation was even then beginning to approach legendary proportions. Born in Iowa, orphaned at the age of nine, later reared in Oregon and educated as an engineer at Stanford, Hoover had made a considerable fortune in mining ventures and was to many Americans the very model of the self-made man. He arrived in Washington from London in 1917 cloaked in immense prestige gained as head of the Commission for the Relief of Belgium. Nearly his entire adult life had been spent outside of the United States. Like any intelligent traveler, he returned to his native country with a finely sharpened sense of its distinguishing characteristics. That sense, further refined by the war, informed all of Hoover's subsequent public career. Beginning with his service as Food Administrator, and extending through his presidency and beyond, he shaped his prescriptions for America against the constantly invoked backdrop of a foreign alternative. "The food ad-

45. Newton D. Baker to Wilson, Nov. 24, 1917, and Wilson to George Creel, Nov. 26, 1917, WWP.

ministrations of Europe and the powers that they possess are of the nature of dictatorship, but happily ours is not their plight, . . ." said Hoover in 1917. Food policy in the United States, he pledged, would be "based on an entirely different conception from that of Europe. . . . Our conception of the problem in the United States is that we should assemble the voluntary effort of the people. . . . We propose to mobilize the spirit of self-denial and self-sacrifice in this country."[46]

Hoover assumed his post at a time of giddily levitating food prices, and amid consequent public insistence that the government somehow restrain the rise. That Hoover purposed to do, but only to an extent compatible with his paramount priority, which was to increase agricultural output. Despite the urgency of the crisis he faced—the 1917 wheat crop threatened to fall short of domestic needs, to say nothing of the estimated 300 million bushels required by the Allies—Hoover characteristically refused to resort to coercive measures. At both the production and the consumption ends of the market cycle, he instead relied entirely on indirect and voluntary means. "No attempt was made to fix prices of retailers by European methods," he later recollected. "The economic policy of the administration was therefore to stabilize prices and reduce speculative profits by purely commercial pressures and business methods as distinguished from legal regulations."[47]

Like his colleague McAdoo at the Treasury, Hoover applied great ingenuity to the task of getting the nation's farmers, middlemen, and grocery shoppers voluntarily to perform their required parts. Ignoring the importunings of the Allies, Hoover rejected out of hand the idea of food rationing. Instead, pleas for the nation's households willingly to suffer "wheatless" and "meatless" days emanated from Hoover's office, just as McAdoo propagandized the public to swallow his low-yield bonds. Half a million persons went door to door to hand housewives pledge cards that enlisted their patriotic cooperation in the drive to conserve foodstuffs. The Food Administration thus literally reached into every kitchen in America, and its measures no doubt accomplished much by encouraging food conservation. But its techniques also intensified the same patriotic fevers on which the Treasury relied to finance the war. "The significance of this broad campaign," said a Food Ad-

46. Herbert Hoover, testimony before Senate Committee on Agriculture, June 19, 1917, quoted in William Clinton Mullendore, *History of the United States Food Administration, 1917–1919* (Stanford: Stanford University Press, 1941), 52–53.
47. Herbert Hoover, "Introduction" to Mullendore, *History.*

ministration pamphlet describing a mass appeal to retailers, "is far deeper than may appear at first thought. It is indeed typical of the whole program of the Food Administration, in its insistence upon cooperation rather than coercion, upon the compelling force of patriotic sentiment as a means to be tried before resort to threats and prosecutions."[48] The mobilization of emotion—or, as Hoover cared to call it, "the spirit of self-sacrifice"—proved preferable to rationing, just as to McAdoo it proved preferable to heavy explicit taxation.

Hoover showed equal inventiveness in dealing with the production and distribution phases of the food situation. Here the commitment to "purely commercial pressures and business methods" meant primarily that the mechanism of price, rather than production quotas, would be the principal device to stimulate production. Hoover cajoled the Allied purchasing commissions into pegging agricultural prices at levels high enough to call out increased production from the profit-conscious American farmer.[49] (In the key commodity of wheat, he later endeavored to reinforce the Allied price offerings by having the United States government guarantee farmers a price of $2.20 a bushel.) In relying on high prices to produce larger harvests, Hoover revealed that production, not inflation, was his first concern. He also, to some extent, made a virtue of necessity. Especially in the great Midwestern grain belt, marked indifference and even outright hostility to the war rendered farmers impervious to Hoover's patriotic propaganda to increase plantings and yields. The same sentiments made foolhardy any government attempt to require such practices or to requisition crops.

Hoover also entered into creative arrangements with processors and distributors. Armed with the Attorney General's opinion that collusive business arrangements to which the government was a party were "obviously not within the mischief at which the Sherman [Anti-trust] Law was aimed," Hoover proceeded to lay down rules stipulating profit margins at each link of the distributive chain. He also regulated storage facilities, and limited speculation in futures. Significantly, "the uniform practice of the Food Administrator therefore was to promulgate rules

---

48. Mullendore, *History*, 221.

49. The Allies agreed to this, despite their insistence that rationing was a more efficient and less costly way to ensure adequate food supplies. They not unreasonably resented the increased costs they felt pressured into bearing, and they moved after the Armistice, with what Hoover regarded as extremely indecent haste, to escape this burdensome system. See Mullendore, *History*, 32, 263.

only after full and free conference with the trade representatives, at which conferences they were notified just what rules were being considered and their suggestions and criticisms were asked. . . . In a very real sense, therefore, the rules and regulations that the licensees were required to observe in the conduct of their business were rules which in many cases the trades patriotically adopted."[50] In promoting that spirit of partnership between business and government, Hoover again in part simply made a virtue of necessity. His power to punish violators was, after all, largely confined to extracting "some public expression of contrition or some sale of food at nominal consideration to the government departments."[51] But in larger measure Hoover's voluntaristic and indirect policies in dealing with both farmers and middlemen followed naturally from his vision of American society. In Hoover's ideal social order, the state's formal power should be small, but its services placed at the disposal of those private interests working to coordinate and rationalize the nation's economic life. Hoover's was among the more articulate versions of a social theory widely shared by war administrators.

As he faced the already well-disciplined milling and marketing sectors in 1917, Hoover had little problem identifying authoritative spokesmen for the interests with which he must deal. But in the countryside farmers still struggled to concert their manifold enterprises, and Hoover therefore undertook to fill the void with a dependable "grass-roots" organizational stratum of his own. He invited the president of the largest bank in each agricultural county to convene other bankers, newspaper editors, and the chief executive of the local commercial club to nominate a county food administrator. For an agency hoping to appeal directly to farmers, that seemed, to say the least, an odd administrative stratagem. Late in 1917, a Wisconsin farmer described his district's reaction to such arrangements. Farmers, he admitted, "have not been as active to participate in Food Conservation, Red Cross Work or Liberty Bond sale, . . . as might be expected."

> I believe the cause to be, that in the selection of those bodies who are supposed to be representatives of the Nation, such as Defense Councils, Safety Commissions and the like, we have surrounded the farmers with the same class of people who have incurred their ill will in former times, the bankers, lawyers, professional politicians, repre-

50. *Ibid.*, 64.
51. *Ibid.*, 60.

sentatives of a business system . . . who now under the guise of Patriotism are trying to ram down the farmers' throats things they hardly dared before.

The remedy, the writer suggested, lay in the creation of an organization of farmers for patriotic purposes. "Why not form an American Farmers Council . . . and there would never be any need to 'shame the Farmers into loyalty' as a recent paper quoted Hoover. . . . Even the men of German descent on the farms would surprise the nation by their loyalty to their adopted country."[52]

Out of an amalgam of Hoover's administrative techniques and the aspirations of farmers to build a businesslike and loyal organization of their own came one of the most striking developments of the war period. American farmers, decisively thrust into a minority position in the nation's councils after the Populist debacle of the 1890s, had groped ever since for a mechanism to make their political weight effectively felt. Legatees of the old Farmer's Alliances, like the Farmer's Union and especially the left-leaning Nonpartisan League, inherited also the active hatred of the cities (and of the Department of Agriculture) for agrarian radicalism, and were consequently able to accomplish little. But about 1911, there had begun to appear in rural districts a new organization, the farm bureau. The bureaus shunned radical rhetoric, cultivated the most intensely commercial elements among farmers, and themselves adapted the methods and values of the farmers' erstwhile business adversaries. In nearly every instance, the genius of a bureau was the county agent. Beginning in many locales as agricultural officers of the Chamber of Commerce, the agents had by 1917 assumed an independent and unique station, simultaneously (and confusingly) sponsored by the federal, state, and local governments, as well as by the bureau itself, a putatively private association. This questionable arrangement meant that a public officer became the paid organizer for a private group, one of whose principal purposes was to influence government policy.

The farm bureaus received great stimulus from the Smith-Lever Act of 1914, which allocated federal money for the expansion of the county

52. H. G. Tank to Carl Vrooman, Assistant Secretary of Agriculture, Oct. 30, 1917, "Correspondence of the Secretaries of Agriculture," Record Group 16, National Archives, Washington, D.C. I am obliged to David Danbom for calling my attention to this item. See David Danbom, *The Resisted Revolution: Urban America and the Industrialization of Agriculture* (Ames: Iowa State University Press, 1979).

agent system. But, writes one student of the subject, "the real change of gradient came in 1917, when the system received the benefits of special war appropriations. . . . This was the period of mushroom-like growth in the numbers and membership of county farm bureaus."[53] In late 1919 and early 1920, bureau representatives from over thirty states met in Chicago and formed the American Farm Bureau Federation, an aggressive lobby that "gave definite evidence of becoming one of the most powerful pressure groups that the country had ever known."[54] Some of the aims in whose service that pressure was to be applied were indicated by the resolutions the conventions passed: condemning labor militancy, offering the Federation's aid in the drive "to rid the country of Bolshevism and other anarchistic tendencies," and praising the American Legion as "one of the most important factors in the life of America."[55]

More significant than those vivid evidences of a newly articulate agrarian conservatism were the curious circumstances of the Federation's genesis. The war had not created the bureau movement, but it had greatly catalyzed it because of the obvious need for increased organization and the relative friendliness of wartime Washington to a body likely to prove more safe, businesslike, and tractable than the militant existing farmers' groups. The Federation later would sometimes press uncomfortably hard on Hoover when he served as Secretary of Commerce and as President, but it nonetheless vindicated his policy of taming the countryside by introducing the soundest banking and commercial elements into agricultural politics. Above all, the formation of the American Farm Bureau Federation demonstrated how public and private elements had been imaginatively commingled in wartime. That creative interpenetration of realms traditionally supposed to be separate exemplified one of the chief structural effects of the crisis, and one of Hoover's principal contributions to the theory and practice of American statecraft.

Ideally, according to Hoover's theory, public authority need never be nakedly invoked. Private pursuits under properly restrained government guidance would naturally orchestrate themselves in the general welfare. But even Hoover recognized the need occasionally to compromise

53. Grant McConnell, *The Decline of Agrarian Democracy* (New York: Atheneum, 1969), 46, 50.
54. Theodore Saloutos and John D. Hicks, *Agricultural Discontent in the Middle West, 1900–1939* (Madison: University of Wisconsin Press, 1951), 258.
55. *Ibid.,* 259.

ideals, a recognition forced on him in this case by the refusal of the nation's farmers to respond to mere exhortation to produce more. The compromise proved small enough, as Hoover sought legislation enabling the government to support agricultural prices at high levels—a potent but still indirect means of calling forth larger harvests. In the Lever Food and Fuel Act of August 1917 Congress officially created the Food Administration, which had existed on the legally dubious basis of exclusively presidential authority since May. The Act empowered the President to peg the price of wheat, and led to the establishment of a government Grain Corporation, capitalized at $150 million, to guarantee that price. The Act also authorized the President to control fuel prices, and Wilson presently named Harry Garfield, president of Williams College, as Fuel Administrator.

Despite its modest and qualified departure from laissez-faire orthodoxy, the Lever bill excited hot controversy. It took more than a month to make its way through Congress, obstructed repeatedly by objections to any aggrandizement of presidential power, by complaints about the failure to extend price controls to other commodities, and by hostility to the very idea of explicit government control over the economy. The bill's passage was further impeded by the action of Senator Weeks, who seized the chance to resurrect his proposal, so noxious to Wilson, for a Joint Committee on the Conduct of the War. The Weeks proposal, wrote Wilson to Asbury F. Lever, would "render my task of conducting the war practically impossible." Referring to the Civil War Wade–Chandler Committee, he noted that "it was the cause of constant and distressing harassment and rendered Mr. Lincoln's task all but impossible." The adoption of the Weeks resolution, Wilson concluded, "I could only interpret . . . as arising from a lack of confidence in myself."[56] The President headed off the resolution only by the most adroit political maneuvering, though he won but a skirmish in the running war-within-a-war for control of the mobilization effort.

In the winter of 1917–18, that war erupted into a major open battle, touched off by the apparent ineptitude of Fuel Administrator Garfield. Shortages of fuel, especially coal, had plagued the country throughout the unusually cold winter. Local officials had begun brazenly to commandeer coal trains in transit through their jurisdictions, so desperate were their constituents for warmth. Police in some cities had to guard industrial coal piles from marauding citizens seeking relief from the

56. Wilson to Asbury F. Lever, July 23, 1917, RSB, VII, 186.

bitter chill.[57] Congressional Republicans hoped to capitalize on the public's considerable discomfort by pressing a vigorous attack on many deficiencies in the management of the war: the chaos in the ship-building program, the failure to supply the AEF with American-made machine guns, airplanes, or artillery, and the allegedly unsanitary and even immoral conditions in the military training camps. "We are struggling here to overcome the mismanagement and incapacity in the preparation for and the conduct of the war," Senator Lodge wrote an English correspondent. "The fact is the President has no administrative capacity. He lives in the sunshine. He wants nobody to tell him the truth apparently and he has a perfect genius for selecting little men for important places."[58] Secretaries Daniels and Baker especially were the targets for most of those salvos, and the Senate Military Affairs Committee summoned Baker on January 10, 1918, to defend himself against charges of manifest incompetence. The Committee obviously intended to give Baker a hiding, but the Secretary, tugging the while on a cigar, calmly deflected the senatorial slings and arrows for three dramatic days. For the moment at least, the administration seemed to have beaten back the attack on its policies.

Then on January 17 Garfield unexpectedly announced that all factories east of the Mississippi were to be shut down for four days. By this drastic means Garfield hoped to move bottlenecked coal to eastern seaports and into the bunkers of ships idled at their moorings for want of fuel. As it turned out, the bottleneck was quickly broken and the fuel situation soon stabilized. But for a time the tempest set off by Garfield's order threatened to engulf the administration in a tidal wave of criticism. "Bedlam broke loose," Colonel House commented. "I have never seen such a storm of protest."[59] "The order itself inflicts a profound mortification on the American people," raged former Harvard President Charles W. Eliot, "which, in my judgment, they will not forget for a long time. No one of the belligerent nations in Europe, except Russia, has been forced to admit such incompetence in public administration."[60] To the already massive and only momentarily silenced Re-

57. Livermore, *Politics Is Adjourned*, 68.
58. Lodge to Lord James Bryce, Dec. 24, 1917, Lodge Papers.
59. Livermore, *Politics Is Adjourned*, 87. For a general account of the fuel crisis, see James P. Johnson, "The Wilsonians as War Managers: Coal and the 1917–18 Winter Crisis," *Prologue* 9 (1977), 193–208.
60. Charles W. Eliot to David Houston, Jan. 18, 1918, Houston Papers, Houghton Library, Harvard University, Cambridge, Mass.

publican barrage against Wilson, Baker, and Daniels, members of the President's own party now added their fire. Oregon Democratic Senator George Chamberlain introduced a bill on January 19 that aimed to wrest control of the war effort from the President and place it in the hands of a War Cabinet of "three distinguished citizens of private ability." The measure would have effectively reduced Wilson to a figurehead. Its implications were so disastrous as to make the earlier Weeks resolution look almost desirable by comparison. Badly shaken, the President sent Baker back into the lists, and in heated testimony before the Military Affairs Committee on January 28, the Secretary managed once again to blunt the force of the congressional attack. "Jesus, you ought to see that little Baker," Senator Ollie James reportedly told the President. "He's eating 'em up."[61]

With his congressional critics thus once again temporarily disarmed, Wilson launched a counter-offensive of his own. He induced Senator Lee Overman to propose legislation giving the President great discretionary authority to reorganize executive agencies without consulting Congress in each case. Though it amplified the President's power at the expense of Congress—the real issue underlying the clashes over the Joint Committee and the War Cabinet—Overman's proposal deftly exploited the critics' own demands for greater administrative efficiency in the Executive, making it difficult for them to stand against it. The Overman Act became law on May 20, marking an important advance in the historic growth of presidential power. It also signified the beginning of the end of Wilson's effective relationship with Congress. As a careful student of the presidency, Wilson had attempted throughout the first year of the war to avoid Lincoln's rather unilateral assumption of extraordinary powers. Preferring to cast himself as a parliamentary leader, Wilson in wartime, as earlier in his presidency, had sought express congressional authority for nearly all his actions. In some ways that strategy had backfired, as Congress became an overheated cockpit for intensely partisan, publicly conducted wrestling over every war measure, as demonstrated in the brawling over the Lever Act. Wilson evidently thought the pain worth enduring until the battles of the winter of 1917–18 pushed him, with the Overman bill, largely to abandon the effort to base war measures in explicit congressional statutes. But there was, it seemed, no refuge from the critical gales the war had loosed. With the Overman Act and the subsequent changes in his ad-

61. RSB, VII, 504.

ministration, Wilson did insulate himself a bit from charges of inefficiency—but thereafter he was increasingly condemned for his high-
handed and "dictatorial" behavior.

The accusations of "dictatorship" were assuredly exaggerated. Though
the Overman Act laid a foundation on which future Presidents were
to erect a more potent Executive establishment, Wilson used its authority only modestly. His most notable action under its terms was the
reorganization of the War Industries Board in the spring of 1918. The
Board was without doubt the most ambitious of the war agencies. As
the focal point for the continuing debate about the government's proper
relation to the economy, it frequently excited extravagant hopes and
fears during the war, and has ever since been the subject of interested
controversy and scholarly inquiry.

In common with so many other significant wartime measures, the
Board emerged out of the turbulent political atmosphere surrounding
the passage of the Lever Act in the summer of 1917. Prior to that time,
the Advisory Commission of the Council of National Defense (CND)
had groped with small success for an acceptable device to manage industrial mobilization. The procurement operations of the several military bureaus were archaic. They were organized according to military
categories, such as ordnance and quartermaster, which bore no relation
to the functional patterns of the economy. They often competed with
one another for scarce goods or transport facilities. They remained too
fragmented to pursue unified pricing policies or to gauge the aggregate
impact of military purchases on the workings of the civilian economy.
The Commission sought to streamline that ramshackle structure by
relying on modern business methods—and businessmen. It encouraged
the creation of so-called "cooperative committees," composed of industry representatives who advised government purchasing agencies on
sources of supply and the quality and costs of materials.

The actions of the cooperative committees soon trapped the Commission in a snarl of disputes. The military bureaus resented any en-
croachment on their domains. Those corporations that were excluded
from the cooperative committees challenged the committees' legality.
And many citizens hotly questioned the propriety of an arrangement
that seemed to allow private businessmen to serve their own interests
under the cloak of public authority. That charge was particularly explosive in light of the radical accusation that business elements had

forced American entry into the war in the first place. "The Attorney-General should put every one of those fellows in jail between now and Saturday night who keep the price up," railed House Speaker Champ Clark in May, and the following month the activities of the Commission's coal committee intensified popular indignation. A conference of coal operators meeting under CND auspices in Washington set the price of coal at three dollars a ton. The agreement prompted effusive plaudits from Secretary of the Interior Franklin Lane, who hailed it as a fine example of patriotically inspired business-government coopera-tion. But the President was soon forced to acknowledge that the price stipulated by the conference "exactly coincides with the agreement which certain operators are now under indictment by the Government for making 'in restraint of trade.' "[62] Business, with government help, seemed to be flouting the anti-trust laws, among the landmark reform achievements of the progressive period.

Moved by the increasingly noisy popular outcry against apparent business infiltration of government, Congress grafted Section Three to the Lever bill, which made it illegal for any government agent to con-tract for supplies in which he had an interest. Wilson strenuously re-sisted the measure, which would instantly unravel the elaborate net-work of informal business-government relationships the Commission had painstakingly patched together. The dismantling of that structure threatened to impale the administration on the horns of a dilemma. On the one side loomed chaos, with government and industry rigidly sepa-rated from one another by a legal wall erected to insulate the public from the private spheres. On the other side lay the implied alternative of a powerful government superbureau, with sweeping authority to commandeer goods and fix prices. Proposals in this vein, granting the government broad price-setting power, were already under discussion in Congress in the summer of 1917, and would be still more vigorously put forward the following winter.

The urgency of the war crisis simply did not permit the acceptance of the first of those alternatives; and a host of ideological and political impediments militated against the latter. The war thus posed, in stark and insistent terms, the characteristic dilemma of the progressive era, indeed of American political economy in the twentieth century. Wilson, buffeted between the shoals of unbridled laissez-faire and full-blown

62. Clark quoted in Cuff, *War Industries Board,* 105; Wilson to Franklin Fort, July 2, 1917, RSB, VII, 140.

state economic control, cast about for a safe middle way. Within the councils of the administration a plan for a War Industries Board began to take shape in June and July 1917. The Board's ostensible assignment was to impart system to the government's war purchases. But the constitution of the Board, the functions it was both assigned and denied, and its operating techniques all indicated that it had other purposes as well. Perhaps the most important of those implicit aims, at least in the beginning, was the attempt to outflank the legislators pushing for Section Three in the Lever bill. "One of the principal things expected," Bernard Baruch jotted in his diary, "is to stop criticism because of relations of business men."[63]

The President announced the formation of the new Board on July 28, 1917. It was to have, besides the chairman and an army and a navy representative, three members, with respective responsibilities for raw materials, finished products, and priorities. Significantly, the authority actually to enter into contracts for the delivery of goods remained with the military bureaus, and the Board was given no price-fixing power. Though heralded by many, then and since, as a strong agency empowered to end the disarray in the industrial procurement program, the Board in fact was largely a cosmetic creation, even a political ploy, intended as much to stymie the administration's critics and hold the line against radical institutional reordering as to render mobilization more efficient.

In its defensive mission the Board did not, at first, have much success. Section Three passed despite Wilson's démarche, and as he feared, the business advisers on the cooperative committees began to desert in droves. Edgar Palmer, president of the New Jersey Zinc Company and chairman of the zinc committee, wrote Wilson that it appeared he must now either leave the committee "or forbid my companies to sell zinc supplies to the Government." Attorney General Thomas W. Gregory reluctantly confirmed that the new law forced that choice, and Palmer, along with many others, speedily resigned.[64] The continuing confusion that beset the Board's operations claimed another major casualty in October, when Chairman Frank Scott, broken in health by his Sisyphean efforts to manipulate the Board's deliberately unwieldy machinery, also resigned. The next chairman, Daniel Willard of the

63. Bernard Baruch Diary, entry for July 13, 1917, Baruch Papers, Firestone Library, Princeton University, Princeton, N.J.
64. Edgar Palmer to Wilson, Aug. 15 and Sept. 20, 1917, WWP.

Baltimore and Ohio Railroad, knew full well that he was being asked to preside over a paper empire. Secretary Baker, who virtually dragooned the railroad executive into taking the post, described Willard's reluctance to the President: "The embarrassment in his mind," Baker reported, "arose from the fact that the War Industries Board as such has no power conferred by statute."[65] Within two months Willard, too, had quit, despairing over the Board's contrived impotence. For the remainder of that crisis-ridden winter of 1918, the Board remained headless. "Like a convulsed person," writes Paul A. C. Koistinen, "the W.I.B.'s limbs twitched without central motor control," until Bernard Baruch assumed the chairmanship in March.[66]

Baruch, like Hoover, was a figure swiftly elevated into prominence by the war. Like Hoover, he too epitomized the ideal of the self-made man. The son of a Jewish immigrant physician, Baruch had grown up in South Carolina and New York in comfortable but modest circumstances. Beginning as an office boy in a New York brokerage house in the 1890s, he had amassed a hefty fortune as a stock speculator with a canny sense of markets and a prodigious grasp of facts. Woodrow Wilson would later call him "Dr. Facts," and draw him into the closest circles of the administration. But again like Hoover, who had lived so long abroad, Baruch passed much of his life on the periphery of the mainstream. Colonel House wondered in 1917, when Baruch was mentioned as a possible head of a centralized purchasing agency, whether the country would tolerate "a Hebrew Wall Street speculator given so much power."[67] As a Jew in a gentile land, a Southerner in New York, and an ardent Democrat inhabiting the densely Republican confines of high finance, Baruch was thrice an outsider. "He was of Wall Street," said Grosvenor B. Clarkson, "but he was its Ishmael."[68] Tall, thin, meticulously tailored, with aquiline features and a courtly but aloof manner, Baruch fitted well his Wall Street sobriquet, "The Lone Eagle." "He was alone," writes his biographer. "He was always alone."[69] Yet his singular status invested Baruch with a unique political utility. He was in the business world but not wholly of it, intimate with its chief-

65. Baker to Wilson, Nov. 17, 1917, WWP.
66. Paul A. C. Koistinen, "The 'Industrial-Military Complex' in Historical Perspective: World War I," *Business History Review* 41 (1967), 394.
67. Edward M. House Diary, entry for May 27, 1917, House Papers, quoted in Cuff, *War Industries Board*, 102.
68. Clarkson, *Industrial America*, 70.
69. Margaret Coit, *Mr. Baruch* (Boston: Houghton Mifflin, 1957), 93.

tains and accustomed to dealing with them, yet not a full-fledged member of their tribe. Thus when Wilson sought to build bridges to the business community in 1915 and 1916, he turned to Baruch, whose familiarity with capital, and simultaneous detachment from it, specially suited him for the assignment. For like reasons, in March 1918 Wilson looked naturally to Baruch to head the War Industries Board.

Perhaps it was that same detachment that made Baruch something of a visionary about political economy. Again in common with Hoover, who has been unjustly characterized as a species of conservative mossback, uncomfortable with ideas that challenged the status quo, Baruch should more properly be regarded as an innovator, even an ideologue. Grosvenor B. Clarkson, secretary and later director of the CND's Advisory Commission, and an enthusiastic admirer of the WIB chairman, sensed the significance of Baruch's ideas, and pointed to the circumstances that helped to crystallize them. "It is little wonder," he wrote after the war, "that the men who dealt with the industries of a nation, binned and labeled, replenished and drawn on at will for the purposes of war . . . meditated with a sort of intellectual contempt on the huge hit-and-miss confusion of peace-time industry, with its perpetual cycle of surfeit and dearth and its eternal attempt at adjustment after the event. From their meditations arose dreams of an ordered economic world."[70] A preference for order over confusion scarcely suffices to mark a man as a visionary; but Baruch had a distinctive view of the optimal economic order and the institutional devices that should be fashioned to manage it. That view was strikingly modern. As Baruch described it, one can hear themes that echo from Thorstein Veblen and resonate vibrantly in the later writings of theorists such as Herbert Marcuse and John Kenneth Galbraith.

Like those other commentators, Baruch lamented not merely the lack of system in the free-market economy, but especially the absence of rationality. He boldly distinguished "civilian *needs*" from "civilian *wants*," in peacetime as well as war. That distinction carried Baruch, in company with other apostles of economic rationality, into an obscure intellectual maze, its corridors continually eclipsed by the shadowy concepts of false needs and false consciousness. In the same manner Baruch distinguished the productive from the distributive sectors. The former he regarded as the locus of economic reason and virtue; the latter he indicted for indulging in practices like model differentiation and manipulative advertising that raised prices "without in the remot-

70. Clarkson, *Industrial America*, 312.

est degree contributing to the well being of the people." Under his guiding hand, one of the WIB's important goals was to "assist in cultivating the public taste for *rational* types of commodities."[71]

Those idealistic notions were heady stuff in a society where the individual was supposedly sovereign. They also carried implications for institutional change that undermined the regnant orthodoxies of competition and laissez-faire. Rationality, Baruch believed, could be achieved only through industrial combination. He consequently blasted the antitrust laws as attempts "to reduce by Government interference the processes of business so as to make them conform to the simpler principles sufficient for the conditions of a bygone day." The workings of the "cooperative committees of industry" and their successor bodies had demonstrated to Baruch the disutility of free-wheeling competition: "Many business men have experienced during the war . . . the tremendous advantages, both to themselves and to the general public, of combination, of cooperation and common action, with their natural competitors. . . . These associations, as they stand, are capable of carrying out purposes of greatest public benefit." Baruch recognized that those same associations "are capable also . . . of carrying out purposes of greatest public disadvantage." The question, therefore, was "what kind of Government organization can be devised to safeguard the public interest while these associations are preserved to carry on the good work of which they are capable." Baruch, of course, had the answer: "The experience of the War Industries Board points to the desirability of investing some Government agency . . . with . . . powers . . . to encourage, under strict Government supervision, such cooperation and coordination in industry as should tend to increase production, eliminate waste, conserve natural resources, improve the quality of products, promote efficiency in operation, and thus reduce costs to the ultimate consumer."[72] Such an agency, in Baruch's view, would pursue those admirable goals under the guiding hands of men like himself and Hoover, men who spoke without embarrassment about "service," self-styled classless men who would skillfully administer the apparatus of an active but disinterested state that somehow stood above its constituent parts.[73]

71. Bernard M. Baruch, *American Industry in the War* (New York: Prentice-Hall, 1941), 29, 71, 105; (italics added).
72. *Ibid.*, 104–6.
73. For a particularly insightful synopsis of this social vision, see Robert D. Cuff, "We Band of Brothers—Woodrow Wilson's War Managers," *The Canadian Review of American Studies* 2 (1974), 135–48.

That vision—of a smooth society, staffed by public servants dedicated to the values of noblesse oblige, a society in which the wheels of private enterprise spun freely even while neatly meshed with those of public authority—has been for much of the twentieth century a peculiarly American obsession. But for all its persistence in modern American culture, it was pursued with greatest intensity in the progressive era. In that age the American people confronted with extraordinary directness the vexatious question of the "public interest," and progressives, among whose allies Baruch must be counted, sought energetically to redefine the relation of public to private. To many such reformers the war seemed almost, in Grosvenor Clarkson's phrase, "a blessing instead of a curse," for the opportunity it afforded to alter that relation.[74] But neither the strivings of reformers before 1917 nor the strenuous exertions of Baruch in wartime could fully overcome obstacles to their views deeply rooted in the structure and ethos of American society. Baruch's experience at the War Industries Board, like Hoover's at the Food Administration, illustrated the enduring impossibility of finding the ideal balance between the public and the private realms.

The new Board established in July 1917, for example, perpetuated the ambiguity surrounding the cooperative committees of industry, a significant point since the effort to clarify their status had been the chief impetus for the Board's creation. Now "dollar-a-year-men" served as formal employees of "commodity sections" in the WIB. They negotiated across the table from their erstwhile business associates, who in turn represented "war service committees," freshly organized under the auspices of the United States Chamber of Commerce—itself a private body formed in 1912 with the active help of the Department of Commerce and Labor.[75] This seemed faint clarification indeed of the boundaries demarking public from private. As Robert D. Cuff concludes: "the war service committees took up positions of even greater intimacy

---

74. Clarkson, *Industrial America*, 218.
75. J. Leonard Replogle, for example, youthful president of the Cambria Steel Company, became head of the steel section and found himself, as Clarkson described it, "called upon to take a position that necessarily brought him into opposition with the chief men and interests of his calling. In serving the government he stood to block his own career. In such a position a man might err on either side; he might drive too hard bargains for the Government or he might be too considerate of the industry." In Replogle's case, concluded Clarkson, he "made the public interest first," though the necessity to state that conclusion indicated Clarkson's reluctant awareness of the possibilities for abuse in these arrangements. See Clarkson, *Industrial America*, 87.

with the WIB than those recently vacated by the cooperative committees. They worked closely with the WIB's commodity chiefs, entering the administrative system in a way that involved a substantial transfer of public authority to them. The chamber provided a very porous buffer between public officials and private business groups, and there was a partial continuation of the same kind of arrangements that many hoped Section Three would eliminate."[76]

The perpetuation of those arrangements represented at least a small victory for Baruch's vision of business-government integration; it also marked a triumph for the Chamber of Commerce, which was consecrated to the aim of finding refuge for its members from the anti-trust laws. "Creation of the War Service Committees," declared the Chamber, "promises to furnish the basis for a truly national organization of industry whose proportions and opportunities are unlimited. . . . The integration of business, the expressed aim of the National Chamber, is in sight. War is the stern teacher that is driving home the lesson of cooperative effort."[77] The Wilson administration attended to that lesson. Attorney General Thomas W. Gregory later recalled the President's opinion about anti-trust suits pending at the time of American entry into the war: "He remarked that if we attempted at that moment to vindicate the law, we would disorganize industry. We both agreed that we should let up on those people so that they would have no excuse for not contributing to their full capacities in the prosecution of the war. . . . We let the cases go to sleep until the war was over."[78]

But Wilson hesitated to go beyond those concessions to Baruch's corporatist vision. Even when he at last put the WIB on a firmer legal basis as an executive agency in the spring of 1918, the President merely consolidated the Board's administrative functions, and refused to extend its power substantially. Responsibility for purchases remained with the War and Navy departments, and Wilson designated a separate price-fixing committee under the chairmanship of Robert S. Brookings. The Board continued to depend for the effectiveness of its edicts on the cooperation of the military purchasing bureaus and the Brookings committee, and on the willingness of the Railroad Administration to honor its priority classifications. Thus from beginning to end the Board had little formal authority. "[A]ll that old speculator Baruch had was an

76. Cuff, *War Industries Board*, 159.
77. Koistinen, "The 'Industrial-Military Complex,'" 393.
78. T. W. Gregory to Ray Stannard Baker, n.d., RSB, VII, 80.

old piece of paper," one contemporary commented. "If he had to, he showed it to people. That was the way he settled disputes. That was practically the only power he had except a personality and the sense other people had of his leadership."[79] That deficiency cast a pall of illegitimacy, even illegality, over many of the Board's operations, and this dubious legal status compelled its nearly instant dissolution after the Armistice, when the discipline of crisis could no longer be counted upon to contain court challenges to the Board's decisions. Some administration officials feared, in fact, that peace would bring a flood of suits against the government for extralegal actions the Board had taken in wartime, a fear that materialized in at least one case.[80]

Devoid of formal authority, the Board sought to work its will on American industry through other devices: cajolery, exhortation, intimidation, and negotiation. Those tactics came clearly into play when the Board confronted the conundrum of price policy. Both the Food and the Fuel Administrations had some congressionally mandated authority over the prices of commodities under their jurisdictions; but the existing legislation left a vast array of goods, supposedly under the WIB's purview, altogether untouched by price controls. Thus, of necessity the Board's price-fixing operations "always took the form of negotiation, and the results were, strictly speaking, agreed rather than decreed prices."[81] Negotiations took place in an environment that guaranteed the widest bargaining latitude to the firms with which the Board had to deal. Over the objections of the military bureaus, who wanted preferentially low prices for their purchases, President Wilson insisted that the bureaus should pay the same rates as the Allies and the public, so as not to penalize companies doing business with the government. The WIB also valued high production levels over low prices, the

79. Coit, *Mr. Baruch*, 173. The "old piece of paper" was President Wilson's letter of Mar. 4, 1918, appointing Baruch chairman of the War Industries Board.

80. The firm was L. Vogelstein Co., which protested the terms of a wartime copper shipment to the government, forced by a WIB that Vogelstein claimed had no statutory standing. See Attorney General T. W. Gregory to Joseph Tumulty, Jan. 12, 1920, WWP. Similarly, Pierre S. Du Pont insisted on the creation of a separate company, Du Pont Engineering, to undertake certain government-contracted war work. The arrangement was intended to limit the liability of the parent E. I. Du Pont de Nemours and Co., in the event "of its being hereafter held that the Ordnance Department exceeded its lawful powers in making the contract." See Alfred D. Chandler and Stephen Salsbury, *Pierre S. Du Pont and the Making of the Modern Corporation* (New York: Harper and Row, 1971), 408.

81. Clarkson, *Industrial America*, 177.

same policy that Hoover was pursuing at the Food Administration. As Baruch put it, "cheap prices could not in wisdom have been the single or even primary aim of Government control. . . . Production in many industries had to be stimulated by every conceivable device; and the business man of America is so imbued with the habit of reaping where he sows, that even admitting for him the highest and most unselfish quality of patriotism, no device is more stimulating to his latent energy than a vision of fair reward."[82] Those considerations moved the Board to follow a horizontal pricing policy—setting a single price for an industry's product, regardless of its specific source. That practice, guaranteeing profits to all, effectively discriminated in favor of the high-volume, low-cost producers. In theory their surplus earnings would be skimmed off by the graduated excess-profits tax, but in practice the biggest firms waxed disproportionately fat. "We are all," admitted one steel executive, "making more money out of this war than the average human being ought to."[83] Occasionally some businessmen, typically industry newcomers for whom price competition provided the most effective avenue for entering a given market, protested the efforts of established firms to stabilize prices at a high level. But more often objections came from smaller producers with high cost-margins, who wanted prices pegged higher still. In the summer of 1917, a band of lesser steel manufacturers refused on those grounds to participate in a pricing agreement concluded between the government and U.S. Steel.[84] The Board's task, therefore, was often almost impossibly complex: to set a price that would maximize production while not flagrantly over-rewarding the biggest firms. "Complicated and difficult," reflected Josephus Daniels after discussing the matter with Baruch, Hoover, Baker, McAdoo, and the President. "Price must if possible be fixed so that it would not be high and that it could be high enough to keep production."[85]

Moreover, the Board had virtually no formal power to make its price policies stick. It largely depended on the voluntary compliance of frequently undisciplined, highly competitive industries whose member firms were not accustomed to operating in concert with one another or with the government. Just as often the Board met with well-organized

82. Baruch, *American Industry in the War*, 83–84.
83. Clarkson, *Industrial America*, quoting Price McKinney of McKinney Steel, 319.
84. See A. C. Dinkley, president of Midvale Steel Co., to Newton D. Baker, July 31, 1917, copy in Baruch Papers.
85. E. David Cronon, ed., *The Cabinet Diaries of Josephus Daniels, 1913–1921* (Lincoln: University of Nebraska Press, 1963), entry for May 28, 1917, 158.

and powerful business opposition. In the case of steel, it took months of pressure from Baruch, the threat of a Federal Trade Commission investigation, and the specter of congressional legislation to drive steelmakers, including U.S. Steel, into price agreements with the WIB. Similarly, Baruch fought a long battle with shoe manufacturers over price stabilization and product standardization, a battle in which the Chairman placed the industry "under the glare of publicity and had it labeled an opponent of the public interest." In the absence of more direct means, this "was one of the board's favorite tactics, to direct public opinion to an industry and force it to go to greater lengths to appease those expectations."[86] On other occasions, Baruch called on his renowned ability to "look any man in the eye and tell him to go to hell."[87] He cooly told a recalcitrant lumber man, for example, that if he failed to comply with the WIB's requests "you will be such an object of contempt and scorn in your home town that you will not dare to show your face there. If you should, your fellow citizens would call you a slacker, the boys would hoot at you, and the draft men would likely run you out of town."[88]

The WIB had somehow to inspire the cooperative spirit among the frequently uncooperative, and as Clarkson summed up the matter, the Board operated "by request rather than by mandate. It is true that few chose to resist those requests, but compliance was based as much upon the compulsion of reasonableness and the pressure of opinion as upon fear of governmental power."[89] It is important to stress this point because considerable confusion has surrounded the history of the WIB and the entire mobilization process. Some have regarded the WIB as the pliant tool of capital. Mark Sullivan, on the other hand, a popular chronicler of early twentieth-century American life, complained: "Of the effects of the war on America, by far the most fundamental was our submission to autocracy in government. . . . Every business man was shorn of dominion over his factory or store, every housewife surrendered control of her table, every farmer was forbidden to sell his wheat except at the price the government fixed. . . . The prohibition of individual liberty in the interest of the state could hardly be more complete."[90] That threnody recalled Republican lamentations during 1917

86. Cuff, *War Industries Board*, 238.
87. Clarkson, *Industrial America*, 44.
88. *Ibid.*, 99.
89. *Ibid.*, 94.
90. Sullivan, *Our Times*, V, 489.

and 1918 that a "dictatorial" President Wilson was burying freedom of enterprise under an avalanche of arbitrary government power. But a close examination of the principal mobilization agencies reveals a quite contrary truth: their inability or unwillingness to invoke formal authority. Both businessmen and government officials, including above all Woodrow Wilson, were ambiguous and hesitant about expanding state control over the economy. By turn they promoted, resisted, or acquiesced in proposals for closer business-government integration. Their irresolution produced in the end a curious apparatus, whose official powers were puny in the face of the enormous tasks with which it was charged.

That ambivalence and that disproportion of means to ends mark the historical uniqueness of American economic mobilization in World War I. The war came at a time of peculiarly intense disagreement about the principles of political economy that American society should embody. Though many hoped the war would finally lay that problem to rest, the conflict only demonstrated its intractable complexity and the relatively fixed equilibrium of the several forces arrayed around it. The WIB, which may be taken as a summary example of that phenomenon, did not constitute a clean administrative stroke aimed at cutting the coils of confusion that threatened to strangle the mobilization effort. Nor did it represent the simple co-optation of state authority by business power. Rather it was intentionally invested from first to last with "the degree of ambiguity appropriate for a response keyed to such a diversity of interests."[91]

The ambiguity characteristic of mobilization in World War I had many sources in addition to the unreconciled state of American economic theory. Wilson's room for political maneuver was closely hedged by the Southern Populistic elements in his own party, devoted as always with equal fervor to the causes of anti-monopoly and states' rights. It was constricted by the advocates of progressive reform to whom he had made explicit appeal in 1916, themselves divided between anti-trusters and regulationists. And it was confined by a vigilant Republican right, closely linked to business interests. Conservative Republicans were recently invigorated by the humiliations inflicted upon their insurgent progressive colleagues, the militant reformers who had followed Theodore Roosevelt into the third-party political wilderness in 1912, only to limp sadly back into the GOP fold by 1916, shorn of power and in-

91. Cuff, *War Industries Board*, 104.

fluence in party councils. Old-Guard Republicans now stood ready and eager to restore the pro-business government of the McKinley and Taft years. Wilson's precise calculations about that constellation of forces contributed to his refusal to make the WIB the superbureau that Baruch advocated. On the one hand, an all-powerful WIB might have provoked an unmanageable backlash both from capital and from traditional states'-righters; on the other, its necessarily centralized administrative structure might have offered too vulnerable a target for business take-over. For reasons of ideological irresolution as well as practical political necessity, Wilson repeatedly affirmed his preference for administrative pluralism. He deliberately dispersed responsibility for purchasing, price-fixing, and determination of priorities, even at the risk of being charged with inefficient prosecution of the war.

That Wilson could take such a risk at all indicated, of course, the great distance that separated America from the fighting front and the consequent lack of urgency in her relation to the war. Indeed it might be argued in general that pluralism, that penchant for decentralization and lax social and economic controls so often alleged to be a character-istically American trait, is permissible only in societies that operate within wide margins of prosperity and security. The federal system, based on purposefully fragmented and weak political institutions, Alexis de Tocqueville long ago observed, flourished in America only "because it has no great wars to fear." America had long been able to afford risks not acceptable to countries with hostile neighbors. "No European nation," Henry Adams had noted of another conflict, "could have conducted a war, as the people of America conducted the War of 1812. . . . A people whose chief trait was antipathy to war, and to any system organized with military energy, could scarcely develop great results in national administration. . . . The incapacity brought into evi-dence by the war was undisputed."[92]

So too with World War I, where an apparently felicitous adminis-trative incapacity was further allowable because of the war's remote-ness from the United States and the brief duration of American military involvement. Had the fighting persisted through another spring cam-paign in 1919, as most strategists anticipated, American society quite likely might have experienced something more closely resembling the

92. Henry Adams, *The History of the United States of America During the Ad-ministrations of Jefferson and Madison,* abr. and ed. by Ernest Samuels (Chi-cago: University of Chicago Press, 1967), 407.

trials visited upon European peoples. But geography and fate spared Americans those tribulations. "To the most casual observer of the effects of the World War," economist John Maurice Clark pointed out in 1931, "one outstanding fact is evident: the greatest catastrophe of modern times touched the United States relatively lightly, compared to its effects on other countries." Here there was no invasion, no destruction of farms and factories, no heavy loss of life, no malnutrition nor educational deficits, no heavy taxation, and none of the massive enervation of the middle class that plagued postwar Europe.[93]

The war, Clark concluded, initially cost the American people about $33 billion; interest costs and veterans' benefits would later bring the total cash outlay to approximately $112 billion.[94] But those gross figures masked the great profitability of the war to America. The government, it appeared, had largely succeeded in its often-stated goal of mobilizing with the least possible disruption to the peacetime economy—indeed, with the purpose of strengthening and improving its competitive position in international trade. Congressional inquiries in the 1930s revealed that the Savage Arms Corporation, for example, made a 60 percent profit in 1917, that the Bethlehem Shipbuilding Company had increased its average annual profits from $6 million in peace to $49 million in war; that the Du Pont Company had multiplied its stock dividends between 1914 and 1918 by a factor of 16. Du Pont also emerged from the war with its assets quadrupled and with a surplus of $68 million to invest in new ventures in chemicals and dyes, an area where German patent control and industrial domination had been broken by the war.[95] Many other firms found their financial structures greatly bolstered at the conclusion of hostilities. Wartime tax laws encouraged the retention of earnings, which led to abnormally rapid upgrading of capital stock and accelerated plant expansion. The War Finance Corporation directly underwrote many capital improvements, including the addition to the nation's energy supply of 2 million horsepower of electrical generating

93. John Maurice Clark, *The Costs of the World War to the American People* (New Haven: Yale University Press, 1931), 1–2.

94. Total final cost for the Civil War to the Union side has been estimated at $13 billion; for World War II, $664 billion; for the Korean "police action," $164 billion; and Vietnam, $352 billion. *Historical Statistics*, 1140. These estimates are as of 1970.

95. See John E. Wiltz, *In Search of Peace: The Senate Munitions Inquiry, 1934–1936* (Baton Rouge: Louisiana State University Press, 1963), 112; and Chandler and Salsbury, *Pierre S. Du Pont*, 428.

capacity.[96] And following the Armistice, the War Department frequently forgave previously made construction advances in return for agreement to cancel war-supply contracts.[97] Real wages, too, had increased modestly, and farm income, at least for the moment, stood at a historically unprecendented high level. All sectors, not just big capital, had profited from the war. "Our condition," exulted a commentator assessing the international business scene in 1919, "is like that of the trained athlete, prepared for the combat."[98] On this count, too, the American war experience stood out from that of all other belligerents.

Those developments, though underwritten in part by the accidents of geography and history, were not entirely fortuitous. McAdoo, Hoover, Baruch, and Wilson had all been keenly interested in the implications of mobilization for America's position in the postwar economic order. McAdoo's promotion of an American merchant marine and his reluctance to allow war financing to disturb the peacetime capital structure reflected that interest, as did Hoover's determination to make the Allies pay for expanded American agricultural production. So, too, did Baruch's hesitation to curtail so-called "non-essential" industries, for fear that throwing the economy completely onto a war footing would rob the United States of her postwar advantage over the fully mobilized Europeans, who would foreseeably lose precious time, money, and markets in a complicated reconversion period.

The war had also directly stimulated the movement toward greater industrial efficiency through standardization. The varieties of steel plows, for example, were reduced from 312 to 76; of planters and drills from 784 to 29; and of buggy axles from over 100 to one, to cite but a few examples.[99] The crisis had tested administrative devices that would be revived, some permanently, in the Great Depression of the 1930s. The Federal Reserve Board's Capital Issues Committee, for instance, would provide a model for the Securities Exchange Commission of the New Deal; President Hoover's Reconstruction Finance Corporation would emulate the example of the War Finance Corporation; and Franklin Roosevelt's National Recovery Administration was frankly patterned on what FDR called "the great co-operation of 1917 and 1918," es-

96. Baruch, *American Industry in the War*, 299.
97. Clarkson, *Industrial America*, 54.
98. J. L. Saunders, "The Outlook for America's Industrial Future," *Annals* 82 (1919), 331.
99. Baruch, *American Industry in the War*, 69.

pecially the War Industries Board.[100] Wartime efforts to gather and systematize information about the economy would persist, both in the activities of government agencies like the Bureau of the Budget, created in 1921, and in private bodies like the National Bureau of Economic Research, founded in 1920.

But the most durable and important economic transformation to come out of the war was an organizational one. The dimensions of this change, though large, were difficult to gauge with precision. But with the Department of Justice's Anti-Trust Division conveniently somnolent for the duration, and under the active prodding of war administrators like Hoover and Baruch, there occurred a marked shift toward corporatism in the nation's business affairs. Entire industries, even entire economic sectors, as in the case of agriculture, were organized and disciplined as never before, and brought into close and regular relations with counterpart congressional committees, cabinet departments, and Executive agencies. Under Hoover's careful cultivation as Secretary of Commerce and President, trade associations modeled on the Farm Bureau Federation and Chamber of Commerce proliferated in the 1920s. And a spate of special-interest legislation in the postwar decade testified to the influence of the war in raising the art of lobbying to new degrees of sophistication and effectiveness. From the war can be dated the origins of the modern practice of massive informal collusion between government and organized private enterprise, a practice in which, John Kenneth Galbraith has observed, "the line between public and private authority . . . is indistinct and in large measure imaginary, and the abhorrent association of public and private organizations is normal."[101]

It is ironic, perhaps, that the origins of the "abhorrent association" Galbraith remarks can be traced to the progressive era, which witnessed such earnest efforts to redefine the relation of public to private. But the war had distorted that process, deflecting it in directions that neither progressive reformers, nor their conservative opponents, nor even visionaries like Hoover and Baruch could have fully foreseen. It left a legacy of institutions and practices—such as the Federal Reserve Board, the income tax system, the giant lobbies, and the seeds, at least, of the now

100. William E. Leuchtenburg, "The New Deal and the Analogue of War," in John Braeman et al., eds., *Change and Continuity in Twentieth Century America* (New York: Harper and Row, 1966), 118.

101. John Kenneth Galbraith, *The New Industrial State* (New York: New American Library, 1967), 305.

familiar array of government-business interconnections—that showed the influence of the reform circumstances in which they were conceived, as well as the impress of the crisis into which they were born. The shaping effect of the crisis was particularly evident in the realm of economic organization. Under the lash of war, public authority not only proved responsive to private associations, but, as in the case of the Farm Bureau and the War Service committees, actively participated in their formation. For the remainder of the century, government in America would be in large measure an affair conducted of, by, and for special-interest groups of that type, to the frequent neglect of the unorganized, and of the "public interest," a concept that would come to be regarded as a quaint vestige of a more innocent era. World War I neither initiated nor perfected that system, but gave it powerful momentum.

The First World War, arresting and transforming the progressive debate over political economy, marked a distinct and formative moment in the history of American society. But economic mobilization also laid bare some timeless features of that society, suggesting that the war deserves attention not merely for the changes it wrought but for the dimensions of the enduring American character it revealed. "The great object of terror and suspicion to the people of the thirteen provinces," Henry Adams once wrote, "was power; not merely power in the hands of a president or a prince, of one assembly or several, of many citizens or few, but power in the abstract, wherever it existed and under whatever form it was known."[102] That fear has run like an electric current through American life, pulsing especially in the politics of the nineteenth century, energizing periodic reform surges of which Populism and progressivism were but two instances in a long and recurrent series. But in the twentieth century that fear of power, so salutary for the founding fathers, has sometimes had perverse effects.

As Adams and Tocqueville knew, eighteenth- and nineteenth-century Americans could indulge their antipathy to power and their preference for pluralism because they were in the main a comfortably united and generally equal people, resting securely behind the Atlantic Ocean. They were thus safely insulated from both the internal and the external dangers that regularly wracked European societies and compelled repugnant concentrations of authority in Old World governments. But as the twentieth century opened, American society was no longer so

102. Quoted in Grant McConnell, *Private Power and American Democracy* (New York: Knopf, 1967), 33.

genially homogeneous. The major cities were
with astonishingly various ethnic ingredier
everywhere opened the ugly fissures of cla
curity any longer be taken for granted, or is
to which the engulfing scale of World War I

Yet to a striking degree Wilson and hi
ministrators tried to base American particip
principles. They avoided unilateral exercises of gover......
sought the barest minimum of statutory bodies; they doggedly diffused
administrative responsibility; they relied wherever possible on the time-
honored principle of contractual agreement; and they affirmed repeatedly the *temporary* character of those few naked instruments of
authority they were reluctantly required to grasp. Because of the continuing dispensations of distance and history, they were largely successful. But the war crisis, despite the relative lightness with which it
touched America, pressed in nonetheless sufficiently hard that feats of
discipline and organization had somehow to be accomplished. Given
the deep-grained reluctance to exercise power in a straightforward,
statutory, and necessarily coercive way, Wilson and his war managers
turned instead to voluntaristic means, to persuasion, propaganda, and
the purposeful fueling of patriotic fires. The sources of the "hysteria"
the war produced, so often condemned and so rarely explicated, lay
partly in that very impulse to shun formal power at all costs. A direct
line led from that attitude toward power to the deliberate mobilization
of emotions in the methods of the Treasury, the Food Administration,
and the War Industries Board. Americans, prizing the weakness of their
ancient institutions, strove to maintain that holy debility in a time of
crisis by substituting aroused passion for political authority.

The war thus demonstrated the distasteful truth that voluntarism has
its perils. Reliance on sentiment rather than strengthened sovereignty
to mobilize a people for total war compounded the problem of requiring all people to do what but few people wished. That kind of coercion,
no less insidious for its indirection—perhaps doubly objectionable on
that count had deep roots in liberal democratic culture, and was to
become a salient feature of twentieth-century American life.

ou're in the Army Now"

Shortly after the declaration of war on April 6, 1917, Major Palmer E. Pierce, an aide to Secretary of War Baker, settled uncomfortably into a chair under the inquisitorial gaze of the Senate Finance Committee. Before the Senators lay a bulky sheaf of documents, presenting in fine detail how the War Department anticipated spending the three-billion-dollar appropriation it was requesting. What, inquired Chairman Thomas S. Martin of Virginia, were the principal items in this unprecedentedly vast and confusing budget? Major Pierce began to recite: "Clothing, cots, camps, food, pay. . . . And we may have to have an army in France."

"Good Lord!" interjected Martin. "You're not going to send soldiers over there, are you?"[1]

Martin had reason to be startled. With other Americans he was still absorbing the President's unexpected request for an army to be raised by conscription, a radical departure from the traditional reliance on volunteering, and from Wilson's own previously expressed position. Now came the suggestion that the conscript army was to be sent overseas—a yet more drastic step that few, whether civilian or strategist, had seriously contemplated. Those two questions—how to bring a large

1. Frederick Palmer, *Newton D. Baker: America at War*, 2 vols. (New York: Dodd, Mead, 1931), I, 120.

144

military force into being and how best to use it, once created—troubled the public and policy-makers alike in the spring of 1917.

On the first issue the battle lines had long been drawn. Since at least 1914 Americans had hotly debated the merits and demerits of universal military training, or UMT. Some advocates of that policy, especially military men, saw it simply as a means to strengthen the nation's armed forces in an increasingly unsafe world. But to that rather straightforward proposition many proponents had added a host of other arguments about the allegedly salubrious social effects of military training: it would Americanize the immigrant, nurture the values of efficiency and "service," and overcome class antagonisms. In time those latter arguments came to dominate the discussion, and the debate on UMT became a debate about the fundamental character of American society, a debate about the meaning of equality and freedom, democracy and individualism, in the modern world. "Universal training," George Creel exclaimed, "will jumble the boys of America all together, shoulder to shoulder, smashing all the petty class distinctions that now divide, and prompting a brand of real democracy. Look at Switzerland! Look at France!"[2] France, indeed, ever more heavily invested with sentiment and symbol in the American mind, inspired many enthusiasts for UMT. "In France," wrote playwright Augustus Thomas, "I saw a much finer democracy than our own . . . a finer intercourse between the different social stations . . . fraternal compliance without mockery or condescension. And after a while I came to learn that that relationship had been acquired by men of those classes working in fine equality in their military training."[3]

But others saw not *égalité et fraternité* in the proposals for universal service, but a "heresy—Prussian to the core—that the State is a kind of overlord which should compel its citizens, instead of inducing them willingly to give."[4] Military service, said the opponents of UMT, did not encourage democracy and individual autonomy, but taught lessons of subordination, and slavish deference to authority. Indeed, when

2. George Creel, "Four Million Citizen Defenders," *Everybody's Magazine* 36 (1917), 553. With typical exuberance, Creel even claimed that conscription would regenerate "the heart, liver, and kidneys of America," which were "in sad need of overhauling."

3. Charles A. Fenton, "A Literary Fracture of World War I," *American Quarterly* 12 (1960), 126.

4. *Literary Digest* 54 (Apr. 21, 1917), 1148.

UMT advocates talked, as one typically did, of "Groton and St. Mark's boys" and "boys from the slums of Philadelphia and New York" each developing "a different attitude toward the other class," in the intimacy of their shared pup tents, they seemed in fact to offer military service not as a means to achieve equality but as a substitute for it, a way to reconcile the different social orders to the enduring fact of their difference.[5] It was no accident, said the opponents, that the principal organizations spreading the UMT gospel were dominated by the wealthy and the privileged. The National Security League, critics accurately charged, was funded by some of the nation's most powerful industrialists. And the Military Training Camps Association, along with the League the most prominent pro-UMT organization, was notoriously an upper-class affair. It had grown from the so-called Plattsburg Camps (named for the first encampment at Plattsburg, New York, in 1915), summer séances of well-to-do businessmen and college boys training at their own expense to be military officers.

"Make no mistake about it," said Amos Pinchot, indefatigable foe of compulsory service. "Conscription is a great commercial policy; a carefully devised weapon that the exploiters are forging for their own protection at home, and in the interest of American financial imperialism abroad. . . . [B]ack of the cry that America must have compulsory service or perish, is a clearly thought-out and heavily backed project to mould the United States into an efficient, orderly nation, economically and politically controlled by those who know what is good for the people. In this country so ordered and so governed, there will be no strikes, no surly revolt against authority, and no popular discontent. In it, the lamb will lie down in peace with the lion, and he will lie down right where the lion tells him to. . . . This, if we cut through the patriotic pretext and flag-waving propaganda, is the real vision of the conscriptionist."[6]

Both President Wilson and Secretary of War Baker had shown decided coolness toward the idea of conscription. Baker owed his very office to Wilson's rejection in 1916 of the pro-conscription views of the previous Secretary of War, Lindley Garrison. As in so many other matters of policy, Wilson only reluctantly modified the voluntaristic premises that always informed his thinking. Though he might not regard

5. Henry S. Hooker to Wilson, Dec. 1, 1916, WWP.
6. Amos Pinchot to Samuel Gompers, Mar. 10, 1917, copy in WWP; this letter was also printed in the *New York Times*, Mar. 13, 1917, 4.

conscription as a capitalist plot, the President shared the feeling that compulsory military service somehow violated what Pinchot called the "American ideal," that it debauched sacred tradition and forced America toward the hated "old European system" of coercion and regimentation. As late as February 1917, both Wilson and Baker had affirmed their faith in the volunteer system, and refused to endorse proposals for universal training. Yet in the same month they had authorized the drafting of a conscription bill, and in May the Selective Service System went into operation.

Several considerations prompted this abrupt reversal. At first, Wilson may have considered such a bill no reversal at all, but simply a precautionary measure to equip him with stand-by powers if volunteering failed to bring the armed forces up to desired strength.[7] The evidence also suggests that a cardinal purpose of the conscription legislation as originally conceived was not to press millions of men into military service but to effect an overall manpower policy. Here England offered an especially compelling example. The British had refused until 1916 to resort to the draft. In the first two years of the war they had seen their best-educated and most talented young men rush willy-nilly to the colors and as quickly and haphazardly die in the mud of Flanders. That non-policy wrought a terrible loss of leadership cadres that seriously crippled the British military effort (and, as some observers were later to argue, permanently deprived postwar British society of adequate political leadership). Britain had also felt the massive disruption of economic production, as skilled and unskilled, needed and unneeded, replaceable and irreplaceable workers all volunteered indiscriminately, leaving yawning breaches in the industrial lines on the home front.

The same casual waste menaced the impending American war effort. Already the greatest enthusiasts for American entry were to be found among the educated classes, the Plattsburgers and college men thought to be best fitted for command. At Princeton University a mass meeting had to be convoked in late March 1917 to restrain undergraduates from flocking to the recruiting stations.[8] Moreover, random volunteering

7. Daniel R. Beaver, *Newton D. Baker and the American War Effort, 1917–1919* (Lincoln: University of Nebraska Press, 1966), 27n.
8. *New York Times*, Mar. 26, 1917, 2. Princeton did make some concessions to the patriotic mood. Military instruction on the campus, said President John Grier Hibben, would henceforward "be given more prominence and the academic work lightened considerably." Hibben also accepted a gift of two "flying machines" so that students might form an all-Princeton "aviation corps."

would only exacerbate the already disruptive effect on industry of rapid turnover. There were "many forms of patriotic service," said the President, and "the military part of the service was by no means the only part, and perhaps, all things considered, not the most vital part. Our object is a mobilization of all the productive and active forces of the nation and their development to the highest point of co-operation and efficiency. . . . The volunteer system does not do this. When men choose themselves, they sometimes choose without due regard to their other responsibilities. Men may come from the farms or from the mines or from the factories or centers of business who ought not to come but ought to stand back of the armies in the field."[9] The idea of the draft, Wilson told another correspondent, "is not only the drawing of men into the military service of the Government, but the virtual assigning of men to the necessary labor of the country. Its central idea was to disturb the industrial and social structure of the country just as little as possible."[10] Such remarks suggested that in the early spring of 1917 the President did not contemplate the draft primarily as a device to raise a huge army and field it in France. Conscription was to serve primarily as a way to keep the right men in the right jobs at home.

But, despite the persuasive logic of those considerations, had it not been for certain political developments, the administration might well have postponed resorting to conscription. Anti-draft sentiment was strong in Congress, especially among Representatives from the South and West who comprised the bulk of the Democratic majority. Many Democratic leaders in the House noisily opposed the Administration's proposed draft legislation. On April 18 the House Military Affairs Committee reported out a military manpower bill that rejected conscription in favor of volunteering by a 13-8 vote. Wilson might have accepted a compromise that permitted at least an interim trial to the volunteer system, had not his arch-rival Theodore Roosevelt been busily establishing himself, with strong Republican backing, as the country's most visibly eligible volunteer. Attended by prodigious publicity, Colonel Roosevelt and his old comrade General Leonard Wood had since early February been organizing a volunteer division—later expanded to a corps—that they envisioned as a kind of showcase specimen of American virility. Some staff positions they intended to offer to scions of the French nobility, as a gesture of respect for the memory of Lafayette.

9. Wilson to Guy T. Helvering, Apr. 12, 1917, WWP.
10. Wilson to Mrs. George W. Bass, May 5, 1917, RSB, VII, 52.

But most of the officers—indeed most of the enlisted men—would be Ivy Leaguers. Places of special distinction were reserved for the descendants of prominent Civil War generals. There would be a German-American regiment and a black regiment (officered by whites). This brave all-American band, with the old Rough Rider at its head, would swiftly move into the trenches, where its vigor and dash would instantly bolster the French and terrorize the Hun.[11]

The scheme was as politically dangerous to Wilson as it was militarily daft. In all probability, the aging Colonel and his ill-trained hodgepodge of glory-seekers would have blustered about in France, and, if the fates were not too cruel, retired with minimum harm done to the Allied cause and only a few lives squandered. Yet there was also a chance that Roosevelt might contrive to make this martial buffoonery appear to be the stuff of genuine heroism and adventure—a demonstration of patriotic success which Republicans could be expected to use to bludgeon the Democratic administration. Accordingly, Wilson determined to nullify the possibility that Roosevelt might lead a volunteer division to France by largely foreclosing all forms of volunteering. At the President's urging, congressional Democrats beat back a Republican amendment to the Selective Service bill that would have instructed Wilson to give Roosevelt an independent command. "If Roosevelt or any other Pied Piper can whistle 25,000 fanatics after him, for Heaven's sake give him the chance," Representative Augustus Gardner pleaded in vain.[12] After weeks of wrangling, the legislators agreed on a provision that merely permitted, but did not require, the President to accept Roosevelt's offer. Wilson lost no time in declining. "This is not the time," he announced on signing the Selective Service Act into law on May 18, "for any action not calculated to contribute to the immediate success of the war. The business now in hand is undramatic, practical, and of scientific definiteness and precision."[13]

The final legislation allowed for volunteering only in the Regular Army and Navy and in the National Guard, but not in the new "National Army," where the great bulk of men (77 percent of the eventual

11. See the accounts in Seward Livermore, *Politics Is Adjourned: Woodrow Wilson and the War Congress 1916–1918* (Middletown, Conn.: Wesleyan University Press, 1966), chap. 2; and Beaver, *Baker*, 28–30.
12. Frederick L. Paxson, *American Democracy and the World War,* 3 vols. (Boston: Houghton Mifflin, 1936–48), II, 7–8.
13. Ray Stannard Baker and William E. Dodd, eds., *The Public Papers of Woodrow Wilson,* 6 vols. (New York: Harper and Brothers 1925–27), V, 40.

wartime total) would be required. The law thus had the additional merit, in the administration's eyes, of containing the size of the several states' militias, which were thought to be heavily Republican in character, their "roots firmly planted," said the *New York Times*, "in the partisan organization of the States."[14]

But though the new army was now clearly to be raised by conscription and subject to direct federal control, the Selective Service System was not without elements of voluntarism and localism. The first order of business was to compile a national roster of eligible men in the designated age-group between 21 and 30. The government quickly decided that the only expedient way to proceed was somehow to induce the men to come forward and register themselves. It was not at all certain that this scheme would work. Memories of Civil War draft riots haunted the administration; Senator James Reed of Missouri starkly predicted that the streets of America would run red with blood on registration day, June 5. "I am exceedingly anxious," Newton D. Baker wrote the President, "to have the registration and selection by draft conducted under such circumstances as to create a strong patriotic feeling and relieve as far as possible the prejudice which remains to some extent in the popular mind against the draft by reason of Civil War memories. With this end in view, I am using a vast number of agencies throughout the country to make the day of registration a festival and patriotic occasion."[15] Governors, mayors, chambers of commerce, and state councils of defense joined in concerted patriotic incantation to urge young men to the registration places on June 5. Wilson himself struck the keynote of this gigantic propaganda exercise when he proclaimed, somewhat disingenuously, that the draft was not really a draft at all, but a "selection from a nation which has volunteered in mass." But just to be sure that this mass volunteering went smoothly, the President requested "every man, whether he is himself to be registered or not, to see to it that the name of every male person of the designated ages is written on these lists of honor."[16]

The administration, in thus launching the Selective Service System amid contrived hoopla and presidential appeals for citizen vigilance over eligible registrants, had vitiated one of the System's supposedly premier virtues. Many persons had favored conscription because they

14. *New York Times,* Apr. 1, 1917, sec. II, 2.
15. Baker to Wilson, May 1, 1917, RSB, VII, 74n.
16. Baker and Dodd, eds., *Public Papers,* V, 39.

feared that reliance on volunteers would necessitate the dangerous whipping up of patriotic emotion. Coaxing millions of men voluntarily into the armed services, Walter Lippmann cautioned the President, would surely require "a newspaper campaign of manufactured hatred that would disturb . . . the morale of the nation." Reluctantly, Lippmann concluded that conscription was "the only orderly and quiet way to accomplish what may be the necessary result."[17] Similarly, the Boston banking house of Lee, Higginson and Co. felt that volunteers would come forward only if the government and the press concocted an unjustified sense of crisis. The country, the bankers urged, "cannot be thus wrought up without a grave and wholly unwarranted disturbance of business. Now that is exactly what we ought to avoid. Calmness, resolution and the application of common sense and business prudence, rather than intense emotion, are what is going to win this war."[18] Wilson had expressed such sentiments himself when he rebuked the flamboyant Roosevelt in favor of a draft that would be "undramatic, practical, and . . . scientific."

But the purposefully dramatic cultivation of intense emotion became nevertheless a cardinal method in the operation of the military draft, as did official encouragement of vigilante activity aimed at non-registrants and "slackers." Secretary of War Baker, like so many of his colleagues in the administration, tended to compensate for his reluctance to exercise formal authority by urging the vigorous excitement of public opinion. Nor was the contrived festival atmosphere of registration day the Secretary's only concession to that characteristic wartime practice. Like McAdoo at the Treasury, Baker and his Selective Service administrator, Provost Marshal General Enoch H. Crowder, were careful students of the American Civil War. The Union Army's experiment with the draft, they knew, had been a disaster, providing fewer than 6 percent of Union troops and provoking wide and deep resentment of the inequitable system of exemptions and often arbitrary and high-handed enforcement. The worst feature of the Civil War draft, Crowder concluded, was its administration by military officers, a policy that "bared the teeth of the Federal Government in every home within the loyal states." So fierce had been the antagonism toward those uniformed officials that

17. Lippmann to Wilson, Feb. 6, 1917, quoted in Beaver, *Baker*, 26.
18. Circular letter from Lee, Higginson and Co., Apr. 28, 1917, copy in Edwin F. Gay Papers, Hoover Institution on War, Revolution and Peace, Stanford University, Stanford, Ca. (hereafter Hoover Institution).

nearly a hundred of them had been killed or wounded, and vicious rioting, particularly by the Irish in New York City, had attended the military enforcement of the draft.[19]

The lesson was not lost on Baker, who insisted that the World War I
draft be administered locally, by civilians. The country thereby avoided
the unpleasant scene, as the chairman of the Senate Committee on
Military Affairs put it, of "a board, sitting up there on a platform, we'll
say, composed of five or seven captains and majors and lieutenant
colonels, deciding who should fight for our country."[20] Instead, Crowder
explained, the setting up of local boards "put the administration of the
draft into the hands of friends and neighbors of the men to be affected.
. . . [I]t was the enunciation of the true democratic doctrine of local
self-government."[21] The boards had political utility, too, Crowder
shrewdly noted, as "they became the buffers between the individual
citizen and the Federal Government, and thus they attracted and diverted, like local grounding wires in an electric coil, such resentment
or discontent as might have proved a serious obstacle to war measures,
had it been focussed on the central authorities. Its diversion and grounding at 5000 local points dissipated its force, and enabled the central
war machine to function smoothly without the disturbance that might
have been caused by the concentrated total of dissatisfaction."[22] Most
significantly, creation of the local boards constituted a brilliant public
relations stroke, deepening the illusion of willing individual service and
community control that Wilson had so fetchingly conjured when he
spoke of the nation volunteering "in mass." Crowder helped to perpetuate that appealing fiction in a postwar assessment of the Selective Service System: "Conscription in America was not . . . drafting of the
unwilling," he wrote, echoing Wilson. "The citizens themselves had
willingly come forward and pledged their service."[23]

This insistence that the draft was in reality a voluntary affair should
not be dismissed as willful buncombe, though the government was assuredly not above a little pious flummery to gain the confidence of a

19. Enoch Crowder, *The Spirit of Selective Service* (New York: Century, 1920),
    78–84.
20. James Wadsworth Memoir, 197, Columbia University Oral History Collection,
    Butler Library, Columbia University, N.Y. (hereafter CUOHC).
21. Crowder, *Spirit,* 120.
22. *Second Report of the Provost Marshal General* (Washington, D.C.: Govern-
    ment Printing Office, 1919), 277.
23. Crowder, *Spirit,* 125.

public whose acceptance of conscription was in considerable doubt. But Wilson and Crowder, when they dwelt affectionately on the term "service," were engaged in something far more significant than a transparent publicity ruse to sell the draft. Few words were so widely bruited in American society in the World War I era as "service," and it is a matter of some importance that the term was incorporated into the official title of the draft agency. "Service" was a kind of rhetorical vessel into which were being poured the often contradictory emotional and political impulses of the day. "The spirit of service," said Crowder, was the "spirit of America . . . the yearning of its inner consciousness." Everywhere Americans agreed that a commitment to "service" was an attribute of the national soul that the war had quickened. Social worker Felix Adler observed that the conflict had generated a "high wave of service," and sometime socialist A. M. Simons professed to see the drive for "social service" displacing the profit motive as the mainspring of American life. "The ideal of service," intoned Herbert Hoover, was a "great spiritual force poured out by our people as never before in the history of the world. . . . Do we not refer to our veterans as service men? Do not our merchants and businessmen pride themselves in something of service given beyond the price of their goods?" The "rising vision of service," Hoover concluded, was the "social force that above all others has advanced sharply during these past years of suffering . . . service to those with whom we come in contact, service to the nation, and service to the world itself."[24]

A word so reverently repeated had obviously been heavily freighted with meaning. Some of that meaning derived from the quite natural wish of Americans, like all peoples, to think well of themselves—especially to think of themselves as an exceptionally altruistic nation. But to a still greater extent, the wide currency of the term "service" reflected the particular dilemmas of the historical phase through which American society was then passing. Men like Wilson and Crowder and Hoover and many more in their generation, including *New Republic* editors Herbert Croly and Walter Lippmann, were acutely aware that they were negotiating a passage between individualistic and collective eras. In his famous book of 1909, *The Promise of American Life*, Croly had

24. *Ibid.*, 299; Adler and Simons quoted in Burl Noggle, *Into the Twenties: The United States from Armistice to Normalcy* (Urbana: University of Illinois Press, 1974), 32, 37; Herbert Hoover, *American Individualism* (Garden City, N.Y.: Doubleday, Page, 1923), 28–29.

argued that the central problem of the age was somehow to substitute an ethos of cooperative nationalism for the obsolescent credo of narrow self-interest—without sacrificing the positive aspects of individualism. Croly therefore called for the application of "Hamiltonian means to Jeffersonian ends," a phrase that neatly bespoke the paradoxical character of the problem that absorbed him. So was "service" a fittingly ambivalent term, at once connoting the autonomy of the individual will and the obligation of the individual to serve a sphere wider than his own. For men deeply committed to individual freedom, but increasingly forced to recognize the necessity of cooperative endeavor, "service" was a marvelously reconciling concept, seeming to stand midway between two equally insistent and apparently incompatible value systems. Small wonder, therefore, that the word crept into the discourse of the day whenever those systems threatened to conflict. In this perspective, calling the draft Selective *Service* and insisting on its voluntary character were not simply propaganda gimmicks. They vividly signified that the society was plagued by painful ideological tensions, made still more acute by the demands of the war.

For all its ambiguity—perhaps because of that very ambiguity—the administration's approach to the distasteful business of military impressment was largely successful. Nearly ten million men presented themselves at their local polling places to be registered on June 5, and the day, somewhat to Secretary Baker's amazement, went by without serious incident. With an almost audible sigh of relief, Baker wrote to a friend on June 9 that "the registration was really a very remarkable demonstration." He took special satisfaction from the fact that Senator Reed's sanguinary predictions had not come true.[25] Then at 10:00 A.M. on July 20, a blindfolded Baker drew the first draft number from a huge glass bowl in a ceremony at the Senate Office Building. College student tellers drew more numbers throughout the afternoon and evening, until by two the following morning a national "order-of-call" list had been compiled and telegraphed to local boards throughout the country. By September, the hastily thrown-up camps began to receive the first draftees, and Baker continued to speak of the system's smooth operation with a certain air of wonderment. When the Assistant District Attorney of New York wired that New Yorkers were supporting the draft with "an enthusiasm never anticipated six weeks ago," and that "the system

25. Palmer, *Newton D. Baker*, I, 218.

is working to perfection," Baker happily passed the word along to the President, with the still partly incredulous notation that some initial feeling against the draft "has disappeared apparently."[26]

Despite Baker's somewhat surprised self-congratulations, the Selective Service System was not trouble-free. Some of the trouble came from Baker's colleagues in the highest circles of government. Secretary McAdoo, for example, groused that his "friends" were inadequately represented on the draft boards in New York state. Later, wearing the hat of Railroad Administrator, McAdoo harried Baker for blanket deferments for railroad employees. Fuel Administrator Harry Garfield and Food Administrator Herbert Hoover pushed similar claims for men working in the sectors under their control. Hoover protested "the operation of the draft law against men who may be styled 'key men' in agriculture, that is, men of the foreman, manager and ownership type." Such men, said Hoover, "have too much patriotism to themselves make application for exemption," and should be exempted as a class.[27] General Crowder made short work of that argument. "Our experience," he told Baker, "is certainly not that patriotic scruples are very materially decreasing claims for exemption." Accepting Hoover's suggestion, he dryly observed, would simply mean that "we should have a great many new owners of very small agricultural enterprises."[28]

A still greater source of difficulty lay precisely in the institution of the local boards, Baker's prize contrivance. Intended to be sensitively responsive to local conditions, they were also susceptible to local political pressures, and not immune to local prejudices. Many aggrieved Democrats, including the President, complained to Baker that Republican governors were abusing their appointment power by placing party hacks on the exemption boards. Republican Governor Martin G. Brumbaugh of Pennsylvania was the most fiercely resented, as he seemed to be pursuing a deliberate policy of fastening Republican-dominated

26. Baker to Wilson, with enclosures from Conklin to Crowder, Sept. 9, 1917, WWP. Some of that anti-draft feeling was made to disappear by force, as in the arrest of more than four hundred draft protestors in Oklahoma's "Green Corn Rebellion," an ill-starred outburst by impoverished tenant farmers and sharecroppers. See H. C. Peterson and Gilbert C. Fite, *Opponents of War, 1917–1918* (Seattle: University of Washington Press, 1957), 40–42.

27. Hoover to Wilson, Aug. 27, 1917, in Francis William O'Brien, ed., *The Hoover-Wilson Wartime Correspondence* (Ames: Iowa State University Press, 1974), 118.

28. Crowder quoted in Beaver, *Baker,* 37. In some states, says Beaver, as many as 80 percent of the registrants claimed exemption.

boards on all the state's most loyally Democratic counties.[29] And in Fulton County, Georgia, a board proved so flagrantly discriminatory— it exempted 526 of 815 whites, and only 6 of 202 blacks—that its members had to be removed.[30]

If such instances of willfully unjust administration of the draft were few, inequities inevitably arose from the poorly guided discretionary power of the boards, from the haste with which the original legislation had been drawn, and—most conspicuously—from the very character of American society. The law, for example, exempted men with dependents. Many boards construed that provision to grant deferments to virtually all married men, a practice that launched a nuptial boomlet in some communities.[31] Other boards applied a much more rigorous definition of dependency, inquiring closely into the wife's means of support, her employability, help available from relatives, and the family's assets. Not surprisingly, this kind of prying into personal affairs often provoked resentment. And in the absence of a uniform national standard, the induction rate of married men varied throughout the several states from 6 to 38 percent.[32] Senator Hiram Johnson (whose son-in-law was denied an exemption) was only one of many persons deeply offended at this snooping and arbitrariness. "The draft law," he growled, "was being administered in such fashion as to make it unfair, unequal, partial, and discriminatory."[33]

Further problems stemmed from the quota system established in the original legislation, which provided that the draft calls should be proportionately levied from the several states on the basis of total population. But that provision ignored the presence in the draft-age population

29. Beaver, *Baker,* 34–35; Palmer, *Newton D. Baker,* I, 334–36.
30. Arthur E. Barbeau and Florette Henri, *The Unknown Soldiers: Black American Troops in World War I* (Philadelphia: Temple University Press, 1974), 35.
31. At the New York Municipal Marriage Chapel, marriages were being performed at ten times the usual rate. Mark Sullivan, *Our Times: The United States, 1900–1925,* 6 vols. (New York: Scribner's, 1933), V, 308–9.
32. *Second Report,* 108–9.
33. Johnson to W. A. Sloane, Sept. 27, 1917, Johnson Papers, Bancroft Library, University of California, Berkeley. The dependency exemption had other unforeseen effects. Frequently, a wife saddled with an idle or unwanted husband refused to declare him to the board as her source of support, and thus consigned him to France. Other cases were reported of truant husbands brought home and kept there in order to secure a "I-B" classification—the deferment category for men with dependent wives. Crowder, ever droll, observed: "In short, as a remedy for domestic delinquencies, Class I-B proved an effective measure." *Second Report,* 113–14.

of two and a half million "non-declared" alien males—men without preliminary citizenship papers who were automatically exempted from
military service.[34] Howls of protest went up from the "native" residents
in those localities where non-declarants were heavily concentrated. One
New York draft board member complained that only about half the
registrants in his district were declarants or citizens, and "this slightly
more than 50% will have to furnish the quota for the entire number."[35]
In Brooklyn, another board discovered that nearly a quarter of its
registrants were non-declared Russian immigrants. "The major part
practically defy us," the board angrily reported, "while many of them
shrug their shoulders, laugh at us and say, 'What are you going to do
about it?' " This situation was plainly intolerable to the board members.
"While the flower of our neighborhood is being torn from their homes
and loved ones to fight," they raged, these "miserable specimens of
humanity . . . remain smugly at home to reap the benefits of the life
work of our young citizens."[36]

Those inequities in the draft were only the beginnings of the Army's
problems with the nation's millions of immigrants. So polyglot were the
American armed forces that some Europeans spoke deprecatingly of
the "American Foreign Legion." A condescending story of the day had
it that when an officer at Camp Meade pronounced the roll of immigrant recruits, not a single man recognized his own name, but when the
officer sneezed ten men stepped forward. The Stars and Stripes, the
doughboys' newspaper in France, reported that the AEF censors were
required to scan letters penned by American troops in forty-nine different languages. By some estimates, nearly one draftee in five was foreign-
born.[37]

34. Second Report, 89.
35. Warren Eberle to Lillian Wald, July 16, 1917, Wald Papers, Butler Library,
    Columbia University, N.Y.
36. Frederic F. Purdy et al., to Wilson, Aug. 16, 1917, WWP. In May, 1918, this
    inequity was adjusted by assessing quotas only on the basis of men in "Class
    I," the most eligible category.
37. Edward M. Coffman, The War To End All Wars: The American Military Ex-
    perience in World War I (New York: Oxford University Press, 1968), 11; Bruce
    White, "The American Military and the Melting Pot in World War I," in J. L.
    Granatstein and R. D. Cuff, eds., War and Society in North America (Toronto:
    Thomas Nelson, 1971), 40; Stars and Stripes, Nov. 1, 1918, 6; Robert M. Yerkes,
    ed., Psychological Examining in the United States Army: Memoirs of the Na-
    tional Academy of Sciences (Washington, D.C.: Government Printing Office,
    1921), XV, 693. The discussion in the following paragraphs is greatly in-
    debted to White, "American Military and the Melting Pot."

American society as a whole had not arrived by 1917 at any settled attitude toward its immigrant members, and it was scarcely surprising that the military authorities failed to formulate a consistent policy toward foreign-born soldiers during the war. At first the Army relegated non-English-speaking recruits, along with others deemed unfit for combat, to "depot brigades," where they were assigned to menial chores in the various stateside camps. But many people saw military service as a means, at last, to effect "Americanization"; that, indeed, had been a principal argument put forward by the proponents of universal military training. Bowing to pressure from those sources, the Army eventually established "development battalions"—special units for substandard but "remediable" recruits. There the men received instruction, usually from a YMCA volunteer, in the English language and American history and government. Recognizing the effectiveness of the Army's Americanizing methods, the government in 1918 simplified naturalization procedures for men in military service.

But if the development battalions promoted a measure of ethnic integration, other pressures pushed the Army in the opposite direction, toward the formation of ethnically segregated units. At Camp Gordon, Georgia, Slavs and Italians were organized into two distinct companies, commanded by officers familiar with the relevant tongues and even graced by cooks competent in their respective cuisines. "It may rightly be claimed that such segregation of races into regiments, etc., does not make American citizens," said a staff report, "and possibly this is true, but we are not in this war to make more American citizens, we are in to win the war." Some foreign governments and "governments-in-exile" exerted more pressure in the direction of separatism when they requested permission to recruit their own nationals resident in the United States. Those efforts focused especially on the minority nationalities of the Austro-Hungarian Empire, technically enemy aliens, but eager to do battle against the Dual Monarchy for the sake of Polish or Yugoslavian or Czechoslovakian independence. Partly to preempt those requests, and recognizing the political impact of fielding "large, powerful, nationalistic units" against the ethnically fissured Austrian forces, Congress in July 1918 authorized the formation of a "Slavic Legion" in the U.S. Army. The swift ending of the war in November, however, cut that experiment short.

Toward black men the white military authorities displayed still greater uncertainty, a compound of fear and contempt. Much of the initial resistance to the draft legislation had come from anxious white Southerners frightened at the prospect of training blacks to arms. Senator James K. Vardaman, peerless racist from Mississippi, snarled that the conscription of blacks would put "arrogant strutting representatives of the black soldiery in every community."[38] "The average white person," one black veteran accurately recalled, "whether buck private or general, didn't want Negro soldiers."[39] Secretary Baker may have wanted black soldiers, but he bluntly stated that "there is no intention on the part of the War Department to undertake at this time to settle the so-called race question."[40] Hence the United States armed forces would continue to be, as they had always been, rigidly segregated along racial lines. But that policy, never officially questioned, posed particular problems for the huge conscript army the War Department was raising. At what level—company, regiment, division—should black troops be segregated? Where should they be trained? How should they be used? Should their officers be black? Baker and his staff found no answers to those questions in the first months of the war. When the four Regular Army and eight National Guard black units were quickly brought up to full strength by volunteers in April, all enlistment of blacks stopped. Further black volunteers were simply rejected, and conscription of blacks was postponed. Meanwhile, the War Department struggled to define its racial policy. Several options were debated: concentrating black draftees in two all-black Southern camps; stationing a single black regiment at each of the sixteen National Army cantonments; giving blacks preliminary training only at the eight camps in the North, then dispatching them quickly to France (where, said General Tasker Bliss, "we do not apprehend trouble arising from social differences"), for service as labor troops and stevedores.[41]

As the Department contemplated those choices, its calculations were suddenly scrambled by the eruption of racial violence involving black troops stationed at Houston, Texas. Seasoned black Regulars of the 24th Infantry's 3rd Battalion, insulted and harassed by the city's Jim

---

38. Quoted in John W. Chambers, "Conscripting for Colossus: The Adoption of the Military Draft in the United States in World War I," paper presented at Organization of American Historians meeting, Washington, D.C., 1971, copy in author's possession.
39. Lester Granger Memoir, 24, CUOHC.
40. Baker to Emmet J. Scott, Sept. 30, 1917, quoted in Beaver, *Baker*, 228.
41. Bliss quoted in Beaver, *Baker*, 226–27. See also the impassioned account in Barbeau and Henri, *Unknown Soldiers*, 42–43.

Crow laws, went on a rampage on the night of August 23 and shot to death seventeen white civilians. Southern politicians, seeing their worst forebodings bloodily fulfilled, exploded in wrath. The Texas congressional delegation begged "that all negro troops in Texas be removed at once and that they be kept out of Texas permanently."[42] Mississippi's Senator John Sharp Williams was soon demanding "that colored troops be sent to Cuba for training."[43] After announcing that no black draftees would be called until the situation in Houston was cleared up, the War Department proceeded to mete out justice to the black troops that was both terrible and swift. The 3rd Battalion was disarmed and sent under arrest to New Mexico. Courts-martial were quickly convened to try over a hundred men. On December 8, thirteen troopers were condemned to death. Three days later, well before an appeal could even be got under way, all thirteen were hanged.

The riot and the Army's rapid retribution stunned the black community. Its leaders feared the War Department might now bow to Southern pressure and permanently suspend black enlistments.[44] At the urging of Tuskegee Institute principal Robert R. Moton and prominent Northern philanthropist Julius Rosenwald, Secretary Baker called a conference on August 31 of "men interested in the Negro question." Out of this meeting came Baker's decisions to appoint Emmett J. Scott, a capable moderate of the Tuskegee persuasion, his special assistant for Negro affairs, and to create a black combat division. The War Department also finally determined to disperse black recruits throughout the camps, including those in the South.[45] At last, on September 22, the first draft call for blacks was issued. Carefully segregated during their journey and after arrival, they began to appear in the camps. White fears were allayed somewhat by the assurance that at least a two-to-one ratio of white to black trainees would be maintained in all integrated camps. That policy meant that even the lone black combat division, the 92nd, would not be trained in a single location, but was to be scattered

42. Texas delegation to Wilson, Aug. 24, 1917, WWP.
43. John Sharp Williams to Wilson, Nov. 13, 1917, WWP.
44. Blacks still bitterly remembered President Theodore Roosevelt's dishonorable discharge of an entire black battalion involved in a racial incident at Brownsville, Texas, in 1906.
45. White Southerners were scarcely pleased with this arrangement. Scott later reported that when the black 8th Illinois National Guard Regiment was dispatched to still-seething Houston, "they were jeered at along the way, stoned in one or two places, and a riot was barely averted at a way station in Texas." Emmet J. Scott, *The American Negro in the World War* (n.p., n.d.), 76.

through seven cantonments. Unique among all the divisions sent over-seas, it never assembled as a division in the United States, which was to prove but one of many handicaps when the men of the 92nd reached the trenches in France.

The sole exclusively black camp was the one for training black offi-cers at Des Moines, Iowa. Blacks had been barred from the Plattsburg officer-training encampments before the war, in part because Plattsburg patron General Leonard Wood gagged at the idea of candidates "with whom our descendants cannot intermarry without producing a breed of mongrels; they must at least be white."[46] Fourteen officer-training camps had opened after the declaration of war, but none admitted blacks, and it had begun to appear that the Army intended to commission only white officers. Black fears of that prospect had deepened in June when the Army rather high-handedly relieved from his command Lieutenant Colonel Charles Young, a West Point graduate and the senior black officer in the Regular Army.[47] Confronted with those facts, the National Association for the Advancement of Colored People (NAACP) had tempered its usual insistence on integration and had importuned Baker to establish a separate training camp for blacks. Some black leaders had assailed the idea of a "Jim Crow camp," but NAACP officials Joel Spingarn and W. E. B. Du Bois knew that a segregated facility was the only realistic possibility. Their persistence had resulted in the establish-ment in July of a black officer-training program at Fort Des Moines. In October, it graduated a single class of 639 officers, all below field rank.

46. Wood to Theodore Roosevelt, Mar. 5, 1915, quoted in White, "American Mili-tary and the Melting Pot."

47. Young, said the Army, had Bright's disease. The discovery of his ailment cer-tainly came at a convenient time for Baker, who was being pestered by com-plaints from white officers that they would not obey a command given by a black superior. On June 25, President Wilson, the recipient of similar com-plaints, inquired of Baker about Young's status. The Colonel, Baker replied, was about to undergo medical tests at San Francisco's Letterman Hospital, "to determine whether his physical condition is sufficiently good to justify his return to active service." Three days later, without awaiting the test results, Wilson assured Senator John Sharp Williams of Mississippi that Young "will not in fact have command because he is in ill health." That conclusion seemed decidedly premature, and strongly suggests, as two students of the episode conclude, that a decision about Young had already been made, for which the medical tests were to furnish the public justification. Young rode on horseback from Ohio to Washington, D.C., to demonstrate his good health, to no avail. After the war, he was reactivated and posted on a mission to Liberia. See the ac-count in Barbeau and Henri, *Unknown Soldiers*, 66–69.

Those men were then assigned to the 92nd Division, whose superior officers remained white. The Army frankly regarded the 92nd as an experiment, and had no immediate plans for additional black combat divisions. There was little further need for black officers, so the training camp at Fort Des Moines was closed.

Only one of every five black men sent to France saw combat, while in the AEF as a whole two out of three soldiers took part in battle. "The mass of the colored drafted men cannot be used for combatant troops," said a General Staff report in 1918, and it consequently recommended that "these colored drafted men be organized in reserve labor battalions."[48] And so they were, taking up the most menial tasks in the Army as in civilian life. They worked as stevedores in the Atlantic ports and common laborers at the camps and in the Services of the Rear in France.

The Selective Service System also treated blacks unfairly, especially with respect to exemptions. Thirty-six percent of black registrants were pronounced eligible for service, compared with only 25 percent of whites. In part that differential derived from the effective ban on black volunteering, which left the black pool of able-bodied men, in contrast to the white, undepleted by voluntary enlistments. But to a great extent the inability of blacks to secure exemptions at the same rate as whites owed to their inferior position in American society. Historically barred from the skilled trades, blacks could claim few deferments on grounds of industrial indispensability. It was a particularly cruel irony that many black family men were too poor to claim the usual exemptions for husbands and fathers. Their meager army pay and compulsory family allotment, which might provide up to fifty dollars a month to an enlisted man's wife and children, would actually *increase* many a black family's income, wiping out any claimed deferment on grounds of economic dependency. In the end, blacks, who comprised 10 percent of the population, made up 13 percent of draftees.[49] Crowder and the War Department earnestly tried to operate the draft in a fair and impartial manner, but no system could nullify inequities that inhered in the very

48. "Disposal of the Colored Drafted Men," report of Colonel E. D. Anderson, chairman of the Operations Branch, General Staff, May 16, 1918, in Barbeau and Henri, *Unknown Soldiers*, 191–201.

49. *Second Report*, 192; Samuel McCune Lindsay, "Purpose and Scope of War Risk Insurance," *Annals of the American Academy of Political and Social Science* 79 (1918), 52–68; Fred Davis Baldwin, *The American Enlisted Man in World War I* (Ph.D. dissertation, Princeton University, 1964), 60.

structure of the society. As in other wars, the distribution of draft exemptions in World War I tended to parallel the distribution of civilian privilege, and the obligation of service fell disproportionately on the powerless and the poor.

Some men resisted their military obligation outright, many for reasons of conscience. The Selective Service Act exempted from combatant service members of "any well recognized religious sect or organization . . . whose existing creed or principles forbid its members to participate in war." On its face that provision seemed liberal enough, but in practice it frequently proved unfair and harsh. Uninstructed about what denominations qualified as *bona fide* pacifist sects, the local boards, as in the case of dependency exemptions, often ruled arbitrarily on the sincerity of a claimant's conscience. Then, too, the law at first made no provision for non-religious exemption, leaving many men—humanitarian and political objectors, or German-Americans loath to take up arms against their own blood—without legal refuge from the draft. Moreover, the government neglected for many months to stipulate what alternative service might be substituted for combat duty. As a result of that neglect, 20,000 conscientious objectors certified as sincere by their local boards were inducted into the Army, sent to training camps, and held there until suitable non-combatant service should be defined.

Putting the objectors under military authority, especially in the charged atmosphere of the camps where tens of thousands of men were being trained for combat, was undoubtedly the most callous feature of the government's policy. The War Department officially instructed camp commanders to segregate the conscientious objectors and treat them with "kindly consideration." But the aim of that policy was not to make the dissenters feel comfortable. Rather, it was to induce them, as the Adjutant General noted, to renounce their objections and "give their best efforts to the service of the United States as soldiers."[50] The policy had some success, as more than 16,000 of the certified objectors, declared by their boards to have a legal right to accept only non-combatant service, decided after a period in camp to relinquish that right and take up arms. Some, no doubt, were persuaded by "kindly consideration." But others were humiliated and hazed, jeered and cajoled, until their consciences could accommodate war. The Civil Liberties Bureau

50. Quoted in Norman Thomas, *Is Conscience a Crime?* (New York: Garland, 1972), 90.

badgered the War Department to define non-combatant service and get the men out of their ill-defined limbo in the camps, where they were generally regarded as quirky recalcitrants whose wills must be broken. Finally, in March 1918, the President designated suitable non-combatant activities. He also for the first time permitted the local boards to recognize other than religious scruples against military service. In June, a Board of Inquiry was established to make uniform determinations about the status of objectors already in the camps.

All those measures evidenced the government's good intentions toward objectors. Baker told the President that their numbers were small enough that the administration could comfortably adopt "a very generous and considerate mode of treatment."[51] After the reforms of early 1918, religious objectors from established sects who accepted service in the Medical, Quartermaster, or Engineering Corps had little trouble. Some were also later furloughed to work on farms. But things went hard for those objectors unable to convince the Board of the authenticity of their church or the sincerity of their beliefs. Indeed, the Board seemed at times, like some camp officers, hell-bent on shaming men out of their declared convictions. Major Walter G. Kellogg, one of the three members of the Board, regularly asked claimants if they had bought Liberty bonds or Thrift Stamps, and, somewhat less pertinently, if they were inclined to "drink," "smoke," or "go around with women."[52] He scolded one claimant for belonging "to some nut society" and told him he did not deserve to live in the United States. He opened an interview with another by saying: "If I didn't know that you were a conscientious objector, I would take you for a good wholesome boy."[53]

Things went harder still for the "absolutists," who refused on either religious or political grounds to do anything, even answer roll call, under military command. A handful of these men—Civil Liberties Bureau Chief Roger N. Baldwin was the most notable—managed to have their cases tried in civil courts. But most of them were inducted into the Army and brought before courts-martial, tribunals interested as much in sustaining military discipline as in dispensing justice. Forty objectors were court-martialed before the reforms of 1918, and nearly

51. Baker to Wilson, Sept. 19, 1917, quoted in Beaver, *Baker*, 232.
52. Other members of the Board were Judge Julian W. Mack and Columbia Law School Dean Harlan F. Stone, later to become an Associate Justice of the U.S. Supreme Court.
53. "Transcripts of Hearings before Board of Inquiry at Camp Lewis, Washington," Oct. 1918; in J. G. Ragsdale Collection, Hoover Institution.

five hundred thereafter. Virtually every one was found guilty and dispatched to military prisons. Regarded as "hard cases," they were often subjected to extraordinarily punishing treatment in those already barbarous institutions.[54]

Clearly, the liberal measures of early 1918 marked the outer limits of the administration's goodwill toward conscientious objectors. Thereafter the War Department's attitude hardened. A month after Wilson's liberal proclamation of March, Secretary Baker directed that any objector whose sincerity was questioned, or who engaged in propaganda, or who was "sullen and defiant" should be "promptly brought to trial by court martial."[55] A few months later, Assistant Secretary Frederick Keppel advised Baker that "good departmental and public policy" dictated lenient discipline and honorable discharges for officers who had severely beaten objectors at Camp Funston, Kansas.[56] Baker and Keppel, wrote prominent pacifist Norman Thomas, "had tried to be liberal; they had been criticized for it; now if objectors could not meet them half-way so much worse for the objectors."[57]

So much worse, too, as time went on, for the less than conscientious objector—the draft evader motivated by no principle more elevated than the wish to save his hide. No one will ever know precisely how many men willfully dodged the draft. The Provost Marshal General estimated that roughly 337,000 men escaped his net during the war, some 12 percent of the men inducted. About half of those men were eventually brought to book, and the government contented itself with simply publishing the names of the remainder. At first the administration proceeded rather hesitantly against "slackers." By mid-1918 the Justice Department had prosecuted only 10,000 persons for failure to register. But in March of that year the Department inaugurated a new tactic, aimed not at the individual offender but designed to round up thousands of delinquents in one swoop. Justice Department agents launched the first "slacker raid" in Pittsburgh, aided by local police and

---

54. It was standard practice in military prisons at the time to manacle prisoners to the bars or grating of their cells for eight hours in every twenty-four. One objector, strung up for days in the "hole" at Alcatraz and promised relief if he would only don the soldier's uniform cast beside him on the floor, held out until he contracted pneumonia and died. As a last cruel stroke, his body was sent home in a military uniform. See Thomas, *Is Conscience a Crime?*, 197–200.

55. Thomas, *Is Conscience a Crime?*, 99.

56. Beaver, *Baker*, 233.

57. Thomas, *Is Conscience a Crime?*, 110.

by the self-styled patriots of the American Protective League. More raids followed in Chicago, Boston, and other cities, most notoriously in New York and northern New Jersey from September 3 through 6. In these last raids, armed soldiers and sailors joined a canvass that detained more than 50,000 apparently draft-age men who were often apprehended at bayonet-point in ball parks, restaurants, or on street corners and made to show their Selective Service documents. In New Jersey alone, this dragonnade turned up more than 13,000 delinquents. Thus rudely was the fiction abandoned that the government merely selected from a people who had "volunteered in mass."[58]

Sharply criticized from many quarters, the slacker raids were but the latest cinching of the knot in a relentless tightening of the draft net. In December 1917, General Crowder had already fined the mesh by introducing a classification system, designed to sort the registrant pool more scientifically into five classes of varying suitability for service.[59] In May 1918, he issued his "work-or-fight" order, compelling the local boards to review the current occupations of all registrants and push the idle or the less essentially employed (waiters, for example) into Class I. The following month a new registration enrolled men who had turned 21 years of age since the first sign-up a year earlier. A supplemental registration in August caught the new 21-year-olds of the preceding two

58. *Second Report,* 200ff; Peterson and Fite, *Opponents* 231–34; Thomas W. Gregory to Wilson, Sept. 9, 1918, Gregory Papers, Library of Congress, Washington, D.C.

59. The first screening of the registrants on June 5, 1917, had simply declared them eligible or exempt, with no gradations. The December questionnaires allowed the System to improve considerably on those crude categories. They also provided a weath of information about the physical, familial, educational, and occupational characteristics of American men. From this classification system as well as the physical and psychological tests administered by the Army to inductees came the disturbing deductions that nearly one quarter of the draft-age men were illiterate, one third physically unfit for military duty, and a considerable number apparently underdeveloped mentally.

Historians have made little use of the Selective Service System questionnaires and registration forms, which are stored at the Federal Records Center .at Atlanta, Georgia. For registrants who were inducted or delinquent and whose surnames began with the letters A-D, all the questionnaire information on nativity, residence, education, occupation, physical condition, and so on is available. For other registrants the information has been destroyed, but the A-D group nevertheless provides more than 6000 microfilm reels of data. For one example of imaginative exploitation of this data, see Charles Garofalo, "Black-White Occupational Distribution in Miami During World War I," *Prologue* 5 (1973), 98–101.

months. Also in August, Congress extended the eligible age limits to 18 and 45, a step that called for a massive new registration on September 12 of the estimated 13 million men under 21 and over 30 now suddenly liable to the draft.

This new enrollment worried the War Department even more than the original registration of June 1917. Enthusiasm was no longer fresh and keen as it had been in the first weeks of American belligerency. Casualty reports from France, now published regularly in the newspapers, had perhaps cooled the itch to don a uniform. Men's willingness to come forward, so tensely relied upon in the spring of 1917, was less certain than ever. But Crowder, for one, was little daunted by those difficulties. He had a characteristic solution. "This," he said, "was where the problem of publicity began—how to reach, in a startling, inspiring and universal appeal, every individual in those 13 million."[60] For a solid week before the appointed day, 30,000 Four-Minute Men orated, newspapers urged and advertised, and military bands played incessantly, all to induce the newly eligible men to enter their names in the registration books on September 12. "We were attempting to do voluntarily in a day," said Crowder, "what the Prussian autocracy had been spending nearly 50 years to perfect."[61] Popular historian Mark Sullivan called this spectacle "a propaganda and publicity campaign of a magnitude never seen before or since in this country."[62] Its extravagant dimensions testified to the continuing fascination with the voluntarist ethos and the techniques of persuasion. But the very superabundance of the hoopla preceding the September registration suggested also that the limits of the voluntarist approach to military mobilization were being reached. The slacker raids around New York, carried out in the same week, suggested that conclusion still more strongly. The quickening pace of the draft calls in the summer of 1918 and the extended registration in September revealed the growing desperateness of the military's manpower needs. Had the crisis continued to deepen, and the government been forced to sift the population ever more finely for men to send to France, it was altogether likely that ballyhoo would have increasingly given way to bayonets. But here, as in so many other areas, the country was spared the resort to more extreme measures by the war's end in November.

60. *Second Report*, 28.
61. *Idem.*
62. Sullivan, *Our Times*, V, 312.

Many Americans had at first believed that the nation would be spared altogether the ordeal of sending millions of its sons to join the Allied armies in the field. "They don't need more warriors," said the New York *Morning Telegraph* in April 1917; "they want money and food, and munitions of war."[63] Professional military men, reported the *New York Times* in the same month, thought it would be impossible in any case to send a significant body of American troops to Europe because of the lack of shipping.[64] The French themselves were initially reassuring on this score. Major James Logan, Jr., had cabled from Paris on March 30, 1917, that the French General Staff had "no particular interest in having American troops in France."[65] Moreover, there appeared to be legal impediments to sending a major force overseas, as the Constitution seemed to preclude deployment of the states' militias outside the United States.[66] Hiram Johnson thought in the early weeks of the war that the President intended "to fight with our dollars to the last Frenchman and Englishman. He expects the war to be ended by the time he can prepare to have an army ready."[67] Even among those who envisioned the

63. *Literary Digest* 54 (April 14, 1917), 1047.
64. *New York Times,* Apr. 3, 1917, 3.
65. Warren S. Tryon, "The Draft in World War I," *Current History* 54 (1968), 339ff.
66. The constitutionality of dispatching overseas an American Expeditionary Force composed of conscripts and federalized National Guardsmen was a question that troubled the administration throughout the early months of the war. Article I, Section 8, Paragraph 15 of the Federal Constitution seemed to preclude overseas deployment of the states' "militias." Charles Evans Hughes addressed the American Bar Association at length on the subject in August 1917, and when former minister to Spain Hannis Taylor publicly questioned the constitutionality of the AEF, the President called the Attorney General's attention to Taylor, asking Gregory if there was "anything we could do to this wretched creature." The question was sufficiently disturbing that Gregory set his staff to preparing a nine-page memorandum on the subject, which concluded that the National Defense Act of 1916 had anticipated the objection and made it possible to send both conscripts and militiamen overseas. For Hughes's speech, see *Congressional Record,* Senate, 65th Congress, 1st sess., Vol. 55, 6837–40; see also *New York American,* Aug. 12, 1917, 5, and Wilson to Gregory, Aug. 27, 1917, and reply, Sept. 1, 1917, Gregory Papers. The Selective Service Act itself was held to be constitutional in the *Selective Draft Cases,* 245 U.S. 366 (1918).
67. Hiram Johnson to Charles McClatchey, May 1, 1917, Johnson Papers. Some Europeans, too, feared that Wilson intended to fight to the last drop of their blood, while holding his own troops safely behind the Atlantic. And it will be recalled that Secretary of the Treasury McAdoo considered dollars "substitutes for American soldiers." See William Gibbs McAdoo, *Crowded Years* (Boston: Houghton Mifflin, 1931); 376–77.

creation of an American Expeditionary Force, many saw it actually taking shape only in the far distant future. Julius Kahn, the manager of the Selective Service bill, declared that "it would be folly to think of sending our boys to the front until they have had a year of training." And General Tasker Bliss, speaking for the General Staff, recommended that the Army be prepared at home for two full years before descending in numbers upon France.[68]

But in the month following those observations, General Pershing was on the Atlantic, headed for France. A full American division began to debark at French ports in June 1917. "Three months ago," wrote an unsettled Hiram Johnson on June 25, "if any man in our State had advocated the conscription of our youth to have them fight in Europe in this war, he would have been hooted from the platform. Today, our men are landed in France and our transports are upon the water. As I look back, the changes seem to me almost incredible."[69]

Still more incredible changes were to come. The force that so strained Johnson's credulity was tiny in June 1917. And though the War College and General Pershing both recommended that a million men be brought to France by the following summer, the War Department calculated that available shipping would only permit transportation of some 650,000 troops by June 1918. Training facilities, too, could not so quickly be made to accommodate such numbers. Thus the first draft call was set at only 687,000. By the end of 1917 only 175,000 troops had reached France, and Selective Service inductions had been virtually halted. Then, in 1918, inductions and troop shipments suddenly shot up. In April, May, and June of 1918, more men were drafted than in all of 1917, and throughout the summer nearly ten thousand men a day crammed themselves aboard the troop transports at Hoboken, Newport News, Boston, and Philadelphia. By Armistice Day, almost four million men were to be in uniform, half of them in France.

The reason for this sudden expansion and acceleration of the War Department's plans was not far to seek. Beginning in the autumn of 1917, the Allies suffered a series of disastrous military reverses. In October, the Germans and Austrians unleashed a spectacularly successful assault against the Italians on the Isonzo front, capturing 275,000 prisoners and driving the defenders in wild disarray back behind the

68. Kahn's remark is in *Congressional Record*, House, 65th Congress, 1st sess., 298; Bliss's recommendation is mentioned in Beaver, *Baker*, 40.
69. Johnson to Charles McClatchey, June 25, 1917, Johnson Papers.

River Piave. This new demonstration of the enemy's capacity to carry out an attack contrasted starkly with the failure of the British drive in Flanders, which ground to a pathetic halt at Passchendaele in November, after an advance of barely two miles bought with 300,000 casualties. In November, too, came the Bolshevik Revolution, and moves toward an armistice in the east. Soon German troops were being shifted from the Russian to the western front, preparatory to a massive offensive launched on March 21, 1918. As those blows successively hammered upon their armies, Allied statesmen and generals, in frantically intensifying rhythms, stepped up calls for American troops. The war had turned into a deadly race, testing whether the Americans could throw enough troops across the Atlantic in time to stem the German tide rapidly flowing from the east.

The desperation of the Allied demands threatened to eclipse the United States' intention to create a separate American army. British and French representatives had requested as early as April 1917 that American troops be simply amalgamated into Allied units, dispensing with a separate command and a separate supply operation. The Allies had even suggested that they be allowed to recruit American citizens directly for their own armies, as they explained to the War Department, "from the surplus you will have over your own needs."[70] President Wilson and Secretary Baker had turned aside those suggestions at the time, but with the mounting urgency of the crisis in the spring of 1918 the Allies insisted ever more shrilly that the best use that could be made of fresh American manpower was to punch it quickly into the battered line under French or British command. The British were now driven even to contemplating conscription in seething Ireland, though American troops were greatly preferred. "It is vital that American troops of all arms be poured into France as soon as possible," British Prime Minister David Lloyd George told his ambassador in Washington. "Please press this fact on the President with all your power. . . . The difference of even a week in the date of arrival may be absolutely vital."[71]

In the highest circles of the Wilson administration considerable confusion and irresolution surrounded the issue of amalgamation. Baker

70. T. Bridges to Major General Hugh L. Scott, Apr. 30, 1917, War Office, Directorate of Military Operations and Intelligence: Papers (WO 106/467), Public Record Office, London, Eng. (hereafter PRO).
71. Lloyd George to Lord Reading, Mar. 28 and Apr. 2, 1918, British Foreign Office Papers (FO 371/3441), PRO.

remained committed to a separate American force, but Wilson seemed to waver, so that the Secretary, concludes his biographer, often "was not sure what the President was doing or desired to have done."[72] Tasker Bliss, American military representative on the Supreme War Council, infected by the gloom of the Allied military men, inclined toward accepting some form of amalgamation. But standing resolutely against all such proposals was the Commander in Chief of the American Expeditionary Force, General John J. Pershing.

Had American troops been fed into French and British units, Pershing, of course, would have become the proverbial general without an army. But his reasons for resisting amalgamation went far beyond the simple desire to secure his own command, and he rebuffed the incessant Allied demands with an unremitting stolidity that infuriated his adversaries. Supreme Allied Commander Marshal Ferdinand Foch warned in May 1918 that Pershing's continued resistance might spell the doom of the western front. "You are willing," asked Foch, "to risk our being driven back to the Loire?" "Yes," Pershing replied simply, "I am willing to take the risk."[73]

The remark was typical of the man and his policies. In looks and manner, as in his strategic preferences, Pershing was the model American soldier: no-nonsense, obedient, quietly forceful, and a little dull. Fifty-six years old in 1917, he was still robust and barrel-chested, and his peninsular jaw and perpendicular bearing made him a paragon of military appearance. Born in Missouri, he had attended West Point in the 1880s, when the Academy was still suffused with the afterglow of the Civil War, occasionally visited by aging heroes like Ulysses S. Grant and William Sherman. In the closing years of the nineteenth century, Pershing had skirmished with a few Indians, earned a law degree at the University of Nebraska, and picked up the nickname "Black Jack" while serving with a black cavalry regiment in Cuba during the Spanish-American War. Posted in the Phillipines in 1902, he had energetically subdued the Moros, and won promotion to Brigadier in 1906. Command of the Punitive Expedition against Pancho Villa in Mexico in 1916 made Pershing the only American officer since the Spanish-American War who had led a large body of troops in the field. That experience, in addition to his cool tact and diplomatic acquiescence in ad-

72. Beaver, *Baker*, 112.
73. John J. Pershing, *My Experiences in the World War*, 2 vols. (New York: Frederick A. Stokes, 1931), II, 28.

ministration policy—qualities markedly in contrast with the flamboyant insubordination of his principal rival, General Leonard Wood—recommended Pershing to Wilson and Baker in 1917, and in May they selected him to lead the AEF.[74]

For virtually the entire tenure of his command, Pershing was so preoccupied with Allied pleas for amalgamation, that his chief of staff later wrote: "a reader fifty years hence might well conclude that this struggle between Allies was more important than much of the fighting that went on in quiet sectors on the Western Front."[75] Pershing took his uncompromising stand for several reasons. As he constantly told the Allied supplicants, amalgamation would be terribly unpopular with the American people.[76] Nor, he privately felt, would it be popular with the troops themselves. They were thought to share the national prejudice against the British, and few of them could understand the French tongue. Moreover, the mutinies in the French army in April 1917 were developments that the American commander in chief could hardly have found inviting. Then, too, Pershing, like all American strategists, was a "westerner," opposed to efforts to reopen the eastern front and to peripheral engagements such as the Allies had mounted in Palestine and, disastrously, in Gallipoli in Turkey. "It was my belief," he later wrote, "that our task clearly lay on the Western Front and that we would have all we could do to beat the enemy there." The Allies, he said scornfully, were inclined "to send expeditions here and there in pursuit of political aims." Pershing had no intention of letting American troops be used to free up French or English units for deployment elsewhere, and he cer-

74. The President and the Secretary of War chose, no doubt for political reasons, to allow Pershing's father-in-law, Wyoming Republican Senator Francis E. Warren, to inform the General of his appointment. In high spirits, Warren telegrammed his son-in-law: "Wire me to-day whether and how much you speak, read and write French." With breathtaking literalness, Pershing soberly replied: "Spent several months in France nineteen eight studying language. Spoke quite fluently; could read and write very well at that time. Can easily reacquire satisfactory working knowledge." Pershing, *My Experiences*, I, 1.

75. James G. Harbord, *The American Army in France, 1917–1919* (Boston: Little, Brown, 1936), 186.

76. Wilson and Baker, too, must have appreciated that amalgamation would have made even more precarious the administration's exposed political position, already riddled by partisan Republican fire in the winter of 1917–18, when, as it happened, the most desperate cries for troops arose. See, for example, William Wiseman's account of his discussion of the subject with Wilson on Feb. 3, 1918, RSB, VII, 520–21. Pershing, however, proved a more intractable opponent of amalgamation than did either the President or the Secretary of War.

tainly did not propose to put his troops under foreign command only to find them dispatched "here and there" away from the Western front.[77] Political considerations also entered Pershing's calculations. "When the war ends," he wrote Baker, "our position will be stronger if our army acting as such shall have played a distinct and definite part."[78]

Most of all, Pershing opposed amalgamation because it would hamper the execution of his singular strategy: a massive, head-on confrontation with the main German force, an open and aggressive assault of such overwhelming strength that the enemy would be annihilated. These precepts, he said, were "the fundamentals so thoroughly taught at West Point for a century."[79] In clinging to that brutally simple doctrine, Pershing showed himself to be the most American of strategists. There is, as Russell Weigley writes, an American way of war: "Indian campaigns early encouraged the notion that the object of war is nothing less than the enemy's destruction as a military power. The Civil War tended to fix the American image of war from the 1860s . . . and it also suggested that the complete overthrow of the enemy, the destruction of his military power, is the object of war. . . . In the history of American strategy, the direction taken by the American conception of war made most American strategists, through most of the time span of American history, strategists of annihilation."[80] Pershing's education at post-Civil War West Point, where the votive fires still flickered in commemoration of Grant's slog to Richmond and Sherman's march to the sea, as well as nearly all the young officer's subsequent combat experience, only deepened his attachment to that primal doctrine. Accordingly, Pershing was utterly contemptuous of the defensive strategy of attrition into which both sides had sickeningly settled along the western front. Amalgamation, in his view, would dribble American blood indefinitely into the deadlocked trenches. What was needed was a knockout blow, delivered by fresh American troops held back from the front until such time as they could crushingly breach it by sheer concentration and mass. It was logical, Pershing said with disdain, that

77. Pershing, My Experiences, II, 149. Over Pershing's objections, some American soldiers joined the Allied intervention in Russia.

78. Pershing to Baker, Jan. 17, 1918, quoted in David F. Trask, The United States in the Supreme War Council: American War Aims and Inter-Allied Strategy, 1917–1918 (Middletown, Conn.: Wesleyan University Press, 1961), 74.

79. Pershing, My Experiences, I, 154.

80. Russell F. Weigley, The American Way of War: A History of United States Military Strategy and Policy (New York: Macmillan, 1973), xxi–xxii.

the French were so enamored of defensive tactics, because "they had been on the defensive, at least in thought, during the previous half century."[81]

In fact it was not some inherited Gallic pusillanimity but the cruel realities of modern military technology that had forced all sides, not just the French, into the stalemated trench warfare of 1914–17. Long-range artillery and especially the deadly concentrated fire of the machine gun had given tremendous advantage to the defensive position, locking the opposing armies in an iron checkmate. Those facts Pershing overlooked. In his view, "the basic principles of warfare had not changed," and he repeatedly urged that the French and British instructors who had been seconded to the stateside training camps be posted back home. He wanted to minimize training for trench fighting, and instead emphasize a program "which laid great stress on open warfare methods and offensive action." Victory, Pershing believed, "could not be won by the costly process of attrition, but it must be won by driving the enemy out into the open and engaging him in a war of movement." Above all, that strategy meant that his troops must have thorough training in the use of the rifle. Nothing, he claimed, could replace "the combination of an efficient soldier and his rifle." Training methods for American troops, he said again and again, "must remain and become *distinctly our own*. All instruction must contemplate the assumption of a vigorous offensive." Pershing wanted nothing of the trench fighting that had enervated both sides on the western front:

> From a tactical point of view, the method of combat in trench warfare presents a marked contrast to that employed in open warfare, and the attempt by assaulting infantry to use trench warfare methods in an open warfare combat will be successful only at great loss. Trench warfare is marked by uniform formations, the regulation of space and time by higher commands down to the smallest details . . . fixed distances and intervals between units and individuals . . . little initiative. . . . Open warfare is marked by . . . irregularity of formations, comparatively little regulation of space and time by higher commanders, the greatest possible use of the infantry's own fire power to enable it to get forward, variable distances and intervals between units and individuals . . . brief orders and the greatest possible use of individual initiative by all troops engaged in the action. . . . The infantry commander must oppose machine guns by fire from rifles, his automatics and his rifle grenades and must close with their crews

81. Pershing, *My Experiences*, I, 152.

under cover of this fire and of ground beyond their flanks. . . . The success of every unit from the platoon to the division must be exploited to the fullest extent. Where strong resistance is encountered, reënforcements must not be thrown in to make a frontal attack at this point, but must be pushed through gaps created by successful units, to attack these strong points in the flank or rear.[82]

So Pershing remained, for reasons of sentiment and politics, strategy and tactics, unbudgeably attached to the policy of a distinct American force, uniquely trained and separately fielded. He gambled that the British and French would hold off the Germans until he could play his own strong hand. But the American commander did not hold all the cards. Of necessity, he had to dicker with the Allies over amalgamation, in a series of confrontations that included elements of double-dealing and bluff. Ships were trumps. The Allies, especially the British, had them; the Americans did not—at least not in sufficient numbers to transport the 100-Division army that Pershing eventually wanted.

Immediately after American entry into the war, Prime Minister Lloyd George had prophetically told an American audience in London that victory was "to be found in one word, ships, in a second word, ships, and a third word, ships."[83] Pershing, who somehow had to float a vast army across 3000 miles of sea, knew the truth of that statement. Without ships he would have no army at all. To get them, he alternately wheedled and browbeat the British, bartering troops for bottoms. "In all these discussions," he later succinctly said, "the British were bargaining for men to fill their ranks and we were trying to get shipping to carry over our armies."[84]

In the winter of 1917–18, discussion centered upon two competing proposals. Pershing wanted the British to transport six complete divisions to Europe in the first half of 1918. At first protesting that they had not the shipping to do so, the English surprised the Americans in January by announcing that they would find sufficient ships—on condition that the vessels carry 150 battalions of infantry and machine-gunners only, to be integrated into the British Army. Pershing and his staff, their suspicions of British forthrightness no doubt aroused, nevertheless agreed in January to a compromise: the British would provide ships for the six divisions, whose infantry units would take their forward training

82. *Ibid.*, I, 150–54 (italics added); II, 358.
83. Lloyd George quoted in Paxson, *American Democracy and the World War*, II, 66.
84. Pershing, *My Experiences*, I, 269.

in the British sector. Those units would be available to be thrown into the line in an emergency, though subject to recall by the American commander. In addition, Pershing agreed to place four black infantry regiments under French control, where they remained, unique among American outfits, until the Armistice.

Matters uneasily rested until the German offensive of March 21, which revived Allied clamoring for American men, even raw and un-trained if need be, to patch the shredded and shrinking forces at the front. At a dramatic meeting of the Supreme War Council at Versailles on March 27, Pershing flatly rejected such proposals, angrily stalking from the conference room in a rare but effective display of temper. At a subsequent meeting at Abbeville in May, Pershing stonily called Foch's bluff about retreating behind the Loire. Finally, in July, an independent American Army was formed and the amalgamation controversy at last subsided.

The American position in that protracted wrangling had been shot through with traditional fears of Old World deviousness. Amalgamation was principally discussed in the Supreme War Council, to which Wilson, emphasizing his distance from Allied war aims, refused (until the final weeks of the war) to assign a permanent *political* representative. It was left to the American *military* representative on the Council, Tasker Bliss, to present his government's views on amalgamation, even though this issue, as many others the Council took up, had far-reaching political implications. For his part, Bliss had harbored since early in the war the suspicion that the "deliberate desire" of the Allied powers was to "have a million [American] men there and yet no American army and American commander."[85] United States military planners also sus-pected the British of deliberately understating the tonnage actually available for trans-Atlantic troop transport, in order to keep ships ply-ing the supply routes to their peripheral operations in the Middle East and Russia, which were unpopular with the Americans. The suddenly revised British shipping estimates of January, thrust at Pershing as a bargaining counter in the 150-battalion controversy, increased his sus-picions of British candor. President Wilson cautioned at the time that "whatever they may promise now, the British will, when it comes to the pinch, in fact cut us out from some of the tonnage they will prom-ise us."[86] Nor were commercial calculations absent from these exchanges

85. Bliss to Baker, May 25, 1917, quoted in Beaver, *Baker*, 44.
86. Wilson to Baker, Jan. 20, 1918, quoted in Trask, *War Council*, 76.

on ships, for each side feared ceding advantage to the other in the anticipated postwar rivalry for supremacy in the shipping business.[87]

In all this, the American leaders proved themselves faithful sons to their Revolutionary forebears, deeply mistrustful of the machinations of Old World politicians, and determined, even in the face of military necessity, to avoid entanglement in the coils of European corruption. Pershing further evidenced his embrace of the mythic American image of Europe when he described Allied strategy as timid and tired, the product of an effete military establishment that "lacked the aggressiveness to break through the enemy's lines." The American concept of open warfare, by contrast, "was based upon individual and group initiative, resourcefulness and tactical judgment."[88] The idiom was military, but the accent was a familiar one in which Americans for more than a century had congratulated themselves for inhabiting a New World, whose vigor happily contrasted with the declining vitality of the Old.

Yet if Pershing suspected the Europeans, and tended to deprecate both their strategic ideas and their culture, he nevertheless recognized the genuine desperateness of their plight. He never really questioned the need for enormous infusions of American manpower on the western front; the argument had been about their disposition on arrival. Thus in late 1917 he requested thirty divisions to be landed in France by the end of the following summer, a proposal so ambitious that Wilson wondered if such a program were even possible. Six months later, prodded by Foch, Pershing *tripled* his estimates and called for a hundred divisions by the summer of 1919. Secretary Baker moved at once to secure extension of the draft age limits, and the British at last made firm assurances about providing shipping.

And so the Americans came. They trickled slowly at first into Liverpool and Brest and Saint-Nazaire, then flooded the ports with swelling waves in the summer of 1918: 245,000 men in May, 278,000 in June, 306,000 in July. By the end of August, Pershing at last stood ready to play his long-anticipated role on the western front. Yet, by November the war would be over. Pershing's barely bloodied troops would soon be stacking their scarcely used arms.

Generals, it is commonly said, habitually fight the previous war, a maxim to which Pershing, with his attachment to Civil War tactics and

87. See Chapter 6, pp. 324–31.
88. Pershing, *My Experiences*, I, 152.

strategy, was no exception. But the common soldier, too, went to France with his head full of ideas and images from the past. Like so many American public places dominated by monuments to battles fought long ago, the American mind in 1917 was filled with memories of a kind of warfare that would never again be waged. Somehow, medieval notions of battle as an arena for individual heroism, for the display of "chivalry," and "honor," survived virtually intact into the early twentieth century. Those vestigial ideas were found throughout Western culture, as the popular English poems of Rudyard Kipling and Rupert Brooke, to cite but two non-American examples, picturesquely testified. But a romantic view of war had a peculiar hold on the American mind, which still throbbed with memories of the Civil War, memories glowing with the light of righteous glory and echoing with John Brown's hallelujahs.

It is easy to forget how vivid the Civil War seemed to Americans in the World War I era. Many men yet living had fought under Grant or Lee. More men still, especially those of an age to occupy influential positions in American life—including Theodore Roosevelt and Woodrow Wilson—had been impressionable boys when Beauregard's batteries fired on Sumter. They were raised by hearthsides where fathers and uncles passed on the lore of Bull Run and Vicksburg, Chickamauga and the Wilderness, Cold Harbor and the Sunken Road, Antietam and the Bloody Angle. On registration day, June 5, 1917, Wilson addressed a convention of Confederate veterans, and spoke evocatively of "the old spirit of chivalric gallantry." That rhetoric and the attitude toward war it bespoke were comfortably familiar to two generations of Americans; but even while Wilson talked, both the language and the sentiment were as near to death as the graying men he faced.

Many of those aging veterans, and even more of their Union counterparts, remained powerful arbiters of popular values. Among the images they urged the young to regard reverently was that of war as an adventurous and romantic undertaking, a liberating release from the stultifying conventions of civilized society. No one had more eloquently articulated that sentiment than Oliver Wendell Holmes, Jr., a young Civil War officer in the 20th Massachusetts, veteran of Fredericksburg and Antietam, and for thirty years after 1902 a magisterial figure on the United States Supreme Court. Only in war, he told Harvard's graduating class in 1895, could men pursue "the divine folly of honor." From war "the ideals of the past for men have been drawn. . . . I doubt if we are ready to give up our inheritance." War might be terrible when you were in it, he said, but with time "you see that its message was divine."[89] In the generation succeeding Holmes's, the charismatic Theodore Roosevelt whole-heartedly embraced those precepts and preached them to his countrymen with unflagging gusto. What American had not heard the account of the old Rough Rider waving his hat and charging up San Juan Hill, gleefully projecting an image of battle as a kind of pleasingly dangerous gentlemen's sport?

This irrepressibly positive and romantic view of war belonged particularly to an older elite, people like Holmes and Roosevelt: old-stock, Northeastern, often Anglophilic or Francophilic. In his study of prewar American culture, Henry May has called them "the beleaguered defenders of nineteenth-century tradition . . . the professional custodians of culture." From this quarter came some of the strongest pressure both for a permanent system of military training and for American intervention in the war. Almost unanimously, says May, "the leading men of letters, the college presidents, the old-line publishers, the editors of standard magazines, and their friends knew where they stood from the start" in 1914. "Instead of seeing the war as the doom of their culture, they believed it would bring about its revival: the war was a severe but necessary lesson in moral idealism."[90] Thus did Princeton President John Grier Hibben speak of the chastening and purifying effect of armed conflict. Thus did novelist Robert Herrick write of war's "resurrection of nobility."[91] Thus did one of Edith Wharton's characters tearfully meditate on the ancient phrase from Horace: "dulce et decorum est pro patria mori."[92] Thus did countless posters depict Dame Columbia or some other drapeaued goddess benevolently shepherding doughboys into battle. And thus, too, did widely distributed movies like *Pershing's Crusaders* and best-selling books like *The Glory of the Trenches* and *My Home in the Field of Honor* continue to trade in the kind of medieval imagery that popular authors like Walter Scott had for generations seeded in the American mind. Everywhere, the vener-

---

89. Mark A. DeWolfe Howe, comp., *The Occasional Speeches of Justice Oliver Wendell Holmes, Jr.* (Cambridge, Mass.: Harvard University Press, Belknap, 1962), 73–80.

90. Henry F. May, *The End of American Innocence: A Study of the First Years of Our Own Time, 1912–1917* (Chicago: Quadrangle, 1964), 363.

91. Robert Herrick, "Recantation of a Pacifist," *New Republic* 4 (Oct. 30, 1915), 329–30.

92. Edith Wharton, *The Marne* (New York: D. Appleton, 1918), 52.

able custodians of traditional culture spoke as if with a single voice:
war was glorious, adventurous; it was manhood's destiny, a strenuous
and virile antidote to the effete routine of modern life. And, as May has
noted, it was the "young acquaintances of these elder idealists who
were early in the field. The older colleges and the more exclusive prep
schools contributed far more than their share to the volunteer units."[93]
Young men from the most prominent families and the most prestigious
universities fought with the French or the English, joined the Lafayette
Escadrille air unit, or the Norton-Harjes Ambulance Service.[94] It was,
in short, the nation's most carefully cultivated youths, the privileged
recipients of the finest education, steeped in the values of the genteel
tradition, who most believed the archaic doctrines about war's noble
and heroic possibilities.

Of all the young men who so believed, none did more passionately
than Alan Seeger. A 1910 Harvard graduate given to writing florid and
portentous verses, Seeger had gone to Paris in 1912, "in the spirit," says
a sympathetic biographer, "of a romanticist of the eighteen-forties."[95]
Swelling with Byronic yearning for glory ("it is for glory alone that I
am engaged," he wrote) and for a poetic death at an early age, in 1914
he joined the French Foreign Legion.[96] For the next two years, huddled in billets in Champagne, he wrote of the war, in verse, in his
diary, in letters to his family, and in articles sent to the New York *Sun*

93. May, *End of American Innocence,* 365.
94. Organized in March 1915 and privately financed by Americans, the Lafayette
 Escadrille was officered by French commanders and integrated into the French
 military service. The Escadrille was made up mostly of well-to-do young Americans, among them Edmond Genêt, avenging the memory of his ancestor Citizen
 Genêt, who had failed to forge a Franco-American alliance in 1793. See Herbert
 Molloy Mason Jr., *The Lafayette Escadrille* (New York: Random House, 1964).
 Of the several volunteer ambulance units, the most publicized was founded in
 1914 by Richard Norton, son of Harvard professor Charles Eliot Norton. Another
 unit, the American Ambulance Field Service, also attracted many volunteers.
 Among the later celebrated persons who served in one or another of the units
 were Ernest Hemingway, John Dos Passos, E. E. Cummings, and Malcolm Cowley. Most volunteers were college graduates. Harvard supplied 325 ambulance
 drivers, Yale 187, Princeton 181, Dartmouth 118, Cornell 105, the University
 of California 68, Stanford 54, and Columbia 48. See Charles A. Fenton, "Ambulance Drivers in France and Italy: 1914–18," *American Quarterly* 3 (1951),
 326–43.
95. William Archer, introduction to Alan Seeger, *Poems* (New York: Scribner's,
 1917), xxi.
96. Alan Seeger Diary, Sept. 1, 1915, Seeger Papers, Houghton Library, Harvard
 University, Cambridge, Mass.

and the *New Republic.* He was, he said candidly, "of a sentimental and romantic nature." His writing alternated between lyrical tributes to the charms of the French countryside and awe-filled descriptions of the grandeur of war. "Will never forget the beauty of this winter landscape," he noted in his diary, "the delicate skies, the little villages under their smoking roofs. Am feeling perfectly happy and contented."[97] He was no less happy to hear "the magnificent orchestra of war" in an artillery cannonade, and he wrote his mother: "You have no idea how beautiful it is to see the troops undulating along the road in front of one in *colonnes par quatre* as far as the eye can see with the captains and lieutenants on horseback at the head of their companies."[98] "What is Virgil's line," he mused, "about the pleasure it will be sometime to recall having once done these things . . . ? I pity the poor civilians who shall never have seen or known the things that we have seen and known. . . . [T]he sense of being the instrument of Destiny is to me a source of greater satisfaction." This, he said, was "the supreme experience."[99]

Men of Holmes's and Roosevelt's generations could recognize those sentiments as kindred to their own, and they also found familiar the language in which Seeger expressed them. When he spoke of undulating lines of troops led by men on horseback, he conjured visions of battle as a panoramic pageant with skirling pipes and streaming gonfalons, "the battalions in maneouvre, the officers, superbly indifferent to danger, galloping about on their chargers."[100] At times his diction was even more frankly archaic, as when he wrote in "A Message to America":

> Not by rough tongues and ready fists
> Can you hope to jilt in the modern lists.[101]

When Seeger was killed in 1916, the custodians of culture instantly transformed him into America's first genuine war hero. His uplifting descriptions of war, cast in the literary conventions of the medieval romance, admirably fitted their own views. Indeed, so admirably did Seeger suit the tastes of the traditional keepers of culture that in 1915 they were already calling him America's Rupert Brooke (the English

97. Seeger Diary, Dec. 22, 1914, Seeger Papers.
98. Seeger to Mother, Oct. 17, 1914, Seeger Papers.
99. Seeger Diary, June 15, 1915; and Seeger to "Harry," June 28, 1916, Seeger Papers.
100. Alan Seeger, *Poems,* xxxviii.
101. *Ibid.,* 163.

poet who died earlier in the war). They completed the comparison by prematurely announcing Seeger's heroic demise in October 1915. When he died in fact on July 23, 1916, some were so eager to invest his memory with all the symbolic freight it would bear that he was often erroneously said to have met his fate—that would have been the phrase—on the Fourth of July.[102]

Seeger's poems were published soon after his death, to extravagant praise from established critics, and his *Letters and Diary* was released to the public the following summer. Theodore Roosevelt, the hero of "A Message to America" ("I would go through fire and shot and shell . . . if ROOSEVELT led"), eulogized him in appropriately archaic accents as "gallant, gifted young Seeger." A Wellesley student surpassed even the medieval metaphors of the dead poet himself: "Had he lived in centuries past," she wrote, "he would have lived a knight, true to his 'idols—Love and Arms and Song.' In the twentieth century he still lived as true as was possible to those idols. So he will live in our hearts—Alan Seeger, Knight."[103]

Seeger's was the authentic voice of late nineteenth-century American high culture, and it spoke powerfully of war's ennobling glory. Other writers couched a similar message in a more popular idiom. Robert W. Service, for example, in *Rhymes of a Red Cross Man*, sang of the

> . . . dream that War will never be ended;
> That men will perish like men, and valour be splendid;
> . . . .
> That though my eye may be dim and my beard be hoary,
> I'll die as a soldier dies on the Field of Glory.[104]

When Hiram Johnson read Service's poems to his family in the evenings, "all of us at times have been rather choked up." When he read them to his fellow Senators, he said, "you could have heard a pin drop."[105]

Seeger's *Poems* and Service's *Rhymes* were both best sellers in 1917,

102. Archer, for example, so gives the date of death in his introduction to Seeger, *Poems*, xliv.

103. Theodore Roosevelt to Raymond Price, Jan. 4, 1917, copy in Seeger Papers; Elizabeth Virgin Trump, *Wellesley College Magazine*, June 1918, clipping in Scrapbook No. 3, Seeger Papers.

104. Robert Service, "The Song of the Soldier-Born," in *Rhymes of a Red Cross Man*, Book Four of *The Complete Poems of Robert Service* (New York: Dodd, Mead, 1942), 179–80. Quoted with permission of Dodd, Mead, and Ernest Benn, Ltd. (*The Song of the Soldier-Born,* © Germaine Service, 1960. Published by Ernest Benn, Ltd.).

105. Johnson to Meyer Lissner, Sept. 17, 1917, Johnson Papers.

as was Arthur Guy Empey's "Over the Top," a runaway success that sold 350,000 copies in its first year of release and was later made into a movie. Empey became a featured speaker at countless Liberty bond rallies. Those developments no doubt pleased his publisher, George Haven Putnam of G. P. Putnam's Sons, a founder of the pro-preparedness National Security League. "Over the Top" was a go-get-'em confection in the Richard Harding Davis vein, a snappy autobiographical account of the New Jersey boy's adventures with the British Army in France. Disappointed that his own country had been "too proud to fight" after the sinking of the Lusitania, Empey went to England to become a "Tommy." Though his account of his exploits among the English was replete with condescending national comparisons—British trains had "matchbox" cars; Americans had "energy and push," the English mere "tenacity"—Empey clearly intended to convey affection for the British soldier and sympathy for the Allied cause. "Tommy Atkins," he said, "has proved himself to be the best of mates, a pal, . . . a man with a just cause who is willing to sacrifice everything but honor in the advancement of the same. It is my fondest hope," he added, "that Uncle Sam and John Bull, arms locked, as mates, good and true . . . will wend their way through the years to come, happy and contented in each other's company.[106]

Empey provided the American public with a kind of primer on life at the front. In a bright, wisecracking style, liberally sprinkled with colorful British Army slang, Empey recounted his initiation into British Army ways, his arrival at the front, his first encounters with "Fritz" (the Germans), his wounding in a trench raid, and his trip back to "blighty" (home). The narrative was not without its accounts of horrors and of gut-grinding fears. In a grudging and stiffly jocular way, Empey even admitted to tears at the death of a mate: "I, like a great big boob, cried like a baby. I was losing my first friend of the trenches."[107] But the tone of "Over the Top" was overwhelmingly positive. Even the scenes of terror and fright could not really terrify or frighten, so briskly were they related, and so swiftly did they sink beneath the glinting surface of Empey's quick-paced story. With unrelenting good humor, Empey portrayed the war as a kind of thrillful sporting adventure, where all the players, on his side at least, were good fellows who knew

106. Arthur Guy Empey, "Over the Top" by an American Soldier Who Went (New York: Putnam's, 1917), v–vi.
107. Ibid., 55.

how to "die game."[108] In the climactic battle scene, Empey was wounded, but his outfit "took the trench and the wood beyond, all right."[109] The story faithfully followed the formula of the popular adventure tale: men expired with athletic grace, the hero proved his manhood by receiving a wound in virtual hand-to-hand combat, as convention required, and in the end his fellows triumphantly seized their objective.

The message was insistently upbeat, and lest his American readers miss its significance, Empey candidly said in his closing pages that he dreamt of the day "when the boys in the trenches would see the emblem of the 'land of the free and the home of the brave' beside them, doing its bit in this great war of civilization." For the boys in the trenches, he said, "the spirit of sacrifice is wonderful." Moreover, "for all the suffering caused this war is a blessing to England—it has made new men of her sons; has welded all classes into one glorious whole." War, he concluded, was "not a pink tea but in a worthwhile cause like ours, mud, rats, cooties, shells, wounds, or death itself, are far outweighed by the deep sense of satisfaction felt by the man who does his bit."[110] The language was less elevated than Seeger's, but the meaning no less affirmative of war's virtues.

From accounts like these, many departing doughboys formed expectations of what awaited them in France. An affirmative and inspiring attitude toward war, preached by guardians of tradition like Holmes and Roosevelt, nurtured by popular writers like Seeger and Empey, filled men's imaginations in 1917. That attitude was sufficiently strong to counter three years of news and propaganda about the atrocities of modern warfare; it was strong enough, even, to temper men's natural fear of death. Historian William L. Langer, for example, went to war as a young man in 1917, and later recalled with wonder "the eagerness of the men to get to France and above all to reach the front."

> One would think that, after almost four years of war, after the most detailed and realistic accounts of murderous fighting on the Somme and around Verdun, to say nothing of the day-to-day agony of trench warfare, it would have been all but impossible to get anyone to serve without duress. But it was not so. We and many thousands of others volunteered. . . . I can hardly remember a single instance of serious discussion of American policy or of larger war issues. We men,

108. *Ibid.*, 255.
109. *Ibid.*, 260.
110. *Ibid.*, 279–80.

most of us young, were simply fascinated by the prospect of adventure and heroism. Most of us, I think, had the feeling that life, if we survived, would run in the familiar, routine channel. Here was our one great chance for excitement and risk. We could not afford to pass it up.[111]

John Dos Passos recollected similar sentiments from 1917: "We had spent our boyhood in the afterglow of the peaceful nineteenth century. . . . What was war like? We wanted to see with our own eyes. We flocked into the volunteer services. I respected the conscientious objectors, and occasionally felt I should take that course myself, but hell, I wanted to see the show."[112]

Brimming with eagerness and enthusiasm, hundreds of thousands of young men embarked in 1917 and 1918 upon what Theodore Roosevelt alluringly called the "Great Adventure." Secretary Baker consciously strove to model the stateside training camps on "the analogy of the American college," and countless contemporary observers noted the keen sense of schoolboyish anticipation and excitement that infected the fresh recruits. "As in similar encampments," said one trainee, "Fort Sheridan was alive with enthusiastic recruits, with an atmosphere somewhat like that of a college campus on the eve of a big game."[113]

Even more than college boys, the young men in the Army were to be protected from wickedness and vice. Temperance crusaders, long devoted to changing the nation's drinking habits, were at war's outbreak riding a wave of recent successes. By 1917 nineteen states had adopted prohibition, and the increasingly powerful Anti-Saloon League was pressing for a prohibition amendment to the federal Constitution. Passionate "drys" shuddered at the opportunities for debauchery that army life might put in the path of the nation's manhood. Their political muscle helped convince the War Department to ban the sale of liquor in the vicinity of the training camps, and to forbid (on paper at least) any man in uniform from buying a drink. These measures imparted further momentum to the temperance cause, and contributed to the ratification of the Eighteenth Amendment in 1919.

111. William L. Langer, *Gas and Flame in World War I* (New York: Knopf, 1965), xviii.
112. John Dos Passos, *One Man's Initiation: 1917* (Ithaca, N.Y.: Cornell University Press, 1969), 4–5.
113. Ira Berlin, ed., "A Wisconsinite in World War I: Reminiscences of Edmund P. Arpin, Jr.," *Wisconsin Magazine of History* 51 (1967), 6.

The Army also undertook a campaign against sexual vice that had substantial influence on postwar life. The American Social Hygiene Association had urged as early as 1914 that the public be educated about venereal disease, though the Association cautioned that the effort should go forward "conservatively and gradually . . . without impairing modesty and becoming reticence in either young or old."[114] Despite widespread concern about the debilitating effects of the "social disease," little had happened by 1917 to advance the Association's cause. Then the Army, determined to get the maximum number of "effectives" from the mass of inductees, and not troubled by questions of modesty, launched a great anti-VD campaign. It assigned the task to the Commission on Training Camp Activities (CTCA), a consortium of civilian service organizations, like the YMCA, Knights of Columbus, and Jewish Welfare Board, that worked under official Army auspices. Wanting results, the Army and the Commission cared little for reticence, and they minced no words about sexual matters. Speaking frankly of "balls" and "whores," one CTCA pamphlet carefully explained that wet dreams were normal and that masturbation, common folk wisdom notwithstanding, would not lead to insanity. The clear implication was that natural emission, or even masturbation, was greatly preferable to potentially infectious liaisons. In the same vein, the Commission placarded the camps with posters proclaiming: "A German Bullet is Cleaner than a Whore." Pamphlets urged sexual purity in the name of patriotism: "How could you look the flag in the face," asked one, "if you were dirty with gonorrhea?" "A Soldier who gets a dose," warned a poster, "is a Traitor!"

The campaign continued with the doughboys in France. The Commander in Chief gave special attention to the venereal report every morning, and venereal infection was made a matter for discipline. "Keeping our men clean," said Pershing, was a matter of the highest importance, "not only from the standpoint of effectives, but from that of morals." But, as elsewhere, Pershing's efforts in the battle for sexual purity were hampered by what the general daintily termed "the difference between the French attitude and our own."[115] In February 1918,

---

114. The discussion that follows is based substantially on "The Other War," a 1962 paper by Larry Kincaid, presented in Eric Goldman's "World War I Seminar" at Princeton University. I am grateful to Professor Goldman for allowing me to see a copy of Mr. Kincaid's paper.

115. Pershing, *My Experiences*, II, 43; I, 177.

Premier Clemenceau magnanimously offered to help establish licensed houses of prostitution, customary in the French army, for what he obviously regarded as the long-suffering American troops. Pershing passed the letter containing the offer to Raymond Fosdick, head of the CTCA. Fosdick, in turn, showed Clemenceau's letter to Secretary Baker, who reportedly exclaimed: "For God's sake, Raymond, don't show this to the President or he'll stop the war."[116] The Americans declined this bit of gracious Gallic generosity, and continued to mete out stern punishment to soldiers suffering from VD. The Army congratulated itself that the campaign drastically lowered the venereal infection rate among the doughboys. The educational drive had further import as well. For many young men, the Commission's pamphlets, films, and lectures no doubt constituted the first thorough sex education they had received. Surely very few had ever been exposed to such frank and open scientific discussion of matters about which the society had been notoriously mute. In its own blunt way, the Army contributed to the demythologizing of erotic life by bringing sexual matters into the arena of public discourse, which was to become a characteristic feature of twentieth-century American culture.

The Army cooperated less eagerly with another social experiment in 1917–18: intelligence testing and classification by mental ability of men who passed through the training camps. Testing people's intelligence was a novel procedure in the prewar era. First developed by French psychologist Alfred Binet in the early years of the century, the method was adopted and improved by Stanford University's Lewis Terman in 1916, and became known in the United States as the Stanford-Binet test. When America entered the war, the American Psychological Association pressured the War Department to use the tests to screen mental incompetents from the Army and to classify all inductees on the basis of their intelligence. Not incidentally, this plan would provide the professional psychologists with data-sets of previously undreamed-of size, the raw material for countless further studies.

The Army at first responded tepidly to these "mental meddlers," as one general called them. But by early 1918 trained psychological examiners were posted to all the camps. There they administered thousands of "alpha" tests to the literate inductees, and "beta" tests to the illiterate. The results were used to designate the recruits "superior,"

116. Quoted in Coffman, *War To End All Wars*, 133.

"average," or "inferior," so that personnel officers might then select potential officer trainees and distribute the remainder of the men proportionately, with reference to their tested intelligence, throughout the various units.

The testers were struck by the extent of illiteracy their examinations revealed—as many as 25 percent of the draftees could be so classified. Examiners were also unsettled by the meager educational backgrounds of the recruits. Most enlisted men had left school between the fifth and seventh grades. The median number of years of education ranged from 6.9 for native whites and 4.7 for immigrants to 2.6 for Southern blacks. In one large sample of native white draftees, fewer than 18 percent had attended high school, and most of those men had not graduated. The typical enlisted soldier, concludes one student, was "an ill-educated unsophisticated young man . . . the opposite of the Harvard boys who volunteered for ambulance duty before America entered the war."[117]

The psychologists were less surprised by their correlation of test performances with racial and national backgrounds. Invariably, men from "native" or "old" immigrant stock scored heavily in the "superior" range, while draftees from "new" immigrant backgrounds fell disproportionately into the "inferior" category. More than half the Russian, Italian, and Polish draftees, for example, showed up as "inferior." Nearly 80 percent of the blacks who took the alpha test were labeled "inferior," and their illiteracy rates were significantly higher than those for whites.

The psychologists, striving for scientific objectivity, denied that their examinations were biased toward certain educational or cultural backgrounds, or toward a particular kind of scholastic skill. Yet it may be doubted whether the native intelligence of recent immigrants or poor rural blacks was fairly tested by questions about the authorship of "The Raven," the talents of the painter Rosa Bonheur, or the city in which the Overland car was manufactured—all standard queries on the alpha test.[118] These examinations were the crudest devices of an infant psychological "science" that even in its maturity has not escaped criticism

117. Baldwin, *American Enlisted Man,* 50–91.
118. Yerkes, *Psychological Examining in U.S. Army;* for a general discussion, see Daniel J. Kevles, "Testing the Army's Intelligence: Psychologists in World War I," *Journal of American History* 55 (1968), 565–81. Test results indicated that 47 percent of white draftees and 89 percent of black were "morons" by the definition then prevailing. Yet this revelation, rather than prompting a redefinition of terms, primarily contributed to fears about the menace of the "feeble-minded." See Baldwin, *American Enlisted Man,* 76.

on grounds of cultural bias. The Army, to its credit, never lost its suspicion of the psychologists, and ended the testing program at the first opportunity, January 1919. But what the Army rejected, the nation's educational system eagerly adopted in the postwar era, as intelligence testing became a familiar procedure in the schools. And to many old-stock, white Americans, the widely publicized results of the wartime tests conveniently reinforced their already disparaging appraisal of the new immigrant groups and blacks.

Forewarned about disease, tested and labeled, introduced to the manual of arms, trained to drill, drill, drill, fitted out with a new-fangled safety razor (the war would change the shaving techniques of a generation), and saddled with packs, the doughboys marched out of the camps and up the ramps of the ships of the "Atlantic Ferry." Most left from Hoboken, and nearly half sailed in British vessels. A lucky few cruised in some style on the *Leviathan*, the former Hamburg-American luxury liner *Vaterland*, impounded in New York harbor since 1914, and in 1917 seized and made to carry troops to battle against the men who built her. Others traveled on various Cunard ships and American ocean liners, but a great many were shipped in converted freighters, hastily refitted, stark, and dirty. "Assigned quarters on lower deck," said a private put on board the British ship *Kashmir;* "the blackest, foulest, most congested hole that I ever set foot into."[119] On arrival in France, the men were shoehorned into the notorious "40-and-8's"—diminutive French railway freightcars supposedly able to carry 40 men or 8 horses —and rumbled slowly away from the ports along the choked rail system to their forward training areas in the interior of France. Once off the train, the men began to walk, and for many it must have seemed that they walked forever. *Stars and Stripes* found no more fertile subjects for humor than the length of hikes and the weight of packs. Billetted in widely scattered areas that required lengthy walks to training facilities, and prodded by officers under orders not to let the troops become restless while Pershing's idle army grew to sufficient size, the men

119. Diary of Eugene Kennedy, May 26, 1918, Eugene Kennedy Collection, Hoover Institution. A few men died on the ships, some of them from anthrax, carried in the horsehair of their newly issued shaving brushes. See *Literary Digest,* 59 (Nov. 9, 1918), 23. In the end, disease claimed more soldiers' lives than did battle. The most common killer was pneumonia, a complication of the influenza epidemic in the fall of 1918 that brought death to nearly 50,000 doughboys and perhaps ten times that many American civilians.

moved constantly—often, it seemed, just to be moving. As the diary of one reads:

> Sat. June 22, 1918: Left Colembert in A.M. and hiked with full packs about 7 kilos to Bellebrune.
>
> Wed. June 26, 1918: Hiked with full packs back to Colembert.
>
> Thur. June 27, 1918: Hiked back to Bellebrune.
>
> Sat. June 29, 1918: Hiked with light packs about 14 kilos to gas school.
>
> Wed. July 3: Hiked about 20 kilos to Bouinngues.
>
> Thur. July 4: Hiked 10 kilos to riffle range.
>
> Fri. July 5: Hiked 18 kilos to Buysschure.
>
> Sat. July 6: Hiked 15 kilos to Oudezeele.[120]

The doughboys spent most of their time in this way until the spring of 1918. Then, in March, German General Ludendorff began the first of a series of offensives, thrusting his armies down the scarred valleys of the Somme, the Oise, the Aisne, and the Marne, in a last desperate drive to burst the western front and end the war. Pershing allowed a few American units to be thrown in under Allied command to brace the buckling French and British lines, and the green American troops fought recklessly but well at Cantigny in late May, and at Château-Thierry and Belleau Wood in June. Perhaps 70,000 Americans had tasted battle by mid-July. The last German drive was checked on July 18, and the initiative passed from Ludendorff to Foch, who immediately took the offensive with vigorous counter-attacks. Foch also at last ordered the establishment of an American First Army, and assigned it to move into the front to the French right, in the sector stretching from near Verdun to the Vosges Mountains. It was now becoming Pershing's kind of war. His gamble for time was about to pay off. The Allies had held back the Germans long enough to permit the assemblage of a great American force in France. It now entered the line, fresh and huge, just as Foch prepared to administer the war's decisive blow against the badly battered foe.

120. Kennedy Diary, June 22 to July 6, 1918.

4

Over There – and Back

The methodical Foch at first intended to press the exhausted Germans back along the five-hundred-mile front that stretched from Flanders to the upper Rhine. The American role in this grinding operation would be to remove the German salient behind Saint-Mihiel, a thorn that had festered for nearly four years in the French flank, then to sweep farther east to Metz, on the Moselle River, and finally to inflame the long-silent front from Metz and Nancy to Switzerland. This assignment well suited Pershing's tactical preferences. Once the wooded heights of the salient were taken, his armies could spill down onto the broad Woevre Plain, an attractive theater for the employment of mobile tactics. Pershing looked forward eagerly to "action on a larger scale between the Meuse and the Moselle."[1]

But before the attack could be launched, Pershing's expectations were thwarted. In early August 1918 British troops near Amiens, crouching behind clanking tanks, had slashed widely and deeply into the enemy line. The mauled Germans had begun a systematic retreat. British Field Marshal Douglas Haig therefore proposed that the Western powers hit hard at the reeling German forces in the center of the front, rather than open up a new battle area to the east. Foch's strategy of slowly squeez-

1. John J. Pershing, *My Experiences in the World War*, 2 vols. (New York: Frederick A. Stokes, 1931), II, 245.

191

ing the "Hun" out of France might give the enemy precious time to regroup and dig in along a new line of defense, perhaps along the Rhine. Haig called instead for simultaneous stabs by the British toward Maubeuge and by the French and Americans toward Sedan, which would cut the German lateral communication lines along the Antwerp-Metz railroad. Foch accepted Haig's suggestion and changed Pershing's orders. The American General was not to strike east toward Metz, but was to prepare for a joint Franco-American thrust northwest toward Sedan. The American First Army would advance through the corridor bound by the Meuse River on the east and by the Argonne Forest and Aire River on the west.

Pershing acknowledged the strategic soundness of this action, though it presented him with several problems. Most obviously, it menaced the independence he would have had in the relatively detached eastern sector, where the Americans had been preparing to fight. Foch, whose staff had long counseled that the American army was a "comparatively weak asset," welcomed Haig's proposal in part because it would keep Pershing on a short leash.[2] Even at this late date, Pershing had to argue heatedly to retain the bulk of his units under his own command; Foch continued to request that some of the American divisions scheduled to take part in the Metz offensive be transferred to French control in the Aisne region. The altered battle plan also deprived Pershing of the opportunity to conduct under optimum conditions the kind of open warfare that he favored. He would now have his principal encounter with the enemy not on the expansive Woevre Plain but in the treacherous Meuse-Argonne area, where the broken terrain would impede swift forward movement, and was too narrow for classic flanking maneuvers.

Most immediately, cancelling the Metz objective meant that the reduction of the Saint-Mihiel salient lost much of its strategic justification. Leaving the salient untouched might jeopardize the rear of the upcoming Meuse-Argonne offensive, but that was a manageable risk. Pershing even considered abandoning the Saint-Mihiel campaign altogether, but eventually concluded that it should go forward because "I believed that its capture by the Americans would immensely stimulate Allied morale."[3] Thus the logic of the first independent American action, even

2. "Note for Colonel Fagalde," translation of a French General Staff memorandum on American military assistance enclosed in W. Kirke to Secretary, War Cabinet, Jan. 27, 1918, War Office, Directorate of Military Operations and Intelligence: Papers (WO 106/467), Public Record Office, London, Eng. (hereafter PRO).
3. Pershing, *My Experiences,* II, 254.

before the event, had passed from the realm of hard strategy into that of psychology.

Above all, a victory at Saint-Mihiel would impress the troublesome Foch, buttressing Pershing's ceaseless effort to play a significant military role with his own command. Accordingly, the American General took no chances. Behind the jump-off line on the rain-drenched night of September 11, 1918, he amassed over 100,000 French troops and nearly half a million mostly unbloodied doughboys, poised to overrun half their number of battle-torn Germans. Stumbling through dark, dripping woods, guided only by his hand on the pack of the man ahead, one enlisted man topped the crest of a hill at exactly 1:00 a.m. on September 12, and "saw a sight which I shall never forget. It was zero hour and in one instant the entire front as far as the eye could reach in either direction was a sheet of flame, while the heavy artillery made the earth quake." Another foot soldier remembered that the barrage was so heavy and constant he could read a newspaper by the light of muzzle blasts from the gun batteries massed behind him.[4]

Strangely, there was almost no answering German artillery fire. When the first great wave of troops shoved off at 5 a.m., they encountered only token resistance. By nightfall the attackers had raced past their scheduled objective for the first day. Early the following morning they captured Vigneulles, in the heart of the salient. On September 16, four days after it began, the battle for Saint-Mihiel was finished.

Pershing exulted in his dramatic victory. He had stunningly vindicated his doctrine of frontal attack in mass force, wiping out in four days a position that had menaced the French for almost four years. The superiority of American arms was irrefutably demonstrated, and Pershing's claim on an independent command secured.

Or so it appeared to the Americans. French and British military observers were considerably less impressed. They noted that the American divisions still lacked important auxiliary units. Not a single artillery piece of United States manufacture had been fired in the preparatory barrage in the early hours of September 12, and only half the gun crews were American. Pershing might justifiably answer that this deficiency owed to the nature of the shipping program, tailored to meet the pri-

4. Diary of Eugene Kennedy, Sept. 12, 1918, Eugene Kennedy Collection, Hoover Institution on War, Revolution and Peace, Stanford University, Stanford, Ca. (hereafter Hoover Institution); Harvey A. DeWeerd, *President Wilson Fights His War: World War I and the American Intervention* (New York: Macmillan, 1968), 335.

ority demand of the Allies for manpower rather than material. But the fact remained that Pershing's ability to conduct a self-sustained operation was severely compromised by his dependence on Allied ordnance.[5]

Nor did the speed of the American infantry advance, on close examination, constitute unqualified proof of Pershing's adeptness at mobile warfare. Intelligence officers soon learned that the Germans had given ground so quickly because the attack had caught them in the midst of a planned evacuation. The Americans had flung their enormous force on the backs of a retreating army.

Worse, despite their vaunted preference for mobile tactics, the Americans appeared pitifully unable to organize rear support for a fast-moving battle line. In the set-piece part of the operation—the positioning of troops and guns before the battle—the Americans had performed effectively. But the behind-the-lines confusion after the fighting had started appalled Allied officers. The offensive could have moved even more quickly, noted a French observer, "but the army was immobilized after the first 12 hours by inexperience in reorganizing under battle conditions."[6] When French Premier Georges Clemenceau arrived to visit the liberated areas, he saw firsthand the chaos in the American sector. Caught in an immense traffic jam in the American rear, he never did reach his destination.

Pershing had taken his physical objective but he had not yet conquered the skeptical minds of his Allied military colleagues. They remained deeply dubious about the fighting effectiveness of the American

5. Though the bloodletting of trench warfare had decimated French and British ranks by 1917, the Allies had not suffered commensurately in material terms. Indeed, the Allied insistence on amalgamating American troops gained much of its plausibility from the claim that amalgamation was the most effective way to make immediate use of the great productive capacity of Allied industry. Equipping a separate American army would lead to duplication of effort and lost time. The AEF in fact purchased more of its supplies in Europe than it shipped from the United States. America, in short, was no "arsenal of democracy" in World War I; the American doughboy in France was typically transported in a British ship; wore a steel helmet modeled on the British Tommy's, and fought with French ordnance. Of the nearly 3500 artillery pieces received by the AEF, for example, fewer than 500 were made in the United States. One lasting consequence of American reliance on French fieldpieces was the reclassification of American artillery according to the metric system. Similarly, only a handful of American-made airplanes saw action at the front; American fliers went aloft in British and French machines. See DeWeerd, *President Wilson Fights His War*, 207–8.

6. "Notes on American Offensive Operations," from information received from French sources, n.d., WO 106/528, PRO.

army, though the success at Saint-Mihiel did brace the morale of their weary men at arms. The victory also inflated—perhaps dangerously— American self-esteem. "[T]he most unfortunate part of an otherwise successful operation," concluded an observing Frenchman, "was that it confirmed the American High Command in an exaggerated estimate of the efficiency of the American military machine—and of their ability to control it."[7]

In the now imminent Meuse-Argonne offensive, American troops would pay dearly for those illusions in the high command. But to a large extent Pershing's problems were not of his own making. His logistical difficulties were compounded by the proximity, in both time and space, of the Saint-Mihiel and Meuse-Argonne operations. Because of Foch's revised plans, Pershing had a fortnight to mount two large attacks with the same army, on battlefields lying at right angles to one another about sixty miles apart. Only three rutted roads connected the two sites, and all movement had to be under cover of darkness. Hence it was small wonder that monumental congestion clogged the American lines of supply, forced as they were to run across one another in an already cramped space. Conditions grew so desperate that soldiers assigned to road control had to brandish revolvers to keep men and vehicles moving.[8]

Nor did the terrain favor the American attackers. They faced a twenty-four-mile front dominated by the heights of the Meuse River on the right and the Argonne Forest and the bluffs of the Aire River on the left. The rolling country between these boundaries was bisected by a long north-south shoulder of land with its high point at Montfaucon, and laterally traversed by another ridge-line near Romagne. This topography greatly advantaged the defending Germans. Entrenched in the area for four years, they had established excellent observation posts and emplaced well-registered gun batteries on all the commanding heights. An attacking force would be subjected to murderous enfilade as it proceeded up the two defiles to either side of Montfaucon. And along the contours of the Romagne heights bristled the most formidable of the three German defense-in-depth lines, the Kriemhilde Stellung.

But Pershing possessed advantages of his own. The American attack would be coordinated with Allied assaults from Flanders to Verdun, leaving the enemy little opportunity to concentrate his scarce reserves

7. *Idem.*
8. Pershing, *My Experiences,* II, 255; "Notes on American Offensive Operations."

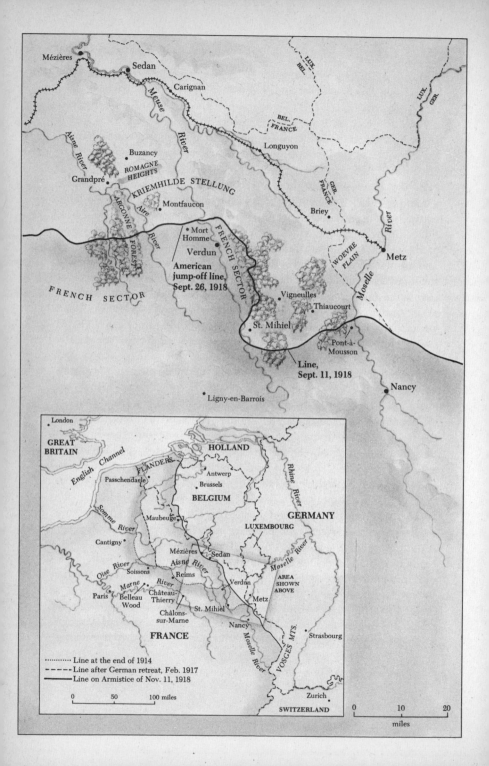

Mézières

Sedan

Carignan

LUX.
BEL.

BEL.
FRANCE

LUX.
GER.

Longuyon

Meuse River

Buzancy

ROMAGNE
HEIGHTS

Grandpré

Aisne River

ARGONNE FOREST

KRIEMHILDE STELLUNG

Aire River

Montfaucon

Mort
Homme

Verdun

FRENCH SECTOR

**American jump-off line,
Sept. 26, 1918**

FRENCH SECTOR

Briey

GER.
FRANCE

Moselle River

Metz

WOEVRE
PLAIN

Vigneulles

Thiaucourt

St. Mihiel

Pont-à-
Mousson

**Line,
Sept. 11, 1918**

Nancy

Ligny-en-Barrois

0   10   20

miles

on a single sector. The five German divisions facing Pershing were undermanned and disspirited, while his own force was more than eight times larger and enjoyed high morale. Even the cancelled drive toward Metz worked to Pershing's benefit, for the Germans had positioned their few available reserves in anticipation of a continuation of the Saint-Mihiel campaign to the east. Speed was therefore a crucial element in Pershing's battle plan. He must catch the Germans off guard, and overwhelm their formidable defense before reinforcements could be brought up. Massed force and swift movement remained Pershing's tactical trumps.

On the night of September 25, the last doughboys moved into position across the nightmarish landscape northwest of Verdun. The siege of 1916 had left the face of the earth here incredibly scarred. For endless acres, not a bush nor even a blade of grass protruded from the shell-churned soil. Rats scratched through the darkness, their dragging bellies fat from feasting on the human offal buried in the reeking mud.[9] At 5:30 a.m., the Americans pushed off into a dense fog. Pershing's plan called for outflanking the high position of Montfaucon and reaching the Romagne heights, ten miles from the starting point, on the first day. Penetration of the Kriemhilde Stellung was to follow on the next morning. The doughboys swept quickly across the old no man's land—one of its principal map reference points was a hill appropriately named Mort Homme, or Dead Man—and the contrast between their quick movement and the devastated deadness passing beneath their boots seemed all the proof needed of the superiority of open warfare over trench tactics.

But the success of that initial movement was delusory. By nightfall the American drive had been effectively halted well short of the Romagne heights, along a line that bulged menacingly in the center around the still untaken prominence of Montfaucon. For several days the advance could only inch forward. Once again the American supply and support units proved incapable of keeping pace with the relatively deep initial penetration of the attack troops. From September 30 to October 4 virtually the entire army had to pause in order to restore communication and control. The Germans used the interval to move reserves into the battle area.

Pershing, so long critical of the immobility of the French, now found

9. See, for example, Ira Berlin, ed., "A Wisconsinite in World War I: Reminiscences of Edmund P. Arpin, Jr.," *Wisconsin Magazine of History* 51 (1967), 23.

himself dunned by Foch to resume the attack. The Supreme Commander also proposed to relieve Pershing of responsibility for his flanks in the Argonne Forest and along the banks of the Meuse, where the American attack had gone especially badly. Pershing was able to fend off this harassment from Foch when he at last breached the Kriemhilde Stellung on October 14—seventeen days later than his initial battle plan had called for.

The American drive now again ground to a near standstill on the slopes of the Romagne heights. For nearly two weeks Pershing could force his lines forward only a few hundred bloody yards per day. Meanwhile, the French and British to the north, fighting on a considerably broader front than the Americans, were making much swifter headway. Frustrated by the stalemate in the American sector, Premier Clemenceau wrote testily to Foch that "our worthy American allies, who thirst to get into action and who are unanimously acknowledged to be great soldiers, have been marking time since their first jump. . . . Nobody can maintain that these fine troops are unusable; they are merely unused."[10] The Premier suggested that Foch appeal directly to President Wilson for Pershing's removal from command. When Pershing years later found out about this request, he dismissed it as "purely a political gesture designed to minimize America's prestige at the peace conference."[11] That, it probably was. Foch, in any case, could see no military advantage in ousting the American commander during what was certainly the war's last campaign. Ignoring Clemenceau's request, he replied with an explanation of the difficulties the American army had encountered in the Meuse-Argonne.

Those difficulties were abundant. Disease had begun to winnow the American ranks, as the world-wide influenza epidemic licked its way into the sopping trenches. Yet the problems of the American army owed at least as much to deficiencies in training and previous battle experience as they did to Dame Nature and to enemy resistance. Some of the men thrown into the forward battle areas in September had been drafted only in July. Pershing had wanted his men to have six months of training in the States, two months in France, and one month in a quiet sector before being exposed to battle. That standard had been roughly maintained until the accelerated troop shipments begin in mid-

10. Clemenceau to Foch, Oct. 21, 1918, quoted in DeWeerd, *President Wilson Fights His War,* 353.
11. Pershing, *My Experiences,* II, 355.

1918. Then the rush to France sucked men ever faster through the camps, across the sea, and into the line. The average doughboy at the Meuse-Argonne had seen perhaps four months of training in camp. Many had seen but a few weeks. Some had been cycled so swiftly from induction center to war zone that they had never handled a rifle, and had to be given a quick ten-day course of instruction upon arrival in France. Other than the "veterans" of Saint-Mihiel, virtually none had ever seen a modern battlefield before the morning of September 26.

Under these circumstances, confusion was guaranteed. Officers frequently lost control of units under their command. The most famous instance involved the so-called "Lost Battalion," an infantry unit that advanced beyond its logistical, artillery, and flanking support in the Argonne Forest in early October and was soon surrounded by Germans. Trapped for five days without food or other provisions, the battalion was rescued after suffering casualties of nearly 70 percent.

On the extreme left of the American sector, units of the black 92nd Division particularly suffered from poor preparation and the breakdown in command control. As the only black combat division, the 92nd entered the line with unique liabilities. It had been deliberately dispersed throughout several camps during its stateside training; some of its artillery units were summoned to France before they had completed their courses of instruction, and were never fully equipped until after the Armistice; nearly all its senior white officers scorned the men under their command and repeatedly asked to be transferred; the black enlisted men were frequently diverted from their already attenuated training opportunities in France in the summer of 1918 and put to work as stevedores and common laborers.

Discipline was severe for all black troops in France. In Bordeaux, unruly black dock workers were herded into a "bull-pen," forced to sleep on cracked limestone rocks, and doused every morning with an ice-cold shower.[12] Four regiments of the incomplete U.S. 93rd Division were brigaded with the French army, which later decorated three of the regiments with Croix de Guerre unit citations. But the French liaison officer at Pershing's headquarters bowed to white American pressure in August 1918 and cautioned French officers not to overpraise black troops, not to treat black officers as equals, and not to allow frater-

12. Berlin, ed., "A Wisconsinite in World War I," 18.

nization among French civilians and black soldiers—which might "spoil the Negroes."[13]

These measures hardly increased the effectiveness of the black fighting units. Yet in the Argonne offensive, the 92nd Division's 368th Regiment was assigned at the last minute to the French Fourth Army, on Pershing's left flank, and given the mission of maintaining liaison between the French and American forces during the advance. It was a tricky assignment that called for close communication and complex coordination. But the inexperienced regiment was provided with insufficient artillery support, was short of wire-cutting implements, and even lacked adequate maps. Battalion commanders repeatedly lost contact with their men, and more than once the forward troops broke and ran for their own lines upon meeting the enemy. The entire 92nd Division was removed in disgrace from the front. Courts-martial convicted five officers of cowardly misconduct in the face of the enemy, and the prejudice against using black combat troops seemed spectacularly confirmed. Forgotten was the valor and competence of the black regiments of the 93rd Division who had fought so well with the French.

Clemenceau's irritation with Pershing turned in large part on the contrast he observed between the behavior of the doughboys under American command and those brigaded with the French and British. Allied military observers sounded this note again and again in 1918. American troops under Allied command "have done splendidly," said a French military report in October, but "owing to inexperience, particularly in the higher ranks, American divisions employed in large blocks under their own command, suffer wastage out of all proportion to results achieved, and generally do not pull more than a small fraction of their own weight." The blame for this sorry state of affairs could be laid to Pershing's "insisting on the premature formation of large American armies."[14] The British cabinet was informed on October 21, 1918, that "The American Army is disorganized, ill-equipped and ill-trained with very few non-commissioned officers and officers of experience. It has suffered severely through ignorance of modern war and it must take *at least a year* before it becomes a serious fighting force."[15]

13. Arthur E. Barbeau and Florette Henri, *The Unknown Soldiers: Black American Troops in World War I* (Philadelphia: Temple University Press, 1974), 114–15; see also Edward M. Coffman, *The War To End All Wars: The American Experience in World War I* (New York: Oxford University Press, 1968), 231–33.
14. "Notes on American Offensive Operations."
15. War Cabinet meeting, Oct. 21, 1918, Appendix II, 210, War Cabinet Papers (CAB 23, Vol. 14), PRO (italics added).

Criticism of "wastage" from the architects of the siege of Verdun and the slaughter on the Somme had an ironic ring. Ironic, too, was the British estimate at the end of October that it might take a year to develop a serious American fighting capacity. In fact, the war was already all but over. On October 3 the new German government, at the request of its military commanders, had appealed to President Wilson for an armistice. By the end of October, Bulgaria, Turkey, and Austria-Hungary had left the war. Almost the entire American offensive in the Meuse-Argonne verged on anti-climax. When Pershing resumed the attack on November 1, it was against a manifestly defeated foe in full flight back toward the German frontier.

Even in pursuit the American army betrayed its inexperience. Sedan lay in the path of advance of the French Fourth Army on Pershing's left; but the American General badly wanted this prize to fall to American arms. As both the French and the Americans accelerated behind the fleeing Germans, there developed a race for Sedan. Some of Pershing's divisional commanders determined to beat not only the French but their own American colleagues. They directed soldiers from the First Division to leave their positions in the center of the American sector and, incredibly, to pivot across the front of the still advancing divisions on their left. This was a military atrocity of the first order: the intermingling American units could easily mistake one another for the enemy. On the night of November 6, in fact, a First Division patrol briefly detained a 42nd Division brigade commander, Douglas MacArthur. When the traversing American troops began to intrude on the French zone, the French commander threatened them with artillery fire. Fortunately for the Americans, the Germans were too preoccupied in removing themselves from the area to exploit this fantastic disarray in the American ranks. The French finally took Sedan.

On November 11 the war was over. For many doughboys, it had barely begun. Some could not believe the end had come. "It sounds like B.S. to me," wrote a sergeant in his diary.[16] But as the big guns stayed silent and the confirming reports came in, disbelief gave way to relief and exuberance. By evening all knew the Armistice to be real. Many built fires, forbidden when the front was embattled, as much to beat the chill as to celebrate. "Talk about fellows hollering," wrote a Washington state draftee; "they certainly had some time. You could build a fire at night and we sure enjoyed it." Others watched as the sky

16. Dixon Wecter, *When Johnny Comes Marching Home* (Boston: Houghton Mifflin, 1944), 257.

flashed endlessly with Very lights and colored star shells, fired in wild profusion by rejoicing artillery batteries on both sides of no man's land. Still others were too tired to care. "Some fellows discharged their arms in the court yard," read the journal of a corporal who was "bunked in a fine big chateau," enjoying his first night off duty in two months. "But most of us were too well pleased with dry bunk to get up."[17]

Until the end of his days Pershing insisted that the Saint-Mihiel and Meuse-Argonne offensives had demonstrated the value of the distinctly American tactic of a highly mobile attack in overwhelming strength. But the facts suggested that Pershing's favorite tactical ploy worked best when directed at the receding backs of a retreating foe. When the enemy chose to stand and fight, as he had across the center of the Meuse-Argonne corridor, motion and mass proved incompatible. Swift attacks might achieve small penetrations here and there, but further exploitation by larger elements was repeatedly frustrated. Conversely, a mass force might be quickly moved a short distance, but was inevitably tugged to a halt by the dragging anchor of its cumbersome supply lines to the rear. The real lesson of the Meuse-Argonne was the same grim lesson learned by the European combatants in four years of trench warfare: in a modern, technologically sophisticated land battle between large forces of equal strength, a breakthrough was exceedingly difficult to effect and almost impossible to sustain.

The forty-seven days of the Meuse-Argonne had also demonstrated the obsolescence of Pershing's belief that the lone infantryman with his rifle remained the ultimate instrument of war. A handful of heroic riflemen did stand out. Alvin C. York, armed only with a modified Enfield rifle and a Colt .45 sidearm, singlehandedly killed or captured nearly one hundred and fifty Germans in one day. Samuel Woodfill, squeezing off single rounds from his trusty Springfield, annihilated several five-man German machine-gun crews in a daring raid on the Kriemhilde Stellung. Pershing praised these exploits lavishly, and later named York and Woodfill, along with "Lost Battalion" commander Major Charles Whittlesey, honorary pallbearers at the interment of the Unknown Soldier. But both these cases were clearly exceptional. York, a converted conscientious objector from Tennessee, was a mountain marksman who had been drilling bullets into targets and turkey heads from

---

17. William H. Barney to Agnes Wright Spring, Dec. 22, 1918, Agnes Wright Spring Collection, Hoover Institution; Kennedy Diary, Nov. 9–11, 1918.

the time he was a boy. Woodfill, a Regular Army veteran whose Springfield was practically part of his anatomy, had as a youth toted a musket
through the woods of Kentucky. Most of the civilian city-boys in the
AEF, however, handled a rifle about as effectively as they would a
broomstick. They were no match for the chattering Spandau guns that
cut them down like cornstalks in a field. Allied observers remarked
with sadness the frequent sight of American rifle companies lying dead
in regular lines.[18] No amount of "individual initiative" could compensate for inadequate training, poor command control, and inexperience.

The Allies found much more to criticize about the AEF. They noted
that green troops in the Argonne had exaggerated the opposition and
had hesitated to advance. When the troops did move forward, they
were handicapped by the poor performance of their artillery batteries.
American gunners were ill-trained to provide the close support of a
creeping barrage, and hence tended to favor long-range fire of dubious
effect.[19] Loose discipline further hampered the American attack, as
small bodies of troops scattered themselves about, under no apparent
control. "Gypsy-like bivouacs" dotted the landscape, with "men stealing
bread off ration lorries, men leaving work to raid the Y.M.C.A., every
wagon and lorry covered with men who should be walking." Straggling
was so severe a problem that a continuous line of military police fine-
combed the rear to keep men moving forward. Ironically, many of the
problems of the AEF stemmed from the fact that it moved too quickly.
Many soldiers were reduced to looting and foraging to feed themselves
when supply columns stalled far in the rear. Worse, eager doughboys
sometimes overran German forward defenses so rapidly that they failed
to mop up properly—leaving still lethal machine-gun nests in their
rear.[20]

But nothing struck Allied observers more emphatically than the sheer
prodigiousness of the American operation. "One is much impressed with
the extravagance of the Americans," reported a British officer, "both in
men and material. For any particular work they seem to have about
five times as much of both as we do." When American engineers were
on the job, remarked an observer, there seemed to be more men than

18. DeWeerd, *President Wilson Fights His War*, 323.
19. "Notes on Argonne Operations," by British Army observer General Wagstaff,
    Sept. 28, 1918, WO 106/530, PRO.
20. *Idem*, and "Notes on American Offensive Operations"; on stragglers, see
    DeWeerd, *President Wilson Fights His War*, 345; on foraging, see Kennedy
    Diary, Oct. 9, 13, 14, 17, 24, 1918.

road. The same approach applied to combat. The AEF had an immense numerical superiority over the Germans in the Meuse-Argonne, and made most of its advances simply by smothering the enemy with flesh. One American commander estimated that ten of his men perished for every dead German.[21]

When the German Supreme Command determined on September 29 to sue for an armistice, they were primarily reacting not to Pershing's advance in the Meuse-Argonne but to the far more successful French and particularly British attacks in the north. The AEF was at that time safely contained in front of the Kriemhilde Stellung, where in fact it remained stalled for more than a fortnight. Pershing never did reach his ultimate objective, the Antwerp-Metz rail line. His contribution to the final victory thus owed far less to his strategic success than to the simple calculus of attrition. German reserves were exhausted. However much punishment the AEF might absorb in the Meuse-Argonne, Pershing had wave after wave of fresh reinforcements to throw into the line, and still more millions ready to come from across the Atlantic. No matter how skillful the enemy's defense, he could not for long endure this costly confrontation that was engaging and slowly but certainly destroying one fourth of his troops on the western front. As the American First Army Chief of Staff wrote in late October 1918, "The gaining of ground counts for little, it is the ruining of his army that will end the struggle."[22]

There was bitter irony in the fact that attrition, not mobile strategy, proved to be Pershing's greatest contribution to the western cause. But the American Commander in Chief nevertheless had reason to be proud. The presence of the AEF had been indispensable in freeing the Allied reserves that made the counter-offensive of 1918 successful. Pershing's triumph at Saint-Mihiel had at a crucial moment lifted the morale of the Allies and equally dampened that of the Germans. He had clung tenaciously, though under a thousand pressures, to his concept of an independent American army—a concept that may have posed military problems but that was most prudent from the standpoint of politics and diplomacy. His men for the most part did not want for courage. Their errors and losses on the battlefield were largely attributable to their lack of preparation and to the inexperience of their officers. Per-

21. "Notes on Argonne Operations"; DeWeerd, *President Wilson Fights His War,* 345.
22. Quoted in Coffman, *War To End All Wars,* 338.

shing knew this. He had planned to use his troops in force only in the anticipated final campaign in the spring of 1919. At Allied insistence, he had prematurely thrust his raw and ill-trained army into the Meuse-Argonne, and it had suffered for its greenness. But the AEF's exertions in 1918 undoubtedly helped shorten the war by perhaps as much as a year, and helped, therefore, to avoid still further bloodletting on both sides. This, as the guardians of the older culture who had cheered the doughboys off from Hoboken might have said, was a worthy sacrifice.

Two million men served in the AEF. The experience struck nearly all of them as an extraordinary moment in their lives—while they passed through it, and when they later remembered it. That they considered it an extraordinary interlude at the time is evidenced by the diaries and journals and strikingly "literary" letters so many of them wrote during their period of service. Americans in 1917, especially those of the age and class who qualified for the AEF, were not the diary-keeping people they had once been. Yet thousands of men who had never before recorded in writing their daily doings, and never would again, faithfully kept journals while they were in the Army. Most of these records began with induction and ended with discharge, neatly delineating the time spent in uniform as a peculiar interval, a moment stolen from ordinary life and forever after sealed off in the memory as a bundle of images that sharply contrasted with "normal" experience. The reactions to France and to war were, of course, as varied as the men who recorded them. But even a modest sampling of the personal documents left behind—a few of them published, many deposited in libraries, more still passed down reverently as family heirlooms to later generations—reveals common responses to the shared enterprise, and common conventions of perception and language to which these men resorted in the effort to comprehend their experience and relate it to others.

They were, first of all, as much tourists as soldiers. Later reflections, governed by the masculine need to emphasize prowess at martial exploits, would tend to blot that fact from the record. But the average doughboy spent more peacetime than wartime in France. And, though as many as 1.3 million Americans came under enemy fire, few saw sustained or repeated battle. Virtually none was subjected to the horror and tedium of trench warfare for years on end, the typical lot of the European soldier. The Americans fought no major defensive battles.

Their two chief engagements were relatively brief, mobile attacks in the closing weeks of the conflict.

Hence, to a remarkable extent—remarkable at least when compared with the war writings of European combatants—the doughboys' accounts deal with topics other than war. It was AEF policy to rotate leave zones "in order to give all an equal chance to see as much of France as possible."[23] Most coveted of all were the pink tickets that permitted a trip to Paris. *Stars and Stripes* felt obliged to caution arriving troops against the "oo-la-la" idea of France as a great tourist playground. Too many men, said the journal, came over "expecting to find a sort of international Coney Island, a universal pleasure resort."[24] "We have been all over France and seen and learn [*sic*] a lot," said one awestruck New Yorker.[25] After the Armistice, the Army organized sporting events and provided educational opportunities for the idle troops. It also endlessly compelled them to solve "problems"—sham attacks against an imaginary enemy. Many men fought more of these mock battles than real ones. One long-suffering soldier reported in April 1919 that "every hill in this vicinity has been captured or lost at least ten times."[26] But the same enlisted man spoke the sentiments of many when, describing his post-Armistice leave to Nice and Monte Carlo, he called it "the most important event in my life over here (from a social standpoint)."[27]

Like previous generations of their traveling countrymen, the doughboys were impressed with the *age* of the Old World. "Its old cathedrals, chateaux and ancient towns have been quite wonderful to my eyes so accustomed to the look of the New World," said one.[28] In countless diaries and letters the soldiers dwelt on the quaint antiquity of this town, or that church or chateau, their imaginations especially fired by the evocation of names from the history books. "The church here," wrote another doughboy, "is very, very old, probably built sometime in the 12th or 13th century. Saint Louis the Crusader, King of France, attended service there on three occasions and Jeanne d'Arc was there several times."[29] "The architecture for the most part seems to represent

23. *Stars and Stripes,* Feb. 8, 1918, 1.
24. *Ibid.,* Feb. 22, 1918, 4.
25. John F. Dixon to "Sister," received Aug. 5, 1918, Anna Russell Collection, Hoover Institution.
26. Eugene Kennedy, letter to Lancaster (N.Y.) *Enterprise-Times,* May 22, 1919, 3, Kennedy Collection.
27. *Ibid.,* 1.
28. Edward B. Egan to Mrs. Martin, June 29, 1918, Russell Collection.
29. Jacob Emery Diary, Aug. 3, 1917, Jacob Emery Collection, Hoover Institution.

a period several hundred years past," wrote another. "We are living, for the present, in barracks built about the time of Louis XIV, though no one here knows anything about them prior to Napoleon."[30]

The France they described was rich with history, an old country inhabited by old people. No observation of French life was more common than remarking the elderly women in black who seemed to be the only residents of the ruined towns behind the front. A tired people in a blighted land, the French pursued antiquated ways. "My but the people are old fashioned," observed one enlisted man. "They still harvest with cradles and sickles. Once in a while you see a binder or mower. I've never saw [sic] a real wagon, they use carts."[31] All signs, in short, confirmed the American myth of the Old World as an exhausted place, peopled by effete and even effeminate races. All this, of course, served as a useful foil for the image of American energy and "pep." "What an impression our boys are making on the French," enthused Raymond Fosdick, head of the Commission on Training Camp Activities. "They are the greatest lot of sheer boys you ever saw. . . . The French, who love to sit and meditate, are constantly gasping at the exuberance and tirelessness of our fellows."[32] "Never was there such a spectacle in all history," exclaimed a New York Times correspondent, "as that of the fresh millions of free Americans flocking to the rescue of beleaguered and exhausted Europe."[33]

But if Europe was exhausted, it was still splendid to behold. Numerous accounts expressed rapt wonder at the sheer physical beauty of France. "Picturesque" was perhaps the most commonly used word in these descriptions. One is struck too by the frequency of panoramic portraits of nature, of efforts to translate a long sweep of the eye into a string of words. If sunrise and sunset were the characteristic themes in the writings of trench-bound British troops in Flanders, as Paul Fussell has observed in his study The Great War and Modern Memory, it was the panoramic landscape that most attracted the eye of Americans.[34]

30. Otis Emmons Briggs Diary, Mar. 4, 1918, Otis Emmons Briggs Collection, Hoover Institution.
31. William H. Barney to Agnes Wright Spring, Aug. 27, 1918, Spring Collection.
32. Raymond Fosdick to family, June 9, 1918, Fosdick Papers, Firestone Library, Princeton University, Princeton, N.J.
33. Quoted in Charles V. Genthe, American War Narratives, 1917–1918 (New York: David Lewis, 1969), 56.
34. Paul Fussell, The Great War and Modern Memory (New York: Oxford University Press, 1975), 51–69.

There were good reasons for these divergent motifs. In the flatness of
Flanders, sunup and sundown provided the only natural relief from the
monotonous landscape. And twice-a-day British stand-to's on the trench
firing step, year after year, in season and out, were timed to take advantage of the long silhouetting light when the sun was low on the
horizon. But the American troops, by contrast, were doubly "summer
soldiers." They were not only civilians temporarily in uniform, but the
bulk of them came to France in the late spring and summer months of
1918. Behind the front, at least, the forests were indeed verdant, the
fields aripple with grain, the roadsides in bloom. "The country is green
and covered with flowers. It is a continuous garden," said a soldier
who arrived in April 1918.[35] Moreover, again unlike the British, the
American troops were on the move, all the way across France from
ports on the Bay of Biscay to their training areas in the north and east.
They traversed the rolling country of north-central France, and when
they at last saw their assigned portion of the front it ran along the
undulating hills from Verdun to the Vosges. From the prominence of
Montfaucon, for example, one could easily see in clear weather virtually
the entire American battle line on the Romagne heights, stretching several miles from east to west. Even the seasons and the terrain conspired
to sustain an image of France as a kind of grand open-air arena suited
to staging battles of operatic movement and theatrical visibility.

Common to many Americans' perceptions of France was a sense of
ceremony, which often had religious overtones. *Stars and Stripes* declared that France was "holy ground," and that more than once in history the French "at Chalons, at Tours, at the Marne—'saved the soul of
the world.' "[36] To many of the doughboys, the great war in which they
were now engaged amounted to a ritual reenactment of those historic
dramas. To the largely Protestant Americans, the exotic rites of French
Catholicism fittingly exemplified the ceremonial attitude they deemed
appropriate to the occasion. Alan Seeger had noted that "the Catholic
religion with its idealization of the spirit of sacrifice makes an almost
universal appeal in these times," and many members of the AEF agreed
with him.[37] The "Marseillaise," too, had the power to "set you quiver-
ing." When French religion and patriotic music were combined, the

35. Briggs Diary, Apr. 14, 1918, Briggs Collection.
36. *Stars and Stripes*, Feb. 22, 1918, 4.
37. Alan Seeger Diary, June 29, 1915, Alan Seeger Papers, Houghton Library,
    Harvard University, Cambridge, Mass.

effect was deeply moving.[38] One American soldier attended high mass on Bastille Day, 1918, and a band at the flag-draped church played the "Marseillaise": "Rene, talk about throwing up your hat and shouting 'To Hell with the Kaiser.' The scene and music impressed me so much that I could hardly get my breath. I cannot describe how grand the whole thing was."[39]

Time and again in the personal narratives of these touring provincials one suddenly hears a different voice. The rough and often wise-cracking American idiom abruptly gives way to a grandiloquent tone that speaks, for example, of the "red-tiled roofs resplendent in the sunlight, resembling huge cameos set conspicuously on the vine covered slopes."[40] This strange diction was the language of the tourist brochures, or of the ubiquitous YMCA guides who shepherded the gawking troops about the various sights. It was not a natural voice. Those wondrous foreign scenes often exceeded the native American capacity for authentic speech, and the confrontation with the unfamiliar was thus almost automatically rendered in clichés and highly stylized prose. To a significant degree, the same was true of descriptions of the war itself.

Reverence toward France and the "cause" was not carried over to the Army. Fellowship of arms gave certain consolation, but the physical conditions of life and the restrictions of the military regime were constant causes of complaint. Most pestiferous were the lice—"cooties"— that occasioned frequent trips to the delousing stations, and almost daily "shirt readings," or close inspections of clothing for nits. Equally wearing on men's bodies and spirits was army food—or lack of it. In vivid contrast with the wooden descriptions of tourist sights are the lively and lavish descriptions of those rare meals eaten somewhere— anywhere—other than the military mess. The careful recording of menus, indeed, took up a great deal of space in many soldiers' diaries and letters. Men frequently noted losses of more than ten percent of their body weight in the weeks after arrival in France. These accounts confirmed Field Marshal Haig's observation that the Americans "hardly knew how to feed their troops."[41] They also suggest that undernourishment may have dulled the fighting effectiveness of the AEF.

38. Jacob Emery to Mother, May 14, 1917, Emery Collection.
39. Joe Downey to "Rene," July 14, 1918, Russell Collection.
40. Eugene Kennedy, letter to Lancaster (N.Y.) *Enterprise-Times*, May 22, 1919, 1, Kennedy Collection.
41. War Cabinet meeting, Oct. 21, 1918.

But the worst feature of military life was the discipline. Military hierarchy and subordination chafed against ingrained American values of equality and individualism. Anti-German propaganda harped on the supposedly slavish subservience of the "Hun" in order to enhance an image of the German soldier as an eminently bayonetable alien. The American resentment of martial authority could be found in all ranks, and sometimes manifested itself in striking ways. Even a pillar of traditional authority such as once and future Secretary of War Henry L. Stimson complained to his diary, while a staff officer in France, that "I am getting a little tired of kow-towing to regulars just because they are regulars."[42] On the returning troop carriers in 1919, the doughboys enacted a ritual "funeral of Sam Browne." To the throaty cheers of the enlisted men, the officers solemnly marched to the ship's rail and threw their leather girth-and-shoulder "Sam Browne" belts, hated symbols of military caste, into the sea.[43] Even the hierarchy of different services prompted resentment, as infantry officers often took potshots at airborne American pilots, the elite and haughty "Knights of the Air." "It is just a gesture of irritation at the air service," opined the commander of an observation balloon squadron, "something like boys throwing a rock at a limousine which is dashing by when they are having to work."[44]

Long idle behind the lines, and then only briefly exposed to battle, the great mass of the American soldiers in France were spectators in the theater of war. They had come to see the "Big Show," and were not disappointed. Nothing in that show was more exciting than the aerial battles. Men approaching the front strained their eyes and ears for signs of aircraft, more out of curiosity than fear. Always they referred to aerial "duels," or "wonderful air battles," or "thrilling air fights." One balloonist described seeing "Richthofen's *circus.*" The famed "Red Baron's" formation approached, "some of the planes with red bodies, and they fly along with some planes climbing and some dropping and give the effect of being on the rim of a giant wheel which is rolling thru the sky."[45]

Artillery fire, too, provided visual spectacle on a colossal scale. In the rear training area, reported one young officer, "the most fun is going

---

42. Henry L. Stimson Diary, No. 4, entry for June 12, 1918, Stimson Papers, Sterling Library, Yale University, New Haven, Conn.
43. Wecter, *When Johnny Comes Marching Home,* 297.
44. Birge Clark, "World War I Memoirs," Nov. 9, 1918, typescript in Green Library, Stanford University, Stanford, Ca.
45. *Ibid.,* Oct. 19, 1918.

out to the artillery range." There, secure in a bomb-proof observation shelter near the target, "you can see the shot appear as a little black speck and follow it down to the earth when it bursts."[46] In the battle area, the long-range guns were usually registered on specific targets, and their effects could be safely observed from beyond the target perimeter. Seen from this distance, the discharge noise partly dissipated, the artillery blasts blended into the natural beauty of the landscape itself: "Later another boy and I from section C walked out to the tip of the strip of woods, where we could see the French guns firing and watch the German replies. The shrapnel was exploding harmlessly over a meadow perhaps 500 yards away from us. In the air you would see a sudden noiseless puff of brown smoke which hung very close together for some time after the explosion, then quite a perceptible time later would come the whistle and then the report. It was all very unreal and spectacular."[47]

But the big guns also brought death. Worse, they brought it without warning, from an unseen distance. In descriptions of shelling, one occasionally finds the faintly dawning realization that modern military combat was something quite different from what the eager troops had been led to expect. And its worst feature was its impersonality. Many men wrote of their sense of outraged helplessness while being shelled. Indeed, "shell shock" may have had as much to do with this feeling of impotence as it did with the physical effects of concussion. Even the irrepressible Alan Seeger found bombardment "distressing," because he was "being harried like this by an invisible enemy and standing up against all the dangers of battle without any of its exhilaration or enthusiasm."[48] William Langer wrote that shellfire "has always seemed a bit unfair to me. Somehow it makes one feel so helpless, there is no chance of reprisal for the individual man. The advantage is all with the shell, and you have no comeback."[49] Enduring shellfire often prompted fantasies of bloody personal reprisal. As one draftee wrote: "we cannot fight artillery. Jerry is a rotten sport. . . . Poor Frank Carr, he was hit with a shell and broken all up. I'll remember that and when it comes my time to run a bayonet into one of the skunks I'll look to heaven and cry out to Frank to watch me do the job up."[50]

46. *Ibid.*, Apr. 15, 1918.
47. Emery Diary, Aug. 3, 1917, Emery Collection.
48. Alan Seeger to Father, Dec. 11, 1914, Seeger Papers.
49. William L. Langer, *Gas and Flame in World War I* (New York: Knopf, 1965), 24.
50. Joe Downey to Brother Jim, Aug. 29, 1918, Russell Collection.

But negative notes in the contemporary reactions to the war were relatively rare. What most strikes the reader of these personal war records is their unflaggingly positive, even enthusiastic, tone. Seeger's sanguine reflection that war was affording him "the supreme experience" was reiterated countless times by those who followed him to France. Raymond Fosdick, arriving overseas during the German offensive in the spring of 1918, wrote that he was "having an experience . . . which dwarfs anything I have ever lived through or seen before. . . . I am just back from a four days' trip at the Front. . . . Needless to say I had a wonderful time—a most exhilarating time—at moments, a most exciting time."[51] One volunteer wrote from France in mid-1917 that "I never enjoyed life as much as I have since I have been over here and if one must be killed to enjoy life—Well. It has already been a wonderful thing for me." After the Armistice the same man could only reflect "what a glorious adventure it has all been to me."[52]

These expressions of exhilaration, wonder, and glory are notable not only for what they say but also for the way in which they say it. The sights of France elicited mostly tourist-brochure boilerplate from the doughboy writers. Similarly, the war itself seemed to overwhelm the power of the imagination to grasp directly, and of language to describe authentically. It is not especially surprising to find Stars and Stripes assuring a soldier-reader that he was the "spiritual successor" to "the Knights of King Arthur's Round Table."[53] But it is to be remarked when countless common soldiers wrote privately of themselves in the same vein. American war narratives, with unembarrassed boldness, speak frequently of "feats of valor," of "the cause" and the "crusade." The memoirs and missives penned in France are shot through with images of knight-errantry and of grails thrillingly pursued. A truck driver in the aviation section of the AEF exclaimed that "war's great caldron of heroism, praise, glory, poetry, music, brains, energy, flashes and grows, rustles and roars, fills the heavens with its mighty being. . . . Oh! War as nothing else brings you back to the adventurous times of old."[54] One of Lillian Wald's "boys" from the Henry Street Settlement proudly announced his enlistment in the "battle to throw down the shackles of Honensollern [sic] and Junkerism."[55]

51. Raymond Fosdick to family, May 30 and June 9, 1918, Fosdick Papers.
52. Emery Diary, Aug. 5, 1917, and Nov. 11, 1918, Emery Collection.
53. Stars and Stripes, Feb. 22, 1918, 4.
54. Quoted in Genthe, American War Narratives, 95.
55. Benjamin Fromberg to Lillian Wald, Feb. 8, 1918, Wald Papers, Butler Library, Columbia University, N.Y.

The ghost of Alan Seeger, and of the nineteenth-century literary conventions he exemplified, haunted these and innumerable similar passages. Faced with the unfamiliar reality of modern war, many young American soldiers tried to comprehend it in the comfortably familiar verbal formulae of their childhood storybooks. In the homeliest lines scribbled by the humblest privates, the war was frequently couched in language that appears to have been lifted verbatim from the pages of G. A. Henty or, more often, those of Sir Walter Scott. That language echoed, however pathetically, the epic posturings of George Creel and the elaborately formal phrasing of Woodrow Wilson. Those accents may ring strangely in the modern ear, but they flowed easily from the tongues and pens of the doughboys in 1918. The ubiquity of that idiom, from the White House to the trenches, suggested a widely made equation between the official and the personal definitions of the war's significance. If the war was to redeem Europe from barbarism, it would equally redeem individual soldiers from boredom; if the fighting in France was the "Great Adventure," the doughboys were the great adventurers; if Creel and Wilson could speak of the "Crusade," then it followed that American troops were crusaders. Not only did many doughboys accept without reflection the official definition of the war's meaning, but, perhaps more important, they translated that meaning into their understanding of their personal experiences, and described those experiences in language transported directly from the pious and inflated pronouncements of the spokesmen for traditional culture. That language pervaded all the vast "literature" produced during the war by members of the AEF.

British troops, eager and exuberant in 1914 and 1915, had at first written of the war in much the same archaic idiom. But they were soon made to see the skull of death beneath the smiling skin of life. As Paul Fussell writes, that "innocent army fully attained the knowledge of good and evil at the Somme on July 1, 1916."[56] There, the Germans inflicted nearly 60,000 casualties on the first day of the British attack; succeeding weeks of the abortive campaign would see casualty lists climb to ten times that number on each side. Haig thereafter settled his armies into the appallingly costly warfare of attrition that the French and Germans had already made infamous at Verdun, and "the possibility that the war might be endless began to tease the mind near the end of 1916."[57]

56. Fussell, *Great War and Modern Memory*, 29.
57. *Ibid.*, 71.

One of the casualties of that warfare was a manner of speech, language itself, the very medium of thought and expression used to comprehend war. The formal phraseology with which the earlier English writers had described battle began to give way. In its place came new images, new diction—indeed, suggests Fussell, a wholly new phase of the literary cycle, in which irony displaced mimesis as the dominant form of understanding.[58] Fussell argues that this transformation marked the passage of English literature from a "low mimetic" phase, in which the hero's power of action had typically approximated the reader's (as in the nineteenth-century novel), to an "ironic" modern phase, in which the protagonist's power of action is less than that of the reader, who has the sense of looking down on scenes of frustration or absurdity (as in many twentieth-century novels and plays).

Fussell additionally observes that British war writing was couched in the conventions of proscenium theater, conventions appropriate "for a war settled for years into fixed positions."[59] All three of the great English war memoirists—Robert Graves, Edmund Blunden, and Siegfried Sassoon—confessed "to entertaining the idea or the image of the war's literally lasting forever."[60]

Those developments on British battlefields and in British literature had no American analogues. Saint-Mihiel was not the Somme, and even Pershing's agonies in front of the Kriemhilde Stellung fade before the enormities of Haig's punishment in Flanders. Almost never in the contemporary American accounts do the themes of wonder and romance give way to those of weariness and resignation, as they do in the British. The narrative devices most characteristic of American war novels were adopted not from proscenium theater but from cinematic film—a source more appropriate to the American experience of movement and rapt incredibility.[61] And while the American narratives may occasionally reflect on the immenseness and incomprehensibility of the war's evil, they much more often crackle with positive excitement—what the authors themselves would be likely to call "zest" or "peptomism." "Our boys went [to] the battle field last night singing," recorded a Regular Army veteran; "you can't beat them they are surely [a] game and happy bunch."[62]

58. *Ibid.*, 35, 311ff.
59. *Ibid.*, 220.
60. *Ibid.*, 73.
61. *Ibid.*, 221.
62. John F. Dixon to Sister, Aug. 5, 1918, Russell Collection.

No doubt the objective circumstances of the AEF's relation to the war helped to sustain this cheerful attitude: the season and the terrain, the lateness and brevity of American belligerency, the relatively open warfare that characterized action all along the front in the final weeks when the American army at last saw combat. But one should note, too, the precise character of American good cheer, the imaginative constructs in which it found expression. English war writing showed the heavy impress of the long and rich tradition of English literature. *The Oxford Book of English Verse* traveled in many a Tommy's rucksack to the trenches, and provided a fund of literary models and allusions in which the scene at the front could be mentally encompassed. By contrast, says Paul Fussell, "American writing about the war tends to be spare and one-dimensional," devoid of allusion, without the shaping mold of tradition to give it proper form. Of Seeger's most famous poem, "I Have a Rendezvous with Death," Fussell notes that it "operates without allusion, without the social instinct to invite a number of canonical poems into its vicinity for comparison or ironic contrast."[63]

This is a telling observation, but it can be carried too far. The canon of English literature, after all, had not been unburdened in the British Isles. It had been exported in bulk to the United States, and consumed avidly by generations of readers (the doughboys may have carried few copies of *The Oxford Book of English Verse,* but *Stars and Stripes* carried Kipling's poems on page one). Thus, in one sense American war writing was different from British only in that its life cycle was truncated. It sprang from the same sources but never, or only later, completed the cyclical devolution from mimesis to irony that British writing accomplished. In another sense, the contemporary American war literature was more attenuated than the British: it drew on a narrower range of allusions, traced its literary lineage to fewer forebears. Why this should have been so is a question whose pursuit would carry well beyond the boundaries of the present subject. But suffice it to say that, Fussell notwithstanding, the contemporary American imaginative response to the war unmistakably took its inspiration from a branch of English literature: the medieval romantic tale. To be sure, the immediate source of this inspiration was most often the nineteenth-century author Sir Walter Scott, a "popular" writer perhaps not of "canonical" stature. But at the level of popular culture, the mind-set of the great mass of doughboys, Scott's influence was prodigious—and lasting.

63. Fussell, *Great War and Modern Memory,* 158.

Raymond Fosdick showed Scott's tutelage, for example, when he wrote: "I saw one of our divisions going into action the other afternoon. . . . The men had decorated their helmets with red poppies from the fields and they swept by like plumed knights, cheering and singing. I could have wept not to be going with them."[64] Heywood Hale Broun, a correspondent for the New York *Tribune*, was still more explicit: "Verdun and Joffre, and 'they shall not pass,' and Napoleon's tomb, and war bread, and all the men with medals and everything. Great stuff! There'll never be anything like it in the world again. I tell you it's better than 'Ivanhoe.' Everything's happening and I'm in it."[65]

Graphic attempts to invest the war with meaning drew from a similar stock of imagery. Cartoons and posters depicted the spike-helmeted Germans as human gargoyles. Against them stood the lantern-jawed doughboys, fighting for the honor of a fair lady—Dame Victory and Dame Liberty were favorites of *Stars and Stripes*, which also counseled its readers "to hold all women as sacred."[66]

In his discussion of British war writing, Fussell concludes that "it is their residence on the knife-edge" between the low mimetic and ironic modes "that gives the memoirs of the Great War their special quality."[67] But the contemporary American accounts reside along a different frontier of the low mimetic mode: the boundary that separates it from the "high mimetic" style of epic, romance, and myth, in which the hero's power of action exceeds that of ordinary people in everyday life.

By war's end, in November 1918, little had happened to dislodge the American imagination from that exotic territory. The Armistice had come so swiftly after Pershing's army at last took the field that many troops in fact registered a desire to continue to dwell in that fantastic landscape. "I have a rather peculiar feeling," wrote one doughboy the day after the Armistice. "Heaven knows I am enormously thankful the war is over, but nevertheless I feel as tho [*sic*] my occupation was entirely gone, and the idea of turning back to civilian life seems like an awful jump. I really have got accustomed to fighting, life in the open, running a balloon company with a lot of men, trucks, etc., and it is going to leave a rather gone feeling for a while."[68] A year later, a

64. Raymond Fosdick to family, June 9, 1918, Fosdick Papers.
65. Quoted in Genthe, *American War Narratives*, 97.
66. *Stars and Stripes*, Feb. 22, 1918, 4. See, for example, cartoons by C. LeRoy Baldridge on May 10, 1918, and Charles Dana Gibson on Feb. 8, 1918.
67. Fussell, *Great War and Modern Memory*, 311–12.
68. Clark, "World War I Memoirs," Nov. 12, 1918.

marine wrote: "I know how we all cried to get back to the States. . . .
But now that we are here, I must admit for myself at least that I am
lost and somehow strangely lonesome. These our own United States
are truly artificial and bare. There is no romance or color here, nothing
to suffer for and laugh at."[69]

For men like these, the war had provided a welcome relief from ordinary life. It had in large measure lived up to the romantic expectations
encouraged by spokesmen for traditional culture like Holmes and Roosevelt. Like the legendary American West, wartime France was a place
where men lived in the open, on the move, in the intensely male com-
radery of adventure and misery and threatening violence. Like the
frontier West, "over there" was a distant land, where men could give
vent to dangerous impulses that must be suppressed in civil society. For
women, by contrast, wartime heroism consisted in preserving their
civilian demeanor. Thus did Raymond Fosdick praise the YMCA girls
and the "Salvation Army lassies" for being "just as cool and calm as if
they were pouring tea at home."[70] This constancy, frequently attributed
to women at the front, bespoke an ideal vision of the true feminine
character. But for many men, the true male character, including the
fancied immemorial imperatives to hunt and to kill, could only be released in war. The mystery and allure of the battleground derived
largely from the fact that it was *not* home. France figured as a kind of
equivalent to Huck Finn's "Territory," a place to light out to in flight
from the artificial constraints of civilized life.

This contrast between civilian problems and military release became
a stock item in the affirmative literature about the war. Even Laurence
Stallings and Maxwell Anderson's play of 1924 *What Price Glory?*,
though it is usually classed with the "disillusioned" literature of protest
against the war, relies on this device. Twice at crucial points in the
plot, as Captain Flagg and Sergeant Quirt deadlock in their rivalry for
the innkeeper's daughter Charmaine, the *deus ex machina* of a summons
to battle breaks the impasse and resolves the dramatic tension.

The war, like the American West, became mythic in the minds of
many who were to remember it. The process of mythicizing began even
before most of the troops had returned home. On February 15, 1919,
Colonel Theodore Roosevelt, Jr., presided over a meeting in Paris of
twenty officers from the AEF. These men formally launched the Ameri-

69. Wecter, *When Johnny Comes Marching Home*, 320.
70. Fosdick to family, June 9, 1918, Fosdick Papers.

can Legion, among whose purposes were "to preserve the memories and incidents of our association in the great war . . . to consecrate and sanctify our comradeship."[71] The Legion, in fact, did not simply spring spontaneously from sentiments like these. It grew from a prewar preparedness society and was subtly encouraged by members of Pershing's staff. They feared that left-wing doctrines might infect the restless troops idled by the Armistice, and that radicalized returning soldiers might link hands with dangerous "bolshevik" elements at home. Far better to promote a "safe" veterans' organization dedicated to commemorating the war and combating reds—which, along with "bonus" agitation, fairly accurately described the bulk of the Legion's activity in the postwar years.

But the ordinary Legionnaires knew little of those designs in the minds of their senior officers. One of the Legion's brilliant organizational strokes was to prohibit military titles, opening membership on an equal footing to all veterans. The Legion thus shrewdly blotted from mind rankling recollections of military hierarchy and discipline, freeing the memory to dwell on more positive wartime themes. And the very name "Legion" perpetuated the romantic idiom in which the official culture had taught the doughboys to think of themselves. (Significantly, the only alternative title seriously proposed for the veterans' organization was "Crusaders.")[72]

The 1923 Pulitzer Prize for fiction went to a novel that encompassed many of the ideas about the war as a romantic realm of male freedom and chivalry: Willa Cather's *One of Ours*. Cather's previous fiction, including *O Pioneers!* and *My Antonia*, had figured the frontier West as a heroic land that was losing its promise and appeal. Claude Wheeler, the hero of *One of Ours*, is a sensitive, prosperous, but frustrated farmer whose vague yearnings can no longer be quelled by the myths of the West. As he sits on the steps of the Colorado State House, watching the sun go down behind the mountains, he broods that "the statue of Kit Carson on horseback, down in the square, pointed Westward; but there was no West, in that sense, any more."[73] There was, however, France, and the war, to which Claude eagerly goes to find fulfillment in a martyr's death.

71. Rodney G. Minott, *Peerless Patriots: Organized Veterans and the Spirit of Americanism* (Washington, D.C.: Public Affairs Press, 1962), 41.
72. Wecter, *When Johnny Comes Marching Home*, 428.
73. Willa Cather, *One of Ours* (New York: Knopf, 1922), 118.

Reviewers complained that Cather had proposed and let the catastrophe of war dispose—a critical flaw in the novel's composition, but a device that appealed to the widespread sense of the monumental anguish of war as a cathartic antidote to the little agonies of ordinary life, and probably did much to ensure the book's popularity. Other critics charged that the war scenes were unrealistic: a "tour de faiblesse," sniffed Gilbert Seldes. Ernest Hemingway grumbled that "Nobody had any damn business to write about it [war], though, that didn't at least know about it from hearsay. Literature has too strong an effect on people's minds. Like this American Willa Cather, who wrote a book about the war where all the last part of it was taken from the action in the 'Birth of a Nation,' and ex-servicemen wrote to her from all over America to tell her how much they liked it."[74]

Despite attacks from some critics, *One of Ours* struck a deeply responsive chord in much of the reading public, as Hemingway grudgingly acknowledged. And the sentiments it commemorated, which translated the "official" meaning of the war into an intensely personal idiom, continued to resonate vibrantly throughout American culture long after the Armistice. Charles Fenton found in the writings of Norton-Harjes Ambulance Service and American Ambulance Field Service volunteers "that the vast majority of the volunteers sustained throughout the war *and into the peace* a firm belief in the validity and necessity of their conduct." In their accounts, both public and private, they frequently invoked poetic imagery from Rudyard Kipling, or Robert Service, or Alan Seeger. The ambulance drivers, says Fenton, "were apparently dismayed after the war by the literary interpretations of their experience by such colleagues as John Dos Passos." To sustain the vividness and value of their overseas experience, drivers in the American Ambulance Field Service established the American Field Service Fellowship to send young Americans to France after the war. Among the fellowship recipients was literary critic Malcolm Cowley.[75]

When Dos Passos's *Three Soldiers*, a novel of unmistakable protest against the official meaning of the war, was published in 1921, Harvard critic Kenneth Murdock reviewed it in the Harvard *Crimson* and found it presented a false picture of the war. In his opinion the pious and reverent *War Memoirs* of Harvard's dead were "the truest record we

---

74. Gilbert Seldes, *Dial* 73 (1922), 438; Ernest Hemingway, *Torrents of Spring*, (New York: Scribner's, 1930), 89.
75. Charles A. Fenton, "Ambulance Drivers in France and Italy: 1914–1918," *American Quarterly* 3 (1951), 334–42 (italics added).

are likely to have of the reaction of our generation to the shocks of the war years."[76] Four years later Yale President Arthur Twining Hadley recalled of the war that "the students as a body were carried outside of themselves by visions of a larger world than that in which they had hitherto moved. . . . Thank God, the vision of 1917 and 1918 led us in the right direction. The lives of those who fell in that great struggle were not wasted." But Hadley also suggested the corrosive effects of time on this positive view of the war experience, when he said of Yale's dead that "it was their good fortune to die while the inspiration under which they fought was at its highest."[77]

By the mid-1920s the high tide of wartime inspiration had receded, but it had not fully ebbed. Countless pools of consciousness still brimmed with shimmering wartime memories. As late as 1933, poet Archibald MacLeish was arguing with Malcolm Cowley in the pages of the *New Republic,* rejecting Cowley's claim that the dead had died in vain, insisting on the nobility of the gesture of dying "generously and in loyalty to a believed-in cause . . . regardless of the success of that cause, regardless even of its validity."[78] A romantic view of the war's meaning on a personal level was still very much alive. One attentive reader of the Cowley-MacLeish exchange, Dartmouth professor Ramon Guthrie, put the matter simply: "The one thing that neither of them seems to consider is the fact that a lot of people were like myself and enjoyed the War. I don't think there was anything monstrous about me for liking it. The things I loved about it . . . are apparently essential to any happiness: i.e., close association with large numbers of one's fellow men in a common purpose, the chance to put forth intensive and disinterested effort in a cause greater than one's own personal concerns, economic equality, freedom from economic worries, adventure. Even the fact that I never did expect the war to 'make the world safe for democracy' or anything else did not keep me from enjoying these features of it."[79]

Guthrie wrote these words nearly a generation after the Armistice, after Wilson's failures at Paris and the rise of European totalitarianism had demonstrated the disillusioning truth that the Crusade had little political utility. But men like MacLeish and Guthrie, even in the face

---

76. Quoted in *ibid.,* 342.
77. George Henry Nettleton, ed., *Yale in the World War,* 2 vols. (New Haven: Yale University Press, 1925), I, ix.
78. Archibald Macleish, *New Republic* 76 (Oct. 4, 1933), 215.
79. Ramon Guthrie, *ibid.* 76 (Oct. 25, 1933), 311.

of the obvious deflation of Wilsonian political ideals, tried nevertheless to salvage their individual sense of the war's significance in their private lives and memories. Here, in contrast with the purely political sphere, "disillusionment" was strenuously resisted. *One of Ours* might appeal only "to those who knew those boys," critic Robert Morss Lovett half-apologized, "but to us that appeal is beyond words. We are proud of them."[80] And for many years after 1918 American Legion halls echoed the lines of "Mademoiselle from Armentières":

> 'Twas a hell of a war, as I recall,
> But a damned sight better than no war at all. . . .

Yet such feelings were far from universal in postwar American culture, as Cowley's bitter attack on a sentimental evaluation of the war showed. One of the last wholly unambiguous affirmations of the war's political and personal meaning was Edith Wharton's *A Son at the Front*, published in 1923. In this novel, a narrow-visioned father, whose character is obviously intended to suggest the smug provincialism of a neutral America, is gradually moved from indifference to commitment toward the war by the persistent idealism of his soldier-son. As R. W. B. Lewis has observed, the book, published five years after the Armistice, seemed largely to be rehearsing an issue long since decided.[81] But the novel was also explicitly built around a theme which came to be the implicit preoccupation of much of the literature of disillusionment: the conflict between generations over the war's significance. Wharton made the son at the front the agent and the father at home the subject of a transformation in attitude, from apathy to affirmation. But increasingly in the post-Armistice period a younger generation of authors wrote of the devolution of soldiers themselves from a kind of parentally instilled enthusiasm and idealism to bitter disillusionment. John Dos Passos developed this theme in *One Man's Initiation, 1917*, published in 1920, and pursued it further the following year in *Three Soldiers*. In the same year as *A Son at the Front*, Thomas Boyd's *Through the Wheat* appeared, depicting combat which did not ennoble the hero, but made him an insensate zombie. In 1924, *What Price Glory?* opened to extravagantly favorable reviews, even though it largely ignored a romantic view of the war and instead portrayed its principal characters as cussing and quarrelsome though amiable drunks. Stallings openly

80. Robert Morss Lovett, *ibid.* 32 (Oct. 11, 1922), 177.
81. R. W. B. Lewis, *Edith Wharton: A Biography* (New York: Harper and Row, 1975), 457.

mocked the wartime rhetoric of chivalry in his novel of the same year, *Plumes.* Its Walter Scott-like chapter titles ("Tourneys," "The Caitiff Knight") and medieval nomenclature—the hero's full name is Richard Coeur de Lion Plume—provide ironic contrast to the downbeat story line about a wounded doughboy come home from the war. Plume befriends a "wiry little wild Jew" who has been imprisoned for his antiwar agitation. The ex-soldier ends up re-breaking his own shattered knee in a furious roundhouse swing at four men in uniform singing "My Country 'Tis of Thee." In 1929 came Ernest Hemingway's *A Farewell to Arms,* in which the action moves *away* from war and into the "civilian" pursuits of love, marriage, and childbirth—a precise reversal of the standard plot line in the romantic war literature.

These and several other novels, including E. E. Cummings's *The Enormous Room* (1922), William Faulkner's *Soldier's Pay* (1926), and William March's *Company K* (1933), are usually taken to represent a literature of protest against the war, a collective expression of "disillusionment" with the war's official meaning. These writings have cast a deep shadow over the historical memory of the war, consigning to the darkness of unfathomable obsolescence those sensibilities that had entertained "illusions" about the war's adventure, or romance, or poetry, or idealism.

But the term "disillusioned" as applied to these postwar writers has troubled more than one critic. Cowley, generally regarded as a leading representative of the orthodoxy of disillusionment, himself observed in 1948 that "I have always felt that the adjective was badly chosen. They [these writers] were something quite different; they were *rebels* in art and life."[82] Stanley Cooperman concluded that "The World War I literary protest was far more *dynamic* than the simple tag of 'disillusion' or 'negation' would seem to indicate."[83] And Alfred Kazin offered the important reminder that Europe "now lay paralytic after four shattering years, where Americans were *merely disillusioned* by the *aftermath*. . . . If it was America that 'had won the war for Europe,' as the popular legend had it, it was the new American literature, seizing the *vitality* that was left in the world, that made the victory its own."[84]

82. Malcolm Cowley, "Two Wars—and Two Generations," *New York Times Book Review,* July 25, 1948, 1 (italics added).
83. Stanley Cooperman, *World War I and the American Novel* (Baltimore: Johns Hopkins University Press, 1967), 214 (italics added).
84. Alfred Kazin, *On Native Grounds* (Garden City, N.Y.: Doubleday, 1956), 148–49 (italics added).

"Rebels," "dynamic," "vitality,"—these terms do not harmonize with the chord that the word "disillusionment" usually strikes in the mind. Nor do they seem remotely applicable to European war writing, such as Erich Maria Remarque's *All Quiet on the Western Front*, in which the hero at the end is "so alone, and so without hope."[85] They suggest, rather, that much of the same energy that is naïvely displayed in the romantic war literature is equally present in the "protest" novels, though harnessed to a different wheel. What John Aldridge said of one of those protest novels, Dos Passos's *One Man's Initiation, 1917*, might be said about the entire body of literature of which it is considered to be a part: "The excitement which Dos Passos seems to have felt when he conceived of war as a great adventure and crusade has apparently been transformed . . . into an immense energy of denunciation." The strong feeling of outrage that dominates the last half of the book springs from the same sources of enthusiasm that inform the first half: "it has simply been reinforced now by hurt feelings and has changed direction."[86]

Toward what objects were that outrage and that "immense energy for denunciation" directed? It is misleading and insufficient to reply that they were directed simply at the brutal facts of battlefield violence. Hemingway and Stallings, for example, maintained a life-long fascination with things military. They both contrived to get into the Second World War, and Stallings in 1963 wrote an anecdotal history of the AEF that was heavily invested with nostalgia and peppered with good old soldier-boy stories. Faulkner's *Soldier's Pay*, in which the grotesquely wounded Lieutenant Mahon drifts mutely through the novel to his waiting grave, might be taken as a rather turgid statement against the war's violence. But it is worth noting that Faulkner himself never got beyond Canada in his quest to see the "Big Show," and that *Soldier's Pay* is formally a long anti-climax, with all the violence preceding the action of the novel. Cummings's *The Enormous Room* concerns the war only in the most indirect and allegorical sense. The story takes place far from any battlefield, and the book as a whole invites a reading as a kind of impish *jeu d'esprit*, a clever exercise that draws only incidental coloration from the proximity of its action to a great historical catastrophe. Cummings himself commented that "When *The Enormous Room*

85. Erich Maria Remarque, *All Quiet on the Western Front* (Greenwich, Conn.: Fawcett, 1968), 175.
86. John Aldridge, *After the Lost Generation: A Critical Study of the Writers of Two Wars* (New York: Farrar, Straus and Giroux, 1951), 64.

was published, some people wanted a war book; they were disappointed."[87]

Of the overt facts of the military experience that drew these writers' rage, it was not so much violence and suffering that provoked them as *authority*. In this they were at one with the least literate of doughboys. Thus Cummings wrote about the arbitrariness of the French military prison at La Ferté Macé, Chrisfield in *Three Soldiers* grenades his hated sergeant, Frederic Henry in *A Farewell to Arms* shoots a retreating Italian, runs afoul of the military police, expiates himself with a dunk in the Tagliamento, and deserts. So too does Dos Passos's John Andrews desert, and one is reminded here of the persistence in American fiction of the imagery of flight, the anti-social rebellion against authority and convention familiar to readers of the *Leatherstocking Tales* and *Huckleberry Finn*. This imagery had been vivid in the minds of many doughboys. Whether or not they had actually read Cooper and Twain, they had nevertheless mentally figured their own flight into the AEF along lines long ago traced in the escape to the western woods by Natty Bumppo and Huck. The theme of desertion simply rotated this traditional American fictional device 180 degrees, making civil society the hero's ultimate refuge.

In the end, the power of the postwar literature of disillusionment principally derived not from denouncing the violence of the actual, historical war, nor simply from exploiting the traditional American motif of resentment at authority. It came, rather, from the enlistment of that literature in another war altogether—a war between two concepts of culture, a conflict whose first skirmishes had been fought even before 1914. An older generation attempted to carry intact into the twentieth century traditional nineteenth-century definitions of morality, the rationality of human nature, and the civic utility of "high culture." Against them were pitted younger intellectuals attracted by notions of absurdity, irrationality, and the possibly subversive implications of art. The youthful John Dos Passos in 1916 scorned the older culture's literary tastes as "wholesome rice-pudding fare . . . a strangely unstimulating diet. . . . Our books are like our cities," he complained, "they are all the same. . . . The tone of the higher sort of writing in this country is undoubtedly that of a well brought up and intelligent woman, tolerant, versed in the things of this world, quietly humorous, but bound tightly

87. E. E. Cummings, *The Enormous Room* (New York: Modern Library, 1934), vii.

in the fetters of 'niceness,' of the middle-class outlook." America, he feared, might "stagnate forever, the Sicily of the modern world, rich in this world's goods, absorbing the thought, patronizing the art of other peoples, but producing nothing from amid our jumble of races but steel and oil and grain."[88] World War I neither initiated that conflict nor set its terms. But both groups of combatants seized upon the war as an occasion to advance the arguments of their respective sides. Behind the attack on military authority in the novels of disillusionment lay a second attack on the cultural authority of the Old Guard—the Old Guard that had promoted American entry into the war, and employed the full force of its rhetorical power to describe the war in terms compatible with its ancient values.

The initial victories undoubtedly went to the custodians of the older culture. Their most spectacular triumph was their success in upholding an idealized view of war, a success that Pershing's policies had abetted. Their achievement was everywhere evident in the war years, and for some time thereafter, in the very language that ordinary soldiers used to describe themselves and their exploits—the inflated rhetoric of an archaic literature of romance.

The postwar writers of disillusionment protested less against the war itself than *against a way of seeing and describing the war.* As writers, they naturally focused their fire on the verbal conceits of the older generation. They insisted over and over again that the war experience —and by extension all modern human experience—could not be contained in the stilted shibboleths and pieties of the traditional culture. This was the field of energy—its poles being two separate cultures, even two distinct systems of speech—across which arced the most kinetic prose of the postwar writers. This was the source of power in Hemingway's famous passage about being "embarrassed by the words sacred, glorious, and sacrifice and the expression in vain," and finding dignity only in the names of places and the numbers of the roads.[89] This was the thrust of Cummings's opposition of "vulgar American idiom" to a parody of Wilsonian rhetoric in the opening chapter of *The Enormous Room:* "To borrow a characteristic cadence from Our Great President: the lively satisfaction which we might be suspected of having derived from the accomplishment of a task so important in the sav-

88. John Dos Passos, "Against American Literature," *New Republic* 8 (Oct. 14, 1916), 269–71.
89. Ernest Hemingway, *A Farewell to Arms* (New York: Scribner's, 1929), 184–85.

ing of civilization from the clutches of Prussian tyranny was in some degree inhibited, unhappily, by a complete absence of cordial relations between the man whom fate had placed over us and ourselves. Or, to use the vulgar American idiom, B. and I and Mr. A. didn't get on well." This was the point of Cummings's describing, again with telling rhetorical juxtaposition, a conversation with Mexique: "When we asked him once what he thought about the war, he replied, 'I t'ink lotta bullsh–t,' which, upon copious reflection, I decided absolutely expressed my own point of view."[90]

From this same field of energy flashed the savage force that illuminated two well-known descriptions of dead soldiers. In *Company K* William March viciously and heavy-handedly mocked the form of the reverent letter written by the commanding officer to the parents of the dead: "Dear Madam: Your son, Francis, died needlessly in Belleau Wood. You will be interested to hear that at the time of his death he was crawling with vermin and weak from diarrhea. His feet were swollen and rotten and they stank. . . . [A] piece of shrapnel hit him and he died in agony, slowly. You'd never believe he could live three hours, but he did. He lived three full hours screaming and cursing by turns. He had nothing to hold on to, you see: He had learned long ago that what he had been taught to believe by you, his mother, who loved him, under the meaningless names of honor, courage, patriotism, were all lies."[91]

In *USA: 1919*, John Dos Passos described the interment at Arlington of the Unknown Soldier. The starched speech of the formal ceremony collapsed into an almost unintelligible blur: "Whereasthe Congressof theunitedstates byaconcurrentresolutionadoptedon the4thdayofmarch lastauthorizedthe Secretaryofwar to cause to be brought to theunited statesthe body of an Americanwhowasamemberoftheamericanexpeditionaryforceineuropewholosthislifeduringtheworldwarandwhoseidentity hasnotbeenestablished. . . ." In vivid contrast was the language of the drill sergeant: "Atten'SHUN suck in your gut you c——r wipe that smile off your face eyes right wattja tink dis is a choirch-social?" And of the mortuary detail: "Make sure he ain't a dinge boys. make sure he ain't a guinea or a kike."[92] *What Price Glory?* shocked New York audiences with frequent repetition of what would later be regarded as mild

90. Cummings, *The Enormous Room*, 3, 181.
91. William March, *Company K* (Concord, N.Y.: American Mercury, 1931), 48.
92. John Dos Passos, *USA: 1919* (Boston: Houghton Mifflin, 1963), 407–9.

obscenities, words like "hell" and "goddamnit." Knights and Crusaders simply were not supposed to talk that way. Had not Secretary of War Baker assured the women of America in 1918 that he had never seen a doughboy who was not "living a life which he would not be willing to have mother see him live?"[93]

But to point to this assault on traditional language as evidence of "disillusionment," and there let analysis rest, is to miss something important about postwar American literature. The war assuredly disabused many writers of their illusions about the romance and nobility of warfare. But for the younger generation of authors that came to the fore after 1918, the war was also a fabulously useful, if expensively purchased, metaphor for the corruption of the culture they had under siege. Somehow it provided them with an infusion of creative adrenalin, an access of energy that set off the 1920s as one of the most remarkable periods in the history of American fiction. To recognize this is to be forced to recognize the curious fact that it was terribly convenient, even necessary, that the war was not entirely a "success." The literature of the 1920s would be impossible to imagine if Wilson had triumphed at Paris, and had progressive expectations been widely fulfilled at home. Those developments would have ornamented the conflict with just the crown of glory and genuine accomplishment that the custodians of the older culture had promised. How difficult it then would have been to find such a rich and concrete metaphor for the worthlessness of the philistine, repressive culture the young were indicting. And how difficult, too, to discredit the speech and the symbols that the older culture had invoked to affirm the war's value.

This suggestion is not entirely conjectural. World War II, a generation later, did not loose the same creative wave in American literature that World War I did—in significant measure because the later war could only with difficulty be figured as a "failure." Thus the post-World War II period saw little stylistic inventiveness comparable to the 1920s, and the anti-war "protest" of writers like Joseph Heller and Thomas Pynchon was pitched often at a high and sometimes wild level of abstraction. There was little of the direct and searing *anger* that pervaded and energized the writing of the post-World War I generation.

The stridency and innovative genius of that generation of writers in America owed perhaps to another source as well. Writing principally

93. Quoted in William L. O'Neill, *Everyone Was Brave: The Rise and Fall of Feminism in America* (Chicago: Quadrangle, 1969), 190.

for American readers, they had to bridge a gap of consciousness that did not yawn nearly so wide for European authors. European readers of Robert Graves or Siegfried Sassoon or Erich Maria Remarque knew largely from grim and long-endured experience the texture of wartime life. They had absorbed through their very flesh the facts of the war, and literature, in a sense, had but to lift those inchoate truths from the viscera into the imagination.

Americans, for the most part, knew nothing of those facts. Civilians were little touched by the distant fighting, and the great majority of the late-arriving doughboys had not tasted battle in ways comparable to the experience of their Old World comrades and foes. American writers had to put forward a "truth" about the war that was not so easily made apparent to their readers. Significantly, the greatest of the American war authors had all served for a time with European armies —Hemingway with the Italians; Dos Passos and Cummings with the French. Small wonder, therefore, that they had to summon extraordinary powers of expression in the attempt to make themselves understood by their own countrymen. They had indeed been travelers in a foreign land, returning home with strange tales to tell.

Yet in another sense their message was not so alien. Writers like Cummings and Dos Passos had in common with the custodians of older culture like Oliver Wendell Holmes, Jr., and Alan Seeger, as well as with Willa Cather's character Claude Wheeler, a brooding hostility toward the vacuity and artificiality of industrial civilization. Where they parted company with their elders was in their appraisal of war as a possible alternative to the modern condition. An older generation had preached that combat offered adventure-filled liberation from the iron trend of peacetime society toward mechanization, routine, and the suppression of the individual. The younger authors protested that war was in fact the supreme embodiment of those hated tendencies. Death-dealing technology, ennui, arbitrary authority, and loss of identity became the leading motifs of their war writing. When officialdom chose to honor the Unknown Soldier as this war's exemplary "hero," his anonymity almost too neatly symbolized what the younger novelists were trying to say. Dos Passos made electrifying use of this imagery in *USA: 1919:* "How can you tell a guy's a hundred percent when all you've got's a gunnysack full of bones, bronze buttons stamped with the screaming eagle and a pair of roll puttees?"[94]

94. Dos Passos, *USA: 1919*, 408.

The postwar writers, in short, inverted the older culture's image of war, even while sharing their forebears' anxiety about the character of the society that had spawned the war. In making war a metaphor for the modern condition rather than a counterpoint to it, writers like Dos Passos and Hemingway and Cummings slammed shut for many of their readers one of the imagination's last remaining exits from the enormously uncomfortable room of modernity. In the last analysis, it was this curiously confining achievement that rendered the literature of disillusionment more moving and more historically durable than the essentially escapist fantasies of authors like Empey, Seeger, Cather, and Wharton.

This artistic victory was neither sudden nor total, nor was it without its costs. Henry May in *The End of American Innocence* has correctly pointed out that many of the elements of modern American culture once thought to have sprung spontaneously to life during and after World War I in fact had deep roots in the ante-war period, which May calls "the first years of our own time." But May's persuasive account has encouraged the mistaken conclusion that the war effectively killed the older nineteenth-century culture. On the contrary, that culture retained a powerful grip on American life during the conflict and for some time thereafter. It had pressed its values and its icons and its figures of speech too deeply down into the popular mind for them to be uprooted in the brief nineteen months of American belligerency. The war may have weakened those cultural forms but it did not destroy them, as the persistently romantic, upbeat view of war in innumerable doughboy diaries and letters and memoirs suggested.

In time, the "high" cultural image of war held by the older custodians of culture did yield to the onslaughts of the "modern" writers who displaced obsolescing verities about morality and heroism and individual sacrifice with a new orthodoxy that dwelt on absurdity and irony and victimization. But at the level of popular culture, there remained a residue, if not of the older values about war, at least of their rhetorical forms. For the former doughboys who clung to those forms, the literature of disillusionment was not only obscure and mystifying, but seemed to deny the very authenticity of their perceptions of their experience in France.

They were right. The postwar novelists of protest saw and remembered a different war than that which most of "Pershing's Crusaders" had witnessed. Most of the young men in the AEF had arrived too late and moved too swiftly to be deeply disabused of their adventurous expectations. Between the sensibilities enshrined in the minds of the American Legionnaires and those expressed in the novels of Hemingway, Dos Passos, Cummings, and the others, there gaped an immense void of incomprehension. This hole in the fabric of American culture, further separating the intellectuals from the "masses," was one of the lasting legacies of the war.

5

Armistice and Aftermath

By the first of November 1918, the end was near. On November 6, Berlin dispatched envoys to carry an armistice proposal to Supreme Allied Commander Marshal Ferdinand Foch. Waiting in his railway carriage in the forest at Compiègne, Foch guided the Germans by wireless to the designated frontier crossing-point. As they approached the French lines on November 7, he ordered his guns in that sector to stand silent, so that the truce party might safely pass.

Somehow, a war-zone correspondent from United Press mistook the momentary stand-down in that single sector for a general cease fire. Excitedly, he flashed a message in cable-ese to New York: "Urgent. Armistice Allies Germany signed smorning. Hostilities ceased two safternoon." The cable arrived in UP's Manhattan office in the Pulitzer Building at noon; by 1:00 p.m. it had been relayed to other cities, and special newspaper editions proclaiming peace were on the stands. In New York, sirens, bells, whistles, and shouts split the clear November air. Clerks abandoned desks, workers put down tools, and thousands of men and women poured into the streets in a wild, whooping dance of celebration. Chicago erupted in a "carnival of noise and ribaldry." A Belgian tenor broke into a Chicago Opera Company rehearsal with the news, and the Italian director—obviously a connoisseur of the *bella figura*—immediately ordered the singing of "The Star Spangled Banner" and the anthems of the Allies. Bartenders everywhere instantly forgot the prohibition on selling drink to men in uniform, as soldiers and civilians in countless soon-to-be-dry saloons toasted each other, their comrades and co-workers, the President, the Congress, the end of it all—anything that justified the lifting of a glass.

In the late afternoon, the State Department denied that an armistice had been struck. The terms, explained the Secretary of State, were still under discussion. Late editions shamefacedly corrected the error. But by that time many citizens did not care. Angry at the official denial, some vented their wrath by violently tearing up the afternoon papers that printed the State Department's correction. Others—"boys who welcomed the release from all inhibitions, hoodlums joyfully seizing any excuse for making a noise, and some who had drunk so much in the afternoon that they neither knew nor cared whether the peace story had any basis or foundation"—roamed the streets far into the night. The afternoon's joy-dance degenerated into dangerous carousing. Two Minnesota revelers injured themselves trying to coax a victory salute from a temperamental cannon. In Columbus, Ohio, worried officials closed the city's saloons until the following day. In Chicago, police finally had to use clubs to contain the surging crowds.

It was, said the New York Times, "the most colossal news fake ever perpetrated upon the American people." The day's events also suggested a parable for the nation's experience in the war. As on that disappointing day, so it was in the years after 1917: hopes inflated only to be crushed; idealistic enthusiasm sliding into intoxicated violence; victory itself an anti-climax, an illusion of triumph soon to be buried in the ashes of the aftermath. Progressives, particularly, the men and women who had so anxiously hoped that a repugnant war would somehow bring victory for their ideals, might have keenly felt the premonitory chill of those ironies on the night of November 7.[1]

For other Americans, Republicans of the Old Guard and the interests they represented, even the false armistice could not dampen their joy. On November 7 they were still luxuriating in the warmth of a great victory of their own, won at the polls only two days before. In the new 66th Congress, Republicans would enjoy an overwhelming preponderance in the House, holding 237 seats. In the Senate the margin

1. Descriptions of the "false armistice" are taken from the New York Times, Nov. 8, 1918; see also Mark Sullivan, Our Times: The United States, 1900–1925, 6 vols. (New York: Scribner's, 1933), V, 513–27.

of victory was narrower, yielding a majority of only two. But every-where Republican satisfaction abounded. The party had been effec-tively reunited for its first national victory since the disastrous Roose-velt-led schism of 1912. The hated Wilson, even as he was about to grasp the palm of military success, had been denied his full measure of glory as a conquering war leader. A Republican Senate would now have a strong fulcrum on the President's treaty-making power. Not least, a Republican Congress would now have a major hand—perhaps ultimately the dominant hand—in domestic reconstruction. No one glowed more exultantly at those prospects than Henry Cabot Lodge. The American people, Lodge observed just after the election, "used us as an instrument to defeat Wilson." As for supporting the President in the difficult peace-making and reconversion period, "we should be false to our duty as Americans if we gave him a blind support and that proposition cannot be accepted for a moment."[2] Lodge stood poised in November 1918 to throw down the glove to Wilson, challenging him for control of policies both diplomatic and domestic. It was a moment for which the Massachusetts Senator had long been preparing.

He and other Republicans had sought since the spring of 1917 to find a means to turn the crisis to their political advantage. The prob-lem was a delicate one. Given the obvious need to close ranks in war-time, the usual partisan tactics were in bad odor. "The fact is," Lodge wrote a friend in early 1918, "we should run the risk of defeating our own ends if we made the attacks on Wilson that we all want to make. We must give no opening for the charge that we are drawing the party line and the cry that we are not loyal to the war. We have to proceed cautiously. . . ."[3] The trick was, as Lodge's Massachusetts colleague John W. Weeks put it, to devise "a program which will, of course, in-clude supporting the Administration in all its war activities but which will give us something to hang party action on when the war is over."[4] The trick, in other words, was to oppose the administration without appearing to oppose the war. And the goal, always, was political com-mand of postwar society.

The program adopted to that end was Doric in its simplicity: pose

2. Lodge to Will H. Hays, Dec. 25, 1918, Lodge Papers, Massachusetts Historical Society, Boston.
3. Lodge to W. S. Bigelow, Feb. 21, 1918, Lodge Papers.
4. John W. Weeks to Nicholas Murray Butler, Dec. 1, 1917, Butler Papers, Butler Library, Columbia University, N.Y.

the Republicans as the party of superior patriotism, nationalism, and administrative acumen; criticize the Wilson administration, accordingly, for its insufficient bellicosity, its parochialism, and its bureaucratic incompetence. Mishandling of the mobilization effort had been the principal battle cry during the intensely bitter Republican attacks in the winter of 1917–18. The breakdown of the railway system and eventual government takeover of the railroads, the coal shortages in the East and consequent shutting of factory gates at government order, the slow progress in the building of ships and in the dispatching of troops to Europe, and the accusations of massive corruption in the aircraft production program, which had not turned out a single airplane by early 1918, all were grist for the Republican mill. But by the spring of 1918 Wilson had put his administrative house substantially in order, and in the summer the tide of battle had begun to turn in favor of the Allies in France.

As the election drew near, Republican criticism shifted to Wilson's peace terms and to the anticipated social and economic issues of the postwar period. Theodore Roosevelt, in a carefully prepared speech to Maine Republicans in March, struck what he hoped would be "the keynote on which the Congressional Campaign can be fought."[5] The Democrats, he said, had sinfully allowed the country to be unprepared for the war, and they had added to their culpability by mismanagement of the mobilization program once war was declared. Republicans, on the other hand, had long advocated preparedness, and after American entry they had supported military measures with far more enthusiasm and consistency than Democrats. Even now, Roosevelt sneered, Wilson persisted in trying to win the war with "kid gloves and fine phrases," when what was needed were "brains and steel." As for peace terms, said the old Rough Rider, "there is but one way to get a righteous and lasting peace, and that is to beat Germany to her knees." But Roosevelt tried to offer his cheering audience more than jingoistic blood and thunder. He also hoped to move them toward his own brand of progressive reform. After the war, he said, the Republican Party should stand for land reform, repeal of the anti-trust laws, federal licensing of interstate businesses, and recruitment of labor representatives into the highest councils of industry. The Grand Old Party, he concluded, "must

5. Roosevelt to Henry Lewis Stimson, Mar. 12, 1918, in Elting E. Morison, ed., *The Letters of Theodore Roosevelt*, 8 vols. (Cambridge, Mass.: Harvard University Press, 1951–54), VIII, 1299.

shun equally the bourbon reactionaries . . . and the sinister dema-gogues and loose-minded visionaries."[6]

Roosevelt, seeking to rebuild bridges between the progressive and conservative factions in his party, strove in 1918 to repair some of the damage he himself had inflicted on the GOP in the immediately pre-ceding years. He circulated early drafts of the Maine speech among a wide spectrum of political leaders, including several Congressmen, labor officials, and party luminaries like Elihu Root, William Howard Taft, Hiram Johnson, Henry Cabot Lodge, and new Republican National Chairman Will Hays. Behind the scenes, he advised the phenomenally peripatetic Hays which progressives he should see during his travels, "so that they shall not feel that they are slighted." Overlooking no pos-sible sources of votes in this critical election, he specifically cautioned Hays, about to embark for the suffragist strongholds of the West, to "be very careful to see prominent women in all those states. . . . [T]here is a very real need that we should begin to take them into our councils generally."[7] Hays, the angel of Republican conciliation, seemed to be everywhere in 1918, "enthusiastically jumping from place to place," noted Hiram Johnson, "vigorously shaking hands with everybody and saying 'How is it?', and 'We're all together.' "[8] If Roosevelt was the greatest Republican war-horse, and Lodge the chief Republican strate-gist, Hays was assuredly the master tactician. The "supreme accolade" for unhorsing the Democrats in 1918, concludes Seward Livermore, "must go to the wily and indefatigable Hays. The dapper and diminu-tive National Chairman performed prodigies in knitting together the shattered fabric of the organization and in developing controversial issues only indirectly connected with the prosecution of the war but capable of inflaming sentiment against the administration over a wide area."[9]

But though Hays, with Roosevelt's assistance, held out the olive branch to both progressive and Old Guard factions, the party's center of gravity had shifted markedly to the right in the war period, and it

6. *New York Times,* Mar. 29, 1918, 4.
7. Roosevelt to Will H. Hays, Mar. 26, 1918, Morison, ed., *Letters of Theodore Roosevelt,* VIII, 1305.
8. Hiram Johnson to Roosevelt, Mar. 16, 1918, Johnson Papers, Bancroft Library, University of California, Berkeley.
9. Seward W. Livermore, *Politics Is Adjourned: Woodrow Wilson and the War Congress, 1916–1918* (Middletown, Conn.: Wesleyan University Press, 1966), 245.

was the former insurgents and Bull Moosers who had to travel the greater distance along the road to reunion in 1918. Lodge might have been briefly conciliatory when he piously reassured an inquirer that "No one here would think of discriminating against any man because he was with the progressive wing of the party and voted for Roosevelt."[10] But in fact Lodge had learned little charity over the years toward the people he contemptuously referred to in 1917 as "the remnants and rags of the old Progressive Party, who fought against us in the last campaign and supported Wilson. . . . They represent the crowd that want to have the initiative and referendum, the recall of judges and every other radical thing, putting the State more completely in the hands of the labor unions and minority organizations."[11] Many progressively inclined Republicans had marched out of their party to stand at Armageddon with Theodore Roosevelt in 1912. Their leader had managed to re-enter the fold, but many of his followers had spent years in the political wilderness, and they never fully regained their seniority, nor their respectability, in the old party. By 1918 conservative elements securely controlled the national party apparatus; they abhorred the regulatory and pro-labor policies the government had embraced in wartime, and they had no wish more compelling than to return to the "normal" conditions of prewar days.

The Democrats, for their part, were peculiarly vulnerable in 1918. Wilson had first taken the White House as a minority President, thanks to the Republican split in 1912, and he held it in 1916 chiefly as "the man who kept us out of war," an appeal that could hardly be repeated. Democrats had the barest majority in the House, as evidenced by the difficulty of organizing the lower chamber in April 1917. In the Senate, the "class of 1912" included many Democrats, elected largely by virtue of Republican divisions in that year, from traditionally Republican states—notably Colorado, Delaware, Illinois, Kansas, and New Hampshire. Wilson, moreover, had experienced painful difficulty disciplining some of the Southern grandees of his own party, whose opposition to certain war measures, especially the draft, caused the administration and the national party extreme embarrassment.

Beyond the Congress, Democrats were still a minority party in most states outside the South, and the President strongly suspected that state Republican organizations were exploiting the emergency mobilization machinery for partisan advantage. "It is becoming more and more evi-

10. Lodge to H. R. McMurtrie, Nov. 23, 1918, Lodge Papers.
11. Lodge to Bigelow, Apr. 19, 1917, Lodge Papers.

dent," Wilson complained to Secretary of War Baker, "that throughout the country the draft organization, the public defense organization and the Fuel and Food Administrations are being made use of for political purposes."[12] In Wisconsin, for example, the President instructed George Creel to bypass the Republican-packed State Council of Defense and to deal instead with a Democratic "Loyalty League" in all matters of publicity and propaganda.[13] Creel thought that "where the State Councils were not Republican, they were reactionary in their very essence," and he recommended to the President just before the Armistice that "as soon as possible steps should be taken to demobilize the Council of National Defense so that the Chauvinistic [sic], reactionary state organizations may be put out of business."[14] Feeling the precariousness of his party's position, and stinging from constant Republican harassment, Wilson was driven to drastic political measures in 1918.

The very fates seemed arrayed against the President's party. Death claimed eight Democratic Senators during the 65th Congress, thinning their already sparse majority. Perhaps the cruelest blow of all was the accidental shotgun killing of Wisconsin's Paul O. Husting on a duck-hunting trip in October 1917. Husting, the first Democrat sent to the Senate from Wisconsin in more than twenty years, had been elected in 1914; in the normal course of events his seat would not have been contested again until 1920. Democratic retention of this one seat would have meant a Democratic Senate in 1919–20, which might have had quite different consequences for the passage of the Versailles Treaty and the history of the postwar world. But it was not to be.

A special election was called for April 1918 in Wisconsin. Wilson, knowing full well the importance of filling Husting's place with another Democrat, threw all his weight into the contest. He induced Joseph E. Davies to resign as chairman of the Federal Trade Commission and return to Wisconsin to stand for the office. In a public letter of endorsement for Davies, the President urged Wisconsin voters to consider the candidates' positions on three neutrality-period measures as the "acid test" of "true loyalty and genuine Americanism."[15] This was a low blow. Victor Berger, the Socialist Party candidate, and Irvine Lenroot, the

12. Wilson to Newton D. Baker, Dec. 6, 1917, WWP.
13. Livermore, *Politics Is Adjourned*, 44.
14. George Creel to Joseph Tumulty, Nov. 14, 1918, and Creel to Wilson, Nov. 8, 1918, WWP.
15. The measures were the McLemore Resolution, warning Americans not to travel on belligerent ships, an embargo bill, and the Armed Ship Resolution of early 1917. See Livermore, *Politics Is Adjourned*, 118.

Republican, had both opposed Wilson on those measures in Congress. But Davies had been safely ensconced at the FTC after 1914 and hence had not been required to take a public stand. The administration further inflamed the opposition at the end of March when Wilson dispatched Vice President Thomas R. Marshall to stump for Davies. Marshall warned Wisconsinites that their state was "under suspicion" of disloyalty, and that Lenroot in particular was appealing to the "sewage vote."[16] Lenroot won the election in April, but Wilson had lost more than a Senate seat. He had lost also a good part of the aura of nonpartisanship that is among the greatest political assets of a sitting President, especially in wartime. He had invited the Republicans, until then at least partly restrained by the war atmosphere, to make more open political battle against him. And he had placed the battle on the ground of loyalty to the war measures of his administration, a ground on which it could be plausibly argued that Republicans had stood more steadfastly than many members of his own party.

Wilson gave further evidence of his political straits in June 1918, when he personally persuaded automobile industrialist Henry Ford to run in Michigan for the Senate. Here was positive proof that the President was desperate, perhaps, suggested some, even unhinged. Were it not for the gravity of its implications, the episode might have provided comic relief to a distracted country. Accustomed to acting innovatively, Ford determined to enter not just the Democratic primary but also the Republican. By a quirk in the Michigan electoral law, a candidate might cross-file in the primaries and, if he swept them all, appear alone on the general ballot in November. Those provisions fitted admirably the purposes of Wilson, who wished to pose Ford as a candidate above partisan entanglements, devoted only to supporting the administration.

That strategy misfired, as it were, from both barrels. Ford lost the Republican primary to Truman H. Newberry, a Detroit businessman, and was made to stand in November not above the battle, but as a Democrat. Moreover, Republican campaigners filled the air with condemnations of Wilson's highly unorthodox personal role in the recruitment and promotion of Mr. Ford. They also filled Newberry's campaign coffers with scandalously large sums of money. Most tellingly, they shrewdly turned Wilson's personal interest in Ford to their own advantage. They resurrected all the outrageous things Ford had ever said about the flag, the war, and the country—and Ford had been

16. *Ibid.*, 120.

loose-mouthed enough in his pre-political days to provide his enemies with a fat anthology of damaging material. They pointed to Ford's abortive "peace ship" mission to Europe in 1915, and roundly denounced him as a peace-at-any-price man, a denunciation, by implication, of the President as well. They claimed that Wilson's bizarre interest in Ford proved the President's autocratic obsession, his intention to subvert the party system in order to bend Congress to his iron will. The Michigan senatorial election, declared Lodge, "is the most important single election now pending in the United States." Newberry, he said, had proved his patriotism by joining the Naval Reserve. "Opposed to him is Mr. Henry Ford, who belongs to no political party, who has been nominated at the request of the President, and whose only claim is that if elected to the Senate he would vote blindly in obedience to the President's directions. He has been notorious throughout the country as an advocate of peace at any price. . . . It is not a party question. It is a question of patriotism; of the honor of the country; and of the winning of the war in the only way which could justify our sacrifices."[17]

Lodge's blast at Ford typified Republican campaign rhetoric. The Ford candidacy, indeed, must have seemed to Republicans virtually a heaven-sent target for the slings and arrows they had been stocking in their political arsenal throughout the war: boost the Republicans as statesmanlike champions of aggressive military efficiency; damn the Democrats as addle-pated Copperheads, and Wilson as a compulsive egomaniac, a man who dangerously confounded his personal pride and the national interest in a relentless quest for dictatorial power. Republican orators endlessly iterated those themes in 1918. The indictment was, like most political pronouncements, overdrawn. But it sufficiently worried Wilson that he was provoked, on the eve of the election, to make a dramatic public appeal.

Nominally, both parties had foresworn partisan activities in the war. In fact, both sides honored the principle far more in the breach than in the observance, but the fiction was officially maintained that overt partisanship was put aside for the duration of the conflict. Wilson himself had given the notion its most articulate expression when he had announced to Congress in May 1918 that "politics is adjourned." That high-minded doctrine was useful to the President when he was trying to keep restless legislators in session long enough to consider his tax bill in the spring of 1918. But as the political season advanced, his

17. Lodge to Clarence L. Ayres, Oct. 26, 1918, Lodge Papers.

commitment to avoid overt politicking became increasingly an embarrassment. Republicans pressed his party hard in a dozen senatorial races and several score of congressional contests. By August, led by Lodge and Roosevelt, they hammered at Wilson's liberal peace plans and demanded that Germany be conclusively crushed. Democratic office-seekers beseeched Wilson to give them the kind of public support any President might normally be expected to give to his party in a congressional election year, and Wilson himself deeply feared the consequences for his diplomatic position if his party were repudiated at the polls.

But 1918 was no ordinary year; the war had supposedly adjourned politics. Wilson had personally urged the adjournment the preceding May. Now, as the election neared, what could he do? Political commentator David Lawrence neatly described Wilson's dilemma. If the President remained silent, Lawrence wrote, "it will be construed as indifference on his part to the outcome, tacit admission that it matters very little to him whether the Republicans get control or the Democrats keep it. If he expresses a preference for his own party, the Republican leaders will bombard him with criticism." Despite the dangers of that bombardment, Lawrence predicted, "Mr. Wilson may go before the country with the same request for a vote of confidence that Lloyd George is shortly to ask in Great Britain."[18]

After much agonizing and extensive consultation with his advisers, Wilson on October 25 asked the voters for just such a vote of confidence. "If you have approved of my leadership," he pleaded, "and wish me to continue to be your unembarrassed spokesman in affairs at home and abroad, I earnestly beg that you will express yourselves unmistakably to that effect by returning a Democratic majority to both the Senate and the House of Representatives." The Republican leadership, Wilson accurately noted, "have unquestionably been pro-war, but they have been anti-administration. At almost every turn since we entered the war they have sought to take the choice of policy and the conduct of war out of my hands and put it under the control of instrumentalities of their own choosing. . . . Spokesmen of the Republican party are urging you to elect a Republican Congress in order to back up and support the President, but . . . Republican leaders desire not so much to support the President as to control him."[19]

18. *Literary Digest* 59 (Oct. 26, 1918), 17–18.
19. Albert Shaw, ed., *The Messages and Papers of Woodrow Wilson*, 2 vols. (New York: Review of Reviews Corp., 1924), I, 557–59.

"Now the President has thrown off the mask," snapped Lodge, "and it is enough to make a Republican pretty indignant to be told that he cannot be trusted to take part in the government of his country, that the only test of loyalty is loyalty to one man no matter what he does."[20] Republicans howled that their patriotism had been impugned, their loyalty insulted, their integrity besmirched by what Will Hays called this "ungracious . . . wanton . . . mendacious" appeal.[21] They rushed into print and onto the hustings to proclaim that here was ultimate proof, if proof were needed, of Wilson's perfidy. The immediate effect of Wilson's statement was thus to elevate the level of rhetorical violence at which the final few days of the campaign were waged. When the ballots were counted on November 5, the Democrats had lost six Senate seats and the Republicans had gained thirty Representatives. Some claimed that the President's appeal had provided the momentum that carried the GOP to victory. But that interpretation, however dear to Republicans pleased to believe in Wilson's tendency to self-destruction, will not bear close scrutiny. If anything, the appeal may have helped some Democratic candidates; Henry Ford, for example, reduced the normal Republican plurality in Michigan by nearly 100,000 votes, losing only narrowly to Newberry. But not even Wilson's rhetorical prowess could fully stem the Republican tide. The party in power in the United States typically loses congressional seats in a non-presidential election year, a rule to which 1918 was no exception. But in that year the usual rule applied with a particularly rigorous logic. The first third of the twentieth century was an era of Republican dominance. The Wilson years constituted an interlude, an aberration made possible only by the temporary disarray in Republican ranks in 1912 and the peculiar political force of the peace issue in 1916. In 1918, therefore, the country simply returned to its normally Republican political condition.

Of all the liabilities that rendered the Democrats a persistently minority party, none was greater than its sectional character. In the Wilson era, the South was not merely solid for the Democratic Party, not merely the party's bankable minimum at the ballot box, but its heart and soul. Wilson himself was a transplanted Southerner. His cabinet was dominated by men from below Mason's and Dixon's line. Sons of Dixie held virtually every committee chairmanship while the Demo-

20. Lodge to Joseph Bucklin Bishop, Oct. 26, 1918, Lodge Papers.
21. Quoted in Frederic L. Paxson, *American Democracy and the World War*, 3 vols. (Boston: Houghton Mifflin, 1936–48), II, 446.

crats controlled Congress. That Southern grip on the government had provoked strenuous criticism during the war. The administration was frequently charged with sectional favoritism—in the location of the army training camps, in the design of revenue legislation, and in the incidence of price controls. It was this last issue in particular that proved the Democrats' undoing.

The Democratic Party in Woodrow Wilson's day still did not have a reliable base in the urban, industrial states of the Northeast. Wilson had achieved victory in 1916 by uniting the "Solid South" with the West. But the attachment of the West to the Democratic Party was extremely tenuous. "There is no necessary natural affinity between the West and the South," noted Secretary of Agriculture David Houston after the 1916 election. "The West will not sustain the Democratic party unless it continues to go in the direction it has been going."[22] The direction Houston had in mind, of course, was upward on the curve of prosperity, with farmers' fortunes buoyed by low tariffs, easy credit, and high agricultural prices. Wilson was quite attentive to the first two of those requirements, promoting legislation to reduce import levies, to establish a Federal Farm Loan Board, and to make agricultural warehouse receipts negotiable instruments for loans or delivery orders. And the war, suddenly thrusting abnormally increased demands on American suppliers, powerfully lifted prices, especially in the great Midwestern grain belt. Dollar wheat was rare in the years before the war, but by 1915 farmers could command upwards of $1.25 a bushel for all the wheat they could supply. In the first year of the war more than ten million new acres were planted to wheat. More than one billion bushels were gathered in 1915, and despite the fantastic bounty of the harvest, prices held firm. The combination of a smaller crop and still rising demand pushed prices toward the two-dollar mark in 1916. Then with American entry into the war, under the authority of the Lever Food and Fuel Act, the President pegged the price for the 1917 crop at $2.20 a bushel.[23]

That price was unprecedentedly high—more than double the average prewar price—and it achieved its cardinal goal of expanding the acre-

22. Houston to Lewis Hancock, Nov. 28, 1916, Houston Papers, Houghton Library, Harvard University, Cambridge, Mass.
23. *Historical Statistics of the United States* (Washington, D.C.: Government Printing Office, 1975), 208; Theodore Saloutos and John D. Hicks, *Agricultural Discontent in the Middle West, 1900–1939* (Madison: University of Wisconsin Press, 1951), 87–94.

age sown to wheat. But almost from the instant the Lever Act was passed grain farmers grumbled that the price was too low. It failed to compensate, they complained, for the even more sharply inflated costs of the necessities of life and of all the factors that went into wheat production, such as wages, fertilizer, and machinery. The winds of discontent rising from the western plains beat especially hard upon Food Administrator Herbert Hoover. At the end of 1917 he told the President that "the farmers justly complain that . . . their income is restricted and no restraints are placed upon the goods they must purchase." The only acceptable remedy, Hoover explained, was "a general price-fixing power vested in yourself or in the Federal Trade Commission."[24] Wilson rather perfunctorily requested legislation to that end in his annual message to Congress on December 4, but the lawmakers showed little interest in granting such sweeping authority, and Wilson, in the low season of his political fortune during that trying winter, was unable to impose his will.

In the meantime, virtually all prices continued to ascend steeply—except that of wheat. In fact, the $2.20 price was not a fixed maximum but a guaranteed minimum, and when farmers asked that it be raised they were seeking not to reestablish a free-market price but to induce the government to raise its "artificial" support level. Congress, more readily disposed to dispense dollars than to expand presidential power, proved amenable to this simple means of placating agricultural unrest, and amended the Lever Act to provide a $2.40 minimum for the 1918 crop. Wilson now faced a painful—and fateful—decision. Approving the amendment would stoke the already raging fires of inflation. The urban press railed against the legislation, and the British ambassador pointedly informed the Treasury that its enactment would require his country to borrow an additional $100 million to finance food imports. Turning down the amendment, on the other hand, would strike a hard blow at the frail links holding the wheat states in the Democratic camp. Scissored between those hard choices, Wilson eventually vetoed the bill. His veto at a stroke carved apart the fragile political coalition that had carried the Democrats to victory in 1916. Not only did his action pinch Western farmers' pocketbooks; it also stood in inflammatory contrast to the administration's failure to restrain the fourfold increase in

24. Hoover to Wilson, Dec. 1, 1917, in Francis William O'Brien, ed., *The Hoover-Wilson Wartime Correspondence* (Ames: Iowa State University Press, 1974), 118.

the price of cotton, the principal crop of the South, the region which was now accused more rancorously than ever of dominating the national government and grossly discriminating against the interests of other sections. In November, the Democratic disaster in the grain belt was nearly total. Outside the West, the party did better than the dominant party usually does in an off-year congressional election, but all across the plains and prairie states the Democrats went down like dead timber. In Indiana, Republicans swept every contested seat. In Kansas, there was but a single Democratic survivor—a conspicuous critic, as it turned out, of the administration's inaction on cotton prices. The veto of the wheat-price amendment, in short, was the blade that cleaved the West from the Democratic South and drove Westerners back into the Republican fold. Many wartime policies were unpopular, but none was more fatally aimed at the weakest spot in the Democratic coalition.

The day after the 1918 election, Theodore Roosevelt crowed that "the Republicans made the fight on the unconditional surrender issue, and their victory serves notice on Germany that Foch will dictate the terms of the Armistice." But the *New York Times* more accurately observed that "the set of the current was against the Democrats for domestic reasons."[25] Not the immediate details of the Armistice but the accumulated resentments at wartime domestic policies had swung the election to the GOP. Republican savant Nicholas Murray Butler professed to see clearly the mandate the voters had given. The new Congress, he told Henry Cabot Lodge (who would be its predominant figure), "will not only bring an end to the tyranny under which we have been living for some years past, but it will erect a barrier against the farther advance of socialism, Bolshevism, and the destructive elements of society." Lodge agreed. "The Republican victory," he replied, "means a country-wide revolt against dictatorship and a desire to return to the constitutional limitations."[26] A few weeks later Lodge explained to his English friend James Bryce that "Mr. Wilson's defeat at the elections and the magnitude of the defeat are almost unbelievable. . . . The underlying cause was the dread deep down in the people's hearts of the establishment of a dictatorship, and in view of the great bureau-

25. *New York Times*, Nov. 7, 1918, 1, 14.
26. Butler to Lodge, Nov. 6, 1918, and Lodge to Butler, Nov. 16, 1918, Lodge Papers.

cratic machine which has been built up the alarm was anything but ill founded."[27]

Actually, the magnitude of Wilson's defeat was rather modest by usual midterm election standards. Moreover, it might be argued that not less but more government bureaucracy—in the form of price controls, at least over cotton—would have soothed Western resentment sufficiently to allow the Democrats to retain control of Congress. Lodge, in the manner of partisans, distorted the facts, and his distortions foreclosed any doubts about his intentions for the postwar period. His duty, as he saw it, was to dismantle as quickly as possible virtually the entire jerry-built edifice of Wilson's wartime powers.

Throughout the war, there had been much talk of the "reconstruction" that would follow the Armistice. The word connoted different things to different people. For some it simply implied the necessary redirection of resources from military to peaceful ends. For others it indicated a sweeping restructuring of the international order along the lines Wilson had sketched, however faintly. For some businessmen, it signified new roads and an expansion of government subsidies to shipping. But many reformers, said the progressive organ, *Survey*, still hoped for "a spiritual regeneration."[28] To progressives especially, reconstruction promised final realization of the reform opportunities the war had made possible at home.

Though the term was widely used, progressives had a particular affinity for the word "reconstruction," with its implied images of post-Civil War radicalism. The word had additional appeal for people associated with the *New Republic* because of its currency in Britain, where a Reconstruction Ministry, pledged to "moulding a better world out of the social and economic conditions which have come into being during the war," had been formed in 1917. Directed principally at the working classes, the British reconstruction proposals were frankly conceived "to allay war-weariness and discontent."[29] Accordingly, the British Labor Party took a keen interest in the matter, and appointed a special committee on reconstruction. Its report, "Labor and the New Social Order," strongly colored by socialist ideas, attracted wide attention in the

27. Lodge to James Bryce, Dec. 14, 1918, Lodge Papers.
28. *Survey* 41 (Nov. 30, 1918), 241–42.
29. Arthur Marwick, *The Deluge: British Society and the First World War* (New York: Norton, 1970), 239–40.

United States. The *New Republic* printed the entire document as a special supplement to its February 16, 1918, issue, and "earnestly recommended" it to readers.

Men and women of liberal persuasion had initially supported the war largely because they saw it as an opportunity to further the fight against drift in the nation's life, to assert mastery over social and economic affairs by strengthening the hand of the state. That was what John Dewey had meant by war's "social possibilities." It was what Walter Lippmann had meant when he portrayed the war as a time to "stand committed as never before to the realization of democracy in America." It was what countless progressives had meant when they earnestly described the war as an occasion to root out Prussianism in American society as well as abroad. At the time of the Armistice, progressives hoped to preserve and even to extend many of the collectivist practices and much of the state authority that had grown up during the war. "The whole issue," said the *New Republic*, "hinges on social control. For forty years and more we have been steadily but too slowly widening the sphere of this control, subordinating the individual to the group and the group to society. Without such control, we should not have been able to carry on the war." Now that peace had come, said the magazine, "we shall require a subordination of class and sectional interests to the interests of the nation, as well as an adjustment of these to the larger world interests. . . . For what we are deciding," the editors warned, "is whether we are to have cooperation in this country or a future civil war, whether we are to erect our building on solid ground or to build it over a volcano."[30]

Though events of the preceding nineteen months had already chastened many reformers, they had not lost their capacity for hope. "It is elementary that after the war America will not be the same America," said the irrepressible Grosvenor B. Clarkson. "Already she has in many directions broken with her past and she is being hourly transformed. . . . [C]hange will be as great in the thought and ideals of the nation as it will be in its strictly material problems. . . ." The entire world had become in the war "one great altar of sacrifice," he claimed, and "soon the spirit of the nation will be a burning flame. . . . Out of the turmoil and the sacrifice will come discipline and orderly living and thinking. . . . Here is the fundamental reconstruction to which the

30. *New Republic* 17 (Nov. 16, 1918), 59–61.

American Government should address itself."[31] In the same vein, the socialistic A. M. Simons cheered what he saw as the wartime passage of power from capital into the hands of government and labor. The government, he wrote, was "the great organizing force . . . toward which all else is oriented, the nucleus about which all social life is turning. . . . It will hereafter be something to use for the common good, to serve the common ends, to defend the common interest, and produce and distribute the common wealth."[32] "Capitalism," opined *Survey*, "will not come back unchallenged and uncontrolled."[33]

Those heady visions ignored some hard realities. The war had not massively dislocated American material life, creating pressure for further change, and though it had violently agitated the nation's spirit, it had not touched it deeply. The conflict was too remote, and American participation too short, to have worked transformations in "thought and ideals" on a scale such as Clarkson anticipated. Noted educator Charles W. Eliot, for one, knew better when he observed toward the end of the war that his countrymen on the whole were not committed to drastic social reconstruction nor even to a truly significant league of nations. "Americans as a rule," he wrote, "are too well pleased with what they have got to venture on vast untried experiments in vague hope of getting more."[34] Even John Dewey, much as he might have wished otherwise, knew this to be the case. "One is building on the sandiest of foundations," he wrote just after the Armistice, "who expects much help in dealing with post-war problems, domestic or foreign, from the community of emotional consciousness generated by the war. Men will resume the opposition of interests where they laid them down." The malleable moment, said the philosopher, had passed. What was not accomplished in the fluid environment of war could not now be wrung from the already rigidifying social structure of the aftermath. Any expectation for the future based on the unrealized hopes of wartime, he concluded, "is doomed."[35]

31. Grosvenor Clarkson, "A Memorandum to the Council of National Defense and the Advisory Council on Further Plans for Future Work . . . ," May 16, 1918, copy in WWP.
32. Algie M. Simons quoted in Burl Noggle, *Into the Twenties: The United States from Armistice to Normalcy* (Urbana: University of Illinois Press, 1974), 37.
33. *Survey* 41 (Nov. 16, 1918), 183.
34. Charles W. Eliot to James Bryce, Oct. 8, 1918, copy in Houston Papers.
35. John Dewey, "The Post-War Mind," in Joseph Ratner, ed., *Characters and Events: Popular Essays in Social and Political Philosophy by John Dewey*, 2 vols. (New York: Henry Holt, 1929), II, 599.

Political obstacles, too, lay in the path of a reform-oriented reconstruction. Woodrow Wilson, distracted by a myriad of other problems, had given only fitful consideration during the war to post-Armistice domestic arrangements. When Secretary Baker had recommended in June 1918 that the Council of National Defense be designated to study and coordinate reconstruction policies, Wilson had replied that "I am ashamed to say I am not clear as to just what you are referring to."[36] Still, the President had expressed some general intentions that offered hope to the reformers. Writing to New Jersey Democratic leaders in March 1918 about "the days of political and economic reconstruction which are ahead of us," Wilson had spoken of "the birth of a new day, a day . . . of greater opportunity and greater prosperity for the average mass of struggling men and women and of greater safety and opportunity for children." The war, he said, "is certain to change the mind . . . of America. . . . The men in the trenches, who have been freed from the economic serfdom to which some of them had been accustomed will, it is likely, return to their homes with a new view and a new impatience of all mere political phrases and will demand real thinking and sincere action."[37]

After Baker clarified his proposal to the President, Wilson gave the Council of National Defense his tepid approval for further studies of reconstruction matters. The ambitious Grosvenor Clarkson, secretary of the CND, immediately formed a reconstruction research group on his staff. In August he reported that the work was going slowly because it was buried and neglected in the bowels of the Council. Without an independent reconstruction agency on the model of the British ministry, he warned Secretary Baker, "if peace were to come today there would be only chaos in our efforts to unscramble the eggs that we have broken." He sketched a broad agenda to which such an agency should address itself, including demobilization of soldiers and sailors, industrial reconversion, labor problems, foreign trade, scientific research, the fate of the merchant marine and the railroads, and "Americanization of Aliens."[38]

Though such suggestions only feebly engaged his attention, Wilson was not entirely deaf to them. In the late summer and early autumn of 1918, he repeatedly evidenced his intention to appoint a special recon-

36. Wilson to Baker, June 12, 1918, WWP.
37. Wilson to New Jersey Democratic leaders, Mar. 20, 1918, WWP.
38. Grosvenor Clarkson to Newton D. Baker, Aug. 20, 1918, copy in WWP.

struction commission. "I have in mind the formation of such a commission as you suggest," he wrote in September to Edward A. Filene of the U.S. Chamber of Commerce; and in October, commenting on Senator Lee Overman's bill to create a federal commission on reconstruction, he said, "I had intended in any case to appoint a commission of this sort."[39] In early November, the newspapers abounded with speculation that the President was on the verge of creating a new commission. But Wilson's interest in a special reconstruction body, never very strong, was abruptly cut short by the Republican victory at the polls on November 5. Republican Senator John W. Weeks of Massachusetts, in Wilson's eyes among the most obnoxious of his political opponents, had already proposed in September to create a joint congressional committee on reconstruction, thus threatening to extend beyond the Armistice the wartime battle between Congress and the Executive for control of extraordinary powers. Wilson observed to Overman that "Senator Weeks' resolution was not intended to be helpful but had a distinct political object."[40] Overman's own bill was designed as a counter-measure to the Weeks proposal. It called for a presidential reconstruction commission, appointed with the advice and consent of the Senate. But now the Senate was to be Republican; any new reconstruction body would not be simply a presidential, or even a Democratic, creature, but would be strongly influenced by the opposition party.

When that reality became clear, Wilson's already slight interest evaporated. The Republicans, he wrote to Senator Key Pittman, were stirring within a few days after the election to emasculate his revenue bill, and this, he thought, "is only a sample of the things that will be attempted."[41] The opposition had been nettlesome enough during the war; Wilson had no desire to prolong his political agonies in peacetime by arming his foes with a new governmental instrument in the form of a powerful reconstruction commission. "I doubt if I shall appoint a new and separate Reconstruction Commission," he wrote to suffragist leader Dr. Anna Howard Shaw in mid-November. By the end of the month he was recommending speedy dissolution of the war-emergency bodies, arguing that "organizations built up for the urgent and pressing occupations of the war would not find enough to do to justify the sacrifices

39. Wilson to Filene, Sept. 7, 1918, RSB, VIII, 390; Wilson to Overman, Oct. 5, 1918, *ibid.*, 452.
40. *Idem.*
41. Wilson to Pittman, Nov. 12, 1918, WWP.

of individual time and effort involved, when peace conditions are re-established."[42]

In his final message to Congress, two days before departing for the peace conference at Paris on December 4, Wilson declared that "while the war lasted we set up many agencies by which to direct the industries of the country. . . . But the moment we knew the armistice to have been signed we took the harness off." The President had heard much, he reported, "as to the plans that should be formed and personally conducted to happy consummation, but from no quarter have I seen any general scheme of 'reconstruction' emerge which I thought it likely we could force our spirited businessmen and self-reliant labourers to accept with due pliancy and obedience." The people, he said, were resourceful and independent. "Any leading strings we might seek to put them in would speedily become hopelessly tangled because they would pay no attention to them and go their own way. All that we can do . . . is to mediate the process of change here, there, and elsewhere as we may."[43]

Wilson thus simply acknowledged the political reality that no new governmental instruments acceptable to him were likely to be forged. But that fact cannot greatly have discomfited him. The President had never pushed vigorously for a reconstruction agency that would institutionalize the reform possibilities of the war, in part because he had largely exhausted his own reform ideas even before 1917. Under his direction, mobilization had gone forward on the principle that the least possible disturbance should be inflicted on the existing economic system. The return to "normalcy" was to be an effective Republican slogan after the war, but in fact throughout the conflict it had been Wilson's main intention to depart from the normal as little as possible, especially in economic matters. Because American participation in the war had been so brief, it had proved feasible to pursue that policy to the very end. At the time of the Armistice, the United States was devoting only about one quarter of its gross national product to military needs. Virtually no enterprises had been completely curtailed; the War Industries Board typically restrained, but did not eliminate, so-called "non-essential" businesses. Economically, the war had not been total but partial.[44]

42. Wilson to Anna Howard Shaw, Nov. 18, 1918, and Wilson to Russell B. Harrison, Nov. 30, 1918, WWP.

43. Shaw, ed., *Messages and Papers of Woodrow Wilson*, I, 564.

44. See Paul A. Samuelson and Everett E. Hagen, *After the War, 1918–1920: Military and Economic Demobilization of the United States* (Washington, D.C.: Government Printing Office, 1943), especially 12, 40.

It followed that "reconstruction" should simply consist in a rapid and relatively painless snapping back into place of business-as-usual.

That, indeed, was the guiding principle of government policy in the days and weeks immediately following the Armistice. Bernard Baruch submitted his resignation in less than a fortnight, and by the end of November the War Industries Board had effectively ceased to function. The Fuel Administration began to liquidate its activities within four days of the German surrender. So went nearly all the major wartime agencies. The swiftness of their passing has often been attributed to economic ignorance and political cowardice—to failure to realize their potentially stabilizing effect on disordered postwar markets, and unwillingness further to challenge big-business interests. But the dismantling was perfectly compatible with the voluntaristic, informal, and incomplete way in which mobilization itself had been effected. And, in fact, the immediate postwar economy was remarkably vital, surging upward in a year-long boom propelled by continuing government deficits and backlogged foreign orders. Moreover, some of the strongest cries for retaining wartime controls came from business interests. They actively lobbied against rapid dismantling and for extension of at least some wartime government practices—especially continuing relaxation of the anti-trust laws. The War Emergency Congress of the U.S. Chamber of Commerce in December 1918 made such recommendations, including a request that government contracting officers remain in the public service long enough to complete contract-cancellation negotiations.

When the fighting stopped, the government held thousands of contracts worth $4 billion in still undelivered—in many cases still unmade—goods that could not be used in peacetime. Thus, on November 12, the telegraph wires fairly hummed with cancellation orders emanating from Washington. Within a month the Department had unburdened itself of $2.5 billion of those obligations, and eventually settled virtually the entire amount for about 13 cents on the dollar. There were potential legal problems here, as suppliers might justifiably balk at the sudden termination of purchase orders, but the government's terms proved generous enough to induce most businessmen to go along. A common form of settlement was to allow a contractor to charge the government for war work already done, including new capital investment, but from which no actual production had resulted. The government assumed those expenses and paid an additional 10 percent of profit on the amount so established. By these "capital allowances," the taxpayers, while relieved of nearly $3.5 billion of purchase obligations, directly subsidized almost half a billion dollars of new plant and machinery for private industry.[45]

No industry had felt the wartime hand of government more heavily than the railroads. Following the Armistice, the future of the government's relation to the railway system was, as Wilson told Congress just before his departure for Paris, "the question which causes me the greatest concern." Senator Albert Cummins of Iowa thought the disposition of the railroads second only to the League of Nations as "the most important and the most difficult of the many problems of reconstruction which the war has bequeathed to the United States."[46]

Always a major factor in industrial life, the railroads in the early twentieth century were uniquely indispensable to the health of the American economy. They had long since displaced canals and other waterways as the chief arteries of internal commerce, and the days of heavy reliance on highways and air freight were still in the future. The very centrality of the railways to the nation's economic system had made them for half a century before World War I the object of intense political activity. It was no accident that railway "brotherhoods" were among the most powerful unions—often called the "aristocrats of labor." Nor was it without significance that the first modern government regulatory body was the Interstate Commerce Commission (ICC)—created in 1887 to act on shipper complaints against railroad management's practices. By 1917, all these groups—labor, railroad management, and shippers—had long histories of skillful organizing and effective lobbying behind them. As in so many other sectors of American life, they were all keenly interested in turning the war to their particular advantage.

The mobilization-induced economic surge in 1917, in addition to the already roaring boom of the neutrality years, badly taxed the capacity of the rail network. Insufficient rolling stock, undermaintained roadbeds, antiquated terminal facilities, and inadequate coordination among

45. See John Maurice Clark, *The Costs of the World War to the American People* (New Haven: Yale University Press, 1931), 54; see also Benedict Crowell and Robert Forrest Wilson, *Demobilization: Our Industrial and Military Demobilization After the Armistice, 1918–1920* (New Haven: Yale University Press, 1921), chap. 8.

46. Shaw, ed., *Messages and Papers of Woodrow Wilson*, I, 570; Cummins quoted in K. Austin Kerr, *American Railroad Politics, 1914–1920: Rates, Wages and Efficiency* (Pittsburgh: University of Pittsburgh Press, 1968), 130. Much of the discussion that follows relies on Kerr's detailed account.

the several lines all threatened to strangle commerce and paralyze the war effort. By the fall of 1917, railcar shortages were forcing coal companies to close their pits and steel mills to bank their furnaces. Railroad management, seeking to put the crisis to good use, blamed the mess on the government. The operators argued that anti-trust laws prohibited reasonable consolidation, and that the rate-regulating powers of the ICC had so crimped profits in the preceding years that the railroads had been unable to expand and modernize their equipment. The solution, they insisted, was higher rates and relief from the threat of anti-trust prosecution. Shippers countered, as they always had, that competition was the guarantor of efficiency and fairness. Moreover, they ascribed the sorry condition of the railroads not to low rates but to over-capitalization. If the railroads were not afloat on a sea of watered stock, they would have adequate revenues to make needed capital improvements. The railway labor unions cared little about stock-watering, but because wages were tied to rate levels, they sided with management in the demand for higher rates. When the ICC refused on December 5, 1917, to allow substantial rate increases, the brotherhoods threatened to add to the already massive transportation chaos by walking off the job.

Coloring all discussion of railroad problems was the status of the railroads as public utilities. Because they held a "natural" monopoly, their services could not be easily substituted, and their functions vitally touched, directly and indirectly, a vast range of other activities. Those considerations created a "public" interest—to be attended to by the government—in the operation of the railway system. That interest, always present, became paramount in wartime. Faced with the near collapse of the nation's chief economic arteries under the weight of the war crisis, President Wilson proclaimed on December 26, 1917, that the railroads should pass under government control. Treasury Secretary William Gibbs McAdoo was named Director-General of the new Railroad Administration.

This was without doubt the most drastic mobilization measure of the war. Closing the hand of government over the country's largest and most essential enterprise, Wilson's action had enormous economic scope. It also had rich potential for lasting institutional change. Certain progressives longed to realize that potential. For years they had advocated outright government ownership of the railroads. That demand, dating back to Granger and Populist days, had enjoyed special popularity in the agricultural regions of the South and the plains and Pacific states. California's Hiram Johnson began immediately after Wilson's proclamation to agitate for permanent nationalization as the logical outcome of the emergency takeover. Now was the time for progressives "to begin the propaganda," Johnson enthused. "If McAdoo can successfully direct and manage the railroads for the government, a tremendous impetus will be given to government ownership."[47] During Wilson's first administration, McAdoo had advocated a federally owned and operated merchant marine, and he was widely presumed to view the railroad takeover, which he had urged upon the President, as another opportunity to test the principle of direct government intervention in the economy.

It was, of course, the successful testing of that principle that the railroad operators most feared. They were prepared to accept McAdoo only as a steamship captain receives a harbor pilot—welcoming his temporary aid to navigate a difficult passage without relinquishing permanent command of the vessel. Catering to those anxieties, Wilson assured the heads of the principal railroad systems that a board selected from their ranks would be appointed to advise the new Director-General of the Railroad Administration. Congress further allayed the fears of capital in the Federal Control Act of March 1918, stipulating that government control of the railroads would run no longer than twenty-one months after the end of hostilities. The Act also guaranteed the railway corporations a "standard return" (in effect, a government rental payment for use of the roads) equal to average earnings in 1915-1916-1917.[48] In addition, Congress effectively abrogated the rate-fixing powers of the ICC for the duration of federal control, a move that shippers loudly protested, since the Commission was historically their chief instrument in restraining the railroads from arbitrarily jacking up rates. But those complaints were in vain, and the way was cleared for the Railroad Administration to set rates on its own authority at whatever level it deemed appropriate to keep the transportation system

47. Johnson to C. K. McClatchey, Mar. 18, 1918, Johnson Papers.
48. Actually, the Railroad Administration proposed 1916–17 as the base period on which to compute the standard return. The suggestion delighted the operators, since those were exceptionally profitable years. Congress, responding to pressure from shippers who feared that too high an earnings base would compel rate increases, added 1915—but the base was still high enough to be acceptable to the railroads.

working smoothly. The first requirement of smooth operation was to pacify the restless railway brotherhoods, whose stirrings in late 1917 had been among the precipitating causes of government takeover. On May 25, 1918, McAdoo ordered wage hikes totalling $300 million for the nation's railway workers; almost immediately thereafter, he ordered a general rate increase to meet those additional costs.

McAdoo thereby revealed that his first priority, like that of his colleagues Hoover at the Food Administration and Baruch at the War Industries Board, was to obtain the highest level of uninterrupted service from the economic sector that he commanded—with small regard for the price. In the process, he swiftly divested reformers of their illusions about the significance of federal control. Appeasing railroad capital and labor with generous financial emoluments, McAdoo then handed the price tag to railroad users and the general public. Shippers' fees went up, and eventually the Railroad Administration was drawing on general federal revenues to make up deficits created by its higher labor costs. The traditionally anti-railroad regions wailed with pain at the announcement of the new rates, pain that Republicans were quick to exploit and that contributed to Democratic losses in the 1918 elections, especially in the Midwest. Progressives, too, quickly grew disgusted at McAdoo's collusion with railroad management and labor at the expense of the general public. Hiram Johnson, so recently enthusiastic about government operation, denounced the Federal Control Act as "one of the most infamous we have ever passed." It was, he protested, "outrageously generous to the railroads and shamefully unjust to the people." After the wage and rate jumps in the spring, Johnson exploded in fury. "Big business with its great profits, and railroad speculators with their stock soaring are content," he fumed, "while, on the other hand, vast increases in wages bring enthusiastic support from the natural opponents of big business." That diabolical alliance was made all the more unholy by the government's adherence. "God pity the forgotten middle class," Johnson raged, "who foot the bill!" Here was the classic progressive lament: the middle class, which presumptively embodied the "public" interest, was being ground between the wheels of special interest groups who had captured and prostituted the authority of the state. Hence many progressives like Johnson, who until the spring of 1918 had been the foremost advocates of public ownership of the railroads, recoiled from the effects of that policy when they saw it actually rehearsed in wartime. Because of McAdoo's administration of the railroads, concluded Johnson in 1919, government ownership "has been postponed for a couple of generations."[49]

But if the Director-General's policies had rapidly cooled the ardor of the progressives for railroad nationalization, the cause was soon taken up by the railway brotherhoods. The American labor movement in general had traditionally been suspicious of direct government intervention in the marketplace. But the brotherhoods found the Railroad Administration such an exceedingly open-handed paymaster that they now sought to make the government their employer in perpetuity. In 1919 they came forward with an elaborate plan, drafted by labor attorney Glenn Plumb, calling for government purchase of the railroads at an estimated cost of $18 billion, and for centralized administration by a tripartite board comprised of representatives of management, labor, and the public. Vigorously promoted by the powerful brotherhoods, the Plumb Plan attracted support from a handful of farm organizations, and from some intellectuals who saw it as the entering wedge for a broad-based socialist transformation in American industrial life. Precisely for that reason, Gompers and the A.F. of L. leadership, notoriously hostile to anything that smacked of socialism, stood aloof from the campaign. Yet by the end of the year, the brotherhoods and Gompers had momentarily buried their differences, not to make common cause in pushing the Plumb Plan, but to protect themselves from a mounting congressional onslaught against organized labor.

Leading the charge was Iowa Senator Albert Cummins. In a gesture of conciliation to Midwestern progressives, Lodge had seen to it that Cummins was installed as chairman of the Interstate Commerce Committee, where he might preside over railroad legislation. The gesture risked little to Lodge's constituents in the banking houses of Boston's State Street, who ministered to billions of dollars of private capital invested in railroad securities. Cummins, like Hiram Johnson, was a progressive of the most limited sort. One might almost say that he was a progressive of opportunity, possessed of no broad social vision, his politics closely fitted to the quite specific interests of his constituents—mainly shippers in thrall to the railroads, burning with resentment at their wartime victimization by government in cahoots with labor. Like Johnson, Cummins had abandoned by 1919 any thought of nationalization; the war experience had only too clearly demonstrated the dangers

49. Johnson to C. K. McClatchey, Mar. 3, 1918; to Meyer Lissner, June 4, 1918; to McClatchey, July 16, 1918, and Aug. 19, 1919, Johnson Papers.

of that policy. He sought simply to restore the rate-fixing powers of the
ICC, the shippers' chief lever on railroad policy. His overall aim was to
secure efficient functioning of the railroads at the lowest possible rates;
his strategy, to effect a détente of sorts between the operators and the
shippers. Conspicuously absent from this political equation were the
interests of labor.

The bill that Cummins introduced in the Senate in the spring of 1919
revealed much about the new equilibrium of political forces struck by
the war and the recent congressional elections. In exchange for restoring controls to the ICC, Cummins proposed to instruct the Commission
to draw rates in such a way as to guarantee to capital a certain "fair
return," calculated as a percentage of investment. Half of a given rail-
line's net earnings in excess of that level were to be "recaptured" by
the ICC for redistribution to financially weaker lines. Here was riskless
capitalism with a vengeance, promising profits to all, with the sound
enterprises shoring up the uneconomical or mismanaged. Nor were
virtual government guarantees of profits the only feature of wartime
largesse to capital that Cummins proposed to continue; his bill also
substantially exempted railroad consolidations from anti-trust prosecutions. Not surprisingly, the investors and managers whose interests
Lodge so faithfully guarded had warm applause for the Iowa Senator.

But toward labor, Cummins's bill was extraordinarily harsh. It simply outlawed strikes against the railroads, depriving the brotherhoods
of their only effective weapon in the perpetual confrontation with capital. Gompers, fearful that the ban on strikes, if enacted, would eventually be extended to all unions, sprang instantly to arms. When the bill
passed the Senate with the anti-strike clause intact, the A.F. of L. and
the railway brotherhoods joined hands in a massive lobbying drive
against the offensive clause. In the stampede for refuge from the anti-
strike statute, the Plumb Plan was left to die of neglect. In the end, the
no-strike feature was deleted from the Transportation Act of 1920, as
the final legislation was called. In its place was substituted a Railway
Labor Board, modeled on wartime boards of mediation. It had authority to arbitrate labor disputes, but supposedly no power to compel
settlements on an unwilling party. For labor, ever fearful of compulsory
arbitration, this seemed an improvement. But one of the Board's first
acts was to order a 12 percent slash in railway shopmen's wages, as
well as to repeal certain shop rules negotiated in wartime. If that were
not enough, the Board in 1922 ordered a further 12 percent cut. When

the shopmen walked off the job, the government declared their strike illegal because it violated the Board's mandated settlement, and the Justice Department secured against them the most drastic and sweeping injunction in American history. This was compulsory arbitration in all but name.

Thus, for the railroads, the war had proved a singularly aberrant moment. Temporarily set askew by the exigencies of mobilization, traditional power relationships in the transportation sector had reasserted themselves by 1920. If anything, the conservative features of those relationships had been deepened, mocking the high reform hopes that government takeover had momentarily engendered. Shippers, largely disillusioned with nationalization of the railroads, now contented themselves with pressing their claims, as before, through the ICC. Management, once fearful of government authority, now luxuriated in an environment where the government effectively guaranteed profitability. And railroad labor, briefly prosperous and even more briefly smitten with the idea that the state could be permanently arrayed on the side of the workers, was now more tightly strait-jacketed than ever.

Few groups during the war had fed so lavishly as labor on hopes for the aftermath. Samuel Gompers had viewed the crisis as a crucible in which he might forge permanent gains for organized workers. He was reportedly heard to express regret on Armistice Day that the war had ended so soon, before all the gains he envisioned could be solidly realized.[50] The story, though perhaps apocryphal, was not without its point. By November 1918, A.F. of L. membership was shooting past the three million mark. In the most heavily unionized sectors—coal mining, manufacturing, and transportation—real wages were rising as much as 20 percent over 1914 levels. The long-sought eight-hour day was at last becoming the national standard. Not least, the war had finally enabled Gompers and the "business unionists" of the A.F. of L. to administer the *coup de grace* to their radical adversaries in the labor movement. "We can afford to ignore what is left of the American Socialist Party," clucked the *American Federationist* in 1919. As for the IWW, it was fast exiting the stage where it had strutted its brief hour,

50. Frank L. Grubbs, *The Struggle for Labor Loyalty: Gompers, the A.F. of L., and the Pacifists, 1917–1920* (Durham, N.C.: Duke University Press, 1968), 129, citing a 1964 interview with Norman Thomas.

and was passing already into the realm of song and story.[51] The war had brought all those boons, which gave Gompers great comfort.

It does not stretch belief to imagine that, amidst the din of Armistice merriment, Gompers might have paused momentarily to wonder with trepidation if his good fortune should continue. By November 1918, many of the conditions that had underpinned labor's rise were rapidly eroding. The Wilson administration had been remarkably friendly, even before the war. It had created a Secretaryship of Labor in 1913, fought to have unions exempted from the anti-trust laws in the Clayton Act of 1914, stood behind the La Follette Seaman's Act in 1915, and in 1916 supported the Adamson Act, which mandated an eight-hour day on the railroads. Inevitably, those advances had provoked a political reaction. Critics harped especially on the unseemly circumstances surrounding the passage of the Adamson Act, when Congress was apparently coerced into action under the threat of a general railway strike. As the United States entered the war, Republicans were already making political capital out of labor's alarming ascendancy. The war deflected their attention to other more vulnerable aspects of Democratic policy, but now, with the fighting over and the Republicans in control of Congress, Gompers knew that the counter-attack would resume. He knew, too, that the evaporation of government war orders, the resumption of immigration, and the flood of returned servicemen onto the labor exchanges would rapidly relax the artificially tight labor market that had allowed him to exercise great power. And though his old radical opponents were largely defunct, who could say what new threats to his conservative leadership might be inspired by the energetic stirrings of the British Labor Party, or even by the revolutionary winds blowing out of Russia? In the humming of the telegraph wires carrying war contract cancellation orders on November 12, Gompers might have heard proof of his fears.

The Wilson administration had been required by the needs of war to treat workers well; work stoppages could not be permitted to retard essential war production. To prevent interruptions, the government might either prevent or persuade workers from striking. There were those who favored the former policy. Military officers and railroad executives, for example, had in 1914 and 1915 discussed plans for drafting railroad workers into the Army in the event of war, thus imposing military discipline on a key element of the labor force, backed by the

51. *American Federationist* 26 (1919), 1140.

threat of court-martial.[52] In late 1917 even some Pacific Coast union leaders were said to favor "the drafting of labor for shipyards."[53] But the administration characteristically chose, insofar as possible, to avoid overtly coercive techniques. Instead, it hoped to mollify labor, and the chief instrument of that policy was the government contract.

The first contracts to reveal the government's attitude toward labor were those let by the War Department for the construction of army camps, or cantonments, in the spring of 1917. The Department wanted the camps built with the utmost speed; that meant attracting workers in great numbers and from any source to hammer the planks and shingle the roofs of the barracks that would eventually house several million soldiers. The building trades were strongly organized, and they were historically adamant against "diluting" union-protected job classifications with unskilled, non-union workers. They could be expected to protect their hard-won positions by insisting on the closed shop—which would pose a fatal obstacle to the swift erection of the camps. The government met the anticipated protest in two ways. It underwrote a high-wage policy by letting the contracts on a "cost-plus" basis, in effect indemnifying the contractor against any profit squeeze from rising labor costs. Then, through memorandum between Gompers and Secretary of War Baker was established a Cantonment Adjustment Commission, to be comprised of members representing equally the Army, labor, and the public. The Commission was empowered to adjudicate all labor disputes arising from the camp-construction work.[54]

More labor commissions, similarly constituted, soon emerged in other areas where the government was fast becoming a major employer or purchaser of goods and services: in the booming shipyards, in the longshore and garment trades, even among leather workers supplying harness and saddlery to the cavalry. All the commissions had several features in common. They were backed by the government's willingness to recompense contractors for whatever wage increases the commissions

52. James Leonard Abrahamson, *The Military and American Society, 1881–1922* (Ph.D. dissertation, Stanford, 1976), 503.

53. L. B. Wehle to Wilson, Nov. 11, 1917, WWP.

54. Louis B. Wehle, "The Adjustment of Labor Disputes Incident to Production for War in the United States," *Quarterly Journal of Economics* 32 (1917), 122–41; the following discussion relies heavily on this article and two others by Wehle in subsequent issues of the *Quarterly Journal of Economics:* "Labor Problems in the United States During the War," *QJE* 32 (1918), 333–92; and "War Labor Policies and Their Outcome in Peace," *QJE* 33 (1919), 321–43.

recommended. They were formed by voluntary agreement between the government and labor leaders. They thus had little legal power to enforce their edicts. With respect to workers, they had virtually no means of compulsion, but could only offer economic blandishments. With regard to employers, the boards themselves had no power, but the War Department might withdraw a contract from a recalcitrant firm, or even, in extreme cases, threaten to commandeer its plant. In practice, the government pushed to include many generous labor provisions in its contracts: a living wage, the eight-hour day, respect for existing craft rules, and equal pay for women doing equal work. But deliberately absent from the list of conditions the boards were mandated to protect was the closed shop. The government's insistence on that principle would have been a revolutionary step, fundamentally altering the structure of power in the industrial system. Gompers, however much he might have desired such an alteration, knew that the resistance to it would be fierce, and contented himself with guarantees on wages and working conditions. The typical labor board arrangement, said a wartime labor administrator, "was a bargain for union scales in exchange for the union shop."[55]

Despite the government's generosity toward labor, enormous problems remained. Some arose on account of that very generosity. Wages were so high and demand for labor so strong in enterprises such as shipbuilding and munitions-making that workers flocked from other jobs and regions into contract-glutted centers like Bridgeport, Connecticut; Wilmington, Delaware; and Norfolk, Virginia. Since the adjustment boards did not stipulate maximum wages, labor-hungry employers even within a given sector bid workers away from one another with wild abandon. In the Pacific Northwest lumber industry, for example, the annual labor turnover rate was in excess of 600 percent— that is, the typical job was held by six different men in a given year. Some plants reported turnovers as high as 1200 percent. England had experienced similar problems early in the war, and had acted decisively to restrict labor mobility by a system of "leaving certificates," whereby a worker could not be reemployed without certifying that he had left his last job with the consent of his employer. Characteristically, the American response to the same problem was far less coercive. Here, instead of leading to forcible restraints on labor, the wartime turnover problem stimulated the development of "personnel management": keep-

55. Wehle, "Adjustment of Labor Disputes," 126.

ing workers contented and on the job not by legal constraints but by loving kindness. One labor administrator drew the familiarly comforting trans-Atlantic contrast. Worker education and "employment management," he said, "have not been borrowed from Great Britain; they are distinctly American." For the British, he suggested, stabilizing the labor force called for compulsory means; but in America, "it is a problem in selling the job to the man every day, a problem in emotional complexes."[56] Encouraged by the Department of Labor, several government contracting agencies established "industrial service sections," designed to teach the arts of scientifically managing the work force without resort to compulsion. Arsenal officers and munitions contractors, for example, attended an employment management program at Dartmouth College. The war gave a sizable boost to the cause of scientific management, significantly moving American industry toward the welfare capitalism of the 1920s. In that decade, as in the war, capital's largesse toward labor was made possible by unprecedented prosperity, by the ability of management to operate within wide margins of profit. In such an environment, benefits could easily be offered as a substitute for unions, an affordable means to purchase the preservation of the existing power relationships.

Still, those open-handed policies did not meet with uniform success. The year 1917 saw 4,450 strikes, the highest number in American history. The trans-Mississippi West, in particular, rumbled and flashed with violence throughout the summer and autumn, as strikes were called in the copper mines of Montana and Arizona, in shipyards up and down the Pacific Coast, and in the forests of the Pacific Northwest. Alarmed at the extent of the disquiet, Wilson appointed a President's Mediation Commission to travel to the troubled regions in the fall. Secretary to the Commission was Felix Frankfurter, on leave from Harvard Law School. Short, always impeccably tailored, quietly but fiercely proud of his rise to scholarly and political eminence from the teeming Jewish ghettos of the Lower East Side, Frankfurter possessed a mind that moved with clocklike precision and would eventually propel him to a seat on the Supreme Court. Just thirty-five years of age in 1917, he had already established himself as a brilliant young man of advanced views, especially on the subject of labor. His appointment was

56. Wehle, "Labor Problems in the United States," 346.

widely perceived as another sign of Wilson's cordial regard for the interests of the unions.[57]

After traveling for several weeks through the West in late 1917, Frankfurter wrote his friend Walter Lippmann that he had gathered "a good deal of content on the industrial issue . . . though so far as the central analysis of the situation goes, it is what you and I have known for many a year."[58] What Lippmann and Frankfurter had long known was that workers who lacked the protection of recognized unions stood naked before the frequently brutal power of capital. That fact, true throughout industrial society, could be especially cruel in the rugged raw-material industries of the West, as Frankfurter rudely discovered in the copper district of Bisbee, Arizona.

Bisbee's copper miners, many of them "Wobblies" (members of the IWW) had walked off the job on June 28, 1917. County Sheriff Harry Wheeler, an ex-Rough Rider, was not disposed to trifle with the strikers. He first asked for federal troops, but when an Army observer sent to the scene reported that there was no disorder and hence no cause for military intervention, Wheeler and the local citizenry took matters into their own hands. In the early morning of June 12, an armed force 2000

57. Though the President hardly knew Frankfurter at this time, he had enough confidence in the young lawyer's reputation to ask him to undertake a delicate mission in addition to his assigned duties as secretary to the Mediation Commission. At the conclusion of a meeting with the commissioners, before they departed for the West, Wilson turned to Frankfurter and asked him to look into the case of Tom Mooney. Frankfurter had scarcely heard of the matter, but he soon learned that Mooney had been sentenced to death for planting a bomb that killed several people during a San Francisco Preparedness Day parade in July 1916. Mooney's case had become a cause célèbre among laborers and intellectuals, and Frankfurter, after investigation, concluded that Mooney had in all likelihood been convicted on the basis of perjured testimony. On receiving Frankfurter's report, Wilson asked California Governor William D. Stephens to suspend sentence and order a new trial. Stephens merely commuted the sentence to life imprisonment, and the issue continued to simmer. Secretary of Labor William B. Wilson drew "long and sustained" applause from an A.F. of L. audience in June 1919 when he assured his listeners that the administration was still trying to obtain a new trial for Mooney. But those efforts, however much they evidenced the administration's strong sympathy with labor on a highly emotional issue, provided small comfort to the hapless Mooney, who languished in a California jail until he was finally pardoned in 1939. See Joseph P. Lash, ed., *From the Diaries of Felix Frankfurter* (New York: Norton, 1975), introduction; and W. B. Wilson, "Address Before the AFL Convention," June 13, 1919, copy in WWP.
58. Frankfurter to Lippmann, Nov. 22, 1917, Frankfurter Papers, Library of Congress, Washington, D.C.

strong, supposedly deputized by Wheeler, swooped down on the workers' quarter in Bisbee, rounded up nearly 1200 men, and herded them at rifle point aboard a train to Columbus, New Mexico. The Columbus authorities refused to allow the men to disembark, and dispatched the train to a sun-baked siding at Hermanas, New Mexico. There the refugees sweltered for two days with practically no food or water until finally rescued by federal troops. Bisbee virtually became a stockade town, with fresh workers brought in to reopen the mines, and the deportees kept out by armed patrols. Some of the exiles were later rearrested as they tried to return to Bisbee to report for their Selective Service physical examination. Frankfurter, acting for the Commission, condemned the deportation as "wholly illegal and without authority in law, either state or federal."[59] Despite the fact that Wheeler and his "deputies" had effectively kidnapped 1200 persons and forcibly shipped them across state lines, Attorney General Thomas W. Gregory professed to see no clear grounds for a federal case.[60] Finally, prodded by the Commission and the President, Gregory rather unenthusiastically brought indictments against the vigilantes, who were shown to have been armed and paid by the Phelps-Dodge Company, operator of the Bisbee mines. No company officers, however, were indicted, and after several months of desultory prosecution, an Arizona federal district court squashed the indictments against the vigilantes. The Supreme Court eventually upheld that decision. Such was justice in the wartime Southwest.

Conditions were no less wretched in the Pacific Northwest. The vast cantonment and shipbuilding programs needed almost limitless supplies of lumber hewn from the great Douglas fir forests of Washington and Oregon, and airplane manufacturers required quantities of Northwest spruce. But in late 1917, it was said, the birds were still singing in the trees from which the lumber for war production should have long since been cut. Labor problems had kept the woods and mills silent for much of the year, as loggers demanded an eight-hour day and improved conditions in the camps. A highly seasonal, migratory, and fragmented business, the lumber industry notoriously treated its workers badly. The camps were unlivable sinkholes, accumulating all the drifting flotsam of a rootless labor force that was "womanless,

59. President's Mediation Commission, *Report on the Bisbee Deportations* (Washington, D.C.: Government Printing Office, 1918).
60. Thomas W. Gregory to R. L. Batts, Jan. 10, 1918, Gregory Papers, Library of Congress, Washington, D.C.

voteless, and jobless," as Frankfurter put it, and provided natural re-cruits for the inflammatory doctrines of the IWW. Mark Twain once remarked that any man worth his salt would fight to protect his home, but who would go to war to defend his boardinghouse? The quip might have been inspired by the condition of the lumberjacks, who were cool toward the war, short on patriotism, and long on bitterness toward the established order. One Northwest Wobbly put it bluntly:

> If you were a bum without a blanket; if you had left your wife and kids while you went West for a job and never located them since; if your job never kept you long enough in one place to vote; if you slept in a lousy bunk-house and ate rotten food; if every person who represented law and order beat you up . . . how in hell do you expect a man to be patriotic?[61]

The Commission's report, drafted by Frankfurter, expressed warm sympathy for the loggers' plight. It endorsed agitation for the eight-hour day as "at bottom the assertion of human dignity," called the camps "disintegrating forces in society," and even acknowledged the appeal of the IWW to desperate men seeking "a bond of groping fel-lowship." Frankfurter clearly blamed the intractable mill and timber owners for failing to deal with a moderate union and thus driving the men into the dangerously radical IWW.[62]

The government could not tolerate continued disruption of such a vital war industry. The root problem, the Commission concluded, was the "bitter attitude of the operators toward any organization among their employees." Yet the one union that commanded some support in the woods was the IWW, anathema to the owners and hardly less dis-tasteful to the administration. The government therefore took a series of decisive and novel steps. It first broke the back of the IWW, in the Northwest and elsewhere, with the raids of September 1917. Then in November the Army posted Colonel Brice P. Disque to the Northwest, in command of the Spruce Production Division—10,000 troops in civilian clothing who were to work in the mills and woods and form the nucleus of a new union, the Loyal Legion of Loggers and Lumbermen, or the 4-L. With President Wilson's backing and, at first, Samuel Gompers's blessing, Disque proceeded to organize the lumberjacks' union, 120,000

61. Quoted in Patrick Renshaw, "The I.W.W. and the Red Scare, 1917–1924," *Journal of Contemporary History* 3 (1968), 68.
62. *Report of the President's Mediation Commission to the President of the United States* (Washington, D.C.: Government Printing Office, 1918), 14.

strong at the Armistice. Members pledged "to faithfully perform my duty toward the company by directing my best efforts, in every way possible, to the production of logs and lumber for the construction of army airplanes and ships to be used against our common enemies." With such assurances Disque won the confidence of the operators and eventually, in February 1918, secured employer agreement to the eight-hour day throughout the region. He also succeeded in establishing the industry's first minimum wage, and in making improvements in the condition of the camps.

All this certainly benefited the loggers, brought peace to the North-west forests, and stabilized lumber production. But the 4-L was a de-cidedly tame union, at the farthest imaginable extreme from the IWW, objectionable even by the conservative standards of the A.F. of L., which was soon complaining that its representatives were prohibited from visiting the camps. The 4-L represented company unionism, pure and simple. It had been organized by the U.S. Army; its leaders were "safe"; managers were eligible for membership; and members were re-quired to sign a no-strike pledge.[63] Small wonder that the owners were able to accommodate it.

Disque's activities constituted a uniquely direct form of government intervention in the economic sphere, but they were not essentially dis-tinguishable from the efforts that the government had made to disci-pline other sectors by inducing organization. The soldier-organizers of the 4-L were essentially performing the same functions as the com-modity men at the WIB or the county agents who helped create the Farm Bureau Federation—calling forth acceptable organization where it did not previously exist. For all its singularity, the 4-L was, in the end, simply a part of the great war-forced march toward a better articu-lated organizational structuring of American life.

That deepening organizational structure did not necessarily alter the existing lines of power in the society; indeed it proceeded scrupulously along those very lines, and even set them more rigidly in place. In that respect, too, and again despite its unique features, the 4-L nicely exemplified the administration's general wartime labor policy. The cardinal aim, always, was to secure maximum, uninterrupted produc-

63. For these reasons, the 4-L expired in 1935 after the passage of the Wagner Act, which effectively outlawed company unions. See Robert L. Tyler, "The United States Government as Union Organizer: The Loyal Legion of Loggers and Lumbermen," *Mississippi Valley Historical Review* 47 (1960), 434–51.

tion. High wages and improved working conditions fitted that aim, but any attempt to force a fundamental change in the distribution of industrial power would have unleashed the full wrath of capital and badly disrupted the flow of war production. For that reason, if no other, the government's labor policy, though magnanimous, was distinctly limited. Frankfurter and the more aggressive union leaders pushed always at the borders of policy. Not content with more pay and shorter hours, they strove to put the weight of the government behind the principle of unionism itself. But their success was small. Gompers seems to have decided early that such a goal was unrealistic, and he agreed to a Council of National Defense statement stipulating "that employers and employees in private industries should not attempt to take advantage of the existing abnormal conditions to change the standards which they were unable to change under normal conditions."[64]

That statement described precisely the government's position. The original cantonment agreements deliberately failed to insist on the union shop; even the 4-L was not really a "union" at all, but a company device to organize the men without granting them appreciable power. When Wilson received complaints in the summer of 1917 that labor leaders were endeavoring to use the war crisis to compel recognition of their unions, he brought the matter before the cabinet and instructed the Secretary of Labor to investigate. The Secretary reported that only an "infinitesimal" number of strikes included the demand for union recognition, and the President was evidently reassured.[65] Workers might organize, said the government—in fact they were encouraged to organize—but the administration was quite unprepared in the midst of war to require employers to recognize truly independent unions. There Wilson drew the line, and there it remained throughout the war, rather anomalously midway between the desires of capital and those of labor.

When the government moved to rationalize its labor policies with the creation of a War Labor Board in early 1918, it further codified this curious arrangement, permitting unions to exist but assuring them no power. President Wilson directed the WLB to protect the right of workers to organize and bargain collectively. Employers could not

64. "Recommendations Made by Committee on Labor, Conservation of Health and Welfare of Workers," of the Council of National Defense (chaired by Gompers), n.d., copy in Bernard Baruch Papers, Firestone Library, Princeton University, Princeton, N.J.
65. Charles W. Eliot to Wilson, July 20, 1917, and William B. Wilson to Wilson, July 26, 1917, WWP.

interfere with organizers, nor discriminate among union and non-union employees. But at the same time the Board was instructed that the open shop "shall not be deemed a grievance," where it was already the practice; moreover, unions were to be prohibited from requiring workers to become union members, and from doing anything "to induce employers to bargain or deal" with them.[66] Thus management might refuse to meet with union representatives, or might choose to deal exclusively with a safe union of its own creation, as in the case of the 4-L. There were some employers who chafed at even those mild prescriptions, sensing perhaps that any organization, once in place, would be impossible to control forever. Against such holdouts the government could be tough. The Smith and Wesson arms plant in Springfield, Massachusetts, and the Western Union telegraph company, for example, flouted the WLB's rules forbidding discrimination against union employees, and Wilson eventually commandeered both firms.[67] But most industries played by the rules, probably because the rules required them to give up very little. Cost-plus contracting allowed many employers to be generous at the government's expense. More significant, the administration's unwillingness to require collective bargaining with a majority-elected union encouraged the formation of company unions, as employers sought the advantage of labor organization without any of its liabilities. By 1926, membership in company unions was to reach half the level of membership in the A.F. of L. A variant on this device was the "shop committee," a small delegation of workers, organized on a plant-by-plant basis, with outside union agents rigorously excluded. In both cases, employers were easily able to maintain final control.

Still, the government's war labor policies greatly stimulated the *bona fide* union movement. The benefits of association became increasingly evident to many workers previously beyond the reach of organization, as union agents went about their work with relative impunity, even with government protection. Against capital the government was armed with the labor provisions written into war contracts, and, ultimately, with the commandeering power. And not until late in the war did the administration lift its hand against the unions affiliated with the A.F. of L. Its restraint derived from legal weakness no less than from genu-

66. Wehle, "War Labor Policies," 328.
67. Gordon S. Watkins, *Labor Problems and Labor Administration in the United States During the World War,* University of Illinois Studies in the Social Sciences, VIII (Urbana: University of Illinois, 1919), 169–70.

ine cordiality. Until May 1918 the government simply had little leverage on labor, other than the blandishments of better wages and hours.

There were some occasions to regret that impotence. When striking carpenters in early 1918 menaced the crucial shipbuilding program by refusing to accept a labor board wage settlement, Wilson was reduced to trying to shame the men back to work. "You are undoubtedly giving aid and comfort to the enemy," preached the President, but he could do little more than jawbone.[68] Wilson's inability to take stronger measures in this case may have been the factor prompting him to consider more closely the potential of the Selective Service System as an instrument for the general control of industrial manpower.

In May 1918, Selective Service Director General Enoch Crowder promulgated a "work-or-fight" order, declaring that unemployed men should go immediately to the top of the draft lists. Organized labor was deeply agitated at the order, seeing it as a brazen attempt to crack the whip over workers with the threat of military call-up. They had seen it happen already in Britain, where "the mailed fist of military authority at once punched . . . strikers into the army."[69] Secretary of War Baker gave assurances that strikers would not be counted among the unemployed, but labor remained uneasy, and was measurably less inclined to strike in 1918.[70] Its unease was not unjustified. When machinists walked out in Bridgeport, Connecticut, the following autumn, Wilson pointedly informed them that their persistence would result in their being barred from any war-related work for a year, during which time "the draft boards will be instructed to reject any claim of exemption based on your alleged usefulness on war production."[71] The machinists scurried back to their lathes and dies, and it seemed briefly that in America, as in Britain, the government was about to reveal to labor the mailed fist beneath the velvet glove it had worn throughout the war. At least one wartime labor official felt that the "underlying principles of the British labor policy . . . must be established in this country if the war continues for any considerable period."[72] But within a few weeks of the Bridgeport strike the war was over, and the fist was never fully ungloved. As in so many areas, the brevity of American

68. Wilson to W. L. Hutcheson, Feb. 17, 1918, RSB, VII, 550.
69. Marwick, *The Deluge,* 206.
70. For Baker's assurances, see *New York Times,* May 26, 1918, 14. There were nearly 1000 fewer strikes in 1918 than in 1917. *Historical Statistics,* 179.
71. Shaw, ed., *Messages and Papers of Woodrow Wilson,* I, 516.
72. Wehle, "Labor Problems in the United States," 338.

belligerency had spared the country the directly coercive measures that
Europeans had so often been driven to adopt. The administration had
succeeded in reaching the end of the war with a minimum exercise of
naked power over labor, which could plausibly dismiss the Bridgeport
episode as an unfortunate and singular aberration.

Unionists like Gompers entered the Armistice period with high hopes
indeed. The war had swelled their ranks, fattened their treasuries, and,
they thought, earned them the government's goodwill. So encouraged,
they determined even before the war was over to take up again American labor's historic Sysiphean effort: to organize in the iron and steel
industry. Thirty union leaders met in Chicago on August 1, 1918, to
form the National Committee for Organizing Iron and Steel Workers.
Gompers, presiding over the assembly, invoked the war-born hopeful
spirit: "The old relation in industry of master and slave is giving way
to new ones where employer and employee meet on the basis of equality. . . . We have established democracy in politics, now we must
establish democracy in industry. . . . And our present purpose is to
establish democracy in the iron and steel industry."[73]

Steel, it was said, was the masterclock of the American industrial
system, the most basic manufacturing industry, its hearths and cruci-
bles pouring life into hundreds of other lines of enterprise, its financial
stature imposing, its management concentrated in the hands of a few
tough men, its indispensability to the modern economy second only to
that of the railroads. Labor strategists had long recognized the critical
importance of steel, knowing what a boost a successful organizing
drive in that sector would give to the workers' movement in general.
But, unlike the railroads, steel had proved implacably resistant to
unionization. The Carnegie Steel Company had ruthlessly crushed the
old Amalgamated Association of Iron and Steel Workers in the Homestead Strike of 1892. From that bloody confrontation, in which seven
men had been killed, came a curt warning: the Carnegie Steel Company "will never again recognize the Amalgamated Association or any
other labor organization."[74] The entire industry followed suit, pursuing
a merciless anti-union policy for the next twenty-five years.

During the same period, steelmakers had aggressively mechanized
the industry, reducing requisite skill levels, even rendering obsolete

73. Quoted in David Brody, *Labor in Crisis: The Steel Strike of 1919* (Phila-
    delphia: Lippincott, 1965), 63.
74. *Ibid.*, 18.

many of the crafts that formed the organizational backbone of the trade union movement. Those developments made steel a natural place of employment for the untrained, often illiterate, work-hungry men of the "new immigration." By the time of World War I, the industry's furnaces were stoked and its mills tended by a great mass of ethnically Balkanized, mostly unskilled workers. Here lay the overriding importance of a successful union drive in steel: as steel had gone, so was going much of American industry. Mechanization was being stepped up everywhere. In the process, traditional skills were deliberately downgraded, and the work force was transformed from a crafts to a mass industrial basis. World War I had greatly accelerated that trend, as rising labor costs on the one hand and investment-tax incentives and subsidies on the other stimulated rapid acquisition of new equipment. At International Harvester, for example, a top priority after the war was "to reduce labor cost by installing revised routing systems and labor-saving devices."[75] Machines were being made to usurp the talents of mere men. Steel, therefore, was a great test case, on which depended American trade unionism's very survival in a capital-intense, mass-production industrial era.

The character of the work force was not the only obstacle facing an organizing drive in steel. The coming of the Armistice left precious few means for the government to make its weight felt on labor's side, however much it might have been inclined to do so. Cancelled contracts and the presumed evaporation of the commandeering power, granted only for the duration of the conflict, broke the government's already tenuous grip on capital. Contrary to its expectations when it launched the steel organizing campaign in August 1918, the National Committee would have to stand alone against its ancient nemesis. With the government effectively neutralized, the scene was thus ominously set for the resumption of bare-handed industrial combat. Against labor's heightened hopes was set the strengthened determination of capital, especially in the steel industry, to resist union demands. "The war has stirred up a consciousness on the part of both classes," noted one observer. "The theoretic status of each may have been very little altered, but the intensity of the beliefs of each class has deepened."[76] The historic indus-

75. Edwin F. Gay Diary, entry for Feb. 1, 1919, Gay Papers, Hoover Institution on War, Revolution and Peace, Stanford University, Stanford, Ca. (hereafter Hoover Institution).

76. Joseph H. Willits, "War's Challenge to Employment Managers," *Annals of the American Academy of Political and Social Science* 81 (1919), 47–50 (hereafter *Annals*).

trial struggle, in short, had been only temporarily contained during the war. It exploded in 1919 in heightened turmoil and violence. In that turbulent year, one in five workers—more than ever before in American history—would put down his tools in protest, and the public outcry to restore industrial peace would grow terribly clamorous. Against that roiling backdrop, alone and unaided, labor launched its assault on the steel industry.

National Committee organizers had no shortage of grievances with which to arouse the steelworkers. Wages, especially in such inflationary times, were a major object of complaint. Even more hotly resented was the twelve-hour day, still common in the mills, its grinding effects made worse by the periodic "turnover" of the night and day gangs, when the men were required to stand a continuous twenty-four hour shift. But, at bottom, as both sides knew, "the dispute was not over wages, hours or conditions, but over unionism itself. Organized labor was demanding the right to represent and bargain for the steelworkers. The industry could not surrender on that point without surrendering managerial prerogatives."[77] Accordingly, management determined to resist the union drive with customary thoroughness. The industry's leading figure, in this as in other matters, was Elbert H. Gary, chairman of U.S. Steel.

Gary had come to the steel business from the world of finance capital, out of the counting rooms of J. P. Morgan and Company, when in 1901 the House of Morgan had helped organize U.S. Steel as the first billion-dollar corporation. Thorstein Veblen would have considered him a "saboteur," more interested in making profits than useful goods. But in the field of labor relations Gary considered himself the sophisticated superior to the primitive executives brought up solely on the production side of the steel business. Where his associates often wanted simply to throttle labor, Gary sought to appease it with high wages, with worker stock-purchase and bonus plans, even with low-interest home loans for faithful employees. But on two important issues Gary would not budge. One was the eight-hour day. The other, enormously more significant, was union recognition. Largesse was one thing, power another. "We know what our duty is," Gary explained, "We know what the rights of our employees are, and we feel obligated . . . in keeping their wages up and in bettering their conditions and keeping them in a position where they enjoy life. . . . The employers, the capitalists, those having the highest education, the greatest power and influence," must shoulder

77. Brody, *Labor in Crisis*, 108.

their obligations toward the workers, he told his colleagues, while at the same time "drawing the line so that you are just and generous and yet . . . keeping the whole affair in your own hands." Therefore, he concluded, there was "no necessity for labor unions."[78]

When three delegates from the steelworkers' organizing committee called on Gary at his New York office on August 26, 1919, he simply refused to see them. "I am not antagonizing unions," Gary later blandly explained to a Senate investigating committee. "I am not saying that they have not a perfect right to form unions, of course they have; but we are not obligated to contract with them if we do not choose to do so." Gary's interrogator sharply asked: "What good is the right to unionizing if the leaders or representatives cannot talk with their employers? . . . Is it simply a social society?"[79]

Gary's refusal to meet with the organizing committee deputation almost certainly meant that the steelworkers would be called out of the mills. The men had already voted overwhelmingly to walk out if their demands—especially the right to collective bargaining—were not met. But before the final strike decision was made, the organizing committee, accompanied by Samuel Gompers, called on President Wilson to seek his intercession. Sympathetic, Wilson dispatched Bernard Baruch, long accustomed to dealing with the imperious steelmaker, to confer with Gary in New York. The strike committee agreed to delay the walk-out and await the outcome of this meeting. But Baruch's mission had scant chance of success.

Even during the war, the powerful steel industry had testily resisted the government's labor policies. Trying in 1918 to secure Gary's agreement to an eight-hour day in steel, Felix Frankfurter had obliquely threatened government intervention. But Gary was not moved. Frankfurter asked:

> Suppose that in some one of your plants some of your employees should bring a matter of complaint before the National War Labor Board. That is a perfectly conceivable situation. And the War Labor Board should make a decision which of course your company would respect as the decision of a branch of the government. I assume I am correct in making that assumption.

78. *Ibid.*, 27, 81.
79. Gary before Senator Thomas J. Walsh, U.S. Senate, Committee on Labor and Education, "Investigation of Strike in the Steel Industry," 66th Congress, 1st sess. (1919), quoted in *ibid.*, 125.

Gary replied:

> I could not answer that question just now, and certainly not in the affirmative. . . . I do not know what I would do under those circumstances.[80]

If Gary balked then, he was now adamantine and unmovable because the government was bereft of even its meager wartime means to force compliance. Baruch got nowhere, and the union organizers set a strike to begin September 22, 1919.

But though he was humiliated by Gary's rebuff and powerless to take direct action, Wilson still strove to influence the situation in steel. He again asked the organizing committee to delay until after October 6, when a scheduled Industrial Conference would convene in Washington. The leaders declined, and on September 22, some 250,000 men came out of the mills.[81]

Wilson was dismayed. Gary's recalcitrance and the persistence of the unionists cast a pall over his efforts to restore order to the industrial field. The President had reaffirmed his friendliness toward labor in a special message cabled from Paris to the opening session of the 66th Congress in May 1919. "The question which stands at the front of all others," he had said, "is the question of labor. . . . How are the men and women who do the daily labor of the world to obtain progressive improvement in the conditions of their labor, to be made happier, and to be served better by the communities and the industries which their

---

80. Memorandum of conversation held Sept. 20, 1918, Frankfurter Papers.
81. At the same moment, the government was rather dubiously exercising its powers of direct intervention in the coal industry. Facing a threatened coal strike in November, and no doubt remembering the political wounds inflicted by the coal shortage of 1917–18, the administration invoked the technical point that since a peace treaty had not been formally signed, the war was still on. Coal workers' wage agreements, signed with the Fuel Administration under the authority of the Lever Act and set to run "to the end of the war," were therefore still in effect, and to violate them was "unlawful." On those disputable grounds, the government secured an injunction against the United Mine Workers, and eventually broke the strike. Organized labor was outraged; Gompers in particular felt he had been betrayed by the President, though Wilson, who had suffered a stroke on October 2, was communicating with his cabinet by indirect means and may have had no direct hand in these decisions. See the excellent account in John M. Blum, *Joe Tumulty and the Wilson Era* (Boston: Houghton Mifflin, 1951), 218–23; see also E. David Cronon, ed., *The Cabinet Diaries of Josephus Daniels, 1913–1921* (Lincoln: University of Nebraska Press, 1963), 452ff; and the speech of Gompers to a mass meeting in Washington, Nov. 22, 1919, copy in WWP.

labor sustains and advances?" Not only did justice demand that this question be faced, he reminded the legislators, but so did the national interest. Industrial peace was no less necessary now than in war, especially if Americans were to realize the "unusual opportunities [that] will presently present themselves to our merchants and producers in foreign markets."[82] Preparing to grasp those opportunities had been a chief objective of American mobilization, and Wilson must have winced to consider that he had shaped mobilization to that end only to see the prize slip away just when it should have been seized. Hence he authorized the calling of the Industrial Conference, to meet in Washington on October 6. Despite Wilson's perception of the magnitude of the industrial problem, he significantly chose this form of address to the question, rather than seeking legislation. No doubt he feared the shape that labor legislation might ultimately take in the Republican Congress. He must also have preferred, if possible, not to legislate at all, but to reinstitute the voluntary agreements of wartime. The conference was thus an effort somehow to re-create in peace the cooperative public spirit that had supposedly prevailed in war. But public opinion was now not so easily managed.

The fifty-seven conferees gathered in the Pan-American Building amidst a rising clamor of concern over the labor situation. A general strike in Seattle in February, a police strike in Boston a few months later, countless smaller strikes in every region, a threatened walk-out from the coal mines, now the massive work stoppage in steel—all these, combined with whiffs of revolutionary ferment coming from across the Atlantic, spun the public mind, raising febrile anxieties about the very integrity of the social fabric. Citizens wrote earnestly to conference co-chairman Bernard Baruch, suggesting innumerable schemes, some plausible, many downright loony, for restoring industrial tranquillity. Many of Baruch's correspondents harbored the characteristically American dream of achieving social harmony through education. "There must be a general system of education in the schools," wrote the vice-president of a Wisconsin paper company in a representative statement, "starting in the Kindergarten, teaching dignity and necessity of labor, economy and frugality, that a few must lead and others work; Americanism and Patriotism; the Golden Rule and Ten Commandments. . . . None of this," he concluded, "can be accomplished by encouraging present day

82. Ray Stannard Baker and William E. Dodd, eds., *The Public Papers of Wood-row Wilson*, 6 vols. (New York: Harper and Brothers, 1925–27), V, 485–96.

unionism."[83] The proposals ranged broadly over the ideological spectrum, but to the extent that they struck a common note, it was the familiar theme of antipathy to power, fear that the general interest would be crushed between the millstones of big capital and big labor. Somehow, said *Survey*, a way must be found to make effective "the assertion of the public interest in . . . all differences about wages."[84] The conference's preliminary statement proclaimed "the plain fact . . . that the public has long been uneasy about the power of great employers; it is becoming uneasy about the power of great labor organizations. The community must be assured against domination by either."[85]

Consonant with that general view, the conference was comprised, as were the war labor boards, of three groups, representing equally employers, labor, and the public. The atmosphere seemed hardly auspicious for labor's cause, and for that reason some union leaders had declined even to attend. But Gompers was there, ready as always to seize any opportunity, however slight, to press his case. Under his tutelage, the labor delegates immediately introduced two resolutions, one affirming the right of workers to collective bargaining through representatives of their own choosing, the other proposing that the conference address itself to mediating the ongoing steel strike. Discussion of the first proposal was so acrimonious and protracted that the second was never taken up. The conferees thus presented the amazing spectacle of a specially convened industrial conference refusing to take official cognizance of the major industrial problem afflicting the country at that very moment.

The employer group tried to emasculate the collective bargaining proposal in two ways. First, they attempted to define the union bargaining unit in such a way as to permit them to deal only with company unions or small "shop committees." A. C. Bedford, chairman of Standard Oil of New Jersey wrote to Owen D. Young of General Electric that at the conference they should stand united behind the principle of "providing adequate machinery for adjusting grievances *within each plant*. . . . We therefore urge the Conference to give greater consideration to plant organizations as the most effective means of adjusting controversies."[86] Gompers recognized *divide et impera* when

83. Elbert H. Neese to Bernard Baruch, Oct. 18, 1919, Baruch Papers.
84. *Survey* 41 (Nov. 16, 1918), 183–84.
85. *Preliminary Statement of Industrial Conference Called by the President* (Washington, D.C.: Government Printing Office, 1919).
86. A. C. Bedford to Owen D. Young, Jan. 14, 1920, U.S. National Industrial Conference Papers, Hoover Institution.

he heard it, and roundly condemned the scheme as "a menace to the workers for the reason that it organizes them away from each other and puts them in a position where shop may be played against shop." Worse, he argued, the shop committees already in existence "are, in fact, almost without exception creatures of employers." Only "organization covering whole industries" would do, he insisted.[87]

Frustrated by Gompers's shrewd opposition, the employers tried a second line of attack, proposing a complex national network of "industrial tribunals," or arbitration boards. Again like the war labor boards, these were to be composed of representatives from management and labor, as well as government-appointed "public" referees. But Gompers quickly denounced this proposal as paving the way to compulsory arbitration, historically anathema to the labor movement. With long-familiar emphasis, Gompers outlined once again the tenets of his philosophy of "voluntarism": labor wanted no government paternalism, only the right to organize and bargain collectively. "Organization of the workers," he repeated for the thousandth time, "is the fact upon which must be predicated the existence of any machinery for the settlement of disputes or the extension of the principles of democracy in industry."[88]

But organization of the workers, as Gompers defined it, was just what the employers were determined to avoid at all costs. This was true, above all, in steel. Elbert Gary, sitting rather incongruously as a "public" delegate, not only joined in the general assault on the collective bargaining principle but declared flatly: "I am of the fixed opinion that the pending strike against the steel industry of this country should not be arbitrated or compromised, nor any action taken by the conference which bears upon that subject."[89] Nor did the conference take any such action; eventually even Gompers gave up. Declaring that "we have nothing further to submit," Gompers led the A.F. of L. delegates out of the hall, and the conference collapsed.

In the end, the much-touted Industrial Conference, meeting in two

87. "Press Comment on the Final Report of the Second President's Industrial Conference," *ibid.*

88. *Idem.*

89. Actually, Gary's presence as a "public" delegate, which occasioned incredulous outcries from the labor press, was a small bit of revenge on Woodrow Wilson's part for Gary's refusal to honor the President's request, made through Baruch, to confer with the steelworker organizers. Thus Gary sat uncomfortably in the same conference room with the very union leaders he had before resolutely refused even to acknowledge. See Brody, *Labor in Crisis*, 117–19.

stages from October through January, accomplished nothing with respect to collective bargaining, arbitration, or the steel strike. The conference passed quietly into history, its only utility being the glimpse its records provide of the state of the national mind, and the tactical array of the interested parties, surrounding the labor question in 1919. The labor movement, the conference made clear, had gained little of lasting value from the Great War. It had made temporary wage gains (many of them soon eroded in the continuing inflation of 1919), but it had not been able, even during the war, to secure government guarantees for the indispensable right of collective bargaining through union representatives. Failing to achieve that historic goal in war, it had failed even more miserably in peace, when public opinion, agitated by the countless strikes of 1919 and inflamed by the Red Scare, turned increasingly hostile to organized labor.

It was in fact the steel strike, still grinding on along the Monongahela and around Chicago, even while the conference delegates futilely maneuvered in Washington, that did much to sour the public against labor and break the already flagging spirits of the unionists themselves. Capital, it seemed, had learned a measure of subtlety since the crude union-busting days of the Homestead Strike, when armed Pinkertons fired wantonly into crowds of strikers. There was still some head-splitting in the strike of 1919, as the steel companies paid and armed 5000 "deputies" in Pennsylvania's Allegheny County, and federal troops under the command of the ubiquitous General Leonard Wood entered Gary, Indiana. But by and large the steel operators eschewed outright mayhem, and relied instead on less direct but no less effective means to break the strike. The premier tactic was to excite the most frightful anxieties of the general public, and of many of the strikers themselves, by accusing the leaders of being radicals and Bolsheviks. Feeding those anxieties was the Red Scare atmosphere, ruthlessly exploited by the steel companies. They had a vulnerable target in William Z. Foster, secretary of the National Committee for Organizing Iron and Steel Workers. Foster, a former Wobbly, had once authored a virulent anti-capitalist tract called *Syndicalism,* now rediscovered and widely quoted as proof of his anarchist ideas.[90] These red-baiting smears gained added plausibility in the public mind, because so many of the strikers were immigrants, especially from those regions of eastern Europe long pre-

90. Foster, though at this time apparently in a moderate political phase, would later be a leading figure in the Communist Party of the United States.

sumed to be fetid breeding grounds of noxious revolutionary doctrines.

The polyglot character of the steelworkers, itself a deliberate consequence of the industry's hiring practices in the preceding two decades, provided further opportunities for the steel companies to divide and conquer, as agents were sent into the steel districts to stir up animosities between native and immigrant workmen. In the most cynical ploy of all, steel operators brought in black scabs—not enough men to reopen the mills completely, but sufficient numbers to fling terror into the ranks of the white workers, especially the least skilled, fearful lest they permanently lose their places to black workers eager to possess previously forbidden jobs. Through such stratagems, the steel strike was decisively broken by the first of the new year. With it collapsed labor's high wartime hopes and all prospects of soon organizing the unskilled workers in the great mass-production industries that increasingly dominated the American economy. It would take another national crisis, more than a decade later, to restore to labor the vitality squeezed from the movement by the defeats of 1919.

The 30,000 blacks who crossed the picket lines and entered the steel mills in 1919 were but a small fraction of the great black northward exodus that the war had set in motion. As in other American communities, black leaders at first offered their people divided counsel about the war. Some, like radical editor and future labor organizer A. Philip Randolph, outspokenly opposed black involvement, a position that earned Randolph a jail sentence. Others, like the Reverend Adam Clayton Powell, Sr., for a time flirted with an explicitly quid pro quo strategy, proposing that black support for the war be exchanged only for concrete government guarantees of civil rights.[91] But the majority of blacks agreed with their most prominent spokesman, W. E. B. Du Bois, who urged them to "forget our special grievances and close our ranks shoulder to shoulder with our own white fellow citizens."[92] Like Gompers, nearly all black leaders came to see the war as a time to submerge fundamental demands. They hoped that blacks might increase their stature in the eyes of the white public, and be better able to realize immediate material gains. "This is not the time to discuss race prob-

91. See Jane Lang Scheiber and Harry N. Scheiber, "The Wilson Administration and the Wartime Mobilization of Black Americans, 1917–1918," *Labor History* 10 (1969), 433–58.
92. W. E. B. Du Bois, "Close Ranks," *Crisis* 16 (1918), 111.

lems," said Emmett Scott, special black assistant to Secretary of War Baker. "Our first duty is to fight. . . . Then we can adjust the problems that remain in the life of the colored man."[93]

Of all the opportunities that the war afforded to blacks, none was more alluring than the prospect of penetrating at last the industrial labor markets of the North, from which blacks had long been rebuffed by the steady current of low-wage labor from abroad. In 1914 that immigrant stream was suddenly choked dry, and in 1917 the military draft further depleted the manpower pool. Northern factory managers began to cast about for a fresh labor supply; Elbert Gary even proposed the systematic recruiting of laborers from Asia. But Gary and his cohorts quickly discovered a source of workers closer to hand in the American South. Beginning in south Georgia and Florida in 1916, Northern labor agents fanned out across the black belt, recruiting workers with promises of free transportation and fat wages on arrival. Soon there developed a spontaneous hegira of Biblical proportions. Word spread from mouth to mouth and town to town that there were jobs in the cities to the north, and by 1920 a third of a million blacks had "followed the drinking gourd" out of the Old South and into booming industrial centers like St. Louis, Chicago, Cleveland, and Detroit. The Pennsylvania Railroad alone drew 10,000 black workers out of Florida and south Georgia; Hattiesburg, Mississippi, scoured of its labor force, was said to have been ruined by the sudden exodus.[94]

The white South reacted to this apparent stampede with undisguised alarm. Three hundred years of mistreatment by whites underlay the black disposition to emigrate, and in some communities the threat of mass black flight fostered more conciliatory relations between the races. In as many other communities, whites resorted to police harassment, illegal detentions, and beatings.[95] "We must have the Negro in the South," said the Macon, Georgia, *Telegraph*. "It is the only labor we have, it is the best we possibly could have—if we lose it, we go bankrupt!"[96] To stem the outpouring tide, many Southern communities passed stiff ordinances against the activities of the "pass riders," the

93. Scheiber and Scheiber, "Wilson Administration," 446.
94. Emmett J. Scott, *Negro Migration During the War,* Carnegie Endowment for International Peace, Preliminary Economic Studies of the War, No. 16 (New York: Oxford University Press, 1920), 30.
95. *Ibid.,* 72ff.
96. Quoted in Dewey H. Palmer, "Moving North: Migration of Negroes During World War I," *Phylon* 28 (1967), 57.

labor agents who seemed to be draining the black belt of its able-bodied men. The Macon city fathers set the license fee for agents at the laughably high figure of $25,000, and compounded the impossible by requiring that agents be recommended by ten local ministers, ten manufacturers, and twenty-five businessmen. The Mayor of New Orleans formally asked the president of the Illinois Central Railroad to stop carrying blacks on its northbound trains. At the request of Southern politicians, the Department of Labor's Employment Service suspended its program of assistance to blacks headed north.[97]

The administration's amenability to that request was but one sign among many of its sympathy with the white South, and its generally indifferent, even hostile, regard for blacks. The South, Woodrow Wilson once remarked, was the only place he felt really at home, the only place where nothing had to be explained to him—including the traditional Southern race system. He had screened the film *The Birth of a Nation* in the White House, and had endorsed its pro-Ku Klux Klan interpretation of post-Civil War Reconstruction as "history written with lightning." The President had raised no objection when Postmaster General Albert S. Burleson had in 1913 widened the practice of segregation among federal employees. When a delegation of black leaders called at the White House to protest Burleson's policy, they were brusquely dismissed because Wilson found their language "insulting." In the election of 1916, Wilson had personally helped to stir racial hatreds in East St. Louis, Illinois, where he accused Republicans of "colonizing" imported black voters in a fraudulent attempt to pad the electoral rolls. The aim of the charges, writes a student of the episode, was to "gain extra white supremacy votes," as well as "to intimidate Negro migrants from casting ballots."[98] In the face of such attitudes at the highest political level, it took a truly vaulting leap of faith for Afro-American leaders to persist in the belief that the war could somehow be made to serve the advancement of their race.

The first warning that their faith was perhaps misplaced came, in fact, in East St. Louis. Thousands of blacks had been drawn out of Mississippi and west Tennessee to East St. Louis in 1916 and early 1917, not by Republican politicians, as the administration cynically charged, but by local manufacturing interests. Especially after the

97. Scott, *Negro Migration*, 72, 78, 53.
98. Elliot M. Rudwick, *Race Riot at East St. Louis, July 2, 1917* (Carbondale: Southern Illinois University Press, 1964), 8.

Aluminum Ore Company had been forced to take a strike in late 1916, the city's employers began methodically to recruit black workers to restrain the demands of the unruly white unions. At Aluminum Ore, at the Missouri Malleable Iron Works, and at other industrial establishments, operators began to pursue a deliberate policy of hiring a mix of blacks, immigrants, and native whites, calculating that the three elements would never combine to strike.[99] The unions, traditionally hostile to blacks, chose not to offer them membership but to regard them as strikebreakers. In late May, an angry mob of white workers appealed to the Mayor and the city council to stop the inflow of black workers, and the city seethed with spasmodic violence during the following month. Then on July 2, full-scale race war swept East St. Louis, leaving nine whites and an even larger number of blacks dead in the streets.[100] Black leaders blanketed the President with requests for federal action against the rioters, but only silence came from the White House. Wilson, not kindly disposed toward blacks in the first place, and perhaps fearing that any investigation would dredge up the shameless Democratic exploitation of the racial issue in East St. Louis in the preceding November, refused even to see the black delegations begging for an appointment.[101] Justice Department lawyers, as well as the local United States Attorney, advised Attorney General Gregory that the Civil Rights Act of 1866 and Section Nineteen of the Federal Penal Code provided ample legal grounds for federal intervention in the face of patent local inability or unwillingness to protect civil rights. Despite those opinions, Gregory informed Wilson that "no facts have been presented to us which would justify Federal action," and there, so far as Wilson was concerned, the matter rested.[102]

99. Scott, *Negro Migration*, 100.
100. See Rudwick, *Race Riot*, 41–57, where he argues that it is impossible to determine the precise number of blacks killed.
101. Presidential adviser Joseph Tumulty warned Wilson: "I am afraid that if you see this delegation the fire will be rekindled." Tumulty to Wilson, July 10, 1917, WWP.
102. Thomas W. Gregory to Wilson, July 27, 1917, WWP. Congress did, however, launch an investigation. Nearly a year later, Wilson received a long and thoughtful memorandum, solicited by Tumulty, from two black leaders who suggested ways that the administration might change its low standing in the black community. The authors argued, not implausibly, that enough blacks had migrated into key Northern and Western states to constitute the crucial swing vote which must be secured by the victorious party in the upcoming congressional elections. Despite Wilson's otherwise keen attention to the political arithmetic of 1918, he ignored entirely the suggestions from these two blacks. J. Milton Waldron and John MacMurray, "Memoranda Concerning the Negro and the Present Political Situation in the U.S.," May 25, 1918, WWP.

But despite the sickening violence, and the administration's contemptible inaction, blacks continued to pour northward. They were lured to Chicago especially, as mariners to a beacon, their ears filled with the siren song of the black Chicago *Defender*, ceaselessly trumpeting its summons throughout the South: "I beg you, my brother, to leave the benighted land. . . . Get out of the South. . . . Come north then, all you folks, both good and bad. . . . The *Defender* says come."[103] By 1918 the circulation of the *Defender* reached 125,000, and copies were widely distributed in the South, passed from hand to hand, reportedly bought even by the illiterate as a token of regard for this voice from the promised land to the north. Thousands of poor rural blacks eagerly took in the newspaper's description of Chicago as "the top of the world," and nearly 60,000 had heeded the *Defender*'s beckoning by the end of the war. Then, in 1919, violence visited the *Defender*'s home city. Anti-black rioting broke out on a Lake Michigan beach on July 27, and a reign of terror descended on the city for thirteen days. Black and white gangs roamed the streets, wreaking fury and vengeance on each other. At the end, thousands of persons had been burned out of their homes, hundreds were injured, and fifteen whites and twenty-three blacks lay dead. More race riots exploded that summer in Knoxville, Omaha, Washington, and other cities that had witnessed sizable black influxes during the war.

Du Bois and other black leaders had entered the war full of hope that it would provide opportunities for the advance of their race. But though the threatened labor shortage might have worked to improve relations between the races at scattered points in the South, the fact remained that as many as two hundred blacks perished at the hands of mostly Southern mobs in the war era. Violence, in fact, seemed to rise on an ascending war-borne curve, as lynching parties took 38 black lives in 1917, some 58 in 1918, and more than 70 in 1919. Rioters, particularly in 1919, claimed the rest. As for the North, once happily regarded as freedom's refuge, it had been the scene of some of the worst riots, and hardly proved the "Land of Hope" that the *Defender* and others had lavishly promised.

The war had nevertheless begun a demographic shift of the black population, a shift with far-reaching implications. However short of black hopes life in the North fell, it still provided more opportunities for mobility and talent and even access to political power than the South had traditionally afforded. Though still discriminated against by the trade unions and held in fearful suspicion by their white neighbors, blacks had gained a toehold in Northern industry and in several urban communities. In the next two decades, those black outposts would continue to swell in size, nurturing an artistic "Renaissance" in Harlem, and breeding a generation of leaders strongly critical of the continuing economic and political subservience of blacks in the South. But in 1919, those developments were but tiny seeds, nearly smothered by the oppression of the summer's violence, destined to lie dormant for many years before they finally came to fruition. The war itself had been no quick tonic for the country's ancient racial trials. Even as late as 1933, Emmett Scott observed that "as one who recalls the assurances of 1917 and 1918 . . . I confess personally a deep sense of disappointment, of poignant pain that a great country in time of need should promise so much and afterward perform so little."[104]

As with blacks, so too with women, though their experience in the war was less touched by drama and violence. Feminist leaders, like black spokesmen, divided on the main issues of the war. A small band of prominent women, including Jane Addams, Crystal Eastman, and Emily Green Balch, courageously persisted in their prewar pacifism, though most of their sisters flocked to the colors. Some actually served in the AEF, usually as telephone operators or nurses, and many more traveled to France as volunteers in the YMCA or other service organizations. The huge National American Woman Suffrage Association, led by Carrie Chapman Catt, had announced its support for American belligerency even before the declaration of war. Mrs. Catt and other women hoped that the war would prove the forcing house in which long-standing feminine aspirations for the vote and economic equality would finally mature. On the suffrage issue they were not disappointed. Woodrow Wilson now unequivocally harnessed the spirit of the war for democracy to the cause of woman suffrage, telling the Senate in 1918 that the vote for women "is vital to the winning of the war."[105] Congress and the country responded, and in 1920 the Nineteenth Amendment was at last secured. Nearly a century of political struggle lay behind that victory, though the war appeared to provide the final push over the top.

104. Quoted in Scheiber and Scheiber, "Wilson Administration," 458.
105. Baker and Dodd, eds., *Public Papers of Woodrow Wilson*, V, 266.

But in the economic field, the results were not so cheering. Like so many other groups in American society, women harbored extravagant hopes for the gains that might be wrought out of the plastic environment of war. "Wonderful as this hour is for democracy and labor," said a speaker at a Women's Trade Union League meeting in 1917, "it is the first hour in history for the women of the world. . . . At last, after centuries of disabilities and discrimination, women are coming into the labor and festival of life on equal terms with men."[106] Still nurturing that hopeful dream at the time of the Armistice, *Survey* buoyantly announced that "among the gains of the war we might count the penultimate stage in the emancipation of women. A few things remain to be done, a few places have got to catch up; but broadly speaking, woman has become a citizen and a worker."[107]

This was largely illusion. In reality, women's employment in the war was limited and brief. About a million women took up war work, and of that relatively modest number, only a handful were "first-time" hires, constituting net additions to the female labor force. Most were single girls who moved up from less remunerative jobs to which they soon returned, or previously employed women, now married, who temporarily reentered the work force to help their families keep pace with inflation. Fewer still took up positions in heavy industry, and of those who did, fully half had abandoned them by 1919. Mary Van Kleeck, director of the Women in Industry Service of the Department of Labor, observed that "the question heard most frequently" in late 1918 "was whether women would now retire from industry."[108] The Central Federated Union of New York bluntly demanded in 1919 that "the same patriotism which induced women to enter industry during the war should induce them to vacate their positions after the war," and many women, whether willingly or not, complied. By 1920, women in fact made up a smaller percentage of the labor force than they had in 1910.

The established trade unions were in the main notoriously opposed to women workers. The traditional attitude of the A.F. of L. toward women, the *New Republic* dryly noted, "has not been unlike that of the United States Senate," which had stood firm for generations against

106. Quoted in William Henry Chafe, *The American Woman: Her Changing Social, Economic, and Political Roles, 1920–1970* (New York: Oxford University Press, 1972), 49.
107. *Survey* 41 (Nov. 16, 1918), 184.
108. Mary Van Kleeck, "Federal Policies for Women in Industry," *Annals* 81 (1919), 87.

admitting women to the franchise.[109] Samuel Gompers only belatedly appointed a Sub-committee on Women in Industry in his Council of National Defense Committee on Labor, and he demonstrated his contempt for the women's trade-union leaders by denying them the chair, awarding it instead to wealthy New York socialite Mrs. J. Borden Harriman. The government, too, only tardily created a Woman's Committee at the Council of National Defense, in April, 1917. Headed by venerable suffragist Dr. Anna Howard Shaw, the Woman's Committee was, in the eyes of many feminists, the vehicle by which they would perform significant war work. It had to content itself, however, with organizing traditional middle-class women's "volunteer" activities—helping to establish children's health-care programs, rolling Red Cross bandages, and distributing food conservation pamphlets. "After a while," writes William L. O'Neill, "it became evident that the government viewed the Woman's Committee as a device for occupying women in harmless activities while men got on with the business of war."[110]

Given the antagonism of the A.F. of L. and the general indifference of the government, it was hardly surprising that even agencies like the Women in Industry Service—mandated to protect women workers, and run by a no-nonsense woman like Mary Van Kleeck—accomplished little. In some industries where the WIS was supposed to safeguard "existing standards" respecting women's employment, those standards simply did not exist, because no women had ever before worked in the industry. Elsewhere, regulations protecting women were flouted with impunity. Only 9 percent of the women workers in New York, for example, received the equal pay to which they were supposedly entitled.[111]

As the war decade ended, women could take comfort from the winning of the suffrage—no small gain, though one which proved far less consequential in women's lives than its proponents had long believed. They might take comfort, too, from the action of Congress in establishing the Woman's Bureau in the Department of Labor, giving institutional permanency to the wartime Women in Industry Service. But the doors of industry had not swung wide to women in the war, and what

109. *New Republic* 15 (July 23, 1918), 304.
110. William L. O'Neill, *Everyone Was Brave: The Rise and Fall of Feminism in America* (Chicago: Quadrangle, 1969), 191.
111. Chafe, *The American Woman,* 52; see also Van Kleeck, "Federal Policies," 90, where she states that in many cases it was not even possible to secure agreement to the equal-pay-for-equal-work principle.

tiny openings had been forced were closed again almost immediately at the Armistice. The newly created Woman's Bureau would oversee a decidedly static and definitely unrevolutionized world of women's work. The postwar position of women was perhaps better symbolized by the 1921 Sheppard-Towner Act, providing for federally financed instruction in maternal and infant health care. That measure, aggressively pushed by feminist groups, aimed not to breach the walls of industry for women but to make women more secure in their traditional environs, the home and the nursery.

As the old order thus settled heavily back into place, it crushed many of the aspirations that the war had so giddily lifted. The reform banners that many progressives, trade unionists, blacks, and women had carried faithfully through the fighting and into the Armistice were shredded by the storm of reaction that began to blow in late 1918. "What a God damned world!" exclaimed ex-Bull Mooser William Allen White in 1920, and his old comrade-in-arms Hiram Johnson agreed that "We're in about the rottenest period of reaction that we have had in many years."[112] To progressives, the most deeply disturbing development of the postwar years was the rising specter of class struggle. "The chief issue," Harold Ickes wrote, "is likely to be the relationship between capital and labor. . . . We sense disturbances way down underneath our social structure."[113] No prospect was more horrifying to men like White, Johnson, and Ickes. They knew not whom to fear more: resurgent capital or restless labor. Both groups menaced the yearning for social harmony and the vision of an orderly middle-class utopia that had energized so much of prewar reform. That America was a classless society, or could be made so, was an axiom that had once tripped from the progressive tongue with Euclidean certainty. But the events of 1919 and 1920—especially the steel strike and the race riots and the seeming discovery of radicals on every side—threatened rudely to disprove that cherished theorem.

Some observers professed to see the origin of those events far from American shores, among the war-lashed peoples of central and eastern Europe. The Bolshevik success in Russia inspired communist groups in

---

112. Quoted in Paul W. Glad, "Progressives and the Business Culture of the 1920s," *Journal of American History* 53 (1966), 78; Johnson to Fremont Older, Jan. 17, 1921, Johnson Papers.

113. Harold Ickes to Meyer Lissner, June 5, 1919, copy in Johnson Papers.

other countries to strike for revolution amidst the chaos of their collapsing governments in 1918 and 1919. Communist movements rumbled in Poland, while extreme left "Spartacists" briefly seized control of Berlin and Russian-style "soviets" temporarily ruled in Hungary and Bavaria. In March 1919, the Russian Communist Party established the Third International, or Comintern, headquartered at Moscow and dedicated to world-wide agitation for universal revolution.

Those developments were remote, but in February 1919 a general strike in Seattle evoked the feverish suggestion that the contaminating wartime contact with Europe had infected even the American body politic with the dreaded radical virus. The exaggerated demands of war had been especially hard on the Pacific Northwest shipbuilding and lumbering industries, as the government's unionizing activities among the loggers testified. In early 1919, housing shortages and high prices prompted 35,000 Seattle shipyard workers to walk off their jobs. The Seattle Central Labor Council, a militant body perpetually at odds with the conservative philosophy of Samuel Gompers and the national A.F. of L. leadership, called for a general strike to support the shipyard laborers. On February 6, some 60,000 workers left their jobs, though the Labor Council ensured the continuation of essential services such as electric power, garbage collection, and fuel and food deliveries. The four-day shutdown was orderly and disciplined, unmarred by violence.

Despite the strikers' bread-and-butter goals and their peaceable behavior, Seattle Mayor Ole Hanson requested federal troops to occupy the city and denounced the strikers as deep-Red revolutionists who "want to take possession of our American Government and try to duplicate the anarchy of Russia."[114] Hanson thus keynoted a rising chorus of voices in the spring of 1919 decrying the Red menace to America.

They had some frightening facts to shout about. On April 28, a bomb arrived by mail at Mayor Hanson's office, and the following day a similar parcel blew the hands off the maid of a Georgia Senator. Mail inspectors, now alerted, quickly intercepted thirty-four additional bombs intended for Postmaster General Burleson, Attorney General A. Mitchell Palmer (who had taken over from Thomas W. Gregory in March 1919), and other officials. On May 1, 1919, radical rallies in Boston, Cleveland, and New York were beset by "patriotic" mobs and

114. Robert K. Murray, *Red Scare: A Study in National Hysteria, 1919–1920* (Minneapolis: University of Minnesota Press, 1955), 63. Much of the following discussion is drawn from Murray's informative account.

degenerated into violent melees that left one person dead and more than two score seriously injured. On June 2, simultaneous bomb explosions in eight cities killed two people. One blast demolished part of Attorney General Palmer's Washington, D.C. residence.

These coordinated dynamitings strongly suggested a terrorist conspiracy, but no one knew its dimensions or its ultimate intentions. There were two communist parties in the United States—both breakaways from the Socialist Party. By late summer of 1919, they had a total of perhaps 70,000 members, most of them foreign-born. By no means all of those persons were dedicated bombers and assassins. Yet, in the face of growing public alarm, both state and federal governments began to move against the communists, and against their alleged Russian "connections." New York state police and federal Justice Department agents on June 12 raided the New York office of the Russian Soviet Bureau. A would-be Soviet Embassy, the Bureau was directed by would-be Ambassador L.C.A.K. Martens. But since the United States government still refused to recognize Martens's Bolshevik government, the Bureau had become little more than a propaganda center, dispensing millions of copies of Lenin's "To the American Workers" and other radical tracts among American laborers. Together with a second raid a few days later on the socialist Rand School and the New York offices of the IWW, the action at the Soviet Bureau yielded truckloads of leaflets, mailing lists, and membership rosters. A special anti-sedition committee of the New York legislature, headed by State Senator Clayton R. Lusk, loudly trumpeted this material as proof of an incipient Bolshevik revolution in the United States. The Lusk committee added a refinement to Mayor Hanson's fear-breeding tactics when it announced that black Americans were among the preferred groups that agitators sought to enlist in the upcoming revolt.

In Washington, D.C., Attorney General Palmer beefed up the Justice Department's Bureau of Investigation with the creation of a new anti-radical unit, the General Intelligence Division, headed by the youthful and eager J. Edgar Hoover. Congress instantly obliged with a special half-million-dollar appropriation to aid in ferreting out revolutionaries.

An unprecedented walk-out by Boston police, and the nationwide steel strike, further agitated the public's disquiet in September, as did a threatened coal strike later in the fall, claimed by coal operators to be directly ordered by Lenin and Trotsky and financed by Moscow gold. Prodded by ever-mounting public anxiety, the House of Representatives showed its anti-radical mettle in November by refusing to seat Victor Berger, a duly elected Socialist Representative from Wisconsin.[115] The Senate, irked to discover that most of the fifty-four alien radicals arrested during the Seattle general strike had not been deported, unanimously requested Attorney General Palmer in October 1919 to explain his failure to prosecute more ruthlessly in the war against sedition.

Palmer moved to satisfy his critics on November 7 with simultaneous raids against the Union of Russian Workers in a dozen cities. These and subsequent strikes by both federal and state agents eventually netted several hundred radical aliens. December 21, 1919, saw 249 of them deported to Russia aboard the *Buford*, or "Soviet Ark," as it was dubbed. Even more massive raids against Communist offices followed on January 2, 1920, bagging 4000 suspected subversives in thirty-three cities.

Palmer's methods, and those of his agents, were high-handed in the extreme. Break-ins and arrests were frequently made without warrants, and prisoners were treated roughly. Palmer concentrated his efforts on aliens because they could be deported through a purely administrative process mandated by the Alien Act of 1918. He thus avoided the formal indictments and public trials that would have been necessary had he prosecuted radical *citizens* under the Espionage or Sedition acts. The Alien Act specified mere *membership* in an organization considered to be advocating violent overthrow of the government as sufficient grounds for deportation. If that standard were not loose enough, in the first days of 1920 Palmer also secured an important change in the administrative procedure leading to deportation: a detained alien would be allowed to inspect the warrant against him and be advised of the right to retain counsel only *after* the "hearing has proceeded sufficiently in the development of the facts to protect the Government's interests."[116] These Star Chamber tactics Palmer later defended: "I apologize for nothing that the Department of Justice has done," he testified to a Senate committee in 1921. "I glory in it. I point with pride and enthusiasm to the results of that work, and if . . . some of my agents out in the field . . . were a little rough and unkind, or short and curt, with these alien agitators, whom they observed seeking to destroy their homes, their reli-

---

115. Berger at the time was appealing his conviction under the Espionage Act for anti-war statements. He eventually won the appeal, but was again refused his seat in Congress even after a special election in Wisconsin had gone overwhelmingly in his favor. Defeated in the regular election of 1920, Berger won in 1922 and finally was duly seated in the House.

116. Murray, *Red Scare*, 211.

gion, and their country, I think it might be well overlooked in the general good to the country which has come from it."[117]

Palmer's supporters and active allies in the Great Red Hunt seemed to be legion in 1919. Most of them came from the ranks of the wartime patriotic societies, such as the National Security League and the American Defense Society. They were joined by the recently reborn Ku Klux Klan, and the newborn American Legion, some of whose members provoked a bloody fracas in Centralia, Washington, on Armistice Day, 1919, which ended in the shooting deaths of several Legionnaires and the brutal razor-blade castration and lynching of a Wobbly. But the most significant groups that made common cause with Palmer's anti-radical drive were the various employers' organizations, such as the National Association of Manufacturers. For them, the spiraling fear of radicalism seemed "made to order," writes historian Robert K. Murray, for it allowed them to tar the entire labor movement with the brush of Bolshevism.[118] In publications like the *Open Shop Review*, these groups denounced the union demand for a closed shop as "sovietism in disguise." Unionism itself, they now preached with fresh boldness, "is nothing less than bolshevism." Even the usually judicious ex-President William Howard Taft contributed to this vicious anti-union campaign when he allowed that advocates of the closed shop were "embracing Soviet methods." This onslaught, poisoning the non-union public's mind against the union movement, and sowing seeds of doubt even among working people themselves, proved especially effective in helping to break the back of the 1919 steel strike. By the fall of 1919, Murray notes, all strikes were regularly branded "plots to establish communism."[119]

By the spring of 1920, this tide of anti-radical hysteria, so unsubstantiated yet so injurious to the cause of labor, finally began to recede. When the ever-vigilant New York legislature expelled several lawfully elected socialist members in January 1920, even the conservative establishment cried foul. Senator Warren G. Harding and Attorney General Palmer himeslf berated the New Yorkers, and former Republican presidential candidate Charles Evans Hughes offered the services of the New York Bar Association to the expelled socialists, so that they might redress the legislature's "serious mistake."[120] Shortly thereafter, Depart-

117. Quoted in *ibid.*, 256.
118. *Ibid.*, 92.
119. *Ibid.*, 121.
120. *Ibid.*, 243–44.

ment of Labor officials began to cancel the deportation orders for most of the aliens rounded up in the January raids. The courts, meanwhile, ordered the release of other radicals incriminated on the basis of evidence illegally seized. In the end, only 591 aliens of the thousands originally arrested were actually deported.

Palmer's reputation as the great Red-catcher began to fade when his prediction of a massive revolutionary upheaval on May 1, 1920, failed to materialize. A meticulously researched condemnation of the "Palmer Raids" by some of the country's most prestigious lawyers, including Felix Frankfurter, Ernest Freund, and Roscoe Pound, published on May 28, sobered many of the Attorney General's remaining supporters. When a bomb blast rocked Wall Street in September, 1920, killing over thirty persons, the nation sadly shrugged it off as the probable work of a lone fanatic, not, as Palmer continued to insist shrilly, the product of a vast subversive conspiracy.

But if American society eventually regained its senses about the real dimensions of the Bolshevik threat to the United States, scars from the Red Scare nevertheless remained. Organized labor had been badly chewed up in the anti-radical frenzy. The conservative leaders of the A.F. of L. had run with the hounds after the radical hare, only to find their own closed-shop movement victimized by the yawping pack of union defamers. Union membership went into steep decline in the early 1920s, as more than two million workers left the ranks of organized labor. Moreover, employer groups continued to blemish the closed-shop idea with the charge of radicalism. In the 1920s, they artfully called their own open-shop campaign the "American Plan," effectively crippling all efforts by union organizers to win sympathy for the supposedly "foreign" all-union shop.

The labor upheavals and the Red Scare of 1918–20 had forced many progressives at last to relinquish their fond belief in a classless society. Divested of that faith, they found nothing to put in its place. They too must be counted among the truly "disillusioned," stupefied at the prospect of class politics, deprived of animating ideas. With their mental synapses badly sputtering, some, like Hiram Johnson, began to display a cranky pseudo-conservatism. Others, like onetime tax reformer Frederic C. Howe, simply lapsed into political torpor.[121]

And yet many struggled on. William Allen White and Harold Ickes,

121. See Frederic C. Howe, *The Confessions of a Reformer* (New York: Scribner's, 1925).

for example, survived to play active parts in the reforms of the New Deal. Too much, indeed, can be made of the notion of "disillusion" among political reformers. The view that all the forces of the liberal left were either cowed into quiescence or stunned into ennui after the war is surely overdrawn. Many reformers, in fact, did not shy from the prospect of frankly class-based politics, the necessity for which the war and its turbulent aftermath apparently demonstrated. Some of them had long harbored a kind of inchoate sympathy for the British Labor Party. Lillian Wald, for example, had congratulated Ramsay MacDonald on his election in 1906: "This victory must mean great things for 'our' party and we shall be eager to watch affairs of state across the pond."[122] Especially among the influential young publicists at the *New Republic*, the writings of British socialists like G. D. H. Cole, Sidney and Beatrice Webb, and Graham Wallas commanded great respect. The presence of the brilliant English socialist Harold Laski in the magazine's offices during the war buttressed the editors' leftward inclination. As early as 1916 the *New Republic* had denounced the existing political parties as devices that permitted "the dominant middle class to perpetuate its domination," and the magazine called for "independent labor and partisan organizations who will agitate on behalf of a perfectly definite class program. . . ."[123] The editors had been deeply engaged by the wartime advances of British labor, and in 1918 had called on "liberal Americans" to emulate their English brethren by "promoting the organization of American workers for the capable exercise of political power."[124]

In 1920 many moderate socialists, trade unionists, and agrarian radicals coalesced to form the Farmer-Labor Party. *New Republic* editor-in-chief Herbert Croly endorsed the new party's presidential candidate, Parley P. Christensen. The "Committee of 48," a loose group of progressives cobbled in 1919 out of the remains of the Bull Moose movement, lent its halting support. Yet the Committee's difficulties in aligning itself with the Farmer-Labor Party illustrated the pain inflicted on the progressive mind when it confronted a candidly class-based political program. The committee would have much preferred to revivify

122. Quoted in Kenneth McNaught, "American Progressives and the Great Society," *Journal of American History* 53 (1966), 512.

123. *New Republic* editorials quoted in Charles Forcey, *The Crossroads of Liberalism: Croly, Weyl, Lippmann and the Progressive Era, 1900–1925* (New York: Oxford University Press, 1961), 217.

124. *New Republic* 14 (Feb. 16, 1918), 71.

the prewar doctrines of social harmony, finding a middle way, as their chairman put it, between "the extremes of radicalism and . . . the extremes of reaction." "You hear people speak of class consciousness," said the Committee's secretary in the midst of the steel strike. "There is no such thing."[125] This was incantation, a ritual effort to exorcise the demons of class politics by religiously repeating the old progressive formulae. Some forty-eighters, in fact, walked out of the Farmer-Labor convention in 1920 because they could not swallow its avowedly class-oriented character. But many, however reluctantly, remained.

Their hopes and strivings came to little in 1920, as Christensen polled a pathetic 290,000 votes, proving conclusively that America was not Britain. But many on the left persisted in the effort to build a party, as Croly put it, "composed primarily of the classes who work."[126] In 1922, unionists, farmers, socialists and the dogged forty-eighters again came together to form the Conference for Progressive Political Action. Two years later that coalition, called now the Progressive Party, nominated Robert La Follette for the presidency. His platform proposed lower tariffs, government aid to agriculture, public ownership of railroads and electrical utilities, abolition of the use of the injunction against labor, more progressive income taxes, and a public referendum on questions of peace or war. The American Federation of Labor, in a rare departure from its usual political neutrality, endorsed La Follette. Fielding only a presidential ticket, a party with a head but no body, the Progressives nevertheless attracted nearly five million votes.

La Follette's campaign thus arose, however incompletely, from the ashes to which the post-Armistice period had reduced progressive hopes. Yet even La Follette's limitless exuberance could not overcome the damage that the war and the aftermath had inflicted on the old progressive coalition, especially its labor elements. Defeated, diminished, and divided by the experiences of the war period, labor was an ineffective political force in the 1920s. Analysis of the electoral results in 1924 showed clearly that La Follette lost primarily because he failed to attract a sufficiently large working-class vote.

But La Follette's impressive tally of nearly five million ballots nevertheless testified dramatically that the war had not entirely killed the

125. *New York Times,* Aug. 15, 1919, 13; and Oct. 13, 1919, 13.
126. Herbert Croly quoted in David Burner, "The Election of 1924," in Arthur M. Schlesinger, Jr., and Fred L. Israel, eds., *History of American Presidential Elections, 1789–1968,* 4 vols. (New York: Chelsea House, 1971), III, 2563.

reform impulse. For some of the people attracted to the Progressive ticket in 1924, the war, for all its disappointments, had been not so much a dispiriting experience as one which struck the scales from their eyes, and made them realize, as Felix Frankfurter put it in 1924, that politics must be "rightly founded . . . on men's interests."[127] If that meant a class-based party, on the British model, so be it. The point is worth emphasizing, given the tendency to believe that the war acted only to befuddle reformers and sap their will, forever confining their thoughts to some lost political past.

For some—Felix Frankfurter is an example—that was not so. His vision, clarified by the war, was fixed firmly on the future. Even the immediate results of the 1924 election, he wrote Walter Lippmann, were not so important as "the directions which we further or retard for 1944. . . . The forces that are struggling and groping behind La Follette are, at least, struggling and groping for a dream, for a different look of things in 1944. That's why I'm for them—and in my small way want to help to give direction and definiteness to the dream."[128]

127. Felix Frankfurter quoted in *ibid.*, III, 2570–73.
128. Frankfurter to Lippmann, July 18, 1924, Frankfurter Papers.

6

The Political Economy of War:
The International Dimension

The world economy in the prewar years was a marvel of growth and interdependence. Though nineteenth-century industrial capitalism showered its benefits unevenly on different social classes, all the developed countries had witnessed amazing leaps in their wealth and standards of living in the several decades before 1914. Much of that material advance owed to the deepening harmony and coordination of international economic relationships. Despite ominously intensifying colonial rivalries in Africa and Asia, the European states allowed goods and capital and even labor to move easily across their own national frontiers. Relative to the movement of raw materials and foodstuffs, trade in industrial products was rising more rapidly, indicating the growing importance of technological specialization to economic growth.

Central to the smooth functioning of this complex international economy was the role of Great Britain. London, the heart of the world financial system, pumped the British pound sterling into all the arteries of global commerce. Sterling was indeed the very lifeblood of the world trading network. Other nations held British pounds as a currency of reserve; foreign merchants maintained large sterling balances at London; and sterling served as a currency of account in the exchange of goods that never touched the shores of Great Britain. So great was the world's confidence in sterling, and so skillful was the British banking system's management of sterling flows, that the Bank of England actually operated with smaller gold reserves than most other central banks.

In the course of the nineteenth century, Britain had accumulated enormous financial surpluses. Rather than hoard or redistribute these resources at home, British capitalists had made them available for foreign loans and investments. Roughly 40 percent of British savings in the late nineteenth century were annually invested overseas, and on the eve of World War I, one third of all accumulated British wealth had taken the form of foreign investment. Most of this sizable sum was placed outside the British Empire, predominantly in the United States and in Latin America.[1] Britons in 1914 held over half of all foreign investment in the world. The return on that investment more than offset the growing British tendency annually to import more than was exported. Moreover, the strategic placement of British overseas capital in the development of sophisticated installations like railroads and electric utilities—built to British specifications and dependent on British engineers for servicing and British factories for replacement parts—guaranteed continuing markets for high-value British technology. Britannia also unarguably ruled the waves. Her merchant ships accounted for one third the world's tonnage, while her far-flung empire provided a global network of bunkering facilities that fueled the vessels of all nations. The income from those maritime services, and from related enterprises such as insurance and commercial banking, played a major role in sustaining Britain's financial health.

The British held other major assets as well. Though the home islands had a limited endowment of natural resources, the globe-girdling empire contained nearly every raw material necessary to modern industrial production. Britons also possessed an intangible advantage that was perhaps the most formidable of all: their long experience in foreign trade, from which they inherited an unparalleled knowledge of world markets, and a matchless expertise in the intricate coordination of investment, credit, and shipping that made for success in international business.

As the twentieth century opened, Britain's seemingly eternal success in dominating the international economy excited strong jealousies in other nations. Two upstart competitors, Germany and the United States,

1. Leland B. Yeager, *International Monetary Relations: Theory, History, and Policy* (New York: Harper and Row, 2nd ed., 1976), 300.

had begun to bid for the crown of world commercial supremacy. Under the pressure of those challenges, Britain's share of world trade had dropped from 20 percent in the 1870s to 15 percent in 1913. The German rivalry was among the causes of the Great War; the intensification of the American rivalry was to be among the chief consequences of that war.

For nearly a century following the American War of Independence, the United States had been forced to accept poor terms of trade with Europe. Americans long remained in a kind of economic colonial status relative to the mother continent—exporting raw materials and foodstuffs, importing finished manufactured goods, and running chronically negative trade balances financed by mounting indebtedness to predominantly British creditors. But since 1896 America had achieved a permanently positive annual balance of payments on current account, and by 1914 had liquidated a large fraction of her foreign-held debt. America's emergence as a net creditor, whose dollars would compete with British sterling for foreign investment outlets, was only a matter of time. Moreover, 1913 was the first year in which finished manufactures headed the list of American exports, edging out crude materials and agricultural products as the leading earners of foreign exchange. In that year also, the American share of international trade stood at 11 percent —an unprecedentedly high level, ranking close behind the British at 15 percent and the German at 13 percent. More directly threatening to British interests was the regional distribution of American exports, which had since the turn of the century begun to shift away from Europe toward Asia and especially toward Latin America. Those exotic lands in the Orient and in the southern hemisphere had long been the preserves of British commerce, shipping, and banking. They now began to take shape as arenas for a fierce economic contest between John Bull and Uncle Sam.[2]

That contest, unlike the Anglo-German competition, would match against one another two remarkably similar combatants. They were alike not merely in cultural and political heritage but also in their eco-

---

2. See Gerd Hardach, *The First World War: 1914–1918* (Berkeley: University of California Press, 1977), 3–6. In 1913, British manufacturers accounted for 31 percent of Latin American imports of manufactured goods. Germans accounted for 25 percent, and Americans for 15 percent. See Alfred Maizels, *Industrial Growth and World Trade* (Cambridge, Eng.: Cambridge University Press, 1963), 196–97.

nomic profiles and ambitions. Britain, through the empire, sold in both raw material and finished product markets; America, the world's only developed continental economy, aimed to do the same. These simple facts seemed to preclude a naturally complementary economic relation between the two countries. Nature and history had apparently left them but two alternatives: competition or cooperation. When the war broke out in 1914, those choices were thrown into stark and insistent relief.

Woodrow Wilson actively encouraged the changing American role in the world economy. He warmly embraced the doctrine, familiar to Enlightenment economists and to the theoreticians of classical British liberalism, that trade promoted both universal prosperity and universal peace. It also, not incidentally, would promote Wilson's political fortunes and American profits. Exports, which accounted for less than 5 percent of gross national product in 1910, reached nearly 6 percent in 1912, and still more in 1913. Woodrow Wilson was not alone in his judgment that expanding exports were necessary to continued American economic growth. The fortuitous identity of principle and interest only deepened Wilson's dedication to the expansion of American commerce—indeed, of world commerce. Fundamental to classical liberal theory, and to Wilson's thinking on the subject, was the conviction that political interference with trade was "artificial" and constricting. Commerce should flow where the laws of the marketplace directed it. Political obstacles, such as tariffs, discriminatory trade agreements, and imperial-preference systems, destroyed efficiency and denied to everyone the fruits of freely developed enterprise. Thus one of Wilson's first acts as President was to call a special session of Congress to revise the tariff downward. Trade, he argued, could only move along a two-way street. Reciprocity was the key to American export growth. As Representative Oscar Underwood of Alabama, author of the administration's tariff bill, put it: "We cannot expect to dispose of our surplus products in foreign markets if we maintain in this country a tariff wall so high that other nations are unable to trade with us on reasonable terms."[3] Wilson's commitment to mutuality in economic relations was in no way inconsistent with his knowledge that in a liberalized international trading system, "the skill of American workmen would dominate the markets

3. Quoted in Jeffrey J. Safford, *Wilsonian Maritime Diplomacy 1913–1921* (New Brunswick, N.J.: Rutgers University Press, 1978), 26.

of all the globe."[4] That domination, Wilson believed, would simply distribute the benefits of American efficiency to other peoples.

At the time of his successful effort to lower American tariff barriers, Wilson was also laboring to revise the nation's banking laws. The antiquated National Banking System had proved terribly inadequate to the financial demands of the modern economy, and not the least of its defects was the inability of member banks to discount import and export acceptances. Moreover, the System made poor provision for the establishment of foreign branch banks. These liabilities prevented American bankers from competing effectively for a share in the international banking business, as even American traders were compelled to look to London, not New York or Boston, to finance their foreign transactions. To remove those impediments, the Wilson administration wrote into the Federal Reserve Act of 1913 provisions allowing Federal Reserve banks to discount drafts on foreign commercial transactions and to trade them in the open market. The Act also provided for the relatively easy establishment of foreign branches by member banks.

Significantly, at about this same time Wilson persuaded Congress to quadruple the budget of the Bureau of Foreign and Domestic Commerce. The new funds were to underwrite an expanded network of American commercial attachés abroad, and finance various studies of American foreign trade opportunities. Fifty million dollars of the Bureau's 1915 allocation of $387 million were earmarked for a special study of trade prospects with Latin America.[5]

Thus, when war erupted in Europe in the summer of 1914, the United States was already becoming a major factor in world markets, and the Wilson administration had already amply demonstrated its ambitions for a still greater expansion of American overseas trade. Those ambitions grew from Wilson's deeply rooted conviction that goodwill flowed along with goods in the channels of trade, that commercial contacts were effective guarantors of pacific relations among states. The President also believed that the time had come for American business to take its rightful place in the international economy—and he was determined to put the power of government beside that of private capital in the effort to secure that place.

4. *Idem.*
5. Burton T. Kaufman, *Efficiency and Expansion: Foreign Trade Organization in the Wilson Administration, 1913–1921* (Westport, Conn.: Greenwood, 1974), 76–80, and chap. 3, *passim.*

The initial news of the European fighting badly jarred the American economy, and the war threatened at first to ruin Wilson's plans for foreign commercial expansion. The New York Stock Exchange closed its doors for nearly four months, freezing billions of dollars in usually liquid assets. Foreign exchange, especially sterling exchange, if available at all, had to be purchased at rates that dipped and soared crazily, making all international transactions speculative in the extreme, and indicating the great vulnerability of the world credit system to disruptions of the London money market. Still more ominously, the outbreak of the war virtually swept from the seas the ships that had carried the great bulk of American foreign commerce. German vessels stayed safely in their Baltic ports, or sought safe moorings in neutral harbors. The British diverted all available tonnage to the war trade, leaving many American exporters and importers without the means to move their goods. Southern cotton farmers watched in alarm as the price of raw cotton, piling up on silent wharves, slumped sickeningly from 12 to 6 cents a pound.

The government moved swiftly in 1914 to counter those blows to American commerce. Secretary of the Treasury McAdoo eased the liquidity crunch by making emergency currency available to the banking system. He encouraged the formation of a Cotton Loan Fund, with government participation, to lift the sagging price of cotton. The Federal Reserve System, scheduled to begin operation in November, was to provide some relief to traders starving for lack of credits. Transactions previously liquidated in sterling bills of exchange at London could then be executed in dollars through American banks. In the meantime, McAdoo established a temporary foreign-bill discount market at the Treasury, which permitted modest revival of the foreign trade flattened by the European crisis.

Administration officials quickly saw that the lack of shipping posed the greatest obstacle to revival and expansion of American trade. Here was the weakest link—one might better say the missing link—in the chain of measures that Wilson hoped would lead to a larger American share in the international economy. The once mighty American merchant marine had so decayed by 1914 that American bottoms then carried less than 10 percent of the nation's ocean-going commerce. When the belligerents, who were also, as it happened, the leading maritime nations, suddenly withdrew their tonnage from much of the world ocean in August, the crippling consequences of America's maritime dependency were quickly and painfully revealed. As early as March 1914, Secretary of Commerce William C. Redfield had urged legislation to facilitate the transfer of foreign-built vessels to American registry. Spurred by the war-born crisis in the carrying trade, Congress passed the Ship Registry Act in August, 1914, which eventually brought 372,000 tons of shipping under the American flag. As a companion measure, Congress mandated the establishment of a War Risk Insurance Bureau in the Treasury Department, to provide government financial protection to shippers against the hazards of conducting commerce on hostile seas.

At this point, in mid-August 1914, even while the war in Europe was but a few weeks old, a significant shift seems to have occurred in the minds of American policy-makers. The crisis had at first compelled measures to *preserve* the teetering structure of American foreign economic relations. But with passage of the Ship Registry and War Risk Insurance bills, a new vista opened. The realization began to spread in both government and business circles that the war represented not so much an emergency as an opportunity—an opportunity to capture trade that had previously been jealously held by the now-distracted European combatants. Latin America seemed especially likely to slip from Europe's financial and commercial grip, and therefore afforded a particularly attractive economic prize to be grasped by the United States. Dramatizing the beckoning prospects for American trade in the southern hemisphere was the opening of the Panama Canal, through which the first ship passed on August 15, 1914. To exploit fully these new opportunities, however, would require unprecedented cooperation between business and government. Thus on August 16, Secretary McAdoo boldly proposed to the President new legislation to create a governmentally owned and operated merchant fleet. McAdoo peered through the smoke of the European conflagration, trying to discern ways to use the emergency to secure permanent American gains. "We have an unusual opportunity for South American trade," he wrote to Wilson, "but without ships we can do nothing. With them we can quickly establish business and political relations that will be of inestimable value to the country perhaps for all times."[6]

The President enthusiastically agreed. Like McAdoo, Wilson envisioned the ships of the new fleet sailing primarily to the ports of "the States, great and small, of Central and South America. Their lines of

6. McAdoo to Wilson, Aug. 16, 1914, quoted in Kaufman, *Efficiency and Expansion,* 99.

trade have hitherto run chiefly athwart the seas, not to our ports but to the ports of Great Britain and of the older continent of Europe." In Latin America, said the President, were "markets which we must supply"; it was "our duty and opportunity" to do so. The United States should purchase the German ships bottled up in American harbors, Wilson wrote privately, "and put them upon the direct trade between this country and South America." "The Government," he insisted to the Congress, "must open these gates of trade, and open them wide . . . open them before it is altogether reasonable to ask private capital to open them at a venture." To promote further those ends, the administration convened a Pan-American Financial Conference at Washington in May 1915, where Wilson admonished the delegates that expanded commerce within the western hemisphere would be insurance for all the American states against being "drawn into the tangle of European affairs."[7]

Many businessmen, covetous like Wilson of Latin American trade possibilities, hailed the administration's general intentions. "Why did the U.S. not jump in and pre-empt those vacated South American markets?" asked one contemporary. "Because Uncle Sam had not the ships. . . . If the U.S. had had a fleet of merchantmen with their own docks and rail connections in South America, not a factory in the U.S. need have run half time, not an industrial worker need have gone unemployed."[8] But the administration's specific proposal for a government shipping corporation raised a flurry of opposition. Maritime interests in the United States decried what they regarded as the socialistic implications of a federally owned merchant marine. The National Foreign Trade Council, no enemy of export growth, considered the shipping bill a premature measure that undesirably stifled new private investment in ship construction.[9] The Allies further objected to the fact that the ships most available for purchase were German merchantmen trapped in American ports by British surface raiders. International conventions forbade the transfer of a belligerent vessel to a neutral flag in order to avoid capture. Neither Britain nor France would countenance any infraction of that rule. "The President of the United States . . .

7. Albert Shaw, ed., *The Messages and Papers of Woodrow Wilson*, 2 vols. (New York: Review of Reviews Corp., 1924), I, 69, 72, 143; Wilson to Charles W. Eliot, Feb. 23, 1915, RSB, V, 77.
8. Agnes C. Laut, "Will the Shipping Bill Help or Hurt Our Commerce?" *The Outlook* 109 (Feb. 3, 1915), 292.
9. Safford, *Maritime Diplomacy*, 45–50.

cannot possibly . . . allow his country thus to take sides against us
. . . ," The French ambassador cautioned Secretary of State Bryan
about the Ship Purchase bill.[10]

The combined weight of this opposition suffocated the shipping bill
in 1915, but events soon breathed new life into McAdoo's and Wilson's
design for a revitalized American merchant marine. Despite the administration's best efforts, trade with Latin America in 1915 grew only
modestly over 1914, failing even to reach prewar levels. As McAdoo
had forseen, lack of shipping was the chief constraint on expansion.
The British sought to concentrate all shipping in the Atlantic war
trade, and not incidentally to keep neutral vessels off of temporarily
neglected trade routes that were traditionally British. Hence they used
their enormous maritime power to set a highly profitable rate scale for
Atlantic shipping. By late 1915 they had drawn an incredible 95 percent
of the world's tonnage to the war trade—leaving precious few bottoms
to haul American goods to the southern hemisphere. In December 1915
the London government tightened its already iron grip on world shipping when it put the entire British merchant marine under centralized
control. In June of 1916, the Allied governments took another menacing
step toward postwar discrimination against American trade when they
announced at the Paris Economic Conference their plans for an exclusive economic union. The following month the British Government
lengthened its already noxious black list of American firms who were
to be denied all access to British markets or commercial facilities.[11]

American business groups observed these developments with mounting anxiety, and their fear of economic isolation eventually overbal-
anced their fear of a "socialist" merchant marine. The National Foreign
Trade Council reversed itself and now supported the shipping bill as
a direct retaliation against the exclusionary program announced at the
Paris Economic Conference. Secretary McAdoo adeptly capitalized on
this sentiment, and at the same time he shrewdly associated his shipping
proposals with the rising campaign for military preparedness. The nation needed modern merchant ships, he preached, not only to carry
commercial cargoes but also to serve as naval auxiliaries. Success
crowned these efforts on September 7, 1916, when Wilson signed the
Shipping Act into law. That same day the State Department jubilantly

10. French Ambassador (Jules Jusserand) to Secretary of State (William Jennings
    Bryan), Sept. 3, 1914, in *Foreign Relations of the United States,* Supplement,
    1914, 492.
11. See Safford, *Maritime Diplomacy,* chap. 4.

cabled every American legation in Latin America that the Shipping Act would permit the establishment of lines "to East and West coasts of South America. . . . Anticipate mutually beneficial results."[12]

The Act established a Shipping Board to own and operate a commercial fleet, and it authorized an Emergency Fleet Corporation to purchase and construct merchant vessels. The Board was to have permanent regulatory powers, but, significantly, its authority actually to operate shipping lines was to expire five years after the end of the European war. The crisis had thus bent but not broken the commitment of American capital to keep the government out of traditionally private business enterprise. McAdoo had nevertheless won a major victory in his campaign to use the power of the government to promote foreign trade; he had also, in however primitive a fashion, demonstrated the political efficacy of promoting economic stimulus in the guise of military necessity.

Wilson's plans for the promotion of American overseas commerce antedated the European crisis, but the war both broadened the scope of American intentions and speeded their implementation. The sudden escalation of the President's shipping program from a modest proposal to facilitate transfer of registry to a full-blown scheme for a government-owned merchant marine vividly illustrated the quickening effect of the war on American economic ambitions; and the utility of the emergency in overcoming congressional reluctance about a state-owned shipping corporation suggested just how fruitful a political climate the crisis had created. With the passage of the Shipping Act, the administration realized one major element in its design for American commercial expansion. There remained now the problems of finance and of stimulating and properly organizing the export sector itself.

The Federal Reserve Act of 1913 had taken significant steps toward improving America's international financial position. But in 1914 the United States was still a net debtor on long-term international account to the extent of about $3.2 billion. Most of that amount was held in Britain. And on short-term account, due largely to constantly maturing commercial obligations on the London money market, Americans owed half-a-billion dollars when an obscure Serbian nationalist assassinated the Austrian Archduke Ferdinand and thus ignited the fuse of war in June 1914.

12. G. R. Cookey to Secretary of State, Sept. 7, 1916, Records of the Department of State (hereafter RDS), Microfilm 743, Record Group (hereafter RG) 59, National Archives (hereafter NA), Washington, D.C.

The explosion of war almost instantly reversed the credit standing of the United States. The European Allies began to buy enormous quantities of American exports, unmatched by an equivalent return flow of imports. At first these purchases were paid for in gold, which poured into the country in previously undreamed-of amounts; by 1917 the national gold stock had nearly doubled. But gold shipments could not long sustain the level of buying to which the war had forced the Allies. Moreover, continued gold transfers threatened to depress the value of sterling, as well as feed an inflationary expansion of the money supply in the United States. The Allies, with American approval, thus sought early in the war to settle their huge negative trade balances with the United States by the movement of capital. Both the British and French governments took steps to control or even acquire dollar-denominated securities in the hands of their own nationals; they then either liquidated these assets at New York for dollar exchange, or, after Wilson in 1915 lifted the ban on loans to belligerents, used them as collateral for dollar credits. Europe's unfunded debt to the United States also grew, as American banks and exporters extended long-term credits to their Old World customers. By the time American neutrality ended in April, 1917, some $1.4 billion in foreign-held American securities had been repatriated to the United States, and Americans then held several billion dollars in newly acquired European debt obligations. Thus, even before the massive loans to Europe from the United States Treasury in 1917 and 1918, the United States had become a net international creditor. This development, too, had been foreshadowed well before 1914, but the distorting effects of the war on international trade had breathtakingly accelerated the process.

American export surpluses created a swelling pool of financial reserves at New York. Simultaneously, the London credit market shriveled as sterling was drained off to the war effort. Hence the trials of Europe also hastened a significant shift of short-term international acceptance financing from London to New York. In the first eight months of the war, the chairman of the National Foreign Trade Council exultantly reported, re-exports through New York, especially of South American products like coffee and cacao, had increased more than 50 percent over the preceding year.[13]

---

13. James A. Farrell, "Central and South American Trade as Affected by the European War," *Annals of the American Academy of Political and Social Science* 60 (1915), 60–68 (hereafter *Annals*).

But many foreign merchants, especially in Latin America, still insisted on payment in sterling—largely because the dollar remained a relatively unfamiliar medium of exchange and because the American banking system had few overseas installations to facilitate dollar trading. The National City Bank of New York pioneered in remedying this situation as early as the spring of 1914, when it decided to open a branch in Buenos Aires. Within two years the City Bank had spread its operations to several other Latin American countries, as well as to the Orient and even to Italy. In 1916 Congress amended the Federal Reserve Act to permit American banks to form foreign banking corporations, and the following year a consortium of bankers organized the American Foreign Banking Corporation to establish branch facilities in Latin America. At the same time, the Bureau of Foreign and Domestic Commerce surveyed its consular officers and commercial attachés worldwide to determine specific opportunities for American banking overseas.[14] Nineteen sixteen also witnessed the creation of a Federal Tariff Commission, designed to give increased flexibility to tariff policy and hence sharpen the nation's bargaining ability in international trade competition. Equally significant, Woodrow Wilson in that same year agreed to support the Webb-Pomerene bill, exempting from the antitrust laws business combinations in the export trade.

By 1917, the mixture of European misfortune and administration policy had opened shimmering prospects for American foreign commerce. Exports were booming; keels were laid on every shipping way in the country as the new merchant flotilla came into being; Americans had liquidated much of their debt to the Old World and stood poised to challenge the British as the world's bankers; and to the south the largely abandoned markets of Latin America beckoned alluringly. "There is present to this nation an opportunity which will probably never again come in its history," urged a spokesman for National City Bank of New York in 1915, "an opportunity for introducing American goods in markets hitherto closed to this country."[15] Secretary of Commerce William Redfield declared that "A new spirit has come into our commercial life . . . a sense of a new financial and industrial power,"

14. Kaufman, *Efficiency and Expansion,* 117–24; Bureau of Foreign and Domestic Commerce, "Field for American Banks," Special Instruction Circular No. 505, Feb. 16, 1917, Records of the Bureau of Foreign and Domestic Commerce (hereafter BFDC), File 620, RG 151, NA; see also Carl P. Parrini, *Heir to Empire: United States Economic Diplomacy, 1916–1923* (Pittsburgh: University of Pittsburgh Press, 1969), chap. 5.
15. William S. Kies, "Cooperation in the Export Trade," *Annals* 60 (1915), 39–51.

But Redfield, aglow with the liberal light kindled by his visionary chief, cautioned against the abuse of that power. "Commerce," he warned, "is mutual exchange to mutual benefit and not a species of industrial war. . . . We shall not gain by grinding, but by growing. The law of grasp and gouge is not the law of business permanence. That which is socially undesirable cannot continue commercially profitable."[16]

Across this bright vista a dark cloud had already begun to move in the spring of 1916. In March of that year the Allied governments, responding to rumors of a long-range plan for the economic integration of central Europe (*Mitteleuropa*) under German aegis, began preliminary discussions of their own about coordinating economic war aims. Secretary of State Robert Lansing sensed approaching danger in these discussions. He instructed the American embassy in Paris to monitor the upcoming talks, where "efforts may be made to apply restrictions possibly affecting American interests."[17] When the full session of the Paris Economic Conference met in June 1916, Lansing's worst fears were confirmed. The war had already, of course, played havoc with the multilateral, interdependent character of the pre-1914 international economy. The allies at Paris now proposed to deepen that disruption by tightening the wartime blockade against the Central Powers. They also announced their intention to perpetuate the economic fragmentation of the world in the postwar period by creating an exclusive trading bloc. Close state supervision in each of the Allied countries would lead to common tariff, banking, and shipping policies, cooperative exploitation of raw materials, and the coordinated allocation of world market shares among producers within the bloc. To implement this design, the conferees established a standing body at Paris, the *Comité Permanent International d'Action Économique*.

These policies ostensibly aimed to counter the *Mitteleuropa* plan and to threaten Germany with permanent economic isolation. But the intensification of economic warfare posed a no less lethal threat to the commerce of the neutral nations excluded from *both* proposed trading blocs. Though the United States had historically opposed any such exclusionary combinations, the character and regional distribution of

16. William C. Redfield, "America's International Trade as Affected by the European War," *Annals* 60 (1915), 9, 16.
17. Lansing to Amembassy, Paris, Mar. 10, 1916, RDS, File 600.001/10, RG 59, NA.

its own foreign commerce rendered the Allied measures much more directly menacing to American interests. Those measures constituted nothing less than "militarism translated into commercial warfare," declared one American official.[18] The American Consul General at Paris reported that "the proposed joining of the Allies' economic forces will be of a more comprehensive and formidable character than that previously existing." He recommended that in self-defense the United States should adopt "similar methods of organization" in the export trade, linking government with business to meet effectively the German and Allied challenges.[19] Just that reaction to the Paris pronouncements, in fact, helped carry the government's shipping bill through Congress later in the summer.

Secretary of State Lansing advised the President that the effect of the Allied actions at Paris "may be very far reaching on the commerce and trade of the whole world after the war is over." The Allied plan might backfire and actually prolong the war by stiffening German resistance, the Secretary opined. More pertinently, Lansing warned, "We neutrals, as well as the Central Powers, will have to face a commercial combination which has as its avowed purpose preferential treatment for its members. It will be a strong combination of nations, which on account of their colonies and great merchant marine will be able, I fear, to carry through their preferential program. The consequent restriction upon profitable trade with these commercial allies will cause a serious, if not critical, situation for the nations outside the union by creating unusual and artificial economic conditions." Lansing suggested convening a conference of neutrals to form a third international trading bloc to offset the *Mitteleuropa* and Allied plans. "[T]he best way to fight combination," he advised, "is by combination."[20]

Wilson appreciated the boost that the news from Paris had given to his shipping program, but flatly rejected Lansing's suggestion that the moment be seized to create a third economic bloc under American leadership. Instead, the President took the occasion to reaffirm his commitment to an open world economy, free of all political constraints on trade, guaranteed "against such economic warfare as would in effect constitute an effort to throttle the industrial life of a nation or shut

18. Federal Trade Commissioner William S. Culbertson, quoted in Safford, *Maritime Diplomacy,* 89.
19. A. M. Thackera, "The Economic Conference of the Allies," June 30, 1916, RDS, File 600.001/24, RG 59, NA.
20. Lansing to Wilson, June 23, 1916, RDS, File 600.001/18, RG 59, NA.

it off from equal opportunities of trade with the rest of the world."[21] Wilson here characteristically took the high ground of principle, denouncing economic discrimination against *any* nation. But he clearly saw that a chief effect of the Paris resolutions would be "to prevent our merchants from getting a foothold in markets which Great Britain has hitherto all but dominated"—especially those Latin American markets that American traders had just begun to enter.[22] Seeking to gauge the strength of the new Allied economic offensive, the State Department in early 1917 requested all its legations to report on the intentions of the governments to which they were accredited with reference to the Paris announcements.[23]

So matters stood on the eve of American entry into the war. The Allied action at the Paris Economic Conference threatened both to check American advances into war-disrupted markets and to freeze American interests out of a postwar world economy divided along political lines. Paradoxically, just as the United States edged nearer to military conflict with Germany, the prospect grew of intensified economic conflict with Britain. The overhanging shadow of that conflict chilled Washington's ardor for the Allied cause and darkened the outlook for Anglo-American cooperation when the United States at last became a combatant on April 6, 1917. When the American legation at Paris suggested in 1918 that Washington send a United States delegate to the *Comité Permanent International d'Action Économique,* they were pointedly reminded that "the Committee exists by virtue of the resolutions of Interallied Conferences of March and June 1916—the latter of which adopted the resolutions looking to an economic 'war after the war' of which we have not approved." There would, therefore, be no American representatives on the Committee.[24]

In economic policy, as in other realms, the United States sought even as a co-belligerent of the Allies to distance itself from their wartime practices and postwar aims. This singular posture raised peculiar problems for American policymakers. Their general goal was to *restore* the prewar multilateral international economic structure, though

21. Wilson to Lansing, Feb. 7, 1917, quoted in Parrini, *Heir to Empire,* 21.
22. Wilson to Edward M. House, July 23, 1916, RSB, VI, 312.
23. "Confidential Instructions" to all legations, Jan. 1917, RDS, File 600.001/150, RG 59, NA.
24. "Memo from Mr. Lay," (Office of the Foreign Trade Adviser) attached to Lansing to George McFadden (War Trade Board representative at Paris), Mar. 16, 1918, RDS, File 600.001/207, RG 59, NA.

with greatly increased American participation. Central to that goal was the reintegration of Germany into the global economy. How, therefore, could American economic might be concerted with that of the Allies in the blockade against Germany, without lending support to the aim of the Paris Economic Conference to extinguish Germany as a world economic power? Then, too, how could Americans preserve and even extend the sizable advantages that they had gained in two and half years of neutrality, and simultaneously maintain cooperative relations with their erstwhile commercial rivals, now their partners in war? And through every aspect of these complex deliberations ran the most intriguing and difficult question of all: How might America's economic means, so enormously bolstered in the neutrality period, be made to serve Woodrow Wilson's comprehensive political ends?

Some of those questions were less troublesome than others. In particular, economic warfare against Germany, whatever Wilson's long-range intentions for a restorative peace, presented irresistible opportunities for permanent American gains at the enemy's expense. Within weeks of the American declaration of war, the Emergency Fleet Corporation confiscated several hundred thousand tons of German shipping in American ports. These vessels not only helped meet wartime American shipping needs, but at Wilson's specific request at the Paris Peace Conference, they were permanently transferred to American ownership. Similarly, in October 1917, Wilson appointed A. Mitchell Palmer as Alien Property Custodian to control enemy assets in the United States. To ensure that proceeds from those assets did not reach German hands during the war, the Custodian was empowered to hold enemy properties in trust until the re-establishment of peace. The original legislation establishing Palmer's office authorized the sale of such properties only to prevent wastage. But in March 1918 the enabling legislation was amended to remove restrictions on the Custodian's power of sale. Palmer thereupon distinguished two classes of enemy properties. The first class was "friendly" individual investments in real property and securities. Those he continued to hold in trust pending the conclusion of the war. The second was large-scale German corporate investments in major industries like chemicals and textiles. Palmer did not even feign to confine his thinking about those holdings to the period of hostilities. He proposed that they should be "separated from their former owners forever," and he actively sought the power of sale in order to effect "their com-

plete eradication as German enterprises and their thorough naturalization into an American character."[25] In this manner, Palmer permanently
divested German owners of several million dollars of direct investment
in the United States. The British, too, had been forced to liquidate many
of their American assets, but the British at least received the cash benefits of the sales. Palmer, by contrast, sequestered proceeds from the sale
of German properties to offset postwar claims for American property
seized in Germany.

This policy paid spectacular rewards to several American industries,
especially chemicals. Probably in no other line of endeavor had German
industrial dominance been so pronounced before the war. German
scientists had pioneered and perfected organic chemical processes that
gave the vast Rhineland dye and pharmaceutical complex undisputed
leadership in world markets. German chemical firms preserved their
formidable technological lead by aggressive marketing abroad—some
said "dumping"—that discouraged the growth of foreign competition.
Thus before 1914 American production of dyestuffs and medicinals
remained tiny, and depended heavily on Germany for supplies of intermediate compounds. When the British fleet interdicted the surface
of the Atlantic after the outbreak of the war, those supplies ceased,
despite daring German efforts to continue them by cargo submarine.

Like the embargo of Thomas Jefferson's day, the British blockade
proved to be the mother of American invention, as American firms by
1917 had largely replaced the German imports with their own production, and had even built up a considerable export business. After the
amendments of March 1918 to the Trading-with-the-Enemy Act, profits
from those operations went in part to buy out German interests in the
American chemical industry. But even those achievements did not satisfy Palmer. In the closing weeks of the war he sought a further amendment to the Act to allow him to dispose not merely of enemy real
property and securities but of enemy-owned patents as well. The Germans, he claimed, had taken out thousands of chemical patents in the
United States, which they then held without exercising, as an obstacle
to the development of an American chemical industry. He secured the
requisite amendment on November 4, 1918, just a week before the
Armistice. Shortly thereafter he sold 4500 lucrative patents at bargain-
basement rates to the Chemical Foundation, a newly minted creation

25. *Alien Property Custodian Report* (Washington, D.C.: Government Printing
Office, 1919), 14.

of the American chemical industry. The Foundation then licensed to member firms production rights under the various patents. Congress obligingly fostered this technological windfall with special protective tariff legislation for the chemical industry in 1921, and wrote stiff duties on dyes into the Fordney-McCumber Tariff of 1922.

Palmer's actions indicated a remarkably ambitious and comprehensive plan to use the war crisis for long-term American advantage. Nothing in the policy of wartime blockade of Germany necessitated the *permanent* transfer of assets and rights to technology that the Alien Property Custodian so energetically effected. But Palmer from the outset fixed his gaze beyond the horizon of the immediate conflict. He aimed at nothing less than the establishment in America of a scientific-industrial complex second to none. "No other industry," he said of dyes and chemicals, "offers a livelihood to any such large numbers of highly-trained scientific chemists nor any such incentive to continuous and extended research." Securing the German patents, Palmer boasted, was "the most important piece of constructive work which has been possible in my department." The Chemical Foundation, he claimed, "may well . . . form the nucleus of the greatest research organization in the country."[26] Here were the rudiments of the kind of government-nurtured research and development activities that would later in the century play such a key role in stimulating economic growth. More immediately, Palmer provoked the German government to complain that his policies "were designed to destroy Germany's economic existence upon this continent."[27] The essential truth of that statement must severely qualify Woodrow Wilson's claim that America alone among the great powers was disinterested in economic gain from the war.

The United States pursued an equally aggressive policy of economic warfare against Germany on other continents. In significant measure, the conflict of 1914-18 was not a "world" war at all. In Europe several countries remained neutral, notably Switzerland, the Netherlands, Spain, and all of Scandinavia. Many Latin American nations were also officially uncommitted, or, after April 1917, only reluctant belligerents. One important goal of American diplomacy was to restrict German access to those markets, much as Britain had sought to shut

26. *Ibid.*, 38, 60, 62. By 1929, the U.S. controlled 18 percent of world chemical exports, up from 11 percent in 1913. See Maizels, *Industrial Growth and World Trade,* 302.
27. *Ibid.*, 16.

off German commercial and financial contact with the United States during the period of American neutrality. Through the banking house of J. P. Morgan, the United States orchestrated bear movements against the German mark on the European neutral money markets, and intervened at Zurich to stop the liquidation of German-held securities for neutral currencies.[28] These actions were taken in concert with the Allies, but the vigor of the world-wide American economic assault on Germany sometimes surprised the British, who for years had suffered Wilson's complaints about the effects on neutral trade of the British blockade and the infamous "black list."

In October 1917 Woodrow Wilson established the War Trade Board as the principal agency empowered to regulate American foreign commerce during the war. Through the licensing of exports and imports, the Board sought to choke off all American trade with the enemy, and, so far as possible, to block neutral intercourse with the Central Powers. The Board also tried to guide the flow of commerce in order to conserve shipping, husband essential commodities, and maintain dollar exchange. Because the British by 1917 had already established an effective system of control over the commerce of the European neutrals, the War Trade Board focused most of its attention on Latin America. There, as elsewhere, the objectives of American policy often seemed to exceed the immediate goal of winning the war against Germany. "It has been the endeavor of this Board," said one member, "to foster our trade with South America in every way consistent with the duty imposed upon us to carry out the provisions of the Trading with the Enemy Act."[29]

Like the Alien Property Custodian in the United States, the War Trade Board in Latin America often tried not simply to cripple German interests for the duration of the fighting, but, as Secretary of State Lansing remarked about Ecuadorian cacao plantations, to "effect the *permanent* elimination of the German interests in the properties in question."[30] The Board also used its export licensing powers in efforts

28. Summary from *Rheinische-Westfälische Zeitung*, No. 481, June 18, 1917; Lansing to McAdoo, Sept. 8, 1917, both in Records of the Treasury Department, Bureau of Accounts, International Fiscal Relationships, Germany, RG 39, NA.

29. C. W. Wooley to Joseph H. Defrees, Jan. 9, 1919, Records of the War Trade Board, Executive Office, General Correspondence, RG 182, Federal Record Center, Suitland, Md. (hereafter FRC).

30. Lansing to R. H. Elizalde, Nov. 12, 1918, quoted in Parrini, *Heir to Empire* 136 (italics added).

to force the sale to American owners of German assets in Peru and Guatemala, despite offers to impound in Latin America all German earnings from those assets until after the war. Significantly, Lansing's directive concerning the plantations in Ecuador went out the day *after* the Armistice, voiding any description of the American takeover as a "war measure." The Secretary and his colleagues in government took the long view of American interests on the South American continent. In April 1918, Lansing had requested The Inquiry, the scholarly group conducting studies preparatory to the peace conference, to pay particular attention to South and Central America, even though those regions would probably not enter directly into peace negotiations.[31] The State Department circularized all commercial attachés in Latin America just weeks before the Armistice, seeking information on possible postwar German trade competition. Immediately following the Armistice, War Trade Board representatives urged the Treasury to insist at the peace conference on the forced transfer of the remaining German investments in Latin America to the United States. Failing that, the American government should at the least "take immediate steps to encourage American capital to invest in such German South American property when it is available. A definite government policy in this respect should be worked out by the United States."[32] By 1919 the Departments of State and Commerce pursued such a policy so aggressively, writes historian Joseph Tulchin, that "at times it looked as if representatives of the United States government were working for finders' fees."[33]

The startling energy with which the United States implemented its economic policies in Latin America troubled the British, who began to fear that British South American holdings, no less than German, were targets of American economic warfare. The United States "desire[s] to extend the Monroe Doctrine into the moral world . . . not merely as far as the Canal but right down to Cape Horn," reported a Brtish diplo-

31. Lansing to Sidney Mezes, Apr. 17, 1918, RDS, Microfilm 743, RG 59, NA.
32. "Memo for Mr. Strauss," Nov. 21, 1918, Records of the Treasury Department, Bureau of Accounts, International Fiscal Relationships, Germany, RG 39, NA.
33. Joseph S. Tulchin, *The Aftermath of War: World War I and U.S. Policy Toward Latin America* (New York: New York University Press, 1971), 165. By 1924, United States investment in Latin America had more than doubled from 1914 levels, and by 1929 had more than tripled. See Cleona Lewis, *America's Stake in International Investments* (Washington, D.C.: Brookings Institution, 1938), 606.

mat in 1918. The "suspicion exists in London, and causes some anxiety to His Majesty's Government, that the United States are inclined to use their political influence in Latin America to further their own commercial interests at our expense." These efforts, he commented, were "out of harmony with the noble attempts they are making to assist us in the overthrow of the Germans."[34] Reports came to London from Paraguay of the rapid expansion of American capital into formerly German-owned meat-packing plants, the anticipated opening of an American bank, and "rumors that the buying up of the controlling interest in the Paraguay Central Railroad, a British Company, has been under consideration."[35] From Argentina came the disturbing news that the Americans had upgraded their embassy personnel, and were doubling their consular representation: "The United States, in a word, is admirably represented here and is carrying out its programme with energy, thoroughness, and unquestioned skill." Particularly troublesome was the fact that "The United States are doing all they can to collar the carrying trade to South America."[36] Latin America accounted for about one quarter of all outstanding British investment abroad in 1918, and British officials recognized that "we need now and shall need after the war all the return we can draw from this source."[37] But, observed the British Chamber of Commerce in Argentina: "The chief danger threatening our rapid and complete post-war recuperation is the extent to which American trade and general penetration may prove to have passed from the transient to the permanent stage." Between 1914 and 1917, the Chamber pointed out, the British share of Argentine imports had dropped more than 30 percent, while the American share had nearly tripled and now far exceeded the British.[38]

These developments stirred British anxieties, and would not yield to simple solutions. "What can actually be done," asked a British official, "when we are so immensely beholden to the Americans for their cooperation in the war?"[39] Yet within the constraints imposed by that wartime dependence, the British did seek to protect their stake in Latin American markets. They took a cue from Wilson's dispatch of a

34. "Memo by T. B. Hohler" [?], Apr. 15, 1918, Foreign Office Files (hereafter FO), 371/3244/08774, Public Record Office, London, Eng. (hereafter PRO).
35. F. Oliver to Reginald Tower, Feb. 13, 1919, FO 371/3857/08768, PRO.
36. File memos, 1918, FO 371/3132/205948, PRO.
37. File memos, 1918, FO 371/3244/08774, PRO.
38. "Memorandum of the British Chamber of Commerce in the Argentine Republic to Sir Maurice DeBunsen, June 18, 1918," FO 371/3132/12574, PRO.
39. "Memo by T. B. Hohler."

high-level trade delegation to Latin America in 1916 and in 1918 sent their own trade mission to South America, led by Sir Maurice DeBunsen. His goal was "to maintain and even largely develop both politically and economically our pre-war position in the South American continent."[40] Sent without the courtesy of a notice to the U.S. State Department, the DeBunsen mission evoked wounded outcries from those seeking to advance American interests in Latin America. The outcome of DeBunsen's junket, predicted the American ambassador to Brazil, might be "a commercial treaty between Brazil and Great Britain . . . which will undermine our commercial and political prestige."[41]

In the eyes of many United States observers, DeBunsen's tour was but the latest affront in a series of wartime British slaps at American trade. Protests flowed to Washington throughout the war from the American legation in Argentina that British officials were abusing the "black list" to discriminate against American commerce. The Consul General at Buenos Aires accused the British of inaugurating "a reign of more or less commercial terror. . . . The British Black List in this part of the world has been aimed primarily at American trade . . . and never more so than since we entered the war."[42] The American minister at Quito complained that the "conduct of the British diplomatic and consular representatives in Ecuador towards American (commercial) interests has been exceedingly hostile and unfair. . . ."[43] British ships, it was charged, refused to carry goods consigned to American commercial houses in Latin America, while they carried identical goods destined for British houses. British bunkering authorities extorted manifests from vessels of all nations and shared the confidential information thus obtained with British traders. The British re-exported to Brazil goods procured as "war necessities" from the United States. They even allegedly used low-interest loans from the American Treasury to purchase high-dividend foreign oil properties.[44] "Unless the United States makes a concentrated and organized effort to retain her trade, a great part of which has come into existence on account of war

40. Quoted in Safford, *Maritime Diplomacy*, 150.
41. Edwin T. Morgan to Secretary of State, May 14, 1918, RDS, File 033.4132/4, RG 59, NA.
42. W. Henry Robertson to Secretary of State, Jan. 4, 1918, RDS, File 600.001/195, RG 59, NA.
43. "Memorandum prepared by Mr. Wesley Frost," transmitted to Vance McCormick, Chairman of the War Trade Board, July 8, 1918, Records of the War Trade Board, Great Britain, General, RG 182, FRC.
44. *Idem.*

conditions," warned the American ambassador in Brazil, "she will lose much of it when the Titanic struggle is over. Whatever advances British trade is able to make during the period of the war will be made at the expense of the United States which, in the absence of Germany, is her principal immediate competitor."[45]

Each of the wartime associates eyed the other with uneasy suspicion and jealousy. Yet for the Americans, as for the British, the restricting necessities of wartime cooperation stayed the hands of policy-makers from overly aggressive competitive tactics. No formal complaint about British abuse of the Black List should be made to London, concluded the Foreign Trade Adviser's office in the summer of 1918. An official protest "would merely constitute an incident hardly pleasant to either party; and might be detrimental to Anglo-American cooperation at London to an extent more than counter-balancing any transitory gain which America could expect.[46] The War Trade Board should quietly recognize the situation, concluded the Foreign Trade Adviser, and Washington should "make clear to our merchants and Government representatives abroad that in many respects our commerce has no proximate connection with the present war, and that in those respects Americans should unobtrusively meet the British with the latter's own weapons."[47] But beyond those rather mild measures the United States should not go. For their part, the British, too, showed a certain willingness to cooperate with their American rivals. DeBunsen, for example, had set in motion negotiations between the Brazilian government and the British firms of Vickers, Ltd. and Armstrong about a contract to build Brazilian naval vessels and other munitions of war. The contract had strategic as well as economic significance, for it would lock Brazilian armaments into dependence on British designs and specifications—a tactic that had helped keep several Mediterranean countries, their navies largely British-built, in the British orbit during the war. Yet when the American ambassador in Brazil protested that the "Vickers Armstrong proposition . . . would close the open door," the British permitted the Bethlehem Steel Company to enter the negotiations as a co-bidder on the lucrative contract.[48]

45. Edwin T. Morgan to Secretary of State, May 16, 1918, RDS, File 033.4132/5, RG 59, NA.
46. "Memorandum Prepared by Mr. Wesley Frost."
47. *Idem.*
48. Edwin T. Morgan to Secretary of State, July 23, 1918, RDS, File 832.3421/38, RG 59, NA; Josephus Daniels to Secretary of State, n.d., RDS, File 620.4115,

A similar pattern of mutual suspicion, tempered by the necessity for cooperation, characterized Anglo-American relations in the realm of finance. Until the spring of 1917, Britain served as banker to all the Allied governments, loaning them nearly $4 billion since the outbreak of the war. In the first several months of the conflict, the British had funded these operations almost entirely out of their own liquid reserves. But after 1915 the ability of the Exchequer to extend credits was sustained only by borrowing against secure collateral from private bankers, principally J. P. Morgan, in New York. After American entry, the Treasury at Washington became the financial nerve center of the Allied and Associated powers, ultimately dispensing $10 billion as general obligations of the Allied governments. Simple enough to summarize, this passing of financial primacy into American hands was a staggeringly complex process that held both advantage and danger for the United States as well as for the entire international economy.

As in other areas of wartime policy, Treasury Secretary McAdoo was quickest among Washington officials to see the opportunities implicit in American financial preeminence. He at first generously opened American coffers to the Allies, advancing nearly one billion dollars in April, May, and June of 1917. Then in the first days of July, the Treasury abruptly barred its vaults to the British. Panic seized Whitehall. The news from Washington was "in the highest degree alarming," the War Cabinet protested to the American ambassador at London. "If this financial breakdown should occur, it would be a deadly and perhaps a fatal blow to the Allies' cause. . . . The whole financial fabric of the Alliance will collapse. This conclusion will be a matter not of months but of days."[49]

. The ostensible reason for the sudden cessation of funds involved an outstanding British debt of some $400 million to J. P. Morgan. As the chief fiscal agent for Great Britain in the United States, the House of Morgan had since 1915 been extending revolving short-term credits for British purchases. In February 1917 that indebtedness had stood at $72 million. In the next two months, perhaps in anticipation of an American declaration of war and easy access to the American Treasury, the British

---

RG 59, NA. See also the correspondence between the British Foreign Office and Vickers, Ltd., May-June 1919, in FO 371/79376, PRO.

49. War Cabinet Minutes, July 16, 1917, CAB 23/3, PRO; unsigned memorandum, July 22, 1917, Records of the Treasury Department, Bureau of Accounts, International Fiscal Relationships, Great Britain, RG 39, NA.

had run up their bill by at least an additional $325 million. They, and the House of Morgan, now sought the liquidation of that loan with Treasury money.[50] When a Morgan partner appeared at the Treasury on June 28 looking for his $400,000,000 check, McAdoo balked. He doubted his legal authority to disburse funds for the settlement of debts that antedated American entry into the war. And he knew with certainty the political liabilities he would incur if it became known that he had bailed out J. P. Morgan, arch-symbol of arrogant capitalism, from a bad debt. Thus, pending assurances from the British that they would not seek to clear the Morgan loan from the books with Treasury dollars, the Secretary stopped all payments to the London government.

Though the Morgan "overdraft" provided the immediate occasion for choking off credits to the Allies, McAdoo soon tried to add to his conditions for turning the financial spigot back on. On June 30 he drafted a note to be presented to the Chancellor of the Exchequer inquiring as to whether the British government intended to use the American loans to augment its navy beyond the needs of the present war, whether "your own government has given or received any preferential trade relations effective either during the war or after . . . ," and "whether any territorial determinations or engagements of any kind have been entered into. . . ."[51]

"Here," notes one historian, "was the potential for iron-fisted diplomacy."[52] The potential was assuredly there, though it is unlikely that this message was ever actually presented to the British government.[53]

50. Thomas W. Lamont to Russell C. Leffingwell, Feb. 19, 1918, *ibid.*
51. McAdoo to American Ambassador, June 30, 1917, *ibid.* The document is reprinted in *Munitions Industry, Hearings* before the Special Committee Investigating the Munitions Industry, U.S. Senate, 74th Congress, 2nd sess. (Washington, D.C.: Government Printing Office, 1936), Part 29, 9222.
52. Wilton B. Fowler, *British-American Relations, 1917–1918: The Role of Sir William Wiseman* (Princeton: Princeton University Press, 1969), 43.
53. This document was introduced into the Munitions Industry Senate hearings in 1936 by Stephen Raushenbush, secretary to the Senate Special Committee. The original copy is in the records of the Treasury Department, Bureau of Accounts, International Fiscal Relationships, Great Britain, File GB 132/17-3, RG 39, NA, which is the source Fowler cites. Since all cablegrams were transmitted through the State Department, this message, like all others, was no doubt reviewed by State Department officials before transmission. Secretary Lansing's opposition to McAdoo's tough-fisted approach is well established, and it is not likely that he permitted the transmission of this document. This possibility is corroborated by several pieces of evidence: 1) no copy of the

McAdoo's heavy-handed effort to bind British policy with American purse strings set off a storm of controversy inside the Wilson administration. McAdoo appears to have received support only from his Assistant Secretary Oscar T. Crosby, who urged that "the power of the United States should be felt in the political field as well as on the field of battle."[54] Yet when McAdoo sought presidential approval for a statement to all the Allies that "financial assistance to your government . . . should not be construed as an approval or disapproval by the United States Government of any particular national objectives which your Government may have in view," Wilson demurred. The President referred the question to the Counselor for the State Department, Frank L. Polk, who advised McAdoo that "if we say anything we may raise awkward questions of policy and it would be better not to have anything on record or have any discussion on the subject at this time."[55]

Still McAdoo persisted. He protested to Secretary of State Lansing that "if we fail to do this we may be confronted at the peace conference . . . with the claim that as we furnished money for the purpose of enabling the powers to prosecute the war to a successful conclusion, we tacitly consented to or acquiesced in the national objectives they had in view."[56] Again Lansing vetoed McAdoo's proposal. "I am more firmly convinced than ever," he wrote, "that such a communication would be a grave mistake." Lansing continued:

> The same argument which is urged in regard to loans might be advanced in regard to the employment of the embargo, the cooperation of our naval vessels about the British Islands, the presence of our military forces in France, and similar active aid of this Government. It seems to me that it is much wiser to avoid statements of this sort, which might be misconstrued.[57]

message is to be found in the State Department decimal files; 2) no mention of receipt of the message, which should have caused considerable turmoil in London, was found in a search of the British Cabinet papers, Series CAB 23 and 24; 3) there does exist in the Bureau of Accounts files (International Fiscal Relationships, Great Britain) a reply from the British government dated July 18, 1917, to "the memorandum by the Secretary of the Treasury, dated July 9th" (not June 30), which responds to all of the points raised by McAdoo in the June 30 document, except those relating to naval construction, trade agreements, and territorial treaties.

54. Oscar T. Crosby to McAdoo, July 21, 1917, *Munitions Industry*, Part 29, 9005.
55. Frank L. Polk to McAdoo, Aug. 11, 1917, *ibid.*, 9000.
56. McAdoo to Lansing, Aug. 14, 1917, *ibid.*, 9001.
57. Lansing to McAdoo, Aug. 20, 1917, *ibid.*, 9004.

There the matter ended. Assistant Treasury Secretary Russell Leffing-well later recalled that "Mr. McAdoo and Mr. Crosby were wisely . . . considering all these problems, but . . . the control of loans by the limitation of financing on one hand and the urgent necessity of the war on the other superseded all the philosophical and thoughtful and pene-trating inquiries and it became purely the pragmatic question of how to raise enough money to support the armies and the navies and carry on the war as it was."[58] None of the opponents of McAdoo's proposal cared to argue that British and American war aims were entirely com-patible; they merely insisted that McAdoo had chosen the wrong time and the wrong weapon for a showdown. "England and France *have not the same views with regard to peace that we have* by any means," Presi-dent Wilson had told Colonel Edward House in the midst of the de-bates on loan policies. "When the war is over," the President concluded, "we can force them to our way of thinking, because by that time they will, among other things, be financially in our hands; but we cannot force them now, and any attempt to speak for them or to speak our common mind would bring on disagreements which would inevitably come to the surface in public and rob the whole thing of its effect."[59] In some unspecified way Wilson believed that American financial power was indeed a potent political weapon; but precisely when, and how, to use that weapon were questions to which no one—save possibly McAdoo —had satisfactory answers in the summer of 1917.

The British meanwhile, if they knew at all what were McAdoo's ulti-mate intentions, never answered the Secretary's queries about naval construction, preferential trade relations, or territorial agreements. They instead tried to convince McAdoo that the Allies were close to total financial exhaustion. They pressed hard for the Secretary's agreement to resume the loans and allow their expenditure for the support of sterling exchange and the liquidation of the Morgan loan, as well as for necessary purchases of war materials and consumer goods. Persuaded that the situation was in fact desperate, McAdoo somewhat grudgingly resumed payments to the British account. He was not allowed to attach specific political conditions, but he did win some concessions. All loans from the United States Treasury were to be expended exclusively in the United States; Treasury dollars might be used to support the sterling-dollar exchange at roughly $4.76 to the pound, but not to sup-

58. *Ibid.*, 9007.
59. Wilson to Edward M. House, July 21, 1917, RSB, VII, 180.

port sterling against other currencies; and the British agreed to channel all their buying in the United States through an Allied Purchasing Commission, which would seek the most efficient and least costly sources of supply, thus expediting the war effort and reducing the demands on the American Treasury.

Not all of these arrangements worked smoothly. Despite the fact that orders placed through the Allied Purchasing Commission could be filled at lower prices, the Allies stubbornly persisted in buying goods through their old commercial connections, short-circuiting the intended American mechanism to achieve efficiency and economy. These maverick orders proved hard to control, prompting one frustrated official "to respectfully suggest that you recommend to the Secretary of the Treasury that they disband the Purchasing Commission and open the back door to the Treasury a little wider and furnish these people with a steam shovel so as to afford every opportunity of easy access to the American cash box."[60] Suspicions also persisted that the British were using dollars for sterling support operations outside the United States, and for the purchase of some commodities, especially wheat, on foreign commodity exchanges. On at least one occasion, these concerns caused the cancellation of a scheduled payment (of $15 million) to the British account.[61] Treasury officials suspected that the British were building cash reserves in the United States with which they might quietly pay down the "Morgan overdraft." Hence the Treasury eventually developed a system of monitoring the expenditures and the bank balances of the British so closely "that they never could accumulate balances big enough in this country to meet such an important maturity."[62]

60. Alex Legge to Bernard Baruch et al., Dec. 8, 1917, Records of the Allied Purchasing Commission, General Correspondence, RG 113, NA.

61. George O. May, "Confidential Memorandum for Mr. Leffingwell," Feb. 8, 1918, and unsigned memorandum, Apr. 18, 1918, Records of the Treasury Department, Bureau of Accounts, International Fiscal Relationships, Great Britain, GB 132/17-10, RG 39, NA.

62. Testimony of Russell C. Leffingwell, *Munitions Industry*, Part 29, 8989. The "overdraft," frequently misrepresented as unsecured, was in fact collateralized by American securities, and was eventually liquidated in part by the gradual sale of some of those securities. The remaining balance was cleared by the sale of British Treasury bills at New York, and by a credit of $86 million in payment for British ships abuilding in American shipyards and requisitioned by the Shipping Board in the summer of 1917. The British complained that they were unfairly prevented from disposing of this debt because they had voluntarily refrained from refinancing it in the American money market, so as not to compete with Liberty Loan sales, and because they had hesitated to

By 1919 the Treasury had loaned over $10 billion to foreign governments, nearly half of it to the British. Though McAdoo and other government officials appreciated the political leverage this creditor status might give to the United States, the record suggests that not diplomatic strategy but financial orthodoxy was the foremost informing principle of American loan policy. As Lansing's rebuff to McAdoo in 1917 showed, Washington conspicuously avoided making its financial aid to the Allies contingent on political agreements. Wilson's government sought above all to keep Allied borrowing to the smallest necessary amounts, so as to minimize the burden on the American Treasury. From that axiom of conservative fiscal management the Treasury never wavered.

But if the Treasury's policies did not serve the kind of diplomatic purposes that McAdoo envisioned, those policies nevertheless served American economic interests in quite specific ways. When Treasury officials compelled the British and the other Allied borrowers to expend all their loan proceeds in the United States, they in effect were providing Treasury financing for American exporters. In this respect the role of the Americans as bankers to the alliance differed significantly from that of the British. Great Britain's loans to the other belligerents had badly strained British financial resources, because most sterling credits had eventually to be exchanged for dollars for purchases in the United States. McAdoo's prohibition on Allied use of Treasury loans outside the United States did away with exchange problems, and meant that the dollar would not be subject to the same devaluative pressures that had buffeted the pound. Moreover, those prohibitions guaranteed that America, not some combination of still neutral nations, would continue to be the principal arsenal and breadbasket to the alliance. McAdoo's policies thus reinforced America's natural advantages of geography and resource endowment—and helped to ensure consolidation of the great economic gains already made in the neutrality period.[63]

Though the British were reduced to begging for American money in 1917, they continued to command the seas. The war had confirmed their claim to possession of the world's premier navy, and even after

---

sell their securities for fear of badly breaking prices on the American stock exchanges. See Thomas W. Lamont to Leffingwell, Feb. 19, 1918, and July 3, 1918, and Eliot Wadsworth to Charles L. Faust, Jan. 26, 1923, in Records of the Treasury Department, Bureau of Accounts, International Fiscal Relationships, Great Britain, RG 39, NA.

63. See Hardach, *The First World War*, 148.

losing millions of tons of shipping to German submarines since 1914, Britons still boasted the world's largest merchant marine. But here too the war had opened the way for an American challenge. Woodrow Wilson in 1916 had declared his intention to build a navy larger than Britain's, including a sizable force of capital ships. These large vessels were of little use in anti-submarine operations, and from the first weeks of American entry into the war the British sought to shift American naval construction from dreadnoughts and cruisers to destroyers. The British cabinet as early as June 1917 discussed offering the United States a postwar naval alliance in return for increased wartime production of anti-submarine craft, and on the eve of the Armistice dispatched a mission to Washington to discuss such an arrangement. But Washington showed no interest in these proposals, and even husbanded in American waters the few destroyers at its disposal. American shipbuilding, concluded the First Lord of the British Admiralty, "is being laid out for a very long war"—or perhaps not for the current war at all, but for a future contest with Britain or Japan.[64]

More immediately alarming was the position of Britain's merchant fleet. At nearly sixteen million gross tons in 1917, it was eight times larger than the American merchant marine. But the combined threats of the Kaiser's submarines and Wilson's maritime policies menaced Britain's historic supremacy at sea. U-boats sank over three million tons of British shipping in 1917 and 1918. New construction could not keep pace with these massive losses. By Armistice Day the British merchant fleet had shrunk nearly 15 percent from its prewar size.

In startling contrast to this steady destruction of British tonnage was the vigorous wartime buildup of the American merchant fleet. Wartime sinkings of American vessels (which were held back, protested London, from dangerous voyages in the war zone) totalled 319,000 tons, less than 10 percent of British losses in the same period. And additions to the American fleet far outdistanced these relatively minor damages. The United States merchant marine expanded by nearly four million tons in 1917–18, while the British were suffering net losses. By war's end, the American merchant fleet had grown to be 40 percent the size of Britain's.[65]

64. War Cabinet Memoranda, June 19, 1917 (CAB 24/16, GT 1090); June 22, 1917 (CAB 24/17, GT 1138); Apr. 16, 1918 (CAB 24/48, GT 4252), PRO.
65. Edward B. Parsons, *Wilsonian Diplomacy: Allied-American Rivalries in War and Peace* (St. Louis: Forum Press, 1978), 47, 120; Hardach, *The First World War*, 45.

These developments spawned a particularly painful dilemma for British policy-makers. On the one hand London desperately needed American-built ships to make up the losses inflicted by German submarines; on the other hand, as the British Shipping Controller told the Cabinet in July 1917, "it is obviously undesirable in view of the post-war position, that the United States should build more rapidly than the United Kingdom."[66]

To make matters worse for the beleaguered Britons, the United States Shipping Board in August 1917 requisitioned 163 vessels abuilding on American shipways for British account. The 1.2 million tons thus brought under American registry, when added to the nearly one million tons of confiscated German shipping, almost overnight gave the United States a commercial fleet of impressive proportions. The British stifled their anger and made no protest, their acquiescence partly purchased by an agreement to credit the cost of the requisitioned ships to the British Treasury account, and to allow its application to the repayment of the infamous "Morgan overdraft."[67]

The muted controversy over the requisitioning of British vessels was but the opening note in a series of muffled Anglo-American wartime clashes over shipping. Mutual suspicions persisted over whether one or the other party was withholding tonnage from the submarine-infested war-supply routes in the North Atlantic and employing it instead on profit-making runs in Latin American or Far Eastern waters. When the Allied Maritime Transport Council (AMTC) was formed at London in early 1918 to coordinate shipping policies, Wilson only reluctantly allowed American delegates to take seats on the body, and he tightly restricted their power to bring American shipping under the Council's control. As in so many other areas, Wilson here resisted fully concerting American resources with those of the Allies. He sought to preserve his own freedom of action, and he remained deeply distrustful of Allied intentions.[68] Even in the closing weeks of the war one American repre-

66. "Memo by the Shipping Controller," July 1917, War Cabinet Memorandum, CAB 24/19, GT 1348, PRO.
67. "Note concerning U.S. requisitioning of ships," War Cabinet Memorandum, Aug. 1917, CAB 24/23, GT 1790, PRO.
68. See Safford, *Maritime Diplomacy*, 149. The President cautioned one Shipping Board member, future Secretary of State Bainbridge Colby, against becoming "Anglicized" and forgetting his American heritage while on business abroad. In this case, at least one other observer shared Wilson's concern. Whitney Shepardson of the Shipping Board's legal division recalled in a postwar

sentative to the AMTC spoke of "the lingering sense of distrust which now disturbs our relations with the British," and he called for a comprehensive study "to settle once and for all the question whether or not there is justification for the American impression that too many British vessels are trading with reference to commercial interests rather than to the paramount demands of the War."[69] Significantly, the study when completed "clearly indicated that Great Britain had not used her ships during the period [June 1914–January 1919] to stimulate her trade unduly. . . . In fact, the American delegation claimed that they had been for some time placed in an embarrassing position before the British because of the relatively uninterrupted service of our merchant marine to the West Indies and Central America."[70] The Americans, in short, had proved more reluctant than the British to sacrifice their peacetime commerce to the cause of winning the war. There appeared to be much truth to the British Shipping Controller's comment that it was the *Americans* who "were out for *post bellum* developments of which they always suspected us."[71]

A notable example of American practice surfaced in the winter of 1917-18, in a dispute over the allocation of oil tankers to supply the European war zone. The British requested in October 1917 that the United States permanently place at least 100,000 tons of additional tanker capacity on the North Atlantic run. The U.S. Shipping Board responded by accusing the British of holding their own tankers off the United States-United Kingdom routes and employing them instead on "inefficient" circular voyages through the Mediterranean, the Persian Gulf, and the Indian Ocean. Only if the British withdrew some of their own tonnage from those eastern routes, the Shipping Board insisted, would the United States provide—on a one-time-only basis—40,000 tons of tanker space in the North Atlantic. The British saw this

interview that "the real trouble with the Shipping Board was Bainbridge Colby. . . . [He] seemed to be greatly worried that England would do something to us if we succeeded in creating a merchant marine." "Memorandum of conversation with Whitney Shepardson," Nov. 8, 1926, Edwin F. Gay Papers, Hoover Institution on War, Revolution and Peace, Stanford University, Stanford, Ca.

69. James A. Field to Edwin Gay, Aug. 21 and Sept. 12, 1918, Records of the United States Shipping Board, Division of Planning and Statistics, General File 030-088, RG 32, NA.

70. Eliot G. Mears to Bureau of Foreign and Domestic Commerce, Mar. 24, 1919, BFDC, File 510-UK, RG 151, NA.

71. War Cabinet Minutes, Oct. 19, 1917, CAB 23/4, PRO.

as a high-handed effort to dislodge them from the Middle Eastern and Indonesian oil fields, and to weaken their grip on Egypt. They countered that the United States tankers engaged in the American coastal trade, hauling crude oil from Gulf ports to Northeastern refineries, constituted a wasteful subsidy to the Atlantic coast petroleum-processing industry. Those tankers could more efficiently be used transporting directly from the Gulf coast to Europe. But these protests were to no avail. The Shipping Board would not budge from its insistence that it was to be British, not American, trade routes that would be disrupted for the war effort. Despite urgings from the British in February that the Americans should undertake "heroic measures," and should consider "how we are helping your troops," the Americans stood firm.[72]

British bottoms in fact carried more than half the American troops who went to France. Transporting those men and their supplies made enormous claims on the maritime resources of Great Britain, and the standard of living of its island-dwelling population measurably dropped as ships were diverted from supplying civilian needs to building the American Expeditionary Force. Some British officials began to grumble in early 1918 that perhaps the sacrifices were not worth the effort, as the AEF was slow to reach fighting condition, and Pershing cautiously held his fledgling army behind the line. But Winston Churchill scotched such murmurings in March 1918, when he told the cabinet that "the immense political and military advantages of drawing American manhood into the war . . . ought to outweigh all other considerations. . . . Quite apart from the imperious military need," Churchill prophesied, "the intermingling of British and American units on the field of battle and their endurance of losses and suffering together may exert an immeasurable effect upon the future destiny of the English-speaking people, and will afford us perhaps the only guarantees of safety if Germany emerges stronger from the war than she entered it."[73]

The London government took what comfort it could from such considerations in the face of mounting American affronts to British maritime superiority. London obliged an American request to share equally any neutral tonnage obtained on charter, even though that 50-50 division was far out of proportion with the ratio of the two nations' exist-

---

72. Joseph Maclay to Bainbridge Colby, Feb. 18, 1918, Ministry of Transport Files, MT 25/19, X/K 5711, PRO.
73. Winston Churchill, "America and Shipping," War Cabinet Memorandum, Mar. 24, 1918, CAB 24/45, GT 3928, PRO.

ing merchant fleets and their relative losses to German submarines. The British also endured painful manpower drains, as the U.S. Shipping Board set high wage rates that lured officers and seamen off British vessels and onto American merchantmen. As seen from London, Washington's policy often seemed calculated to make Britain carry an unfair portion of the war burden, while the Americans conserved their resources for a commercial "war after the war." Even when the huge German offensive in the spring of 1918 threatened the western powers with defeat, Wilson proved reluctant to increase American shipping commitments in the war zone. Informed in April 1918 that a stepped-up program of troop shipments would necessitate diverting vessels from the Brazilian and Japanese trade, the President gave instructions to "tell Great Britain how many we can send not taking out Japan and Brazil tonnage and then ask England and France to furnish ships for balance."[74]

While the British worried about the modest, even stingy, American maritime contribution to the war, shipyards in the United States were steadily gearing up to unprecedented levels of production. After a year of mismanagement and confusion, the Emergency Fleet Corporation by mid-1918 presided over a small empire of shipbuilding facilities that was beginning to put finished hulls in the water at the rate of nearly one hundred a day. In the last six month of 1918, almost three million tons of new ships splashed down American ways, equalling total world production in a typical prewar year.[75]

Those fantastic figures fired the commercial ambitions of many American policy-makers, especially Shipping Board Chairman Edward N. Hurley. A former Chicago machine tool and appliance manufacturer, Hurley had long been prominent in the movements for scientific management and industrial rationalization. He deserves to be counted along with Baruch, McAdoo, and Hoover as among the leading apostles of that corporatist vision that conjured a bright future of increased efficiency and prosperity through business combination and government cooperation. He differed from his wartime colleagues only in a lesser degree of political sophistication and a more narrow-minded devotion to exports as the exclusive key to American economic health. As vice chairman of the Federal Trade Commission, Hurley had lob-

74. E. David Cronon, ed., *The Cabinet Diaries of Josephus Daniels, 1913–1921* (Lincoln: University of Nebraska Press, 1963), 296, entry for Apr. 3, 1918.
75. Safford, *Maritime Diplomacy*, 153.

bied actively for legislation to relax the anti-trust laws in the export field, and to facilitate American overseas banking. He had helped to found the National Foreign Trade Council, and had toured South America to scout trade prospects.

As the war approached its climax in 1918, Hurley began to agitate more and more excitedly for aggressive use of the new commercial fleet for overseas trade expansion. He increasingly appeared to be less of a "war manager" than a phenomenally kinetic promoter of American exports. In his view, the war had opened opportunities that must be exploited now to ensure American commercial competitiveness after the Armistice. In March 1918 Hurley urged Woodrow Wilson to send trade missions to South America, the Far East, and Scandinavia, signaling "that America is about to use the great [commercial] weapon which has been held in reserve."[76] Wilson did not think the time was ripe to call up that weapon from reserve, and vetoed the idea. But Hurley took heart from the passage of the Webb-Pomerene Act the following month, exempting export combinations from anti-trust prosecution. In May he wrote to Bernard Baruch that the new legislation would enable American businesses to combine effectively against British trusts and German cartels in the postwar struggle to control the world's supplies of raw materials. "If America would invest stubstantially in the essential raw materials of all foreign countries," Hurley urged, "we would soon be in control of 60% of the cotton of the world, 73% of the copper, and, together with Mexico, 75% of the oil of the world."[77] Hurley circularized virtually every commercial organization in the United States, announcing the birth of a new American merchant fleet that was eventually to reach twenty-five million tons, and urging American businessmen "to put themselves solidly behind American ships." Manufacturers must now "think of customers in Latin America as being as accessible as those in the next state. The farmer must visualize ships carrying his wheat, cotton, breeding animals, dairy products and fruit to new world markets. . . . We must dispel indifference and keep our flag on the trade routes of the world."[78]

No American official more provoked the British than Hurley. His

76. Hurley to Wilson, Mar. 2, 1918, Records of the United States Shipping Board, File 34514, RG 32, NA.
77. Hurley to Baruch, May 21, 1918, *ibid*.
78. "Letter to Business Organizations," July-Aug. 1918, RDS, File 103.95/1760, RG 59, NA.

aspirations for American maritime expansion touched the seafaring Britons on their most sensitive nerve, and Hurley, who regarded Great Britain as "our ally in war, but our antagonist in peace," showed no inclination to handle the issue gently.[79] Secretary of Commerce William C. Redfield accused Hurley of cultivating "an atmosphere of suspicion and fear which seems to surround much of our commercial thought," and the American commercial attaché at London confirmed that Hurley's statements and activities stirred deep resentment in England.[80]

At last, President Wilson intervened to restrain his energetic shipping chairman. The English, Wilson acknowledged, were assuredly seeking "every economic advantage that is within their reach." But, the President suggested, "they are stimulated to do this by their consciousness that our shipbuilding programme will give us a very considerable advantage over them . . . after the struggle is over." Wilson therefore directed Hurley to cease speaking publicly about "the use we shall make of our shipping after the war, because . . . the impression made by past utterances has been that we, like the English, are planning to dominate everything and to oust everybody we can oust."[81] The President reiterated this note of moderation at the time of the Armistice, when he observed that Britain "was a nation that depended on ships and foreign trade," and was consequently "very fearful that we were going to interfere." Diplomacy now necessitated commercial restraint, lest England be given the opportunity to say that America "is also anxious to get all the business she possibly can." When Secretary McAdoo called in November 1918 for the immediate release of all available United States ships to the South American trade, Secretary Redfield, reflecting the President's more comprehensive views, exploded: "Shall we play the hog with our feet in the trough and our eyes on the ground, or shall we play the eagle, soaring with a wide vision?"[82]

With respect to shipping, as with respect to credits and to trade policy generally, there were evident limits to Wilson's inclination to

79. Secretary of Commerce William Redfield so characterized Hurley's attitude. Quoted in Safford, *Maritime Diplomacy*, 147.
80. Redfield quoted in *idem*; Philip Kennedy, "British Trade Attitudes Towards the United States," Nov. 22, 1918, BFDC, File 413.1-UK, RG 151, NA.
81. Wilson to Hurley, Aug. 29, 1918, RSB, VIII, 365.
82. Wilson and Redfield both quoted in Safford, *Maritime Diplomacy*, 161–62.

allow his countrymen to exploit for narrow national advantage the opportunities cast up by the war. Many businessmen, including those serving temporarily as war bureaucrats (like Hurley), chafed at those restraints, and sought ceaselessly to overleap them. But at the highest levels of policy-making, short-term economic gains were decidedly subordinated to long-term political goals.

Yet Wilson did seek ways to press his nation's new economic power into the service of his larger diplomatic objectives. He well appreciated that the growing American merchant fleet and shipbuilding industry, as well as the mounting Allied indebtedness on the Treasury's ledgers, might constitute potent bargaining tools in negotiating the postwar settlement. Anticipating Allied requests for merchant vessels and loans after the Armistice, Wilson told his cabinet that "I wish no ships and nothing done till peace . . . I want to go into the Peace Conference armed with as many weapons as my pockets will hold so as to compel justice."[83] There was no mistaking the kind of economic justice that Wilson sought. He had repeatedly affirmed his aspirations for the postwar international economy, never wavering from the views he had expressed at the time of the Paris Economic Conference in 1916. In his Fourteen Points address of January 1918 he had again enunciated those views with compelling clarity, calling for "the removal, so far as possible, of all economic barriers and the establishment of an equality of trade conditions among all the nations consenting to the peace."[84]

But the President found at Paris that his pockets held too few weapons to command agreement to his goals, despite America's swelling economic might. In a sense, the war ended too soon for the accomplishment of Wilson's objectives, ended before the United States had developed its shipping, commercial, and financial arsenals to full effective strength. The shipbuilding program had reached full stride only months before the November Armistice. The Shipping Board's Division of Planning and Statistics was still straining in December 1918 to complete a study of trade routes on which the new merchant marine might bid for business.[85] And the British still held powerful maritime assets of their own. Their merchant fleet, despite heavy war-

83. Cronon, ed., *Cabinet Diaries of Josephus Daniels,* 347, 342, entries for Nov. 6 and Oct. 17, 1918.

84. Shaw, ed., *Messages and Papers of Woodrow Wilson,* I, 468.

85. William C. Ward, "Memo for Mr. Colby," Dec. 17, 1918, Records of the United States Shipping Board, File 65380, RG 32, NA.

time losses, remained the world's largest. "From our own selfish point of view," warned a U.S. Shipping Board Commissioner in late 1918, "we cannot afford to enter into . . . a competitive fight [with British shipping] for some time to come."[86] Moreover, the two-million-man American Expeditionary Force in France constituted a kind of hostage that could be marooned in Europe if the British should decide to deny the use of their transport vessels to the United States. Influential British shipping interests urged just this course of action as a device to check Hurley's aggressively expansionist policies.[87] Alert to America's vulnerability on this score, McAdoo cautioned the President that "it is most necessary that we arrange to secure such use of British or other foreign ships as may be requisite to bring our soldiers home expeditiously."[88]

Similar considerations restrained Wilson from brandishing the financial weapon upon which he had counted so heavily. The President had looked forward to having the recalcitrant Allies "financially in our hands" at war's end. But though the British and French were deeply in the Treasury's debt-grip in 1918, they had managed to secure an effective counter-hold of their own. Treasury loans to the Allies, which served to finance American exports, had evoked lusty expansion in many sectors of the American economy, notably agriculture. When the Treasury moved after the Armistice to stop the flow of funds to the Allies, the European governments responded by cancelling contracts for the purchase of American pork, leaving a huge surplus in the hands of American farmers and threatening ruinous price deflation throughout American agricultural districts. John Maynard Keynes observed Washington's plight with some relish, noting that Food Administrator Herbert Hoover "had promised the American farmers a minimum price for their hogs [a price to be guaranteed by Treasury-financed Allied purchases]; the promise had over-stimulated the sows of that continent; the price was falling; and . . . when Mr. Hoover sleeps at night visions of pigs float across his bedclothes and he frankly admits that at all hazards the nightmare must be dissipated."[89] The

86. Quoted in Safford, *Maritime Diplomacy*, 173.
87. R. F. Houston to Shipping Controller, Nov. 22, 1918, Ministry of Transport Files, MT 25/12, X/K 5711, PRO.
88. McAdoo to Wilson, Oct. 26, 1918, RSB, VIII, 516.
89. John Maynard Keynes, "Dr. Melchior: A Defeated Enemy," in *Two Memoirs* (New York: Augustus M. Kelley, 1949), 25–26.

nightmare was eventually dissipated in part by new legislation that allowed the War Finance Corporation to furnish credits for exports. But the episode vividly illuminated the limitations of financial diplomacy. War debts might formally and legally be the obligations of foreign governments, but Treasury policy had ensured that the practical effect of those debts was to underwrite American economic growth. Thus to use financial coercion against the Allies was to put at risk the health of the American economy itself.

The pork crisis highlighted another difficulty confronting Washington policy-makers in the immediate postwar period. They were almost unanimously committed to the doctrine that private means were to be preferred to public ones in the economic realm. That belief had clearly informed all aspects of wartime mobilization, including the voluntaristic practices of the War Industries Board, the five-year "death sentence" imposed by the 1916 Shipping Act on the government's authority to operate merchant vessels, and the severe limits on the Treasury's ability to extend foreign credits after the Armistice. Hence the decision to allow the War Finance Corporation to engage in export financing was taken only under great duress, and was singularly distasteful. Indeed, among the reasons most persuasively invoked for cutting off government credits to the Allies after the Armistice was the fear "that a continuation of liberal loans from the United States Treasury to the existing governments would strengthen the hands of those who stand for the policies of centralization . . . and would in fact constitute a large force in shaping both the domestic and international policies of European countries." An international order shaped by heavy government intrusion was anathema to Americans, because it "supposes a continuation of strong governmental control in the United States of our domestic activities."[90]

Thus, though Wilson had anticipated playing strong economic trump cards at the peace table, several factors combined to weaken his hand when he eventually took his seat at Paris: the premature climax of the fighting, the vulnerability of the American economy itself to sudden disruptions of the wartime economic regimen, and the ideological aversion of the President and his circle to perpetuating war-born governmental and inter-governmental controls over trade and investment. This last consideration was the most paradoxical and paralyzing of all.

90. Oscar T. Crosby to McAdoo, Nov. 13, 1918, Records of the Treasury Department, Central Files, General Correspondence, "Chamber of Commerce," RG 56, NA.

Wilson had preached throughout the war the need for a new, co-operative international political order. Yet he and all of his war managers had at the same time fought shy of cooperative *economic* arrangements that would provide necessary undergirding to the political structure they hoped to erect. The Americans had objected to the Paris Economic Conference resolutions in 1916; they had declined to seat a representative on the inter-allied *Comité Permanent International d'Action Économique;* they had participated only haltingly in the deliberations of the Allied Maritime Transport Council, continually exciting British suspicions about the real purposes of United States maritime policy. Now, as the peace discussions began to take shape, Wilson persisted in the exceedingly contradictory policy of trying to effect a new international political multilateralism by economically unilateral means. Those means were not merely too feeble for the task, for the reasons noted above; they were fundamentally at odds with Wilson's larger goals.

The British had shrewdly foreseen this development in mid-1918. "The President . . . will hardly look at the 'economic weapon' from an economic standpoint," noted a Foreign Office analyst.

> The shaft of the weapon may be economic, but its point will be political. . . . The United States . . . seem ready to link the idea of co-operation in an economic defensive with the broader political idea of a League of Nations and to deepen co-operation into something verging on an internationalization of resources. *No doubt their desires will, in this as in previous spheres of joint action, outrun their own performance.* Past experience has shown that their hesitation to participate unreservedly in the international deliberations which they have themselves advocated arises partly out of uncertainty as to the general character of the allied policy of which such deliberations form only one branch.[91]

The accuracy of that forecast was fully confirmed as American policy unfolded in the days surrounding the Armistice. On November 8, 1918, the War Trade Board Chairman reported that President Wilson "had expressly requested that the WTB should make no commitments nor enter into any arrangements with any of the Allies with respect to commodities or other trade arrangements."[92] When the WTB represen-

91. "Further Notes on the United States and the Economic Defensive," July 25, 1918, FO 371/4360/08798, PRO (italics added).
92. Minutes of the War Trade Board, Nov. 8, 1918, Records of the War Trade Board, RG 182, FRC.

tative at Paris cabled the following day to inquire "what economic pressure can the United States exert . . . to persuade the adoption by the Allies of our policies at the peace conference," Wilson authorized an ambiguous reply. "In dealing with the new problems which are arising," he instructed, "you should be governed by two major considerations: on the one hand, the prevention of any breakdown before peace of the spirit and practice of inter-allied co-operation; on the other hand the scrupulous avoidance of any commitments which would restrict our liberty of action at or after the peace conference . . . . At the peace conference the economic power of the United States must be entirely unrestricted, as this force in our hands may be of powerful assistance in enabling us to secure the acceptance of our views."[93] Other considerations, in addition to diplomatic tactics, contributed to a post-war policy of American economic unilateralism. Continuing international economic controls would have proved disproportionately costly to the United States, the most richly endowed, the most efficient, and the most ambitious of the major industrial powers. Herbert Hoover adamantly insisted that his government "not agree to any programme that even looks like inter-Allied control of our economic resources after peace. After peace over one-half of the whole export of food supplies of the world will come from the United States and for the buyers of these supplies to sit in majority in dictation to us as to prices and distribution is wholly inconceivable. The same applies to raw materials. Our only hope . . . will revolve around complete independence of commitment to joint action on our part."[94]

Woodrow Wilson has frequently been accused, especially in reference to his neutrality policies, of wanting to be economically in the world but not politically of it. Yet in the immediate post-Armistice period, Wilson seems to have pursued almost an opposite policy—seeking American political participation in the international order but hesitating to integrate American economic resources fully into that order. In the end that curiously contradictory policy produced a kind of diplomatic paralysis. Wilson held his economic weaponry so long in reserve that it obsolesced before it could be deployed. He never did find the opportunity, as he had hopefully contemplated in 1917, to

93. George MacFadden for War Trade Board, Nov. 9, 1918, RDS, File 600.001/591, RG 59, NA; reply, Nov. 20, 1918, Records of the War Trade Board, File 401, RG 182, FRC.

94. Hoover to John P. Cotton, Nov. 8, 1918, *Foreign Relations of the United States, 1918,* Supplement 1, I, 616–17.

"force [the Allies] to our way of thinking" by means of economic compulsions. Rather, he was compelled to follow a largely negative policy of limiting American participation in the wartime inter-allied control bodies, and withdrawing it almost entirely after the Armistice. True, this strategy did frustrate the realization of the full postwar program announced by the Allies at Paris in 1916. Without American cooperation Germany could not be subjected to all-out economic isolation, and the projected new Allied trading bloc could not be summoned into being. But neither the force of Wilson's ideals nor his country's economic strength could prevent the Allies from imposing a punitive peace on Germany or from perpetuating what Bernard Baruch called the "economic inequality and barriers [that] were among the causes of war."[95] Mighty though her role in the great conflict had made her, America was not at war's end the supreme mistress of world politics whose emergence Wilson and others had too confidently awaited.

In the strictly economic sphere, the war's impact on America's international position was at first glance more dramatic. The merchant fleet had grown by 1919 nearly 60 percent over its prewar size, and by 1922 would swell to two and one-half times its gross tonnage in 1913. In 1919, for the first time since before the Civil War, the United States employed more tonnage on foreign routes than on the coastal and internal trade. As the decade of the 1920s opened, fully 43 percent of American foreign commerce was being moved in American vessels.[96]

Exports, too, boomed ahead, nearly doubling in value in the ten years after 1914, as the American share of world trade climbed to about 15 percent. Much of that gain came at the expense of the British, whose world market share continued to slip, especially in Latin America and Asia.[97] The war had accelerated the shift of United States trade away from Europe, despite the heavy wartime buying of the belligerents. Though the mother continent remained America's chief foreign customer, its relative importance declined. The United States by the mid-1920s doubled its prewar trade with Asia, and increased its exports to Latin America by at least 20 percent. By 1929, American ex-

95. Baruch to Wilson, May 7, 1919, Baruch Papers, Firestone Library, Princeton University, Princeton, N.J.
96. Historical Statistics of the United States (Washington, D.C.: Government Printing Office, 1975), 749, 761.
97. League of Nations, Memorandum on International Trade and Balances of Payments, 1912–1926, 2 vols. (Geneva: League of Nations, 1927), I, 12–13.

porters far outpaced both Britons and Germans in Latin American markets, supplying 38 percent of imported manufactured goods, compared to 22 percent for the British and 16 percent for the Germans.[98]

The war worked its greatest economic transformation on the international financial role of the United States. Net debtors in the amount of $3.7 billion at war's outbreak, Americans were net international creditors by an almost identical amount in 1919, excluding government loans. By 1924 the private credit balance mushroomed to nearly $7 billion, and topped $8 billion in 1929.[99]

Much of the initial shift in America's relative financial position could be attributed to the repatriation of foreign-held American securities. But after 1919, American private overseas lending soared, as bankers and businessmen sought to replace the colossal level of wartime Treasury export financing with private funding. During the war, the Treasury had essentially absorbed the surplus dollars of millions of American savers and made them available, through war loans to the Allies, for purchases by foreigners. The sheer scale of that operation had prodigiously stimulated the American export sector. After the Armistice, American financiers hoped to create private equivalents of that mechanism through the Edge Amendment to the Federal Reserve Act.

The Edge Amendment encouraged American banks to combine in the operation of acceptance corporations, facilitating short-term dollar financing of foreign trade. More ambitiously, the Edge Act permitted Federal Reserve member banks to combine in the creation of foreign investment corporations. These new financial entities would make long-term loans to foreign governments and corporations. They would raise capital through the sale of debentures to the American public—following the wartime example of the Treasury in bidding for the confidence, and the dollars, of American investors. "In this way," writes historian Carl Parrini, "the Edge investment corporations would assume the role played by the government during World War I. American industry . . . would be stabilized at a high level of productivity" without direct reliance on government financing.[100] Passed in December 1919, the

98. *Commerce Yearbook, 1925* (Washington, D.C.: Department of Commerce, 1926), 112; Maizels, *Industrial Growth and World Trade,* 196–97.

99. Lewis, *America's Stake in International Investments,* 455. The Treasury also held some $10 billion in foreign government obligations in 1919.

100. Parrini, *Heir to Empire,* 82; Parrini's chapters 4 and 5 provide comprehensive accounts of the war's impact on American financial institutions, though he tends to exaggerate the dimensions of that impact.

Edge Act in many ways exemplified post-Armistice economic policy. It sought as rapidly as possible to replace governmental with private means, and to direct those means to the same ends that the government had desired during the war: consolidating and advancing the opportunities for gain that the conflict had created for the American economy.

Those gains were assuredly large; yet, with reference to foreign trade and investment, their dimensions and their permanence, as well as the degree of purpose and coordination with which they were pursued, have frequently been exaggerated. The Wilson administration had clearly demonstrated its willingness to place the power of government at the disposal of private capital in the quest for expanded overseas commerce. But in the last analysis, the traditional aversion to government intervention confined to rather modest proportions America's postwar advance into the world economy. The Merchant Marine Act of 1920, for example, largely took the government out of the shipping business, relegating the Shipping Board to a regulatory role somewhat analogous to that long played for railroads by the Interstate Commerce Commission. The Act mandated the sale of government ships to private operators and directed the Board to promote ship construction and the improvement of port facilities. Those mildly supportive measures were no substitute for the kind of subsidy to American shippers that direct government ownership and operation had entailed. The removal of that subsidy, combined with a worldwide slowdown in trade and consequent shipping glut in the early 1920s, drove American cargoes once again into foreign holds. By 1926, the proportion of American foreign commerce that moved in American ships had slid to less than 25 percent, and the wartime dream of a merchant fleet strong enough to challenge the British went aglimmering.

The attempt to displace the British as bankers to the world met with similarly incomplete results. The war had exhausted the financial reserves of most of America's overseas customers, and had crippled their ability to pay for American exports with a compensating return flow of imports. Only substantial American foreign investment could provide potential buyers with the dollars necessary to sustain the high level of American wartime exports—and, not incidentally, to restore the volume of prewar *world* trade once financed by London capitalists. That investment, Americans insisted with their customary financial orthodoxy, "could not be effectively promoted by government activity,

but would have to be developed by private initiative." The Edge Act
in 1919 tried to stimulate that initiative, encouraging American financiers to seek overseas investment opportunities, in the manner of the
British before the war. But in the State Department's Office of the Economic Adviser officials had correctly foreseen in 1919 "that the opportunities for the employment of capital at home are relatively so much
greater than has been the case, for instance, in Great Britain before
the war that there was not the same incentive to the private investor
to seek foreign investments."[101]

Americans annually loaned between $300 million and $700 million
to foreign borrowers in the five years following the Armistice. After the
Dawes Plan reorganized reparations payments in 1924, the level of
lending rose to an annual average of more than one billion dollars,
until the Great Depression, beginning in 1929, virtually suspended all
international trade and money flows.[102] Yet even this unprecedented
infusion of dollars could not stimulate the world economy to regain its
prewar vitality. The volume of international trade only reached its 1914
level in 1929, when its creeping ascent was swiftly reversed by the Depression.

American postwar foreign investment, huge though it was, was not
large enough to offset the weight of the liabilities under which the international economic system struggled in the 1920s, especially the crippling of the key German economy and the overshadowing burden of
reparations payments. In the face of those conditions, the world system
needed unusually vigorous economic leadership, on a scale even more
massive and active than Great Britain had provided before the war.
For a variety of reasons, the Americans did not assume that role.

The long-term Edge foreign investment corporations never did come
into being in the postwar decade. Even the effort of the American
banking system to substitute dollar acceptances for sterling drafts
in the day-to-day financing of foreign transactions proved severely
limited in most parts of the world. Though Latin American trade came
increasingly to be conducted on a dollar basis through American branch
banks, even there the British proved tenacious. Throughout the 1920s
the value of British exports to Brazil and Argentina virtually equalled

---

101. "Minutes of a conference at the office of Mr. Lay," Apr. 22, 1919, RDS,
Office of the Economic Adviser, RG 59, NA.
102. Lewis, *America's Stake in International Investments*, 630-31; Charles P. Kindleberger, *The World in Depression, 1929–1939* (Berkeley: University of
California Press, 1975), 56.

the American share of those countries' markets, and by 1938 the British had regained their position as Argentina's principal foreign customer.[103] After a spurt of openings of American overseas branch banks in 1920, many of those foreign houses closed their doors in 1921 and 1922.[104]

Many factors worked to restrict the overseas placement of American capital in the postwar years. Foreigners, especially Europeans, already owed enormous sums to the United States Treasury as a result of war borrowing. Amidst the constant clamor of the indebted governments in the 1920s that those sums were painful or even impossible to repay, more conservative bankers hesitated to send good dollars in pursuit of bad. Even those observers who believed the Europeans to be certainly capable of meeting their debt obligations to the Treasury worried that the United States government would insist on the priority of its own obligations, and would not in case of crisis support private demands for a precedent claim on the debtors' assets. The government in fact actively discouraged loans to either public or private enterprises in those countries that were not taking steps to settle their war debts to the Treasury.[105]

Most important, the attractions of the home market were so dazzling as nearly to blind most American investors to foreign opportunities. While new foreign loans increased by slightly less than $4 billion in the five years following the war, new capital formation in the United States raced ahead at an average *annual* rate of some $18 billion.[106] In these circumstances, it was hardly surprising that much foreign investment took on a very speculative character, encumbering poor-risk borrowers with oversize burdens of debt at high rates of interest.[107] That development not only saddled American investors with many bad debts that eventually went sour, breeding pressure for dollar-salvaging intervention; it also shunted money away from more soundly based enterprises that could have made real contributions to the world's stock of goods

103. By the same date Germany had outpaced both Britain and the United States in Brazilian markets. Ingvar Svennilson, *Growth and Stagnation in the European Economy* (Geneva: United Nations Commission for Europe, 1954), 190.
104. Parrini, *Heir to Empire*, 96–99.
105. Herbert Feis, *The Diplomacy of the Dollar, 1919–1932* (New York: Norton, 1966), 20ff.
106. Lewis, *America's Stake in International Investments*, 605; *Historical Statistics*, 231. These figures actually understate the difference in magnitude, since the figures for foreign investment are given in current dollars, and those for domestic capital formation in constant 1929 dollars.
107. Kindleberger, *World in Depression*, 55.

and services. Many commentators then and later have pointed to the contrast between the prudent character of prewar British overseas lending and the "carbonated swagger" of American lenders in the 1920s, operating "with much enthusiasm, no experience, and little in the way of guiding principles."[108]

Shipping Board Commissioner Henry M. Robinson was one prescient observer who had predicted these developments as early as 1918. He wrote to a West Coast banking associate:

> I do not believe that our foreign trade from a percentage standpoint, except as reflected in figures for supplies for the armies and for feed for the people of Europe, will amount to much for a considerable time. . . . Our difficulties in foreign trade will be due to our lack of experience and lack of knowledge of how to handle our banking relations; disposition on the part of producer and exporter to treat the foreign trade as heretofore, to wit: as a place to dump rather than as a place to build up a continuing trade as producers endeavor to do at home. . . . We must have a much better knowledge of commercial requirements of foreign countries; knowledge of their seasonal produce which we import; experienced negotiators; a better understanding of the banking needs—in all of which Great Britain leads us so far that we are not in any sense comparable. . . . In other words, in all foreign trade and banking matters, we are still "country bankers." We have certain advantages, but they lie in the fact that we have the materials and the money. We are far from equipped—in the sense of wisdom, knowledge or courage—to compete with Great Britain in foreign trade.[109]

Robinson, to a significant degree, was right. The United States did increase its share of world trade to 15 percent in the postwar period, eclipsing Britain (though just barely) as the world's most important trading nation. Propelled by the demands of European relief and reconstruction, exports reached record heights in 1920. American foreign lending annually averaged nearly two times that of the British by the mid-1920s. But despite those significant advances into the international economy, Robinson had correctly foreseen the *relative* unimportance of foreign commerce and financing to American business. Exports fell off sharply after 1920, stabilizing at a plateau roughly equal to two times prewar levels.[110] Surprisingly, in light of widespread expectations

108. Feis, *Diplomacy of the Dollar,* 4; and Kindleberger, *World in Depression,* 32.
109. Henry M. Robinson to Henry S. McKee, Nov. 26, 1918, Records of the United States Shipping Board, Henry Robinson File, RG 32, NA.
110. *Historical Statistics,* 903. Discounted for inflation, these figures in fact suggest that the real value of American exports remained about constant in the prewar and postwar periods.

about the boost the war would give to America's commercial position, exports actually accounted for a *smaller* percentage of gross national product in the first half of the 1920s than they had in the five years before America entered the war.[111] Export trade expanded between 1921 and 1925 at a rate of 2.5 percent annually; but in the same years the average annual growth rate of gross national product reached nearly 9 percent.[112] Some War Trade Board officials, fearful that foreign demand, especially from war-rich neutrals, might inflate prices and distort the domestic economy, even advocated at war's end that "some organization must be maintained to *restrain* exports to the volume of our surplus."[113]

The administration neglected that recommendation. But that it was made at all suggests that those historians who have tried to explain the diplomacy of this period with reference to the relentless outward thrust of American capital have surely misplaced their emphasis. Their emphasis has also obscured the persistent asymmetry in America's relation to the world economy. Despite the manifestly expansionist hopes of some officials and businessmen, it was in fact even more true after the war than before that the United States was more important to the international economy than was the international economy to the United States. Americans accounted for 15 percent of world trade in the 1920s, but foreign commerce in the same years never accounted for as much as 10 percent of American gross national product.[114]

That lopsided relation, resulting from the sheer size and vigor of the American domestic economy, stood in vivid contrast to the nine-

---

111. *Ibid.*, 224, 226–27, 889.
112. *Historical Statistics*, 887. There is an apparent tendency for exports to account for a decreasing fraction of gross national product in nearly all developing economies, as unexportable services assume greater importance, relative to manufactures, in the nation's economic mix. In the United States, the ratio of foreign trade to GNP has long been smaller than in other countries. That ratio may have started its secular decline as early as 1799. In the 1830s it stood at about 17 percent, declining to around 11 percent in 1913. Comparable figures for Britain and Germany in the 1830s are about 21 percent and 28 percent, respectively, and 66 percent and 35 percent, respectively, in 1913. Germany by that later date had already entered a phase of declining relative economic interdependence. See Karl W. Deutsch and Richard L. Merritt, "Transnational Communications and the International System," *Annals* 442 (1979), 84–97.
113. Unsigned memorandum, Oct. 28, 1918, Records of the War Trade Board, "Post-War Trade" File, RG 182, FRC.
114. *Historical Statistics*, 887.

teenth-century British international role. The absolute value of American foreign investment reached the prewar British sum of some $20 billion only in 1930. Yet even that figure then represented less than 5 percent of American national wealth, compared with the 30 percent of British assets that took the form of foreign investment in 1914.[115] And while Britain had typically exported more than one third of domestic manufactures in a given year, the United States annually exported only about 6 percent of her manufactured products in the 1920s.[116]

The asymmetry of America's relation to the world economy carried troubling implications for the health of the international system. Prewar Britain had helped to invigorate that system both by the scale and productivity of her lending and by maintaining a large open market for imports from her foreign customers. Moreover, British lending and imports had tended to move in counter-point. Domestic recession released funds for foreign investment; domestic boom withdrew funds from overseas placement, but simultaneously stepped up import consumption.[117] Postwar America, by contrast, pursued no such counterbalancing policies. United States foreign investment moved with the general business cycle: up in the 1920s and disastrously down in the 1930s. American lending, in other words, worked to exacerbate, not dampen, swings in the global business cycle.

Even more damaging was American import policy. In 1922 Congress passed the highly protectionist Fordney-McCumber Tariff, effectively penalizing foreigners who wanted to do business in American markets. Coming just a few years after Woodrow Wilson's call for "the removal . . . of all economic barriers," the new tariff strikingly illustrated the perennial problems at the heart of American economic diplomacy. Carl Parrini may be correct that some American policy-makers envisioned the Fordney-McCumber legislation as a "bargaining tariff" for use in negotiations to force acceptance of "open door" policies by trading nations.[118] But to a considerably greater extent, the forbiddingly high levies of 1922 reflected the continuing preoccupation of the great majority of American businessmen with their home markets, and their

115. *Ibid.*, 869, 225.
116. Maizels, *Industrial Growth and World Trade*, 223.
117. Kindleberger, *World in Depression*, 292–93.
118. Parrini, *Heir to Empire*, 219–20. Parrini emphasizes the importance of Section 317 of the Fordney-McCumber Tariff, permitting tariff adjustments up to 50 percent, as proof of the "bargaining" character of the 1922 law.

relative disinterest in foreign trade. "Britain's empire is abroad; America's is at home," announced a prominent Chicago banker in 1921.[119] Connecticut Republican Frank Brandegee, advocating the Fordney-McCumber bill, called exports a mere "drop in the bucket . . . of . . . American prosperity," and one of his Republican colleagues argued that "to give up our home market, which is the best in the world, for the encouragement of foreign trade would be not only a poor but a perilous policy."[120]

No doubt many of Woodrow Wilson's countrymen agreed with him about the desirability of the open door, and in some corner of their being hoped that it would come to pass as the rule of international commerce. But their desire was not informed by the compelling necessity of *interest*. The domestic market simply had too many of them too bedazzled to think seriously of meshing that market more deliberately with the volatile and uncertain global economy. From this perspective, all of Wilson's efforts to force American trade and ships and capital into the international system might best be understood not as a quest for profit but as an effort to break down the parochialism of American businessmen and stitch their interests permanently into the new international fabric the President hoped to weave out out of the tangled skein left by the war. Without the creation of such an interest, without the creation of a large internationally oriented constituency in the business community, there would be scant political support for a truly internationalist and enlightened American diplomacy.

That constituency and that support did not materialize, and in significant ways America remained aloof from the postwar world, to the Wilsonians' bitter regret. That aloofness wrought painful consequences for the international order. The British had helped to sustain the global economy with policies of free trade, import surpluses, and well-managed overseas investment. But Americans, whatever they professed in theory, in practice preferred protectionism to free trade, and appeared not to understand the impossibility of long remaining in surplus on both export and capital accounts. They also preferred, to a far

119. C. H. Crennan, "The Meaning and Manner of Business Revival," *Annals* 47 (1921), xiii. I am indebted to Susan Pannell for this and the following reference.
120. Brandegee quoted in *Congressional Record*, Senate, 67th Congress, 2nd sess., Vol. 62, Part 12 (Sept. 14, 1922), 12560; the second remark is by Iowa Representative Horace Mann Towner, House, *ibid*. (Sept. 13, 1922), 12516.

greater degree than the British, to invest their surplus capital not in Capetown or Cairo, but in Dallas or Detroit—or in stock market speculation.[121]

The Americans, in short, disproportionately employed their profits from the war years to fuel a spectacular expansion of the home economy, rather than extending still farther their position in the world economy. They then proceeded largely to shut off that booming domestic economy from foreign access. With its richest market walled off by a high tariff barrier, and its principal source of credit increasingly closing in upon its own speculative attractions after 1928, the world economy no sooner regained its prewar dimensions than it was immediately plunged into the abysmal crisis of the 1930s.[122] Even the alleged internationalist Franklin Roosevelt appeared for a time to believe that the remedy to that crisis lay in revivifying, not repudiating, American economic isolationism. "Our international trade relations," he declared in his inaugural address in 1933, "though vastly important, are in point of time and necessity secondary to the establishment of a sound national economy."[123] So saying, Roosevelt scuttled the London Economic Conference and helped to foreclose the possibility of a concerted international solution to the world depression.

The war had quickly catapulted the Americans close to the position of world economic leadership that the British had taken nearly a century to reach. Perhaps the very speed of that advance helped to frustrate its final success, as did the markedly different structure of the American economy compared to the British, and of the postwar global system compared to that before 1914. Despite the vastly increased role that America was now called upon to play in the international eco-

121. The Du Pont Corporation, for example, accumulated immense cash reserves during the war period, especially in the years of American neutrality. (Net earnings declined by nearly 50 percent after the declaration of American belligerency and the acceptance of substantial U.S. government contracts.) Of the $90 million of reserves in 1917, $40 million was earmarked for diversification into chemicals, dyes, and paints, in anticipation of permanently displacing from American markets German manufacturers of those items. Another $25 million was used to purchase a large interest in the General Motors Corporation. See Alfred D. Chandler and Stephen Salsbury, *Pierre S. Du Pont and the Making of the Modern Corporation* (New York: Harper and Row, 1971), 430–54.
122. Hardach, *The First World War*, 290–91.
123. Quoted in Kindleberger, *World in Depression*, 26–27n.

nomic order, she had neither the skills, nor the wisdom, nor the compulsion of interest, to play that role as productively as Great Britain had played her part in the nineteenth century. And despite the dreams of some men at the time, and the claims of some historians later, the United States was not in 1919, nor even in 1929, yet heir to the mantle of "empire" that history was stripping from the backs of the British. America was still a pretender to the title. Her time was yet to come, in another war, a generation later.

Epilogue: Promises of Glory

On December 4, 1918, the former North Germany Lloyd Company liner *George Washington*, confiscated during the war by the Americans, steamed out of New York harbor, bearing Woodrow Wilson to the Paris Peace Conference. Small boats crowded the Hudson channel, tooting their hopeful farewells. Airplanes soared above, and thousands of cheering people jammed the docksides. Standing at the ship's rail, the President waved his hat to the exulting well-wishers, while the *George Washington* slipped past the Statue of Liberty and out onto the gray Atlantic.

Several days later, far at sea, Wilson acknowledged to his advisers the difficulties he would face in persuading the Old World statesmen who awaited him at Paris to accept an American peace plan. The President knew that Pershing's modest military successes against Germany had given him little diplomatic leverage on the Allies, and the war's sudden end had virtually struck from his hands the economic "weapons" he had hoped to flourish. But Wilson still had the force of his ideals, and undiminished faith in his favorite political tactic: a direct popular appeal. He still felt confident of his ability to forge from humanity's devotion to his promised peace the most powerful of political instruments. "If necessary," he had said in July 1918, "I can reach the peoples of Europe over the heads of their rulers."[1] Now, as his ship plied toward a tumultuous reception at Brest, he reaffirmed his attachment to that tactic, noting, he later recalled, that "the men whom we were about to deal with did not represent their own people."[2]

Yet neither, in an important sense, did Wilson represent *his* own people. Just weeks earlier they had repudiated his party at the polls, scorning the President's personal plea for a Democratic Congress so that he might "continue to be your unembarrassed spokesman in affairs at home and abroad." The defeat of the Democrats had severely embarrassed Wilson; if America had had the parliamentary system of government that he so much admired, Wilson would no longer have been entitled to represent his country.

Equally important, Wilson's own wartime policies had already damaged the *European* constituencies to whom he hoped to appeal over the heads of their governments, especially the labor and socialist elements favorably disposed toward a liberal peace settlement. At the time of American entry into the war, Wilson was widely perceived, both at home and abroad, as reaching out his hand to the European left, stirring ever more restlessly for a negotiated peace. Many signs had confirmed that belief in early 1917: the President's call in January, implicitly repeated in his April war message, for "peace without victory"; his refusal to enter into formal alliance with the Allied governments, a gesture that suggested his sympathy with the opposition laborite and socialist parties in Britain and France, perhaps even in Germany itself; his cordial praise in his war address for the March Revolution in Russia, which again seemed to underscore his alignment with the international left, the "forces of movement" agitating for an end to the war and a liberal peace.

That perception of Wilson helped to speed much of the American left into the pro-war ranks. John Dewey had declared in the spring of 1917 that America could not fight the "European war" with its full "heart and soul" until "the almost impossible happens, . . . until the Allies are fighting on our terms for our democracy and civilization."[3] It had been just that remote prospect—of the American presence raising the Allied effort to a higher moral level—that Wilson had conjured

1. Arthur Walworth, *America's Moment: 1918* (New York: Norton, 1977), 138.
2. Thomas A. Bailey, *Woodrow Wilson and the Lost Peace* (Chicago: Quadrangle, 1963), 109.
3. John Dewey, "In a Time of National Hesitation," *Seven Arts* 2 (1917), 5–6.

so effectively. "What is it that has changed the focus and meaning of the war?" asked Will Durant on the first anniversary of America's entry. "Two factors chiefly: first, American participation, under the guidance of a President whose intelligence impels him to liberalism; second, the growth in every European country of liberal forces standing on the power of labor."[4] For the American progressives, those had been sufficient reasons for beating plowshares into swords. Americans, John Dewey exhorted, must "see to it that these ideals are forced upon our Allies, however unwilling they may be."[5]

Wilson's claim to leadership of the international left had won the confidence of American progressives as the United States entered the war, and heartened the forces of movement throughout Europe. But almost immediately after the American war declaration, Wilson found his hold on the loyalty of those forces rudely shaken. Out of the fast-moving confusion of events in Russia, the Petrograd Soviet issued a call on May 15, 1917, for an international conference of socialist party members from all the warring countries to meet in neutral Stockholm to discuss "peace without annexations or indemnities on the basis of the self-determination of peoples."[6] Soon labelled the "Petrograd formula," this pronouncement raised havoc in the Allied and American governments for the next two years. With it, the Petrograd Bolsheviks electrified the peace-seeking and liberal parties in all the warring countries. They also frontally challenged Woodrow Wilson's unique patronage of an enlightened, non-punitive peace program. The American President was thus forced to react according to the dictates of a first principle of ideological warfare. As Harold Lasswell described it: "A propagandist must always be alert to capture the holy phrase which crystallizes public aspiration about it, and under no circumstances permit the enemy to enjoy its exclusive use and wont."[7]

Wilson had therefore launched, as early as May 1917, a massive propaganda campaign against the Petrograd formula and all who

---

4. Stanley Shapiro, "The Great War and Reform: Liberals and Labor, 1917–1919," *Labor History* 12 (1971), 323–44.
5. John Dewey, "The Future of Pacifism," in Joseph Ratner, ed., *Characters and Events: Popular Essays in Social and Political Philosophy by John Dewey,* 2 vols. (New York: Henry Holt, 1929), II, 581–86.
6. Arno J. Mayer, *Political Origins of the New Diplomacy 1917–1918* (New York: Vintage, 1970), 194–95.
7. Harold D. Lasswell, *Propaganda Technique in the World War* (New York: Peter Smith, 1938), 66.

hearkened to it, including the very forces of movement who were his own natural allies. He sternly chided the Russian Provisional Government for even countenancing the Stockholm scheme. "The day has come," the President bluntly advised the Russian leaders, "to conquer or submit."[8] The vigor of Wilson's condemnation of the Petrograd proposal stunned many of his would-be supporters on the left. In their eyes the prospective inter-belligerent socialist conference seemed directed toward a peace along the same liberal lines that Wilson himself championed. American socialist Morris Hillquit announced that Wilson's "attitude has been officially endorsed by Socialists on both sides of the Atlantic," and Hillquit accordingly offered to lead a delegation of American socialists to Stockholm.[9] But Wilson had other ideas. "I do not like the movement among the Socialists to confer about international affairs," he informed Secretary of State Robert Lansing, and the State Department refused to issue them passports. Wilson would allow no hands but his own to grasp the banner proclaiming a peace of moderation and restraint. From this time can be dated the origins of the increasingly vicious government attack on the American left, an assault that climaxed in the Pyrrhic victory for Wilson that Oswald Garrison Villard noted at war's end: "At the very moment of his extremest trial our liberal forces are by his own act scattered, silenced, disorganized, some in prison."[10] The note to the Provisional Government and the refusal of passports to the American socialists, Randolph Bourne wrote, portended "that the entire strategy of the negotiated peace has passed out of American hands into those of Russia, and that this country is committed to the new strategy of the 'knockout blow.' "[11]

Wilson in fact proposed one possible alternative to the knockout blow: a revolution inside Germany, bringing to power a new, liberal government with which he might negotiate for peace. Yet that scheme bristled with perils of its own. The very idea of promoting revolution anywhere shivered the spines of conservative statesmen in the Allied

8. Albert Shaw, ed., *The Messages and Papers of Woodrow Wilson*, 2 vols. (New York: Review of Reviews Corp., 1924), I, 408.

9. Quoted in Ronald Radosh, *American Labor and United States Foreign Policy* (New York: Random House, 1969), 119.

10. Quoted in Michael Wreszin, *Oswald Garrison Villard: Pacifist at War* (Bloomington: Indiana University Press, 1965), 101. For a discussion of the war against the American left, see Chapter 1 above.

11. Randolph Bourne, "The Collapse of American Strategy," in Carl Resek, ed., *War and the Intellectuals: Essays of Randolph S. Bourne, 1915–1919* (New York: Harper and Row, 1964).

capitals, frightened at the rising revolutionary temper among their own peoples in that third year of war.[12] But Wilson envisioned only a modest revolution, moving Germany from medieval Junkerdom to modern bourgeois democracy—and no farther. Therein lay another difficulty. The largest opposition group in Germany was socialist, and it contained a militant wing more attuned to radical voices from the Russian east than to Wilson's moderate reform urgings from far across the western sea. Especially after the Bolshevik revolution in November 1917, Wilson's was not the only revolutionary summons on the wind. The blasts blowing out of Russia, beating first upon Germany, but reaching the ears of workers everywhere, terrorized conservatives and gave Wilson, the merely *liberal* revolutionary, considerable pause.

Wilson stood in an exceedingly precarious diplomatic position. Opposed to the imperialistic designs of the conservative Allied governments, he had effectively embraced their demand for total victory, for the knockout blow. Opposed as well to the radical doctrines of the Bolsheviks, Wilson appeared at first to have joined them in his appeals for a liberal peace and a German revolution, only then to compete with them for the proper definition of peace and revolution—and for ideological leadership of the international forces of movement.

Wilson's diplomatic dilemma was, in a sense, the domestic political dilemma of the progressives in the American Union Against Militarism writ large. They, too, had decided for war on hopeful and moderately liberal grounds only to find themselves suddenly thrust rightward into unholy collaboration with the domestic forces of reaction they had long opposed. And on their left, they found their moral authority challenged by the steadfast pacifists and the more militant radicals in the Civil Liberties Bureau and the Socialist Party. So with Wilson on the world stage. In early 1917 he was the only belligerent chief of state who did not lead an avowedly conservative party. On the foreshortened spectrum of American politics, Wilson's Democrats *were* the left, and it was the distinctly attenuated values of American progressivism that Wilson hoped to champion in the world at large. At the head of the international left, he would face down the reactionaries gathering to impose a vindictive peace on prostrate Germany. Just that appeal had tied liberals everywhere to the President in 1917.

As the war progressed, the Committee on Public Information's Foreign Section undertook to bind worldwide opinion still more tightly to

12. See Mayer, *Political Origins of the New Diplomacy,* 333ff.

the American leader. In essence, write the historians of the Creel Committee, "the foreign mission of the CPI was to convince the people of the world:

1. That America could never be beaten. . . .
2. That America was a land of freedom and democracy; and therefore that it could be trusted. . . .
3. That, thanks to President Wilson's vision of a new world order and his power of achieving it, victory for the Allied arms would usher in a new era of peace and hope. . . .[13]

To those ends, George Creel's colleagues mounted a global advertising campaign, as Creel was pleased to call it, designed "to convince all the world that hope for the future lay in Wilson alone."[14] In neutral countries, despite official renunciation of tactics that would not bear public exposure, they bribed editors and secretly subsidized publishers in order to insert pro-American articles in the press.[15] Balloons, kites, and artillery pieces carried the "paper bullets" of American propaganda into Germany itself, preaching "incitement to both political and social revolution." Capitalizing on the universal appeal of a characteristically American industry, the CPI arranged with film distributors to release no movies to foreign customers who did not agree to screen the Committee's "educational" material along with entertainment features.[16] Josephine Roche's Division of Work with the Foreign-Born organized immigrant speakers and writers to spread the Wilsonian gospel to their old-country kinsmen. The doughboys landed in England and France under what amounted to a covering barrage of leaflets, speeches, and films, seeking "to acquaint the people . . . with the war aims of America, and to gain their support, over the heads of their own governments, for a peace of moderation and hope, not a peace of vengeance and Old World nationalism."[17] Thus, at war's end, "the adulation that the President received en route to the Peace Conference was at least in part a tribute to the thoroughness with which the CPI Foreign Section had done its work."[18]

13. James R. Mock and Cedric Larson, *Words That Won the War: The Story of the Committee on Public Information, 1917–1919* (Princeton: Princeton University Press, 1939), 247.
14. *Ibid.,* 237.
15. *Ibid.,* 238, 263–84.
16. George Creel, *How We Advertised America* (New York: Harper and Brothers, 1920), 276.
17. Mock and Larson, *Words That Won the War,* 286.
18. *Ibid.,* 235–36.

In all that propaganda the chief American aim was the wooing of the left, constantly in danger of deserting the fight, as the Bolsheviks eventually did in early 1918. The masterpiece of Wilsonian wooing was the proclamation of the famous Fourteen Points peace agenda. The Bolsheviks, the President told Congress in December 1917, were making great propaganda hay out of the Petrograd formula. "But the fact that a wrong use has been made of a just idea," he declared, "is no reason why a right use should not be made of it."[19] Accordingly, moving to wrest the "holy phrase" from the possession of the Bolsheviks, Wilson announced the Fourteen Points on January 8, 1918. They were his own amplified version of the no annexations, no indemnities, self-determination formula proclaimed at Petrograd the preceding May. Wilson had no doubt long held such sentiments as he then expressed on the plane of high diplomatic principle. But the context of his announcement clearly marked it as a counterstroke against the Russian revolutionaries in the war for people's minds.

The Fourteen Points address had four principal objectives: to induce the Russians, at that moment negotiating an armistice with the Germans, to stay in the war; to bolster the German dissidents; to lift the sagging morale of the Allied peoples; and to appease the American liberals, chafing for some sign to offset their disquiet at the advancing engines of domestic repression. Together with a similar address by British Prime Minister David Lloyd George at about the same time, Wilson's speech had the desired effect, for the moment, in the Allied countries. It also temporarily firmed up his lines of support at home, where even Socialist Party chief Eugene Debs declared that the Fourteen Points "deserve the unqualified approval of everyone believing in the rule of the people, Socialists included."[20]

But Wilson's success was limited. The Russians proceeded to conclude a separate peace treaty with the Germans at Brest-Litovsk in March 1918, and the German government, restrained neither by Wilsonian principles nor by its own dissident parties, dictated a hard settlement to the temporarily helpless Bolsheviks. Meanwhile, the war in the West dragged on, entering its most ominous phase with the renewed German offensive of March 21, 1918.

In this atmosphere, British Labor Party leader Arthur Henderson worked feverishly in the spring and summer of 1918 to revive interest

19. Shaw, ed., *Messages and Papers of Woodrow Wilson*, I, 446.
20. Quoted in David A. Shannon, *The Socialist Party of America: A History* (Chicago: Quadrangle, 1967), 119.

in the Petrograd Soviet's proposal for an inter-belligerent socialist conference at Stockholm. Wilson moved just as smartly to squelch Henderson's effort. The socialist conference, Wilson believed, would either lead to a premature peace, preventing the final extinction of the German Imperial Government, or it would encourage a runaway leftward shift, perhaps careening all the way to Bolshevism, throughout Europe and possibly even the United States. Equally important, the Stockholm idea continued to menace Wilson's exclusive proprietorship of the liberal peace program.

The State Department refused a visa to Henderson (though he was a member of the British cabinet) in April 1918, lest he infect American labor with the socialist peace virus. For this, Samuel Gompers was duly grateful. His government's intransigence ensured that his American socialist adversaries would not be bolstered by reinforcements from overseas. Gompers, in turn, proved eagerly receptive when the administration agreed to subsidize an A.F. of L. delegation that traveled to Europe in the summer of 1918. Their mission was to slake the thirst for peace of European labor, and especially to head off Henderson's agitation for an inter-belligerent conference. Gompers spared no effort in pursuit of those goals. At the Inter-*Allied* Labor and Socialist Conference in London in September, he instructed his lieutenant, John Frey, to take a tough stand against proposals for an inter-*belligerent* conference. "Start the fight from the drop of hat," Frey remembered Gompers's telling him. "Don't call a spade a spade, call it a son-of-a-bitch. Fuck them."[21] Thanks largely to this onslaught, the Stockholm conference never materialized.

Gompers's hard-nosed approach did not endear the A.F. of L. representatives to European labor. The Allied left, far more war-weary and desperate for an end to the fighting than Gompers, regarded his position as little different from the policies of their own governments, which they increasingly distrusted. Ray Stannard Baker, a Wilson intimate sent on a special reconnaissance mission to Europe in 1918, reported that to bring "a message of interminable war, and for no clear or democratic or socially constructive purpose, as Gompers would probably do, was not very promising."[22] British socialist Sidney Webb

21. John Frey Memoir, Columbia University Oral History Collection, Butler Library, Columbia University, N.Y.
22. Quoted in Arno J. Mayer, *Politics and Diplomacy of Peacemaking: Containment and Counterrevolution at Versailles, 1918–1919* (New York: Vintage, 1969), 44.

bluntly warned that "it would not be desirable that any more American labor delegates, preaching the doctrine of the 'Knock-out blow' and of complete non-intercourse with the German socialists, should come to this country or to France at the present time."[23]

Gompers, in short, by clinging fast to the doctrine of Wilson's sole sponsorship of a liberal peace, worked to divide the forces of liberalism in Europe. In effect, writes historian Arno Mayer, "Gompers strengthened those leaders and forces which were *least* inclined really to oppose their own governments and to appease defeated Germany as well as revolutionary Russia. . . . The net result was that the center faction which triumphed stood right rather than left of center in the Allied Socialist and labor movements. As the three Allied premiers headed toward armistice and peace negotiations with the Wilson administration, they were not about to be excessively alarmed by this divided and temperate opposition to carthaginianism."[24]

On December 13, 1918, the *George Washington* nudged into its berth at Brest, France, while warships in the harbor boomed their many-gunned salutes and bands bugled "The Star-Spangled Banner." Wilson disembarked from his ship, made his way between rows of cheering soldiers, and stepped aboard the train that carried him in triumph, past peasants kneeling in grateful prayer beside the tracks, to Paris. There two million French men and women roared their grateful welcome to "Wilson the Just." Several days later, flag-draped youngsters strewed flowers in Wilson's path when he landed in Dover, England. Tens of thousands of Italians greeted Wilson in Rome, and in Milan they jammed the streets and piazzas for a glimpse of the American President. Here, Wilson felt, in these throbbing, chanting multitudes, was the great force to be marshaled against the diplomats he was soon to meet in Paris.

Yet that characteristically Wilsonian hope was doomed from the start, despite the delirious effusion touched off by the President's arrival in Europe. The Allied governments were forewarned of Wilson's desire to use "the laboring masses on both sides of the Atlantic" in support of his diplomacy.[25] Accordingly, they tried to keep his contact with the masses to a minimum, scheduling his days to preclude too much exposure of their peoples to the American leader. Allied states-

23. Quoted in Radosh, *American Labor and U.S. Foreign Policy*, 146.
24. Mayer, *Politics and Diplomacy of Peacemaking*, 44 (italics added), 52.
25. Walworth, *America's Moment*, 147.

men, anxious about Wilson's mass following, "are beginning a sort of campaign to undermine his popularity," remarked Secretary of State Robert Lansing.[26] The peoples of Europe seemed in any case more grateful for American help in achieving victory than they were eager for American meddling in the peace. "A lot of people would like to see European affairs settled by Europeans. Above all else they would like to have Wilson go back to Washington . . . ," noted one American observer.[27] Even as Wilson prepared to visit England, the British were counting the last ballots from an election that returned Lloyd George to the Prime Minister's chair with strong Conservative support, pledged to seek vast reparations payments from the defeated Germans. And when Wilson in April resorted to his master tactic, appealing to the Italian people, over the head of their premier, to renounce irredentist claims to Fiume, his maneuver badly misfired. Premier Vittorio Orlando stalked out of the Paris conference. He returned to Italy to ask: "Have I properly interpreted the will of the Italian people?" The Italian Senate responded with a unanimous resolution of confidence, matched by an overwhelming vote of approval, 382-40, in the Chamber of Deputies. In the streets of Italy, the people covered with cloth the plaques and tablets they had erected only weeks earlier in Wilson's honor.[28]

All those liabilities Wilson might have mitigated had he firmly grasped the outstretched hand of the European socialists in 1917 and 1918. In all the Allied countries he might thus have braced those constituencies most sympathetic to his vision of peace and most disposed to challenge the reactionary designs of their own governments. But Wilson, scenting the taint of Bolshevism in the socialist camp, and in any case unwilling, perhaps temperamentally unable, to share leadership in the crusade for world reform, spurned the proferred hand of alliance. His truculent wartime policies toward the European left, aggressively executed in part by Samuel Gompers, helped to ensure the President's political impotence when he finally sat down to the Peace Conference table in Paris on January 12, 1919.

Given the weakness of the military, economic, and political cards that the American President held, the wonder is that he managed to

26. *Ibid.*, 138.
27. *Ibid.*, 139n.
28. Bailey, *Woodrow Wilson and the Lost Peace*, 263.

shape the final peace settlement as much as he did. In the first round of discussions at Paris, Wilson won two major points: the establishment of a mandate, or trustee, system to govern the former German overseas colonies (avoiding their outright transfer to the victors); and the incorporation of the League of Nations Covenant as Section I of the peace treaty (foiling the Allied desire to postpone creation of the League until after the finalization of peace terms).

In mid-February Wilson returned to the United States, where Republican Senators ardently denounced the President's accomplishments in Paris. They warned that the Senate would not approve a treaty containing the Covenant of the League as then drafted, which they believed badly compromised American sovereignty. Wilson hurled defiance at his Republican critics on the eve of his return to Paris, telling a New York audience that "so many threads of the treaty [are] tied to the covenant that you cannot dissect the covenant from the treaty without destroying the whole vital structure."[29]

Back at the Peace Conference table in mid-March, however, Wilson negotiated important amendments to the League Covenant in order to appease the senatorial opposition. He secured Allied agreement that the League should have no power to interfere in "internal" matters like tariffs and immigration; that any nation should have the right to withdraw from the League; that American claims under the Monroe Doctrine should be beyond the League's jurisdiction; and that America should be allowed to refuse unwanted mandate territories.

Wilson's demand for these concessions encouraged the European and Japanese representatives to strike harder for the realization of their own national ambitions. The French and the British pressed for formal admission of war guilt and heavy reparations payments from the defeated enemy. France not only reclaimed the "lost provinces" of Alsace and Lorraine but also insisted on occupying Germany's coal-rich Saar Basin. Premier Clemenceau won Wilson's agreement to a security treaty guaranteeing American military aid to France, which Wilson knew faced certain rejection in the United States Senate. The Italians annexed the Brenner Pass, absorbing some 200,000 German-speaking Tyroleans into their Latin state, and clamored for the largely Slavic seaport of Fiume. Japan adamantly refused to relinquish captured German holdings and trading rights in China's Shantung Province. The

29. *New York Times,* Mar. 5, 1919, 1.

treaty's final draft, explicitly incorporating many of these arrangements and silently acquiescing in others, was sullenly signed by the Germans in the Hall of Mirrors at Versailles on June 28, 1919.

Despite those defeats for his precious principles of a just peace based on self-determination, the presence of Wilson at Paris no doubt helped to soften the wrath of the victors against Germany. On the other hand, the presence of the Americans on the battlefield had provided the extra weight in the military hammerhead whose final blow left the Germans completely crushed—and set the stage for a peace of vengeance rather than compromise. The final treaty thus ironically embodied the counter-poised consequences of American belligerency. The settlement was harsher than it might have been if the Europeans, left to their own fate, had simply collapsed into a peace of exhaustion; but its harshness was mitigated by Wilsonian ideals, above all by the promise of enduring international comity under the aegis of the League of Nations.

The dual, even contradictory, character of the Versailles Treaty ignited controversy from the moment of its publication in America in the late spring of 1919. *New Republic* editor Herbert Croly was already worrying privately that the Allied governments "have not the slightest intention of writing anything but a punitive peace. . . . If this anticipation proves correct," he warned, "our attitude will necessarily become one of agitation against the League then existing and in favor for the time being of a resumption of our isolation in foreign affairs."[30] That prophecy proved correct when the *New Republic* a few weeks later sadly urged the Senate to repudiate the Versailles Treaty, "this inhuman monster" hatched by the political servants of "inhumane and complacent capitalist society." For Croly and his fellow editors of the liberal journal, Walter Weyl and Walter Lippmann, the decision to oppose the Treaty was particularly painful and humiliating. They had been among the leading proponents of American intervention, outspoken advocates of Wilson and his peace program. But they were forced to conclude that their great gamble on the liberal leader had failed, that America's "national promise" was "still unredeemed." As good pragmatists, they now withdrew their allegiance from an idea—the

30. Charles Forcey, *The Crossroads of Liberalism: Croly, Weyl, Lippmann and the Progressive Era, 1900–1925* (New York: Oxford University Press, 1961), 285.

Wilsonian idea of a new, liberal world order—that had failed to be realized.[31]

Other Americans attacked the Treaty as too liberal or too internationalist. Giving new life to the wartime cry of "100 per cent Americanism," isolationists like William Randolph Hearst especially denounced Article X of the League Covenant, which pledged the signatory states to preserve against external aggression "the territorial integrity and existing political independence of all Members." Article X, charged the supernationalists, constituted a blank check on American men and guns, a surrender of sovereign independence.

Added to these abundant hostilities toward the Treaty were the resentments of several American ethnic groups, incensed at Wilson's "betrayal" of the aspirations of their various homelands. Irish-Americans cried that the Treaty did nothing to free their ancestral island from English oppression. Italian-Americans shared their old-country brethren's indignation at Wilson's meddling in the Fiume affair. German-Americans echoed the complaint of their European kinsmen that the treaty had been brutally and cynically forced on the vanquished at gunpoint.

Most ominous was the opposition to the Treaty in the Senate, which was constitutionally required to ratify the agreement before it became binding on the United States. The elections of November 1918 had delivered the Senate leadership into the waiting hands of Henry Cabot Lodge. Perhaps for this reason, Wilson had declined to name any Senators to the American delegation at Paris—an omission that deprived him of key political support in the upcoming struggle for ratification. Lodge fully intended to use his power to "Republicanize" or "Senatorialize" the document that the Democratic President brought home from Versailles in July 1919. Lodge at first stalled for time in the Committee on Foreign Relations by consuming two weeks in reading the 264-page Treaty aloud. Meanwhile, he put in motion a massive anti-League propaganda campaign, amply funded by industrialists Henry Clay Frick and Andrew Mellon, to overcome the public's presumed sympathy for Wilson's pet plan. Throughout the month of August, the Committee on Foreign Relations sat in the sleep-inducing Washington heat, taking tedious and often irrelevant testimony that, as historian

31. *New Republic* 19 (May 24, 1919), 100–101; and Forcey, 291. Forcey correctly notes that this action by the *New Republic* men "took real courage." It also seriously qualifies—perhaps even cancels—Randolph Bourne's conclusion that the pragmatic liberals had no fixed principles save their hunger for influence.

Thomas A. Bailey notes, threatened to drown the Treaty in a sea of words.[32]

By early September, Woodrow Wilson knew that the Treaty's ratification by the Senate was in mortal danger. Summoning what little strength the war and the peace negotiations had left in his sixty-three-year-old body, Wilson determined to resort yet again to the dramatic performance that he always considered his most effective political role. He would take his case directly to the people, on a barnstorming tour of the Western states that had elected him in 1916, where he would rouse the force of public opinion against the stalling Senators.

On September 3, 1919, Wilson set out by train from the capital, raising the curtain on what was to be the last act of his political and personal tragedy. He was shadowed a few days later by two "irreconcilable" anti-League Republican Senators, Hiram Johnson of California and William E. Borah of Idaho, who dogged the President's trail to contradict his claims for the treaty. Yet on the Pacific Coast and especially in Johnson's home state of California the crowds at last seemed to warm to Wilson's message. Encouraged, the fatigued President plunged back into the heart of the continent, over the Sierra Nevada and across the Great Basin to a triumphant reception at Salt Lake's famed Mormon Tabernacle. Then on September 25 he rose before a lustily cheering crowd in Pueblo, Colorado. His own eyes moist as he described the American military cemeteries in France, the President brought many persons in the audience to tears.

Exhausted and shaken, Wilson that night suffered headache and insomnia as his train bore him away from Pueblo toward Kansas. He was forced to cancel his remaining speeches in the Midwest and upper South. The presidential train made full speed back to Washington. At home in the White House, Wilson awoke on the morning of October 2 complaining of numbness in his left hand. Minutes later he slumped unconscious to the floor, felled by a stroke that left him thick of speech and partly paralyzed. He was, said Lloyd George, "as much a victim of the war as any soldier who died in the trenches."[33] The President now become a reclusive invalid in the White House, his once-clear mind clouded by illness, his political judgment marred by sickly petulance.

At this critical juncture Senator Lodge consummated his strategy for

32. Thomas A. Bailey, *Woodrow Wilson and the Great Betrayal* (Chicago: Quadrangle, 1963), 79.
33. *New York Times*, Feb. 4, 1924, 1.

denying the full laurels of victory to the Democratic President. On November 6, Lodge reported out of the Committee on Foreign Relations a resolution of ratification, accompanied by fourteen "Lodge reservations" that circumscribed America's obligations under the League Covenant. The most important of the reservations concerned Article X. Lodge proposed to limit the American pledge to defend other nations against aggression, and to make that pledge in any case contingent on congressional approval. Though this was a technical point that might, if accepted, have had little impact on America's relation to the League, it struck a sensitive Wilsonian nerve. Lodge's reservation on Article X, Wilson thought, compromised America's moral commitment to make the new body work soundly; it was a "knife thrust at the heart of the treaty."[34] Though he now faced the prospect of having a treaty with the Lodge reservations attached or no treaty at all, Wilson urged the Democratic Senators to vote against Lodge's resolution of ratification. On November 19, 1919, almost exactly a year after the cease-fire in Europe, the Senate rejected the Versailles Treaty. Another vote on March 19, 1920, saw many Democrats shun their President's advice and vote in favor of the Lodge-amended version, but there were too few of them to bring the total pro-treaty ballot to the necessary two-thirds majority. The crowning irony came soon thereafter when Wilson vetoed a congressional joint resolution declaring an end to American belligerency. If there could be no treaty other than a purely Wilson treaty, then there would be no legal close to the war itself except on Wilson's terms. It finally fell to Republican President Warren G. Harding, elected in 1920 by the largest majority to date in an American presidential election, to proclaim an end to the state of hostility against the Central Powers in the summer of 1921.

At last, the American crusade to redeem the Old World was officially over. As for the League, Harding declared in 1923 that the issue was "as dead as slavery. . . . Let it rest in the deep grave to which it has been consigned."[35] A few months later the waiting grave closed over the body of the League's great champion. "I am a broken piece of machinery," Wilson muttered from his sick bed on February 2, 1924, and the next morning he was dead. "He lived his purgatory on earth," said Le Temps of Paris; he was a heroic figure whose tragic fault "was to love glory and love to hold the stage alone." The London Daily

34. Bailey, Woodrow Wilson and the Great Betrayal, 157.
35. New York Times, June 22, 1923, 2.

Express stated simply: "Blessed are the peacemakers, for they shall inherit the earth."[36]

On September 10, 1927, another former German ship, the *Leviathan*, slipped her hawsers at her Hudson River pier and pointed her bow on the familiar bearing toward France. A brass band boisterously pumped out the old war tune "Over There," while the dirigible *Los Angeles* hovered festively overhead. A onetime luxury liner refitted as a troop carrier during the war, *Leviathan* had for this journey again become a troop transport of sorts. Jammed around the railing on her promenade deck as she made her way downriver were hundreds of members of the "Second A.E.F.," headed for a nostalgia-rich American Legion convention in Paris. *Leviathan* was the flagship of a fleet of fifteen liners carrying some 25,000 Legionnaires and their families on a "sacred pilgrimage" to France.

The Legion had principally busied itself since the Armistice in promoting 100 percent Americanism and badgering Congress for privileged access by veterans to the public purse. After pursuing a government-financed "farms-for-veterans" scheme in the immediate postwar months, the Legion had soon realized the irrelevance of that plan in an increasingly industrial America, and shifted its agitation to a proposal for straight cash payments to ex-servicemen. Designed to recompense veterans for the difference between their service pay and what they might have earned as wartime civilian laborers, an "adjusted compensation," or "bonus" bill passed over President Calvin Coolidge's veto in 1924.

In the eyes of the Legion's leadership, that accomplishment, though gratifying, paled in symbolic significance next to the holy return to the now-silent battle sites of 1917 and 1918. National Legion Commander Howard P. Savage announced as he boarded *Leviathan* that the Legionnaires would "visit the battlefields where we offered our all on the golden shield of duty," remembering always "the sacred bonds of communion we will hold with the dead in the cemeteries of the World War."[37] In those accents there survived intact the romantic rhetorical conjurings of war's glory that had been so common a decade earlier.

In mid-September the Legionnaires began to descend upon waiting Paris, adorned for the occasion with flickering gaslamps along its rooflines, tens of thousands of colored lights strung in the *grandes rues*, and majestic Notre Dame beflagged with billowing fields of red, white,

36. *Ibid.*, Feb. 4, 1924, 4; Feb. 3, 1924, 1.
37. *Ibid.*, Sept. 11, 1927, 12.

and blue bunting. Only months earlier all Paris had excitedly embraced another traveling American, Charles Lindbergh, when he set his frail single-engine aircraft down on Le Bourget field after a world-shrinking trans-Atlantic flight. The boyish, lanky Lindbergh had been endlessly compared with those earlier American boys who had bridged the Atlantic in 1917. At a stroke he wiped out much of the bitter anti-Americanism that had built up in postwar France, which was resentful of Uncle Sam's tight-fisted insistence on war debt repayment, of American tariff barriers, of America's continuing aloofness from the League of Nations, and of the smug provincialism of American culture, perpetually on display in the form of swelling hordes of dollar-rich tourists. Now the Legionnaires hoped to strike up a sentiment similar to that which Lindbergh had kindled, cancelling a decade of postwar recriminations in shared remembrance of the time when the doughboys and the poilus had been comrades-in-arms. To a large extent they succeeded, as Parisians warmly welcomed the exuberant and free-spending convention-goers.

In their official speeches and statements, the Legionnaires resurrected all the reverent verbal conventions of wartime. "They laid the sacrifice of the nation on the altar of freedom," incanted the aging John J. Pershing as he stood amidst the rows of white crosses in the American military cemetery at Suresnes, near Paris. "No soldier could ask for a sweeter resting place than on the field of glory where he fell."[38] The *New York Times* sent along with the Legion three of its former war correspondents, who vied with each other in rewriting their old war dispatches in a style that in the intervening years had grown still more cloying and sentimental. One of the journalists reported a conversation with a pensive veteran surveying the graves at Villers-Cotterets: "'Maybe they are lucky at that,'" mused the ex-serviceman. "'I am selling leather goods wholesale in Chicago and—damn it—getting fat.' . . . That is what we were seeking this afternoon in the quiet, green, peaceful forest," the correspondent commented, "our youth that had left us. That is what the American Legion is seeking in France—hard days, dangerous days, mud and blood and lice and thirst and pain and hunger; yes, but youth also."[39]

The Legionnaires were not about to let graveyards and somber philosophizing get in the way of a good time. Many of them, "refugees

38. *Ibid.*, Sept. 18, 1927, 3.
39. *Ibid.*, Sept. 22, 1927, 5.

from the Eighteenth Amendment," forsook the convention proceedings to haunt the bars and bistros, slaking their seven-year thirst for legal liquor. "There was no sadness among the visitors," noted one observer. "Serious things are burdening but lightly the minds of the Legion delegates. They have started the convention as one grand, gay party and they intend to keep it going that way."[40]

Things got going in earnest with a mass parade down the Champs Élysées on September 19. Karl Marx once wrote, of another Parisian event, that history repeats itself as farce. That thought might have passed through the minds of Frenchmen as they witnessed the triumphal return of the "Second A.E.F." Some twenty thousand strong, the Legionnaires passed under the Arc de Triomphe, each dropping a red, white, or blue flower at the tomb of France's Unknown Soldier. That duty done, they emerged onto the crest of the gently sloping Élysées and poured down its broad expanse in a wildly colorful river of Americana. They stepped "with characteristic American pep," thought a British observer, in a wondrous display of the "American character and spirit . . . democratic, humorous and free-hearted." There was none of the "excessive dignity which marks the usual European convention."[41] Feathered Indians from Oklahoma marched alongside whooping, cowboy-clad Texans, hailed as "Tom Mixes" by the curbside crowds. Gaudily uniformed marching bands, a forest of banners, flamboyant flappers in the ladies' auxiliaries, countless flag-draped figures of Dame Columbia, and "two lonely Negroes drowned in the mass" flooded past a million astonished Parisians.[42]

"It was difficult for the French," remarked the *Literary Digest,* "to understand the holiday gaiety—the almost carnival spirit—of the former doughboys on their war pilgrimage to scenes and mementoes which are invested with a sad sacredness in the French mind." Some Frenchmen reportedly thought that the Americans were "making fun of Europe's age-old militarism," that the parade was "America's big laugh at Europe."[43] To the French, the *Nation* soberly observed, war was assuredly not "a grand parade," and the Legion "spectacle" was "as tasteless and as shocking to French sensibilities as would be jazz on the battlefields."[44]

40. *Ibid.,* Sept. 19, 1927, 1.
41. *Ibid.,* Sept. 20, 1927, 1.
42. *Nation* 125 (Oct. 19, 1927), 420–21.
43. *Literary Digest* 95 (Oct. 15, 1927), 38.
44. *Nation* 125 (Oct. 19, 1927), 422.

Yet the Legion's Parisian "spectacle" honestly reflected the difference between the American and the French experiences with the war. The late-arriving Americans had not suffered the endless ordeal of the Europeans; the New World and the Old World had, in reality, fought different wars. So too, in remembrance, did their citizens preserve different images of the conflict and derive different meanings from it. The Great War had compromised, but far from cancelled, America's peculiar historic immunity from the deepest wounds of modern warfare.[45]

Other episodes in that anniversary year of 1927 also marked the gulf that the war era had ironically widened between the New World and the Old. On August 23 the state of Massachusetts had electrocuted for bank robbery and murder two Italian anarchists, Nicola Sacco and Bartolomeo Vanzetti. Their execution followed seven years of protest, much of it noisily emanating from the European left, against the postwar American atmosphere of nativism and Red-baiting in which the immigrant radicals had been sentenced to death. French authorities had feared violent leftist attacks on the convening American Legion, notorious for its anti-immigrant and anti-radical activities, but the French left confined itself to a small demonstration in the Paris suburb of Clichy. There, on the very morning of the Legion march down the Champs Élysées, a small gathering of mourners dedicated the Place Sacco-Vanzetti. Among the participants was Roger Baldwin of the American Civil Liberties Union, which had fought futilely to save the condemned men. His solitary and defeated figure poignantly testified to the impotence of the postwar American left, just as the ceremony at Clichy exemplified the despair and even the contempt with which Old World radicals now contemplated America, once the beacon of hope to liberal Europeans. Baldwin's sad voice, no matter how eloquent, was no match for the throaty exuberance of the Legion marchers a few miles away.

European businessmen also despaired of America in 1927. Congress earlier in the year had declined to appropriate fifteen thousand dollars to send an American delegation to the World Economic Conference at Geneva, called to lower tariff barriers and liberalize international trade. President Coolidge had eventually dispatched five American observers to the Conference, paying their expenses from the President's contingency fund. But the stinginess and indifference of Congress was

45. For extended discussion of this idea, see David M. Kennedy, "War and the American Character," *The Stanford Magazine* 3 (Spring/Summer 1975), 14.

emblematic of the American indisposition throughout the 1920s to accept the role of world economic leadership by lowering its prohibitively high import schedules. Repeatedly frustrated in efforts to pierce the American tariff wall, the French government announced, just as the Legionnaires were setting sail from New York, that it had concluded a new trade agreement with Germany. The agreement would effectively disadvantage American firms in lines that competed with German goods. Washington threatened to respond by invoking the retaliatory provisions of the Fordney-McCumber Tariff, hiking duties on French imports by 50 percent. Thus, even in the midst of the Legion's Parisian revels, a French delegation set out for Washington, seeking to placate the Americans. After much acrimony, the French finally backed down in November and agreed to restore the old duties on American goods. These developments mocked the hollow sloganeering of the Legionnaires and their properly decorous hosts about the war-born bonds of blood and sentiment that tied the New World to the Old.

And yet for some, those bonds remained unforgettably real. Thirty thousand American soldiers lay in Europe, their corpses disinterred after the Armistice from scattered, hastily dug pits and gathered into eight military cemeteries. Many families had begged the War Department in 1919 to ship the bodies home, but most had eventually consented to leave the dead where they lay. "It is just as near from France to heaven as from Indiana," concluded one mother.[46] Then in 1930, Congress appropriated five million dollars to send the "Gold Star mothers" to visit their sons' graves. In an omission consonant with the sentiments of the age, no provision was made for bereaved fathers to travel to France.

The War Department dutifully sent some thirty thousand letters to the last-listed next of kin of the doughboys buried in Europe. A full 40 percent of these letters came back stamped undeliverable as addressed, striking evidence of the uprooting fluidity of postwar American society. Of those who responded, nearly 6000 accepted the government's invitation. Some black mothers who wished to make the voyage objected to the government's plan to consign them in a group to a single ship, and to segregate them in separate trains and hotels throughout

46. G. C. Brindle to M. E. Lafoe, n.d. I am grateful to James Kloppenberg for sharing this family letter with me.

the journey. Preferring "to remain at home and retain our honor and self-respect," several black Gold Star mothers sadly declined the War Department's offer.[47]

On May 7, 1930, another band of Americans once again climbed the gangways at Hoboken, setting out on the journey to France that the long-ago war had so often occasioned. This time there was small fanfare. The group numbered just 234, mostly elderly women, the first of more than a score of contingents that would make the ocean crossing under the War Department's auspices over the next three years. Their departure shared the headlines with reports of the movement through Congress of the Smoot-Hawley tariff bill, lifting the levies against foreign imports higher still over the already trade-strangling rates of the Fordney-McCumber Tariff. But the women on shipboard cared little for such commercial topics as they contemplated the somber rendezvous that awaited them in France.

They arrived in Paris on May 16 amidst expressions of worry for their health and emotional state. Then in still smaller groups they went, without speeches or ceremony, to seek their sons' graves at the various military cemeteries. The task of their guides was complicated, the War Department reported, by the fact that so many of the visiting mothers spoke no English. At Suresnes on May 19, six mothers were chosen to lay wreaths at the crosses inscribed "Here Rests in Honored Glory an American Soldier Known But to God." Among the six was a German-American woman accompanied by relatives from Munich. Her son and their son, cousins, might have died fighting one another for the sake of their respective flags.[48]

On May 20 one hundred eight mothers traveled by motor coach to the largest American cemetery at Montfaucon, on the Romagne heights in the stubborn center of the old Meuse-Argonne battlefield. Along the way they passed through Châlons-sur-Marne, where they were told the story of choosing the Unknown Soldier for interment at Arlington. Six unidentified bodies had been brought from as many cemeteries, the coffins laid out in a room at the Hôtel de Ville. ("Make sure he ain't a dinge boys. make sure he ain't a guinea or a kike," John Dos Passos mocked.) A blindfolded sergeant had dropped a white carnation on one of the caskets.

47. *New York Times*, Feb. 23, 1930, sec. IX, 8; May 30, 1930, 12.
48. *Ibid.*, May 19, 1930, 1.

The next morning the mothers took their own flowers to the trim little valley of the Meuse-Argonne cemetery, where 14,000 white Carrara marble crosses and Stars of David marched in repeated rows up the green slopes. As their caravan passed Verdun, the guides pointed out the beacon of the immense mausoleum atop the hill at Douaumont, holding the bones of over one million unidentified French and German soldiers killed in the wartime sieges.

When they finally alighted from their buses, a gentle rain was falling. The mothers walked silently out into the field of marble. Most knelt when they finally found the marker with the familiar yet strangely waiting name. Some scattered soil or flowers from yards where their sons had played as boys. Then the rain began to pour hard and cold. The women were escorted back to the buses, leaving their children alone again in the peaceful French countryside to await their promised glory. They wait there still.

Bibliography

Unpublished Official Documents

WASHINGTON, D.C. NATIONAL ARCHIVES
Records of the United States Shipping Board, Record Group 32.
Records of the Bureau of Accounts, Treasury Department, Record Group 39.
General Records of the Treasury Department, Record Group 56.
General Records of the Department of State, Record Group 59.
Records of the Allied Purchasing Commission, Record Group 113.
Records of the Bureau of Foreign and Domestic Commerce, Department of Commerce, Record Group 151.
Records of the War Finance Corporation, Record Group 154.

SUITLAND, MD. FEDERAL RECORD CENTER
Records of the War Industries Board, Record Group 61.
Records of the War Trade Board, Record Group 182.

LONDON, ENG. PUBLIC RECORD OFFICE
War Cabinet Minutes, CAB 23.
War Cabinet Memoranda, CAB 24.
Ministry of Shipping Files, MT 25.
Documents of the Advisory Committee to the Department of Overseas Trade, BT 90.
War Office Registered Papers: General Series, WO 32; Directorate of Military Operations and Intelligence: Papers, WO 106.
Foreign Office General Correspondence: Commercial, 1906–20, FO 368; Political, 1906–, FO 371; Contraband, 1915–20, FO 382.

Personal Papers

BERKELEY, CA. BANCROFT LIBRARY. UNIVERSITY OF CALIFORNIA
Hiram Johnson Papers.

BOSTON, MASS. MASSACHUSETTS HISTORICAL SOCIETY
Henry Cabot Lodge Papers.

CAMBRIDGE, MASS. HOUGHTON LIBRARY. HARVARD UNIVERSITY
David Houston Papers.
Alan Seeger Papers.
Oswald Garrison Villard Papers.

NEW HAVEN, CONN. STERLING LIBRARY. YALE UNIVERSITY
Edward M. House Papers.
Vance McCormick Papers.
Charles Nagel Papers.
James R. Sheffield Papers.
Henry L. Stimson Papers.

NEW YORK, N.Y. BUTLER LIBRARY. COLUMBIA UNIVERSITY
Columbia University Oral History Collection
    John Frey Memoir.
    Lester Granger Memoir.
    Walter Lippmann Memoir.
    A. J. Muste Memoir.
    Arthur M. Schlesinger Memoir.
    Norman Thomas Memoir.
    James Wadsworth Memoir.
Nicholas Murray Butler Papers.
George Haven Putnam Papers.
Lillian D. Wald Papers.

PRINCETON, N.J. FIRESTONE LIBRARY. PRINCETON UNIVERSITY
Ray Stannard Baker Papers.
Bernard Baruch Papers.
Arthur Bullard Papers.
Raymond B. Fosdick Papers.

STANFORD, CA. GREEN LIBRARY. STANFORD UNIVERSITY
David Starr Jordan Papers.

STANFORD, CA. HOOVER INSTITUTION ON WAR, REVOLUTION AND PEACE. STAN-
    FORD UNIVERSITY
Jacob Emery Collection.
Otis Emmons Briggs Collection.
Eugene Kennedy Collection.
J. G. Ragsdale Collection.
Anna Russell Collection.
Agnes Wright Spring Collection.

Edwin F. Gay Papers.
Mark Sullivan Papers.
United States National Industrial Conference Papers.

WASHINGTON, D.C. LIBRARY OF CONGRESS
Felix Frankfurter Papers.
Thomas W. Gregory Papers.
William Gibbs McAdoo Papers.
Woodrow Wilson Papers.

Published Documents and Papers, Collected Letters

Baker, Ray Stannard. *Woodrow Wilson: Life and Letters.* 8 vols. Garden City, N.Y., and New York: Doubleday, Page, and Doubleday, Doran, 1927–39.

———. *Woodrow Wilson and World Settlement.* 3 vols. Garden City, N.Y.: Doubleday, Page, 1922–23.

———, and Dodd, William E., eds. *The Public Papers of Woodrow Wilson,* 6 vols. New York: Harper and Brothers, 1925–27.

Bane, Suda Lorena, and Lutz, Ralph Haswell, eds. *The Blockade of Germany After the Armistice, 1918–1919.* Stanford: Stanford University Press, 1942.

———. *Organization of American Relief in Europe 1918–1919.* Stanford: Stanford University Press, 1943.

Cronon, E. David, ed. *The Cabinet Diaries of Josephus Daniels, 1913–1921.* Lincoln: University of Nebraska Press, 1963.

Howe, Mark A. DeWolfe, ed. *Holmes-Laski Letters: The Correspondence of Mr. Justice Holmes and Harold J. Laski, 1916–1935.* Cambridge, Mass.: Harvard University Press, 1953.

———. *The Occasional Speeches of Justice Oliver Wendell Holmes, Jr.* Cambridge, Mass.: Belknap Press, 1962.

Lash, Joseph P., ed. *From the Diaries of Felix Frankfurter.* New York: Norton, 1975.

Morison, Elting E., ed. *The Letters of Theodore Roosevelt.* 8 vols. Cambridge, Mass.: Harvard University Press, 1951–54.

O'Brien, Francis William, ed. *The Hoover-Wilson Wartime Correspondence.* Ames: Iowa State University Press, 1974.

Peabody, James Bishop, ed. *The Holmes-Einstein Letters: Correspondence of Mr. Justice Holmes and Lewis Einstein, 1903–35.* London: Macmillan, 1964.

Perry, Bliss, ed. *The Life and Letters of Henry Lee Higginson.* Boston: Atlantic Monthly Press, 1921.

Seymour, Charles, ed. *The Intimate Papers of Colonel House.* 4 vols. Boston: Houghton Mifflin, 1926–28.

Shaw, Albert, ed. *The Messages and Papers of Woodrow Wilson.* 2 vols. New York: Review of Reviews Corp., 1924.

Spiller, Robert E. *The Van Wyck Brooks-Lewis Mumford Letters: The Record of a Literary Friendship, 1921–63.* New York: Dutton, 1970.

Surface, Frank M., and Bland, Raymond L. *American Food in the World War and Reconstruction Period.* Stanford: Stanford University Press, 1931.

U.S. Alien Property Custodian. *Alien Property Custodian Report,* 1919.

U.S. Committee on Public Information. *Official U.S. Bulletin,* 1917–19.

U.S. Congress. *Congressional Record.* 65th–67th Congresses, 1917–22.

——. House. Special Committee. *National Security League. Hearings.* 65th Congress, 3rd session, 1919.

——. Senate. Special Committee. *Munitions Industry. Hearings Before the Special Committee Investigating the Munitions Industry.* 74th Congress, 2nd session, 1936.

U.S. Department of Commerce. *Commerce Yearbook,* 1925.

U.S. Department of Justice. *Annual Report of the Attorney General of the United States for the Year 1918.*

U.S. Department of State. *Foreign Relations of the United States,* 1914–22.

U.S. President. *Preliminary Statement of Industrial Conference Called by the President,* 1919.

——. President's Mediation Commission. *Report of the President's Mediation Commission to the President of the United States,* 1918.

——. President's Mediation Commission. *Report on the Bisbee Deportations,* 1918.

U.S. Provost Marshal General. *Second Report to the Secretary of War on the Operations of the Selective Service System,* 1919.

U.S. War Department. *Annual Reports of the Secretary of War,* 1917–20.

Contemporary Works, Works by Participants, Fiction, Poetry

Adams, Ephraim Douglass. *Why We Are at War with Germany.* San Francisco: Liberty Loan General Executive Board, n.d.

Allen, Hervey. *Toward the Flame: A War Diary.* Pittsburgh: University of Pittsburgh Press, 1968.

Ayres, Leonard P. *The War with Germany: A Statistical Summary.* Washington, D.C.: Government Printing Office, 1919.

Babson, Roger W. *W. B. Wilson and the Department of Labor.* New York: Brentano's, 1919.

Baruch, Bernard M. *American Industry in the War.* New York: Prentice-Hall, 1941.

Berlin, Ira, ed. "A Wisconsinite in World War I: Reminiscences of Edmund P. Arpin, Jr." *Wisconsin Magazine of History* 51 (1967), 3–25.

Brooks, Van Wyck. *Three Essays on America.* New York: Dutton, 1970.

Cather, Willa. *One of Ours.* New York: Knopf, 1922.

Clark, Birge. *World War I Memoirs.* Typescript, Green Library, Stanford University, Stanford, Ca.

Clarkson, Grosvenor B. *Industrial America in the World War: The Strategy Behind the Line, 1917–1918.* Boston: Houghton Mifflin, 1923.

Cobb, Humphrey. *Paths of Glory.* New York: Viking, 1935.

Creel, George. *How We Advertised America.* New York: Harper and Brothers, 1920.

Croly, Herbert. *The Promise of American Life*. New York: Macmillan, 1909.

Crowder, Enoch. *The Spirit of Selective Service*. New York: Century, 1920.

Crowell, Benedict, and Wilson, Robert Forrest. *Demobilization: Our Industrial and Military Demobilization After the Armistice, 1918–1920*. New Haven: Yale University Press, 1921.

Cummings, E. E. *The Enormous Room*. New York: Modern Library, 1934.

Davis, Richard Harding. *With the Allies*. New York: Scribner's, 1919.

Dawson, N. P., ed. *"The Good Soldier," A Selection of Soldiers' Letters, 1914–1918*. New York: Macmillan, 1918.

Dos Passos, John. *One Man's Initiation: 1917*. Ithaca: Cornell University Press, 1969.

———. *Three Soldiers*. New York: George H. Doran, 1921.

———. *U.S.A.* Boston: Houghton Mifflin, 1963.

Elliott, George Ray. *Our Progress-Idea and the War*. Boston: Richard D. Badger, 1916.

Empey, Arthur G. *"Over the Top" by an American Soldier Who Went*. New York: Putnam's, 1917.

Faulkner, William. *Soldier's Pay*. New York: New American Library, 1951.

Graves, Robert. *Goodbye to All That*. Garden City, N.Y.: Doubleday, 1957.

Harbord, James G. *The American Army in France, 1917–1919*. Boston: Little, Brown, 1936.

Hemingway, Ernest. *A Farewell to Arms*. New York: Scribner's, 1929.

———. *Torrents of Spring*. New York: Scribner's, 1930.

History of Company "E", 303d Engineers of the 78th Division, 1917–1919. Rochester: John P. Smith, 1919.

Hoover, Herbert. *American Individualism*. Garden City. N.Y.: Doubleday, Page, 1923.

———. *The Memoirs of Herbert Hoover: Years of Adventure, 1874–1920*. New York: Macmillan, 1953.

Houston, David F. *Eight Years with Wilson's Cabinet, 1913 to 1920*. 2 vols. Garden City, N.Y.: Doubleday, Page, 1926.

Howe, Frederic C. *The Confessions of a Reformer*. Chicago: Quadrangle, 1967.

Jordan, David Starr. *The Days of a Man*. 2 vols. Yonkers-on-Hudson, N.Y.: World Book Co., 1922.

Keynes, John Maynard. *Two Memoirs*. New York: Augustus M. Kelley, 1949.

Langer, William L. *Gas and Flame in World War I*. New York: Knopf, 1965.

Lippmann, Walter. *Drift and Mastery*. New York: Mitchell Kennerley, 1914.

———. *Public Opinion*. New York: Free Press, 1965.

March, William. *Company K*. Concord, N.Y.: American Mercury, 1931.

Mattox, W. C. *Building the Emergency Fleet*. Cleveland: Penton, 1920.

McAdoo, William Gibbs. *Crowded Years*. Boston: Houghton Mifflin, 1931.

McLaughlin, Andrew C. *America and Britain*. New York: Dutton, 1919.

Nearing, Scott. *The Making of a Radical: A Political Autobiography*. New York: Harper and Row, 1972.

Nettleton, George Henry, ed. *Yale in the World War*. New Haven: Yale University Press, 1925.

Pershing, John J. *My Experiences in the World War*. 2 vols. New York: Frederick A. Stokes, 1931.

Ratner, Joseph, ed. *Characters and Events: Popular Essays in Social and Political Philosophy by John Dewey*. 2 vols. New York: Henry Holt, 1929.

Remarque, Erich Maria. *All Quiet on the Western Front*. Greenwich, Conn.: Fawcett, 1968.

Resek, Carl. *War and the Intellectuals: Essays by Randolph S. Bourne, 1915–1919*. New York: Harper and Row, 1964.

Roosevelt, Theodore. *Fear God and Take Your Own Part*. New York: George H. Doran, 1916.

[Roszel, B. M.] *The Commanders' Tour, September 24th–October 11th, 1927*. Richmond: Garrett and Massie, 1928.

Schlissel, Lillian, ed. *The World of Randolph Bourne*. New York: Dutton, 1965.

Scott, Emmett J. *The American Negro in the World War*. N.p., n.d.

———. *Negro Migration During the War*. Carnegie Endowment for International Peace, Preliminary Economic Studies of the War, No. 16. New York: Oxford University Press, 1920.

Seeger, Alan. *Poems*. New York: Scribner's, 1917.

Service, Robert. *The Complete Poems of Robert Service*. New York: Dodd, Mead, 1942.

Small, James Louis, comp. *Home—Then What? The Mind of the Doughboy, A.E.F.* New York: George H. Doran, 1920.

The Soldier's Progress: From the War Letters of Carnegie Tech Men. Pittsburgh: Carnegie Institute of Technology, 1918.

Stallings, Laurence. *Plumes*. New York: Harcourt, Brace, 1924.

Stearns, Harold E., ed. *Civilization in the United States: An Inquiry by Thirty Americans*. New York: Harcourt, Brace, 1922.

———. *Liberalism in America: Its Origin, Its Temporary Collapse, Its Future*. New York: Boni and Liveright, 1919.

Sullivan, Mark. *Our Times: The United States, 1900–1925*. 6 vols. New York: Scribner's, 1926–35.

Thomas, Norman. *Is Conscience a Crime?* New York: Garland, 1972.

Thwing, Charles F. *The American Colleges and Universities in the Great War*. New York: Macmillan, 1920.

Wald, Lillian D. *Windows on Henry Street*. Boston: Little, Brown, 1934.

Walling, William English. *American Labor and American Democracy*. New York: Harper and Brothers, 1926.

Watkins, Gordon S. *Labor Problems and Labor Administration in the United States During the World War*. University of Illinois Studies in the Social Sciences, VIII. Urbana: University of Illinois, 1919.

Wehle, Louis B. "The Adjustment of Labor Disputes Incident to Production for War in the United States." *Quarterly Journal of Economics* 32 (1917), 122–41.

———. "Labor Problems in the United States During the War." *Quarterly Journal of Economics* 32 (1918), 333–92.

————. "War Labor Policies and Their Outcome in Peace." *Quarterly Journal of Economics* 33 (1919), 321–43.

Weyl, Walter E. *The New Democracy: An Essay on Certain Political and Economic Tendencies in the United States.* New York: Macmillan, 1912.

————. *Tired Radicals and Other Papers.* New York: B. W. Huebsch, 1921.

Wharton, Edith. *The Marne.* New York: D. Appleton, 1918.

————. *A Son at the Front.* New York: Scribner's, 1923.

White, William Allen. *Autobiography.* New York: Macmillan, 1946.

Yerkes, Robert M. *Psychological Examining in the United States Army. Memoirs of the National Academy of Sciences*, XV. Washington, D.C.: Government Printing Office, 1921.

Young Men's Christian Association. *Service with Fighting Men: An Account of the Work of the American Young Men's Christian Associations in the World War.* 2 vols. New York: Association Press, 1922.

Contemporary Periodicals

Annals of the American Academy of Political and Social Science, 1914–24.
The Atlantic Monthly, 1917–18.
The Crisis, 1917–19.
Literary Digest, 1914–27.
Masses, 1917.
The Nation, 1914–27.
The Nation's Business, 1917-18.
The New Republic, 1914–27.
New York American, 1917.
New York Times, 1914–30.
The Outlook, 1915–18.
Seven Arts, 1917.
Stars and Stripes, 1918–19.
Survey, 1915–18.

Secondary Books and Articles

Abrahams, Paul P. "American Bankers and the Economic Tactics of Peace: 1919." *Journal of American History* 56 (1969), 572–83.

Abrams, Ray H. *Preachers Present Arms: The Role of the American Churches and Clergy in World Wars I and II, with some Observations on the War in Vietnam.* Scottdale, Pa.: Herald Press, 1969.

Adams, Henry. *The History of the United States of America During the Administrations of Jefferson and Madison.* Abr. and ed. by Ernest Samuels. Chicago: University of Chicago Press, 1967.

Aldridge, John. *After the Lost Generation: A Critical Study of the Writers of Two Wars.* New York: Farrar, Straus and Giroux, 1951.

American Battle Monuments Commission. *American Armies and Battlefields in Europe: A History, Guide, and Reference Book.* Washington, D.C.: Government Printing Office, 1938.

———. *A Guide to the American Battlefields in Europe.* Washington, D.C.: Government Printing Office, 1927.

Anderson, Benjamin M. *Economics and the Public Welfare: Financial and Economic History of the United States, 1914–1946.* New York: D. Van Nostrand, 1949.

Arnett, Alex Mathews. *Claude Kitchin and the Wilson War Policies.* Boston: Little, Brown, 1937.

Bailey, Thomas A. *Woodrow Wilson and the Great Betrayal.* Chicago: Quadrangle, 1963.

———. *Woodrow Wilson and the Lost Peace.* Chicago: Quadrangle, 1963.

Barbeau, Arthur E., and Florette, Henri. *The Unknown Soldiers: Black American Troops in World War I.* Philadelphia: Temple University Press, 1974.

Beaver, Daniel R. *Newton D. Baker and the American War Effort, 1917–1919.* Lincoln: University of Nebraska Press, 1966.

Birdsall, Paul. *Versailles Twenty Years After.* New York: Raynal and Hitchcock, 1941.

Blakey, George T. *Historians on the Homefront: American Propagandists for the Great War.* Lexington: University Press of Kentucky, 1970.

Blum, John Morton. *Joe Tumulty and the Wilson Era.* Boston: Houghton Mifflin, 1951.

———. *Woodrow Wilson and the Politics of Morality.* Boston: Little, Brown, 1956.

Bourke, Paul F. "The Status of Politics 1909–1919: *The New Republic,* Randolph Bourne, and Van Wyck Brooks." *Journal of American Studies* 8 (1974), 171–202.

Brand, Carl F. *The British Labour Party: A Short History.* Stanford: Stanford University Press, 1964.

Brittain, Joan T. *Laurence Stallings.* Boston: Twayne, 1975.

Brody, David. *Labor in Crisis: The Steel Strike of 1919.* Philadelphia: Lippincott, 1965.

Brown, Richard Maxwell. *Strain of Violence: Historical Studies of American Violence and Vigilantism.* New York: Oxford University Press, 1975.

Burner, David. *Herbert Hoover: A Public Life.* New York: Knopf, 1979.

Cary, Francine Curro. *The Influence of War on Walter Lippmann, 1914–1944.* Madison: State Historical Society of Wisconsin, 1967.

Chafe, William H. *The American Woman: Her Changing Social, Economic, and Political Role, 1920–1970.* New York: Oxford University Press, 1972.

Chafee, Zechariah, Jr. *Free Speech in the United States.* Cambridge, Mass.: Harvard University Press, 1941.

Chalmers, David Mark. *The Muckrake Years.* New York: D. Van Nostrand, 1974.

Chambers, Clarke A. *Paul U. Kellogg and the "Survey": Voices for Social Re-*

form and Social Justice. Minneapolis: University of Minnesota Press, 1971.

Chandler, Alfred D. *The Visible Hand: The Managerial Revolution in American Business*. Cambridge, Mass.: Belknap Press, 1977.

——, and Salsbury, Stephen. *Pierre S. Du Pont and the Making of the Modern Corporation*. New York: Harper and Row, 1971.

Chatfield, Charles. *For Peace and Justice: Pacifism in America, 1914–1941*. Knoxville: University of Tennessee Press, 1971.

Clark, John Maurice. *The Costs of the World War to the American People*. New Haven: Yale University Press, 1931.

Clarkson, Jesse D., and Cochran, Thomas C., eds. *War as a Social Institution: The Historian's Perspective*. New York: Columbia University Press, 1941.

Clifford, John Garry. *The Citizen Soldiers: The Plattsburg Training Camp Movement, 1913–1920*. Lexington: University Press of Kentucky, 1972.

Coben, Stanley. *A. Mitchell Palmer: Politician*. New York: Columbia University Press, 1963.

——. "A Study in Nativism: The American Red Scare of 1919–1920." *Political Science Quarterly* 79 (1964), 52–75.

Coffman, Edward M. *The Hilt of the Sword: The Career of Peyton C. March*. Madison: University of Wisconsin Press, 1966.

——. *The War To End all Wars: The American Military Experience in World War I*. New York: Oxford University Press, 1968.

Coit, Margaret L. *Mr. Baruch*. Boston: Houghton Mifflin, 1957.

Cooperman, Stanley. *World War I and the American Novel*. Baltimore: Johns Hopkins University Press, 1970.

Cowley, Malcolm. *Exile's Return: A Literary Odyssey of the 1920s*. New York: Viking, 1951.

——. "Two Wars—and Two Generations." *New York Times Book Review* (July 25, 1948), 1.

Cuff, Robert D. "Organizing for War: Canada and the United States During World War I." Canadian Historical Association. *Historical Papers* (1969), 141–56.

——. *The War Industries Board: Business-Government Relations During World War I*. Baltimore: Johns Hopkins University Press, 1973.

——. "We Band of Brothers—Woodrow Wilson's War Managers." *The Canadian Review of American Studies* 2 (1974), 135–48.

Danbom, David. *The Resisted Revolution: Urban America and the Industrialization of Agriculture*. Ames: Iowa State University Press, 1979.

Davis, Allen F. *American Heroine: The Life and Legend of Jane Addams*. New York: Oxford University Press, 1973.

——. "Welfare, Reform, and World War I." *American Quarterly* 19 (1967), 516–33.

Deutsch, Karl W., and Merritt, Richard L. "Transnational Communications and the International System." *Annals of the American Academy of Political and Social Science* 442 (1979), 84–97.

DeWeerd, Harvey A. *President Wilson Fights His War: World War I and the American Intervention*. New York: Macmillan, 1968.

Dubofsky, Melvyn. *We Shall Be All: A History of the Industrial Workers of the World*. Chicago: Quadrangle, 1969.

Duffield, Marcus. *King Legion*. New York: Cape and Smith, 1931.

Dupree, A. Hunter. *Science in the Federal Government: A History of Policies and Activities to 1940*. New York: Harper and Row, 1964.

Feis, Herbert. *The Diplomacy of the Dollar, 1919–1932*. New York: Norton, 1966.

Fenton, Charles A. "A Literary Fracture of World War I." *American Quarterly* 12 (1960), 119–32.

———. "Ambulance Drivers in France and Italy: 1914–18." *American Quarterly* 3 (1951), 326–43.

Filene, Peter G. "An Obituary for the Progressive Movement." *American Quarterly* 22 (1970), 20–34.

Forcey, Charles. *The Crossroads of Liberalism: Croly, Weyl, Lippmann and the Progressive Era, 1900–1925*. New York: Oxford University Press, 1961.

Fowler, W. B. *British-American Relations 1917–1918: The Role of Sir William Wiseman*. Princeton: Princeton University Press, 1969.

Fredrickson, George M. *The Inner Civil War: Northern Intellectuals and the Crisis of the Union*. New York: Harper and Row, 1968.

Freidel, Frank. *Over There: The Story of America's First Great Overseas Crusade*. Boston: Little, Brown, 1964.

Friedman, Milton, and Schwartz, Anna Jacobson. *A Monetary History of the United States, 1867–1960*. Princeton: Princeton University Press, 1963.

Fussell, Paul. *The Great War and Modern Memory*. New York: Oxford University Press, 1975.

Galbraith, John Kenneth. *The New Industrial State*. New York: New American Library, 1967.

Garofalo, Charles. "Black-White Occupational Distribution in Miami During World War I." *Prologue* 5 (1973), 98–101.

Garraty, John A. *Henry Cabot Lodge, a Biography*. New York: Knopf, 1965.

Genthe, Charles V. *American War Narratives, 1917–1918: A Study and Bibliography*. New York: David Lewis, 1969.

Gilbert, Charles. *American Financing of World War I*. Westport, Conn.: Greenwood, 1970.

Ginger, Ray. *The Bending Cross: A Biography of Eugene Victor Debs*. New Brunswick, N.J.: Rutgers University Press, 1949.

Glad, Paul W. "Progressives and the Business Culture of the 1920s." *Journal of American History* 53 (1966), 75–89.

Goldman, Eric. *Rendezvous with Destiny: A History of Modern American Reform*. New York: Vintage, 1956.

Granatstein, J. L., and Cuff, R. D., eds. *War and Society in North America*. Toronto: Thomas Nelson, 1971.

Gray, Justin. *The Inside Story of the Legion*. New York: Boni and Gaer, 1948.

Grubbs, Frank L. *The Struggle for Labor Loyalty: Gompers, the A.F. of L., and the Pacifists, 1917–1920.* Durham, N.C.: Duke University Press, 1968.

Gruber, Carol S. *Mars and Minerva: World War I and the Uses of the Higher Learning in America.* Baton Rouge: Louisiana State University Press, 1975.

Gunther, Gerald. "Learned Hand and the Origins of the Modern First Amendment Doctrine: Some Fragments of History." *Stanford Law Review* 27 (1975), 719–73.

Hackett, Alice Payne. *Seventy Years of Bestsellers, 1895–1965.* New York: Bowker, 1967.

Hall, Calvin. "The Instability of Post-War Marriages." *Journal of Social Psychology* 5 (1934), 523–30.

Harbaugh, William H. *Lawyer's Lawyer: The Life of John W. Davis.* New York: Oxford University Press, 1973.

Hardach, Gerd. *The First World War: 1914–1918.* Berkeley: University of California Press, 1977.

Hartmann, Edward George. *The Movement To Americanize the Immigrant.* New York: AMS Press, 1967.

Herman, Sondra. *Eleven Against War: Studies in American Internationalist Thought, 1898–1921.* Stanford: Hoover Institution Press, 1969.

Higham, John. *History: The Development of Historical Studies in the United States.* Princeton: Princeton University Press, 1965.

———. *Strangers in the Land: Patterns of American Nativism, 1860–1925.* New York: Atheneum, 1963.

Hilton, O. A. "Freedom of the Press in Wartime, 1917–1919." *The Southwestern Social Science Quarterly* 28 (1948), 346–61.

———. "Public Opinion and Civil Liberties in Wartime, 1917–1919." *The Southwestern Social Science Quarterly* 28 (1947), 201–24.

Himmelberg, Robert F. "The War Industries Board and the Antitrust Question in November, 1918." *Journal of American History* 52 (1967), 378–403.

Hirschfeld, Charles. "Nationalist Progressivism and World War I." *Mid-America* 45 (1963), 139–56.

Hirschfeld, Magnus. *The Sexual History of the World War.* New York: Falstaff Press, 1937.

Hobsbawm, E. J. *Industry and Empire: The Making of Modern English Society,* Vol. II, *1750 to the Present Day.* New York: Pantheon, 1968.

Hoffman, Frederick J. *The Twenties: American Writing in the Postwar Decade.* Rev. ed. New York: Free Press, 1965.

Hofstadter, Richard. *The Age of Reform.* New York: Knopf, 1955.

———. *The Progressive Historians.* New York: Knopf, 1968.

———, and Metzer, Walter P. *The Development of Academic Freedom in the United States.* New York: Columbia University Press, 1955.

Hogan, Michael J. *Informal Entente: The Private Structure of Cooperation in Anglo-American Economic Diplomacy, 1918–1928.* Columbia: University of Missouri Press, 1977.

Hough, Emerson. *The Web: The Authorized History of the American Protective League*. Chicago: Reilly and Lee, 1919.

James, Marquis. *A History of the American Legion*. New York: William Green, 1923.

Jensen, Joan M. *The Price of Vigilance*. Chicago: Rand McNally, 1968.

Johnpoll, Bernard K. *Pacifist's Progress: Norman Thomas and the Decline of American Socialism*. Chicago: Quadrangle, 1970.

Johnson, Donald. *The Challenge to American Freedoms: World War I and the Rise of the American Civil Liberties Union*. Lexington: University of Kentucky Press, 1963.

Johnson, James P. "The Wilsonians as War Managers: Coal and the 1917–18 Winter Crisis." *Prologue* 9 (1977), 193–208.

Kaplan, Sidney. "Social Engineers as Saviors: Effects of World War I on Some American Liberals." *Journal of the History of Ideas* 17 (1956), 347–69.

Kaufman, Burton I. *Efficiency and Expansion: Foreign Trade Organization in the Wilson Administration, 1913–1921*. Westport, Conn.: Greenwood, 1974.

Kazin, Alfred. *On Native Grounds: A Study of American Prose Literature from 1890 to the Present*. Garden City, N.Y.: Doubleday, 1956.

Keegan, John. *The Face of Battle: A Study of Agincourt, Waterloo, and the Somme*. New York: Vintage, 1977.

Kellogg, Charles Flint. *NAACP: A History of the National Association for the Advancement of Colored People, 1909–1920*. Baltimore: Johns Hopkins University Press, 1967.

Kennedy, David M. "Overview: The Progressive Era." *Historian* 37 (1975), 453–68.

————. "The Political Economy of World War I." *Reviews in American History* 2 (1974), 102–7.

————. "War and the American Character." *The Stanford Magazine* 3 (1975), 14ff.

Kernek, Sterling J. *Distractions of Peace During War: The Lloyd George Government's Reaction to Woodrow Wilson, December, 1916-November, 1918*. Transactions of the American Philosophical Society. N.s. 65 (1975), pt 2.

Kerr, K. Austin. *American Railroad Politics, 1914–1920: Rates, Wages and Efficiency*. Pittsburgh: University of Pittsburgh Press, 1968.

Kevles, Daniel J. "Testing the Army's Intelligence: Psychologists and the Military in World War I." *Journal of American History* 55 (1968), 565–81.

Kindleberger, Charles P. *The World in Depression, 1929–1939*. Berkeley: University of California Press, 1973.

Koistinen, Paul A. C. "The 'Industrial-Military Complex' in Historical Perspective: World War I." *Business History Review* 41 (1967), 378–403.

Kolko, Gabriel. *The Triumph of Conservatism*. New York: Free Press, 1963.

Konefsky, Samuel J. *The Legacy of Holmes and Brandeis*. New York: Macmillan, 1956.

Kuznets, Simon. *Capital in the American Economy: Its Formation and Financing.* Princeton: Princeton University Press, 1961.

La Follette, Belle Case, and La Follette, Fola. *Robert M. La Follette.* 2 vols. New York: Macmillan, 1953.

Lary, Hal B. *The United States in the World Economy: International Transactions of the United States During the Interwar Period.* Washington, D.C.: Government Printing Office, 1943.

Lasch, Christopher. *The American Liberals and the Russian Revolution.* New York: Columbia University Press, 1962.

———. *The New Radicalism in America (1889–1963): The Intellectual as a Social Type.* New York: Knopf, 1965.

Lasswell, Harold D. *Propaganda Technique in the World War.* New York: Peter Smith, 1938.

League of Nations. *Memorandum on International Trade and Balances of Payment, 1912–1926.* 2 vols. Geneva: League of Nations, 1927.

———. *Statistical Yearbook, 1930–31.* Geneva: League of Nations, 1931.

Leonard, Thomas C. *Above the Battle: War-Making in America from Appomattox to Versailles.* New York: Oxford University Press, 1978.

Leuchtenburg, William E. "The New Deal and the Analogue of War." John Braeman et al., eds. *Change and Continuity in Twentieth-Century America.* New York: Harper and Row, 1966.

———. *The Perils of Prosperity, 1914–32.* Chicago: University of Chicago Press, 1958.

Levin, N. Gordon, Jr. *Woodrow Wilson and World Politics: America's Response to War and Revolution.* New York: Oxford University Press, 1968.

Lewis, Cleona. *America's Stake in International Investments.* Washington, D.C.: Brookings Institution, 1938.

Lewis, R. W. B. *Edith Wharton: A Biography.* New York: Harper and Row, 1975.

Liddell Hart, Basil Henry. *A History of the World War, 1914–1918.* Boston: Little, Brown, 1935.

Link, Arthur S. "What Happened to the Progressive Movement in the 1920s?" *American Historical Review* 64 (1959), 833–51.

———. *Wilson.* 5 vols. Princeton: Princeton University Press, 1947–65.

———. *Wilson the Diplomatist: A Look at His Major Foreign Policies.* Chicago: Quadrangle, 1965.

Livermore, Seward W. *Politics Is Adjourned: Woodrow Wilson and the War Congress, 1916–1918.* Middletown, Conn.: Wesleyan University Press, 1966.

Luebke, Frederick C. *Bonds of Loyalty: German-Americans and World War I.* DeKalb: Northern Illinois University Press, 1974.

Lyons, Timothy J. "Hollywood and World War I, 1914–18." *Journal of Popular Film* 1 (1972), 15–30.

Maizels, Alfred. *Industrial Growth and World Trade: An Empirical Study of Trends in Production, Consumption and Trade in Manufactures from*

1899–1959 with a Discussion of Probable Future Trends. Cambridge: Cambridge University Press, 1963.

Mandel, Bernard. *Samuel Gompers.* Yellow Springs, O.: Antioch Press, 1963.

Marchand, C. Roland. *The American Peace Movement and Social Reform, 1898–1918.* Princeton: Princeton University Press, 1973.

Margulies, Herbert. "Recent Opinion of the Decline of the Progressive Movement." *Mid-America* 45 (1963), 250–68.

Marks, Sally. *The Illusion of Peace: International Relations in Europe, 1918–1933.* New York: St. Martin's Press, 1976.

Marwick, Arthur. *The Deluge: British Society and the First World War.* New York: Norton, 1970.

Mason, Herbert Molloy, Jr. *The Lafayette Escadrille.* New York: Random House, 1964.

May, Ernest R. *The World War and American Isolation, 1914–1917.* Chicago: Quadrangle, 1966.

May, Henry F. *The End of American Innocence: A Study of the First Years of Our Own Time, 1912–1917.* Chicago: Quadrangle, 1964.

Mayer, Arno J. *Political Origins of the New Diplomacy, 1917–1918.* New York: Vintage, 1970.

——. *Politics and Diplomacy of Peacemaking: Containment and Counterrevolution at Versailles, 1918–1919.* New York: Vintage, 1969.

McConnell, Grant. *The Decline of Agrarian Democracy.* New York: Atheneum, 1969.

——. *Private Power and American Democracy.* New York: Knopf, 1967.

McGovern, James R. "The American Woman's Pre-World War I Freedom in Manners and Morals." *Journal of American History* 55 (1968), 315–33.

McNaught, Kenneth. "American Progressives and the Great Society." *Journal of American History* 53 (1966), 504–20.

Minott, Rodney G. *Peerless Patriots: Organized Veterans and the Spirit of Americanism.* Washington, D.C.: Public Affairs Press, 1962.

Mock, James R., and Larson, Cedric. *Words That Won the War: The Story of the Committee on Public Information, 1917–1919.* Princeton: Princeton University Press, 1939.

Moley, Raymond, Jr. *The American Legion Story.* New York: Duell, Sloan and Pearce, 1966.

Mooney, Chase C., and Lyman, Martha E. "Some Phases of the Compulsory Military Training Movement, 1914–1920." *Mississippi Valley Historical Review* 38 (1952), 633–56.

Mullendore, William Clinton. *History of the United States Food Administration, 1917–1919.* Stanford: Stanford University Press, 1941.

Murray, Robert K. *Red Scare: A Study in National Hysteria, 1919–1920.* Minneapolis: University of Minnesota Press, 1955.

Noble, David F. *America by Design: Science, Technology, and the Rise of Corporate Capitalism.* New York: Oxford University Press, 1979.

Noble, David W. "*The New Republic* and the Idea of Progress, 1914–20." *Mississippi Valley Historical Review* 38 (1951), 387–402.

Noggle, Burl. *Into the Twenties: The United States from Armistice to Normalcy.* Urbana: University of Illinois Press, 1974.

O'Neill, William. *Everyone Was Brave: The Rise and Fall of Feminism in America.* Chicago: Quadrangle, 1969.

————. *The Last Romantic: A Life of Max Eastman.* New York: Oxford University Press, 1978.

Packer, Herbert L. *The Limits of the Criminal Sanction.* Stanford: Stanford University Press, 1968.

Palmer, Dewey H. "Moving North: Migration of Negroes During World War I." *Phylon* 28 (1967), 52–62.

Palmer, Frederick. *Newton D. Baker: America at War.* 2 vols. New York: Dodd, Mead, 1931.

Parrini, Carl P. *Heir to Empire: United States Economic Diplomacy, 1916–1923.* Pittsburgh: University of Pittsburgh Press, 1969.

Parrish, Michael E. *Securities Regulation and the New Deal.* New Haven: Yale University Press, 1970.

Parsons, Edward B. *Wilsonian Diplomacy: Allied-American Rivalries in War and Peace.* St. Louis: Forum Press, 1978.

Paxson, Fredrick L. *American Democracy and the World War.* 3 vols. Boston: Houghton Mifflin, 1936–48.

Pelling, Henry. *Origins of the Labor Party, 1880–1900.* 2nd ed. Oxford: Oxford University Press, 1965.

Peterson, H. C. *Propaganda for War: The Campaign Against American Neutrality, 1914–1917.* Port Washington, N.Y.: Kennikat Press, 1968.

————, and Fite, Gilbert C. *Opponents of War, 1917–1918.* Seattle: University of Washington Press, 1968.

Preston, William, Jr. *Aliens and Dissenters: Federal Suppression of Radicals, 1903–1933.* New York: Harper and Row, 1966.

Radosh, Ronald. *American Labor and United States Foreign Policy.* New York: Random House, 1969.

Ratner, Sidney. *Taxation and Democracy in America.* New York: Science Editions, 1967.

Renouvin, Pierre. *War and Aftermath, 1914–1929.* New York: Harper and Row, 1968.

Renshaw, Patrick. "The I.W.W. and the Red Scare, 1917–1924." *Journal of Contemporary History* 3 (1968), 63–72.

Rochester, Stuart I. *American Liberal Disillusionment in the Wake of World War I.* University Park: Pennsylvania State University Press, 1977.

Roth, Jack J., ed. *World War I: A Turning Point in Modern History.* New York: Knopf, 1967.

Rothwell, V. H. *British War Aims and Peace Diplomacy, 1914–1918.* Oxford: Clarendon Press, 1971.

Rudwick, Elliot M. *Race Riot at East St. Louis, July 2, 1917.* Carbondale: Southern Illinois University Press, 1964.

Safford, Jeffrey J. *Wilsonian Maritime Diplomacy, 1913–1921.* New Brunswick, N.J.: Rutgers University Press, 1978.

Saloutos, Theodore, and Hicks, John D. *Agricultural Discontent in the Middle West, 1900–1939.* Madison: University of Wisconsin Press, 1951.

Samuelson, Paul A., and Hagen, Everett E. *After the War, 1918–1920: Military and Economic Demobilization of the United States.* Washington, D.C.: Government Printing Office, 1943.

Saposs, David J. "The American Labor Movement Since the War." *Quarterly Journal of Economics* 49 (1935), 236–54.

Scheiber, Harry N. *The Wilson Administration and Civil Liberties, 1917–1921.* Ithaca: Cornell University Press, 1960.

Scheiber, Jane Lang, and Scheiber, Harry N. "The Wilson Administration and The Wartime Mobilization of Black Americans, 1917–18." *Labor History* 10 (1969), 433–58.

Schlesinger, Arthur M., Jr., ed. *History of United States Political Parties.* 4 vols. New York: Chelsea House, 1973.

———, and Israel, Fred L., eds. *History of American Presidential Elections, 1789–1968.* 4 vols. New York: Chelsea House, 1971.

Shannon, David A. *The Socialist Party of America.* Chicago: Quadrangle, 1967.

Shapiro, Stanley. "The Great War and Reform: Liberals and Labor, 1917–1919." *Labor History* 12 (1971), 323–44.

Sklar, Martin J. "Woodrow Wilson and the Political Economy of Modern U.S. Liberalism." *Studies on the Left* 1 (1960), 17–47.

Slosson, Preston William. *The Great Crusade and After, 1914–1928.* New York: Macmillan, 1930.

Smith, Daniel M. *The Great Departure: The United States and World War I, 1914–1920.* New York: John Wiley, 1965.

Smith, John S. "Organized Labor and Government in the Wilson Era, 1913–1921: Some Conclusions." *Labor History* 3 (1962), 265–86.

Smith, T. Lynn. "The Redistribution of the Negro Population of the United States, 1910–1960." *Journal of Negro History* 51 (1966), 155–73.

Smuts, Robert. *Women and Work in America.* New York: Columbia University Press, 1959.

Soule, George Henry. *Prosperity Decade: From War to Depression, 1917–1929.* New York: Rinehard, 1947.

Spear, Allen H. *Black Chicago: The Making of a Negro Ghetto, 1890–1920.* Chicago: University of Chicago Press, 1967.

Speier, Hans. *Social Order and the Risks of War.* New York: George W. Stewart, 1952.

Stallings, Laurence. *The Doughboys: The Story of the AEF, 1917–1918.* New York: Harper and Row, 1963.

Stansky, Peter, ed. *The Left and War: The British Labour Party and World War I.* New York: Oxford University Press, 1969.

Stein, Herbert. *Government Price Policy in the United States During the War.* Williamstown, Mass.: Williams College, 1939.

Strout, Cushing. *The American Image of the Old World.* New York: Harper and Row, 1963.

Svennilson, Ingvar. *Growth and Stagnation in the European Economy.* Geneva: United Nations Commission for Europe, 1954.

Taft, Philip. "The Federal Trials of the IWW." *Labor History* 3 (1962), 57–91.

Tillman, Seth P. *Anglo-American Relations at the Paris Peace Conference of 1919.* Princeton: Princeton University Press, 1961.

Timberlake, James H. *Prohibition and the Progressive Movement, 1900–1920.* New York: Atheneum, 1970.

Tindall, George B. *The Emergence of the New South, 1913–1945.* Baton Rouge: Louisiana State University Press, 1967.

Tobey, Ronald C. *The American Ideology of National Science, 1919–1930.* Pittsburgh: University of Pittsburgh Press, 1971.

Todd, Lewis Paul. *Wartime Relations of the Federal Government and the Public Schools, 1917–1918.* New York: Bureau of Publications, Teacher's College, Columbia University, 1945.

Trask, David F. *Captains and Cabinets: Anglo-American Naval Relations, 1917–1918.* Columbia: University of Missouri Press, 1972.

————. *The United States in the Supreme War Council: American War Aims and Inter-Allied Strategy, 1917–1918.* Middletown, Conn.: Wesleyan University Press, 1961.

Trattner, Walter I. "Progressivism and World War I: A Re-Appraisal." *Mid-America* 44 (1962), 131–45.

Tryon, Warren S. "The Draft in World War I." *Current History* 54 (1968), 339ff.

Tulchin, Joseph S. *The Aftermath of War: World War I and U.S. Policy Toward Latin America.* New York: New York University Press, 1971.

Tyler, Robert L. "The United States Government as Union Organizer: The Loyal Legion of Loggers and Lumbermen." *Mississippi Valley Historical Review* 47 (1960), 434–51.

Urofsky, Melvin I. *Big Steel and the Wilson Administration: A Study in Business-Government Relations.* Columbus: Ohio State University Press, 1969.

Vandiver, Frank E. *Black Jack: The Life and Times of John J. Pershing.* 2 vols. College Station: Texas A. and M. University Press, 1977.

Waller, Willard, ed. *War in the Twentieth Century.* New York: Random House, 1940.

Walworth, Arthur. *America's Moment: American Diplomacy at the End of World War I.* New York: Norton, 1977.

————. *Woodrow Wilson.* 2nd ed., rev. Baltimore: Penguin, 1969.

Ward, Robert D. "The Origin and Activities of the National Security League, 1914–1919." *Mississippi Valley Historical Review* 47 (1960), 51–65.

Wecter, Dixon. *When Johnny Comes Marching Home.* Cambridge, Mass.: Riverside Press, 1944.

Weigley, Russell F. *The American Way of War: A History of United States Military Strategy and Policy.* New York: Macmillan, 1973.

Weinstein, James. *The Corporate Ideal in the Liberal State: 1900–1918.* Boston: Beacon Press, 1968.

————. *The Decline of Socialism in America, 1912–1925*. New York: Vintage, 1969.

Whitfield, Stephen J. *Scott Nearing: Apostle of American Radicalism*. New York: Columbia University Press, 1974.

Wiebe, Robert H. *Businessmen and Reform*. Cambridge, Mass.: Harvard University Press, 1962.

————. *The Search for Order, 1877–1920*. New York: Hill and Wang, 1967.

Williams, John. *The Home Fronts: Britain, France and Germany, 1914–1918*. London: Constable, 1972.

Wilson, Joan Hoff. *American Business and Foreign Policy, 1920–1933*. Boston: Beacon Press, 1973.

————. *Herbert Hoover: Forgotten Progressive*. Boston: Little, Brown, 1975.

Wiltz, John E. *In Search of Peace: The Senate Munitions Inquiry, 1934–1936*. Baton Rouge: Louisiana State University Press, 1963.

Wittke, Carl. *German-Americans and the World War*. Columbus: Ohio State Archaeological and Historical Society, 1936.

Wolff, Leon. *In Flanders Fields: The 1917 Campaign*. New York: Ballantine, 1960.

Wreszin, Michael. *Oswald Garrison Villard: Pacifist at War*. Bloomington: Indiana University Press, 1965.

Yates, Lamartine P. *Forty Years of Foreign Trade: A Statistical Handbook with Special Reference to Primary Products and Under-Developed Countries*. London: George Allen and Unwin, 1959.

Yeager, Leland B. *International Monetary Relations: Theory, History, and Policy*. 2nd. ed. New York: Harper and Row, 1976.

Unpublished Studies

Abrahamson, James Leonard. *The Military and American Society, 1881–1922*. Ph.D. dissertation, Stanford University, 1976.

Axeen, David. *Romantics and Civilizers: American Attitudes Toward War, 1898–1902*. Ph.D. dissertation, Yale University, 1969.

Baldwin, Fred D. *The American Enlisted Man in World War I*. Ph.D. dissertation, Princeton University, 1964.

Chambers, John W. "Conscripting for Colossus: The Adoption of the Military Draft in the United States in World War I." Paper presented at Meeting of Organization of American Historians, Washington, D.C., 1971.

Index